D0215913

WITHDRAWN
STATE LIBRARY

Minorities and the Military

WITHDRAWN
UTSA LIBRARIES

Recent Titles in
Contributions in Ethnic Studies

Series Editor: Leonard Doob

Nations Remembered: An Oral History of the Five Civilized
Tribes, 1865-1907
Theda Perdue

Operation Wetback: The Mass Deportation of Mexican
Undocumented Workers in 1954
Juan Ramon García

The Navajo Nation
Peter Iverson

An Unacknowledged Harmony: Philo-Semitism and
the Survival of European Jewry
Alan Edelstein

America's Ethnic Politics
Joseph S. Roucek and Bernard Eisenberg, editors

Minorities and the Military

A CROSS-NATIONAL STUDY IN WORLD PERSPECTIVE

Warren L. Young

CONTRIBUTIONS IN ETHNIC STUDIES, NUMBER 6

 Greenwood Press

WESTPORT, CONNECTICUT . LONDON, ENGLAND

Library of Congress Cataloging in Publication Data

Young, Warren L.
  Minorities and the military.

    (Contributions in ethnic studies, ISSN 0196-7088 :
no. 6)
      Bibliography: p.
      Includes index.
      1. Armed Forces. 2. Ethnic groups. 3. Sociology,
Military. 4. Minorities. I. Title. II. Series: Con-
tributions in ethnic studies ; no. 6.
UB416.Y68   306'.2   81-4246
ISBN 0-313-22900-7 (Lib. bdg.)   AACR2

Copyright © 1982 by Warren L. Young

All rights reserved. No portion of this book may be
reproduced, by any process or technique, without the
express written consent of the publisher.

Library of Congress Catalog Card Number: 81-4246
ISBN: 0-313-22900-7
ISSN: 0196-7088

First published in 1982

Greenwood Press
A division of Congressional Information Service, Inc.
88 Post Road West
Westport, Connecticut 06881

Printed in the United States of America

10 9 8 7 6 5 4 3 2 1

LIBRARY
The University of Texas
San Antonio

CONTENTS

TABLES

BRITAIN

UNITED STATES

SERIES FOREWORD

"Contributions in Ethnic Studies" focuses upon the problems that arise when peoples with different cultures and goals come together and interact productively or tragically. The modes of adjustment or conflict are varied, but usually one group dominates or attempts to dominate the other. Eventually, some accommodation is reached, but the process is likely to be long and, for the weaker group, painful. No one scholarly discipline monopolizes the research necessary to comprehend these intergroup relations. This analysis, consequently, is inevitably of interest to historians, sociologists, psychologists, and psychiatrists.

Like any other significant social institution, the military establishment reflects and affects the society whose existence it would defend, extend, or stabilize. When minorities are present, when a country is multi-ethnic, or when a colonial government calls upon natives to supply manpower, critical decisions are made concerning the number of men conscripted or permitted to enlist; their ranks and duties within the forces; and their relation, whether or not segregated into separate units, to other enlisted men and officers. The decisions stem in part from the military situation, but they depend also upon the political structure and the prejudices prevalent in the society. The role of American blacks in the four branches of the services has changed with their changing status in society, so today there is less segregation in those services and in the country as a whole, but obviously, discrimination persists in both areas. As volunteers or as draftees, soldiers, sailors, marines, and all servicemen must submit to preexisting regulations and obey their commanding officers; as a result, they undergo new experiences and may acquire new, perhaps useful, skills. They become changed persons in some respect, and if they survive and are discharged, they carry over into civilian life a portion of what they have endured, enjoyed, or learned. Whether they or their country then gains or loses is another matter and a very perplexing one.

After a broad historical overview of the military arrangements created in multinational countries such as the Hapsburg Empire and the Soviet Union, Warren L. Young concentrates upon four detailed case histories: Belgium, Canada, the British Commonwealth, and the United States. In each instance, the solution to the existence of minorities or the less privileged in the military is found to be different and to have resulted from the varying historical, social, and political circumstances he delineates. He places the four cases in wide perspective by surveying additional countries such as Switzerland and Malaysia and by alluding to the scholarly literature on the functioning of the military in general. Unquestionably, therefore, this volume provides a significant vantage point from which to examine military establishments—and to observe, in yet another way, the dynamics both of ethnic minorities and of social change.

Leonard W. Doob

ACKNOWLEDGMENTS

Thanks for the crucial and constructive criticism of Ray Jobling of St. John's College, John Barnes of Churchill College, Timothy Leggat of King's College, Cambridge, and Philip Abrams of Durham University and Peterhouse, Cambridge, are both sincere and heartfelt. Without their assistance, my Cambridge Ph.D. dissertation could not, and would not have reached the level they expected of me.

I also want to thank Cynthia Enloe of Clark University; Barry Newman of North-East London Polytechnic; and John James, principal psychologist, RAF Technical Training Command, who both encouraged and helped me during my stay in England. Pierre Bonarens of the University of Ghent and Louis Duinslaeger, secretary to the Belgian minister of defense, were of immense help during my field trips to Belgium to gather material, where research was carried out with financial assistance from the Political Science Fund of Cambridge University's History Faculty and a travel grant from Churchill College, Cambridge.

Lawrence Eagleburger, former United States deputy assistant secretary of defense for international security affairs; Zahava Blum; Ralph Canter; Eli Flyer; Dave Hoffman; and Capt. Harvey Greenberg, U.S. Air Force, helped me a great deal during the United States stage of my research. Barry Newman, David Stephen, and John James assisted me in gathering material in the United Kingdom, and L. A. Bourgeois, director-general, information,

xii   ACKNOWLEDGMENTS

Ministry of Defense, and Pierre Coloumb enabled me to gather Canadian material. Morris Janowitz, through much constructive criticism, also assisted my efforts during his tenure as Pitt Visiting Professor of American Institutions in the University of Cambridge.

I also benefited from the encouragement, advice, and comments of Capt. Bill Gould, Malcolm Barnett, Tuku Mukherjee, and Miriam Roth. Rachelle Schmidt-Barad, whose excellent typing job lifted a "burden" off my shoulders, also deserves mention here.

Finally, James T. Sabin, vice-president—editorial of Greenwood Press, through his kindness and understanding of my persistent difficulties—both personal and professional—has enabled this work to reach the publication stage.

But above all, I owe the greatest debt to my wife, Sara; my daughters Shani and Natalie; and to my parents, who made it all possible.

Minorities and the Military

INTRODUCTION

According to Mao Zedong, "the army is to the nation as the sea is to the fish." Without the sea, not only can't the fish survive; it hasn't any identity. It seems, therefore, in Mao's view, that a nation cannot exist without an army, for not only does the army defend the nation's existence; it provides the element of national unity and identity, thereby building the nation itself. But even in Mao's China, the army has not yet provided an effective basis for amalgamating "national minorities." In fact, these groups have served in separate units in both militia and regular military forces. The contradiction between the potential integrative function of the military as recognized by Mao—among many other observers—and its apparent failure to catalyze national integration in many cases in reality exists not only with regard to nationwide divisions such as class or region; it also applies to the problem of minority groups and military service.

Military service, and issues relating to this aspect of societal participation, can prove to be of fundamental importance as regards the nature of and prospects for society in the respective case. In this book, I focus upon four case studies to formulate generalizations across cases regarding the minority-military-societal interaction. In chapter 1, I present a general historical survey, some themes that provide the basis for my approach, and a critique of the role of the military as regards modernization and national integration. In chapters 2-5, the case studies are presented: Belgium, Canada, the United Kingdom, and the United States. In chapter 6, I approach the case studies by generalization across cases with respect to patterns, parameters, and politicization of minority-military participation. In this chapter, I also deal with intercase variations, and the generalizations formulated are put into world perspective by reference to situations in other national contexts. Finally, I deal with the considerable literature on minority groups in general in an appendix.

1

HISTORICAL BACKGROUND
AND ANALYTICAL PERSPECTIVE

Insofar as "power grows out of the barrel of a gun" or has emanated from the strength of arms, and force has been one of the more traditionally accepted and successful ways of resolving conflict in history, so a need for the "management of violence" has brought with it the development of military institutions and armed forces—the organization, sophistication, and destructive capability of which is unparalleled in human "achievement." Throughout history, however, and concomitant with the development of these paragons of power, certain groups—minorities—have also emerged. Their presence in society as a whole, and the nature and extent of their participation in military organizations in particular, provides a fertile area for inquiry of both a general and case-specific nature.

GENERAL HISTORICAL SURVEY

The tradition of using troops other than those who are "indigenous" or members of the "dominant" group in the specific case is well established throughout the ancient world and persists to the historical present, for whether impressed into service or actively recruited, various minorities have participated in military conquest, empire building and maintenance, and war, from the classical period onwards. In some cases, when recruited as "mercenaries," these troops were one of the props that supported the classical empire. After the sixth century B.C., for example, the Carthaginian Republic relied almost entirely upon such mercenary troops to maintain itself, and Hannibal used Ethiopian soldiers, among other nonindigenous troops, when crossing the Alps in his campaign against Rome. The "pillars of royal authority" in the Hellenistic kingdoms rested upon mercenaries recruited or impressed into service from among vanquished allies. There is also substantial evidence relating to the use of Ethiopian troops by the Egyptians, Myceneans, Persians, Greeks, and Romans.[1]

In Imperial Rome, the use of minorities in mercenary capacities was institutionalized with the formation of the *Auxilia*—units composed of mercenaries to complement the home-recruited legions. Both impressment and active recruitment were used to fill the ranks of these auxiliary forces. Caesar, after the conquest of Gaul, for example, put large numbers of Gallic horsemen to good use in his struggle with Pompey. Although they were taken as hostages, he "turned them around" in the best military sense, rapidly, seeming to value their fighting qualities over any possible threat their newly won but momentary freedom would have posed to his legions. In time, the Auxilia was given regular status. The main incentive for enlistment, it seems, was the granting of Roman citizenship upon honorable discharge. Although this did not come into full effect until the reign of Claudius, the incentive among noncitizens to enlist in the auxiliary forces and serve to the best of their ability in the first century seems to have been the realization that "the direction of social mobility for the soldier was normally upward; even the unpromoted auxiliary infantrymen advanced in status." Among Oriental Auxilia units, for example, the children of soldiers were enfranchised, and if qualified, they were accepted for service in the Oriental regiments of the Roman legions, thereby preserving the "national character" of these units. Manpower shortages and the need for populating the frontier also resulted in the active recruitment of Germans during the later Roman Empire, who served as soldier-farmers in many cases, performing the dual function of colonizing and guarding the borders of the Roman colonies in the West.[2]

The Byzantine Empire also used various minority groups in

military capacities. These groups were, for the most part, recruited from the surrounding territories of the Near and Middle East. The multinational characteristic of Byzantium resulted in cases where "careers . . . were open to talent," and members of the non-Greek-speaking population could rise to high positions in the military establishment. In fact, the core of the empire's military organization—the "thematic," or provincial armies—were based on these non-Greek peoples. As such, Walter Kaegi noted that "one of the most crucial aspects of Byzantine history is that of civil-military relations," resulting from the ethnic and regional cleavages in the military, which "had their origins, or at least their precedents, in the Roman Empire and Republic." In addition, as Stanislaw Andreski maintained, there exists a danger inherent in the use of "unassimilated ethnic minorities" against a population that is "politically apathetic" in order to maintain rule, a danger of military intervention and revolt, as was the case in Rome and Byzantium itself. In other words, Gaetano Mosca is justified in stating that

to declare in principle that all citizens are soldiers without providing for a sound military organization . . . means in practice that in the moment of peril there will be no soldiers at all. . . . On the other hand, to entrust the bearing of arms exclusively to elements in a society that are temperamentally best suited to military trade . . . [means that] the standing army will absorb all the more belligerent elements and, being capable of prompt obedience to a single impulse, it will have no difficulty in dictating to the rest of society.[3]

The tradition continued, however, with the Mamlukes, Circassians, and Armenians impressed into the service of Ottoman Constantinople and Cairo. In the latter case, the Mamluke element in the Sultan's army revolted and were, in turn, dethroned, but only after establishing a significant dynasty. Troops of North African origin, for example, were used as far afield as Palestine, although under the *Millet* systems of the Ottomans—regional government, a legacy of Byzantium—military manpower procurement was not very centralized. Each regional government recruited its own forces, usually mercenary. In some cases, rulers recruited from loyal local elements, thereby resulting in a heterogeneous system that proved to be fairly effective in combat, but inherently weak on the organizational level.[4]

Among the modern European nation-states, France used "exotic" troops most effectively, being first to use them for mercenary purposes both within and outside its colonial empire. Black African troops, for example, were used by the French to a much greater extent than by the British, a point discussed in greater detail below. In South Asia, on the other hand, the British Indian Army was based on the recruitment and use of "martial races," and when manpower shortages made it necessary, even outcaste "untouchables" were recruited, although they were restricted to special units and certain military occupations to ensure "efficiency." Troops from among various European minorities have been used throughout the course of the continent's history as mercenaries, such as the Scots, Swedes, Irish, Croats, and Poles, and certain people, such as the Swiss, "a nation of mercenaries," have served in these capacities until the present, providing, for example, the Papal Guard.[5]

In other European cases, the problem of minority-military participation also arose. In the Austro-Hungarian Empire, for example, according to the 1867 agreement that created the dual monarchy—subsequent to the defeat of the Hapsburgs by the Prussians the previous year—the Hungarian parliament agreed to provide Magyar contingents for the common army. In 1903, however, the Hungarians demanded that Magyar become the language of command in Magyar units and refused to provide contingents until their demand was met. Until then, German was the language of command in the common army of the Austro-Hungarian Empire, where only some 36 percent of the population was German speaking, but accounted for 95 percent of the officer corps. In early 1906, the emperor turned out the Hungarian parliament using troops and annulled the constitution. However, by a combination of threats to enfranchise the Croats, thereby encouraging Croation independence, and promises of continued Magyar domination over the Croats in Hungary, the older order was restored. In return for their manpower contribution to the common army, the Magyar magnates kept their rule over the subject nationalities in Hungary.[6]

Minorities have also served in other military contexts, such as in sub-Saharan Africa, the Arabian peninsula, and the Far East. In the Ashanti, Fulani, and Nupe African kingdoms, for example, locally recruited slaves and mercenaries from militaristic tribes were used extensively. In Arabia, although certain outcaste tribes were prohibited from bearing arms in earlier periods, manumitted slaves, slaves taken from more "noble" tribes, and even outcaste elements were armed and used in the state-building effort of Ibn Saud in the early 1900s.[7] In Asian contexts other than the Indian subcontinent, minorities have also been excluded from military service as a result of in-group/outcaste differentiation. The Korean minority and the outcaste Burakumin in Japan are good examples of groups excluded from military participation or channeled into specific military occupations until manpower shortages dictated their full utilization in the closing stages of World War II.

In pre-World War II Japan, in contrast to the particularistic membership criteria extant in civilian society, universalistic criteria for recruitment and promotion in the army were ostensibly, and ideally, maintained. In theory, the conscription system provided that all men over the age of twenty were either in active service or in the reserves. Indeed, one competent observer of the Japanese case has claimed that

in contrast to some European armed forces where officers were drawn mainly from the aristocracy, in the Japanese army opportunities to climb the military ladder were open equally to the sons of peasants and the sons of nobility. Social mobility within the army . . . functioned as "an anesthetic" to alleviate the sense of dissatisfaction arising from the strict class distinctions which persisted in the civilian society after the Meiji Restoration. Among conscripted men, who constituted the bulk of the rank and file soldiers and non-commissioned officers, universalism prevailed.[8]

In practice, however, both the Korean minority and the outcaste Burakumin were not included in the Japanese army's universalistic membership criterion.

In the former case, a not insignificant number of Koreans requested that they be able to volunteer or be drafted for military service as early as 1937. It was not until 1942, however, that the Japanese war cabinet decided to initiate conscription of Koreans, and even then this was to go into effect only in 1944. By late 1942, however, the first Koreans were drafted. Those Korean conscripts who were inducted, however, were channeled into naval labor-support units. In return for being granted the "gift" of being able "to die for the Empire in which they were not yet first class citizens," some Koreans also asked "for enforcement of the compulsory education system, suffrage, equal rights, and the abolition of crossing (martial) regulations."

The case of the Burakumin—Japan's "invisible race"—is complex. Although these outcastes were ostensibly granted full citizenship rights in 1871, in fact, they are still the focus of discriminatory practices in Japan. With regard to their military service, although they were subject to conscription, they were specifically identified in their personnel records. This was done by means of a red circle before their name or by the Japanese word *toku*, indicating that they were "special." The Burakumin conscripts were channeled into service occupations such as shoe repairing or latrine duties that were deemed suitable for their social status, and that paralleled the traditional Burakumin occupations in civilian society. Organized protest by Burakumin groups against discrimination by the military occurred as early as 1923, but this was not effective. In 1926 the Burakumin struggle against military discrimination reached its peak, when the Japanese police arrested Burakumin leaders on charges of plotting to blow up the barracks of an infantry regiment in which discrimination was widespread. The Burakumin leaders were imprisoned, and the protest movement lost its impetus soon afterwards.[9]

Indians, Negroes, and even Asian immigrants in Latin America (especially Japanese in Brazil) provide other relevant examples of minority military participation. Andreski noted this phenomenon in describing the situation of Latin American peasants in military service, the majority of whom are of Indian origin: "In Latin American, the lowest ranks are either mercenary (as they were in Cuba . . . being recruited from among Negroes of African origin), or recruited among illiterate peasants. In Peru, Colombia, and other mestizo countries, these peasants have the further advantage [sic] of being Indians who have to be taught Spanish.'' Negroes and mulattos in both North and South America have a long history of participation in military service as members of both standing armies and colonial militias. This participation in most cases, however, was limited to the ranks, although even before the abolition of slavery throughout the New World by the end of the nineteenth century, "free" Negroes had, in a number of cases, attained both position and wealth through mercenary service in the colonial militias of Spain and France. Thus, as Lyle McAlister pointed out, "Historically, the Latin American armed forces have provided opportunities to break traditional class or caste barriers. The 19th century success story featured the Indian, Negro, or mixed blood who had enlisted or was dragooned into the army, won a commission, and—through ability, ruthlessness, or luck—rose to the rank of General and became President of the Republic." But upward mobility for members of these groups though military service was limited, in some countries, to only those "special cases" McAlister described. In other countries, however, at various times, military service has been a vehicle for group mobility or instrumental as a catalyst in making the dominant group(s) realize that the minority was an integral part of the nation as a whole.[10]

In countries as far afield as the Soviet Union and New Zealand, for example, minorities have served in the military on an involuntary or voluntary basis.

With regard to the USSR, as one competent observer wrote, "like the Soviet Union as a whole, the army has a nationalities problem." The difficulties posed by the existence of a multinational Russian Empire—an entity distinct from Russia itself—as regards military organization and participation are evident at the levels of both the officer corps and other ranks. In the former case, for example, there was an ongoing conflict during much of the nineteenth century between the ethnic Great Russians and the Baltic-German nobility for dominance over military leadership. This was due to the fact that "the regular army had come to include a large number of officers and generals from the various nationalities of Russia (including Baltic Germans), while the Guards schools and officers were, at the turn of the century, about 90% staffed by Russian officers (the balance being largely from certain favoured minorities such as Baltic Germans and the Georgian princely families)."[11]

Despite the attempts at "Russification" made by the Tsarist regime in its last decades of power, both the Cossacks—whether Ukranian, Don, or Ural—and some Moslem mountain tribes in the Caucasus willingly served, in distinct units, in the Imperial Army. However, other Moslem groups, such as those in Turkestan, for example, were much less willing to be conscripted, not sharing "the Orthodox religion which gave the Tsarist army most of its moral cement." Opposition to conscription, which in the reign of Nicholas I was set at twenty-five years, also came from a small religious groups, such as the Doukhobors, who simply refused to serve and were severely punished by the government.

The advent of the Bolshevik revolution and the Soviet state brought about immediate controversy regarding the formation of a national army as against the continued existence of contingents based on the various nationalities themselves. As early as 1917, there was acrimonious debate at the military conference of the Bolsheviki over the issue. Opinions ranged from those who opposed all national contingents to those who supported the creation of a separate Ukranian army. Stalin, for his part, presented a compromise resolution, passed by the conference, that stated that although the existence of national formations in the Red Army was not necessarily in the worker's interest, the nationalities could not be denied the right to form their own contingents, provided that these contingents would not be turned into separate armies. In 1922 the Red Army was still almost completely dominated by the Russians, who comprised some 80 percent, with Ukranians numbering 10 percent, and the remaining 10 percent composed of other nationalities. By 1925, however, the proportion of Russians had fallen to some 65 percent, and that of Ukranians had risen to 20 percent, with all other nationalities comprising the remaining 15 percent.

In late 1924, the Soviet Military Council drew up a plan for national contingents. This was approved in 1925 by the Third

Soviet Congress and promptly put into effect. The plan entailed the formation of national units up to the divisional level based on nationalities that had been subject to military conscription in the prerevolutionary Russian Empire. Cadres of commanders were also formed on a national basis. As regards nationalities that had not been subject to conscription in the Tsarist empire, much less progress was made, due to the shortage of commanders for such national units.[12]

At the Twenty-Eighth Party Congress in 1939, however, the decision was taken to disband the national contingents and merge them with other units in the Red Army. This occurred concomitant with the total reorganization of the Soviet military system. Under the new organizational scheme, the territorial system of recruitment was totally abandoned. The reason for this was that "the existence of separate small national military formations, permanently attached to their respective territories, was in contradiction to the fundamental principles of the Stalin Constitution and the principle of extraterritoriality in the recruitment of the army." In practical terms, the decision also "solved the problem of attaining efficient commanders for the national units, who were at times difficult to secure." On the eve of World War II, then, the Red Army had totally altered its orientation, becoming "one and indivisible." However, as Michel Garder pointed out, "the Russianisation of the army following the setback of 1941 gave the Russian solder . . . superiority over the non-Russian," this becoming "even more pronounced since the war."

Since September 1939, universal compulsory military service has been in effect in the Soviet Union. Members of non-Russian nationalities, therefore, serve in military units where the language of command is Russian. In the case of Moslem groups such as the Uzbecks, Tartars, and Kazakhs, national service may be their first contact with Russians and the Russian language. Although the Russification process that takes place during compulsory service may or may not wear off when the non-Russian conscript returns home, as Garder noted, the non-Russian minorities seem to "find themselves in not so much a Soviet as a Russian army which clings to the military traditions of the old Imperial army. They may well wonder if they are not simply serving Russia and the dominance of the Russian nation over the Soviet Union." In his study of the Soviet military, Thomas Wolfe, in concise terms, summed up the situation regarding the participation of minority nationalities in the Soviet armed forces. He wrote that although minority nationalities "theoretically and legally . . . have an equal chance with others to rise from private to Marshall" so that "occasionally talented individuals from minority groups, especially Armenians and Georgians rise to the top," the situation as a whole shows that "education, political acceptability, nationality background, and other factors operate to discriminate against some and favor the selection of others." The result of this, he concluded, is that "cultural and educational factors have operated to leave the officer corps dominated mainly by Great Russians and Ukranians."[13]

Maori military participation in New Zealand is an interesting example of a minority group—considered a "warrior race" and subdued by colonizers only after a prolonged armed struggle—that has maintained its martial tradition through military service, first in separate units and then in integrated ones. As early as 1858, even before the complete subjugation of all of the Maori tribes, the governor of New Zealand forwarded a proposal to the British War Office offering to raise a Maori contingent for service against the Kaffirs in South Africa. The proposal was, however, turned down. The final Maori wars that began in 1860 and were to last for over a decade gave both the British War Office and colonists due respect for Maori military prowess. Although many soldiers of part-Maori origin served in the New Zealand contingent during the Boer War, a Maori contingent was not deemed necessary, despite numerous offers from Maori volunteers to serve the crown.

With the outbreak of war in 1914, the Maori leadership offered to raise a contingent of troops for overseas service. The official response at the time was that although Maoris could join the New Zealand Expeditionary Force on a voluntary basis, there was no immediate need for a separate Maori contingent. According to a recent study on the recruitment of Maori soldiers during World War I, "the main reason for this was the known unwillingness of the Imperial government to use native troops in wars between Europeans." However, as soon as it became known in New

Zealand that Indian soldiers had been posted to Suez, the government formally requested that the Army Council accept a Maori contingent. The Imperial authorities initially agreed to the formation of a 500-man contingent, 200 for duty in Egypt and the rest to reinforce New Zealand forces in occupied German Samoa. The Maori contingent was to be used in noncombatant capacities, and the choice of officers, except for the unit's commander and second-in-command, was to be left in the hands of a committee composed of Maori MPs and leaders called the Native Contingent Committee.

The appointment of both senior officers and Maori junior officers, however, turned out to be problematic and proved to be an issue of contention between the Native Committee and the New Zealand military throughout the war. Although a voluntary quota system for enlistment, by Maori electorates, was originally set up, the entire recruiting effort was, in fact, based on tribal traditions. Thus Maori volunteers came mainly from tribes that had been neutral or had fought alongside the Europeans in the 1860s. The two Maori companies formed were subsequently divided into platoons according to their geographical, that is, tribal, origin. The Maori contingent, which followed the New Zealand Expeditionary Force to Egypt in February 1915, was almost immediately sent on to Malta for dispatch as reinforcements to Gallipoli, despite the initial decision to maintain it as a support unit only.

By August 1915, the Maori contingent had been sent into action at Gallipoli. The unit's first combat experience was very costly, with over one hundred soldiers killed or wounded, but it won high praise for its bravery. The commander of the New Zealand Expeditionary Force, however, thought the contingent too small to operate independently. This, in addition to questions about the conduct in action of four Maori officers, led to the splitting up of the contingent and its attachment to the New Zealand Infantry Brigade, while the officers suspected of incompetence were sent back to New Zealand. The issues of the contingent's unity, and whether injustice had been done regarding the returned officers, significantly affected Maori recruitment. The Native Committee, for its part, saw no reason to stress recruiting, only to have Maoris "scattered" within the Expeditionary Force.[14]

In March, 1916, however, the stalemate between the Native Committee and the military was broken by the commander of the Expeditionary Force. He decided to establish a new Pioneer Battalion within the New Zealand Division then being organized. It was to be based on the former Maori contingent and an equal number of "surplus" Maori volunteers from other units. All Maori soldiers were to be posted to the new battalion, and it was hoped that the unit would become almost entirely Maori. During the first half of 1916, the New Zealand military authorities realized that reinforcements for the Expeditionary Force could not be raised solely on a voluntary basis. The original conscription act as proposed exempted Maoris, but after protest from the Native Committee, conscription was ostensibly extended to include them. The National Registration that had been conducted in 1915, however, had not been applied to Maoris, so a complete and up-to-date list of potential conscripts was unavailable.

There was an additional problem regarding Maori participation within the framework of conscription. During the period that military participation was voluntary, there were large differences in recruitment from the Maori tribes. In fact, almost no recruits were forthcoming from two large Maori tribes that were engaged in a long-standing dispute with the government over lands they claimed were confiscated for the purpose of European settlement. In a heated parliamentary debate over the issue of whether members of the Maori tribes reluctant to serve should be conscripted, one Maori MP stated that confiscated lands not yet settled by Europeans should be given to Maori veterans of those tribes in return for their military service. However, this idea was not put into practice. In any event, the most recalcitrant Maori tribes simply refused to allow their members to serve, and conscription was finally imposed on them.

In early June 1917, the government formally extended the Military Service Act to all Maoris and set up a Maori reserve for the Expeditionary Force. By April 1918, a conscription register including the recalcitrant Maori tribes was put into effect. The government, for its part, expected at least some passive resistance from those

Maori tribes opposed to conscription. By the end of August 1918, over seventy Maoris had been arrested and conscripted. Thirty-four of them refused to don uniform and were brought to trial. The leaders of the group—six activists in all—were subsequently court-martialed and sentenced to two years' hard labor, and the remaining defaulters were given prolonged periods of detention. The total of Maori defaulters arrested was over one hundred by the end of the war, and fourteen Maoris were sent to prison for their refusal to serve.

On the front, the situation was entirely different. Although the Maori Pioneer Battalion was essentially a noncombat unit, it did all of the combat engineering work for the Expeditionary Force in France and Flanders over the period 1916-1918. Between February 1915 and November 1918, over 2,000 Maoris had served with the Maori contingent and Pioneer Battalion. Of them, almost 340 were killed in action, with over 730 wounded. Total Maori casualties, then, amounted to nearly half of those sent abroad.

Before the outbreak of World War II, the Maori leadership proposed the formation of a Maori unit, citing the precedent of the Pioneer Battalion. The government initially hesitated but in October 1939 decided to organize an infantry battalion recruited from Maoris. The key officers and NCOs of the unit were to be Europeans, with the intention of replacing them as soon as Maori officers and NCOs could be trained. The Maoris, however, strongly objected to this. Although they accepted that the unit be commanded by a European, they asserted that European company commanders and NCOs were unnecessary. According to them, there were both enough veterans from World War I and young Maoris with higher education and paramilitary (territorial) training from which to choose. The government response was to reiterate its initial position, but it also deliberately channeled Maoris with military experience or prior military training to the New Zealand Army School for officer or NCO training.

By mid-October 1939, recruitment started, and almost 900 Maoris immediately volunteered. Maori military service remained voluntary throughout the war, and since Maori recruiting officers worked in close cooperation with tribal leaders, the battalion was organized along tribal lines. During World War II, the Twenty-eighth Maori Battalion saw active service in Greece, Crete, Libya, and Italy, distinguishing itself especially in the Western Desert and at Cassino.

In the post-World War II period, the government decided that Maoris were to serve throughout the New Zealand Defence Forces, rather than in their own unit. Maoris served in the New Zealand contingent, which formed part of the Commonwealth antiterrorist forces in Malaya in the late 1950s and early 1960s. In 1964 the New Zealand secretary of defence, in his address to the reunion of veterans of the Twenty-eighth Maori battalion, presented the government's reasons for not wanting the reconstitution of the unit. He took the position that the desire for such a unit was backwards, rather than forwards, looking, claiming that to influence the young Maori soldier to join a unit composed of his own group would, in effect, be unfair. He stressed the importance of integration and said that he rejected any effort that would bring about what he saw as cleavage between Maori and European. The reaction of the Maori leadership to this was expressed in a parliamentary debate in June 1964, during which Maori MPs concurred that a Maori unit should be set up. In fact, one Maori MP attacked the government and secretary of defence for their refusal "to allow a Maori unit to be formed," going on to say that "those who suggest that this would be segregation can find their answer on the battlefields of Greece, Crete, the Desert and Italy. . . . I hope this important matter will not be determined on the contentious basis of integration." By the 1970s, however, no such unit had been formed.[15]

In the four cases I focus upon—Canada, Belgium, Britain, and the United States—numerous minorities have been involved in military service. In the United States case, for example, the pattern of Negro military participation and exclusion has received attention only at various critical periods in the course of American history, as has the service of other groups such as American Indians and Hispanic (Mexican and Puerto Rican) and Asian minorities. In Belgium both major linguistic groups have provided military manpower, although significant differences existed in their degree of participation until recently. In Canada the military contribution of French-Canadians has been significant, although they would seem to be "antimilitaristic." In Britain the willingness of immigrant and second-generation Indian and Pakistani youth seems to be somewhat less than their fathers' attachment of serving "the Regiment," as manifest in the seemingly small number of Asians in H. M. Forces. On the other hand, however, some West Indian youth join the armed forces to escape from the squalor of their urban surroundings and the lack of job opportunities open to them.

The examples given provide only a partial listing of the numerous cases that can be cited regarding minority-military participation worldwide throughout history. I refer to some of them when considering the case studies in world perspective. What is clear at this point, however, is that the nature and extent of military participation can prove to be a crucial factor in the social-integration process in general and in the integration of the minority group and its members in particular, and thus the necessity for both systematic case-specific and general analysis. The linkage and feedback between societal cleavage or cohesion on the one hand and minority-military participation on the other hand, therefore, assume a relevance—as regards the prospect for societal stability in general—above the importance that would be attributed to such interactions at first glance, since the degree to which integrative processes take place in a society can result from or be reflected in conflicts of various types and magnitudes. Alternatively, a situation of equilibrium can, in turn, either foster integrative processes or delay them. The characteristics of minority military participation are, therefore, implicitly related to both problems of effective manpower utilization at the organizational level and effective social mobilization at the societal level.

A PROPOSED APPROACH TO THE ANALYSIS
OF MINORITY GROUPS AND MILITARY SERVICE

ASPECTS FOR EXAMINATION

In a recent survey and propositional inventory regarding minority groups in military organizations presented in the *Handbook of Military Institutions*, Charles Moskos stressed that "a high priority must be given to collecting data and formulating propositions on minority groups in military organizations which have generality extending beyond the particulars of a single national entity," concluding that "perhaps the most important, the development of a valid analytic framework for understanding minority groups in military organizations requires systematic comparative research." I believe, however, that to limit consideration solely to "minority groups *in* military organizations" could result in overlooking a number of social phenomena, the understanding of which could, in turn, prove crucial to an understanding of the interactive processes that characterize the relationship between a minority group and its members and the military. In other words, the subject of minority groups and military service should be dealt with not only in terms of a study of such groups in military organizations; rather, it should also be examined in terms of the societal context within which the interaction between the group and the military organization operates, including those social processes that delineate the nature and describe the effects of minority-military participation on the military organization, society as a whole, and the group itself.[16]

As for the situation of minorities in the military, Moskos suggested that the following "topics [be] covered: (1) recruitment, (2) assignment, (3) performance, (4) attitudes towards service life, (5) inter-group relations, and (6) armed forces and society." Since I intend to formulate generalizations going somewhat beyond specific aspects of minorities in military service, I have divided the topics that Moskos suggested into three broad aspects and also enlarged their scope to encompass (a) *patterns*, (b) *parameters*, and (c) *politicization* of minority-military participation. Regarding (a), I attempt to derive a descriptive framework for dealing with this aspect of minority-military participation based on a developmental typology relating to military-societal interactions presented by Moskos in his seminal paper on "the emergent military." Regarding (b), I delineate various forms of participation situations and unit organization. These forms can range from total exclusion on the one extreme through segregated, mixed, or separate units, to dual or plural military structures on the other extreme. Quotas and channeling of minority-military manpower comprise additional parameters to be reviewed. Regarding (c), I illustrate the process of politicization by reference to both case-specific episodes and general characteristics across cases, so that its significance and importance for minority-military participation can be stressed accordingly. All of these aspects relate, however, to the challenging question: is there a penalty or bonus for segregating or integrating minority groups in the military? The explicit nature and characteristics of these general aspects are outlined in detail in chapter 6 after the case studies are presented. Such an approach enables us to deal with cases as diverse as Canada and Belgium, on the one hand, in the same focus as the United States and the United Kingdom, on the other hand.[17]

SCOPE AND LIMITATIONS OF STUDY

In using the material gathered in the course of this inquiry, it was not my intention to present a detailed history of the military institutions in the specific case under consideration or an in-depth analysis of "minority-majority" relations in the case involved. Rather, based on the material collected, I attempted to delimit and describe some fundamental structures and processes that seem to characterize the military-minority interaction in the cases considered and in general.

To bring the scope of this study into manageable proportions, I had to adopt a suitable point from which to proceed as regards the term *military*, that is, what is meant here by *military* and its role and function in general and in the societal-stratification system in particular. As for the definitional problem regarding what constitutes a minority group, due to the large volume of material and anomalous arguments about definitions, it is best, for the sake of continuity and clarity in presentation, to deal with this in an appendix, where it can be discussed in detail.

With regard to the first point, I consider the military to be the only institution of formal, legitimate, and permanent nature at the disposal of the national government that functions as an instrument of armed coercion. In other words, since the military is the only institution charged with the specific task of national defense, as Bernard Barber noted, "military roles are . . . functionally required in society insofar as armed force is necessary to maintain internal order and external security." The difference between the military and a civil-national guard or militia, if it exists in the specific case, would be the degree of professionalization the former exhibits. Furthermore, in terms of organizational function, it seems that the primary responsibility of the latter institutions is the maintenance of internal order, that is, a "police" rather than a "national defense" function as such. Thus I limit detailed consideration to the military. Of course, it must be remembered in this context that the definition of *national guard* varies between the American system, ranging over the French gendarmerie to the Latin American-type of organization. If we accept the "constabulatory-force" concept proposed by Morris Janowitz as the direction in which modern military forces are moving, a clear distinction between military and police functions is established, insofar as the latter activity not only can involve the military in political conflict in the short term but is perceived by the military itself as actually preventing the performance of its role as the nation's guardian.

Regarding the military's role and function in the system of societal stratification, it is, of course, case-specific. However, there still exists some correlation between military rank and rank in the social hierarchy, depending on the degree to which the military is isolated from civilian society and polity. This, of course, implies that military participation in politics or nation building means that there exists a dysfunction in the societal system and polity necessitating it, notwithstanding that, as Samuel Finer maintained, the military in all cases pursues its goals through bargaining and negotiation with the polity's civilian sector.[18]

MODERNIZATION AND NATIONAL INTEGRATION: THE ROLE OF THE MILITARY—CONVENTIONAL APPROACHES AND A CRITIQUE

Following the above, an implicit and underlying question involves the issues of whether military criteria of ascription and assignment basically differ from those in the civilian sector when it comes to minority-military participation. In other words, although we know that the ascriptive systems of military organizations differ from those in nonmilitary institutions, does this necessarily result in *integrative* processes taking place to a greater extent than in civilian life or other institutions? The question then arises regarding the characteristics of military organizations that enable integrative processes to take place. Now, the military in developing countries, at least, has been proposed as the model of an institution that, as a result of its inherent nature and characteristics, is both modernizing and integrative. It follows, therefore, that the more developed the country, the more integrative the military will be, or the more it can be assigned integrative functions. But is this really the case, or has a "projective fallacy" occurred, and if the latter contention does not hold, what are the implications for countries still along the road to advanced or postindustrial development?

Can it be, then, that due to the high degree of military "representativeness" in most cases where minority groups are present in society, the ideal characteristics of the military engendering integrative processes, as described by observers such as Edward Shils, Lucien Pye, and Janowitz, for example, do not exist and thus such processes simply do not occur? These questions can be answered only after considering the conventional approach to the military and national integration and its shortcomings and determining whether integrative processes have indeed taken place in the case studies of minority-military participation. In any event, the discussion here concerns the two extant models of military organization, ascription and assignment, which have been said to engender national integration, and a critique of their analytical and descriptive relevance in terms of both explanatory rigidity and projective fallacy.[19]

THE FORMAL ORGANIZATIONAL
MODEL AND ITS IMPLICATIONS

The properties of the formal organizational model have been outlined by a number of observers. For example, Shils, in his essay on "the military in the political development of the new states," claimed that the "military organization has little to do with the structure of . . . society, from which it is set off by its technology, most of its ethos, its organization and its training," and Amos Perlmutter noted that "the salient characteristic of modern military organizations . . . is their professionalism. The professionalism and institutionalization of the military entails the establishment of military colleges, specialized training, the formation of a unified professional group and of a national army." Kurt Lang also noticed the transformation of the military organization over time from what Janowitz termed "a relatively self-contained ('primitive') organization" to a "competitive" and more "complex and civilian interrelated" organization.[20]

In writing about "military organizations" in the *Handbook of Military Institutions*, Janowitz stated that "military organization reflects the social structure and political and cultural values of each particular environment," and thus "because military formations are organized as national units, they reveal the consequences of historical and traditional values." Earlier, however, in dealing with "armed forces and society in world perspective," Janowitz noted a tendency toward overemphasizing the "formal" perspective of the organizational model he presented himself in both *The Professional Soldier* and *The Military in the Political Development of New Nations*:

In the past . . . when . . . social scientists approached the study of armed forces they did so with an expression of civilian ideology which tended to distort the differences between military and civilian organizations. They tended to overlook what is commun [sic] to large scale organizations in general, both civilian and military. In the current intellectual climate, the reverse distortion is the danger. The social scientist runs the risk of overemphasizing the special characteristics of the military establishment.[21]

Even so, Marion Levy, in his book *Modernization and the Structure of Societies*, stated that "the generally accepted kind and level of isolation of armed forces personnel is extraordinary and it becomes the more extraordinary the more modernized the society." He qualified this statement, however, by noting that "in relatively modernized contexts, armed forces personnel may in fact be less isolated and are certainly less isolable than in relatively non-modernized contexts, but interdependency in general is so high in the former that any isolation becomes more extreme in its implications—whether for good or for evil.'' He continued:

> If action in terms of armed forces organizations is to be effective, it is necessary not only to isolate new members of the organization from the general civilian populace in order to teach them new skills and to integrate them with the going members of the organization, but to some extent it is also necessary to keep them relatively isolated during their membership in order to keep their skills at the readiness. . . .[22]

Levy concluded, therefore, that "given the general isolation of armed forces personnel and given the special emphasis on this isolation until basic training, at least, can be imposed on the new members, the general social origin of the personnel has a special relevance for their behavior while members."

Following from this, if both the minority group and its members are considered to be, in Lang's terms, "resources" for "mobilization," then, according to Levy, if they do participate militarily, their minority origin would be of relevance. Thus the formal organizational approach has also been extended to problems of national integration, as specified by Shils, who claimed that:

1. The military, being of necessity technically oriented, is thus also oriented toward modernization and development, which can only proceed with national integration.
2. The integrative functions of the military are reflected in its national "symbolism" and in the fact that it can act as a "nation-building institution."

Thus according to Shils:

3. The military is capable of playing a constructive part in the provision of some of the elements of a coherent modern, and even democratic society. It can serve to integrate diverse ethnic groups into a national community; it can teach skills useful in economic development; it can keep young men from being infected by nationalistic ideology and give them a greater concern for the nation as a whole.[23]

Janowitz is more explicit regarding the role of formal organizational properties in the military-minority interaction. Given that the military has a specific organizational character resulting from its goal orientation and "combat ideology," "it tends to stress the personal worth of the individual man and to ignore his social background." *As such, the modern military—"in a new nation or an old—*has certain organizational features which result in the recruitment of personnel from more representative and humbler social origins than other professions," that is, "the military attracts recruits from aspiring social groups." He concluded, therefore, by saying that "the military also tends to attract the ambitious who recognize that career success in the military is less likely to be affected by their humble social origins than in other professions. In the ethos of the profession, as inherited from Western professional contacts, social background is de-emphasized once a man has been accepted into military service."[24]

Pye noted an additional characteristic of military service in dealing with the political significance of acculturation in a military setting in terms of citizenship training. He described this process as follows: "recruits with traditional backgrounds must learn about a new world in which they are identified with a larger political self. They learn that they stand in some definite relationship to a national community. In this sense the army experience tends to be a politicizing experience." He concluded, therefore, that "armies in newly emergent countries can thus provide a sense of citizenship and an appreciation of political action."[25]

THE REFERENCE-GROUP APPROACH AND THE MILITARY-SOCIALIZATION PROCESS

One of the factors common to both the formal organizational model and the reference-group approach is the socialization process that occurs in the military. On the most general level of analysis, the systemic, formal model provides one basis for propositions regarding the role of "institutional" means in desocialization out of civilian value systems and resocialization into a military mold. For example, in speaking about the basic training process, Samuel Stouffer indicated the importance of maximizing the internalization of organizational controls in military settings through the process of "habituation" or, in other words, the stripping down of the civilian exterior of the new soldier and the rapid inculcation of military mores. As Stouffer related, the fear of being rejected by one's reference or peer group, however, during the military-socialization process—that is, the fear of failure in task performance in the basic training period and its inevitable outcome—is so paramount as to function as a factor of informal control reinforcing the internalization of the organization's social norms. It is here, then, that reference-group theory attains relevance, that is, during the military-socialization process itself.[26]

According to some observers, in the military context, therefore, becoming a member of a primary group may even transcend particularistic criteria of ascription, that is, if group goals and their achievement take precedence over individual characteristics. In other words, since "primary" group norms are not necessarily or consistently in conflict with "secondary"-group norms, they can give rise to social control of an informal nature, which can prove to be of greater effectiveness in attaining organizational goals than any formal control stemming from the larger organization itself. Some commentators, however, have claimed the process of socialization to be a response to adjustment problems raised by the socialization context itself and not the outcome of values that extended into the situation. Thus the concept of the military as a "total institution," within which a socialization process takes place, also becomes relevant here.[27]

According to Erving Goffman, total institutions are organizations or "entities whose total character is symbolized by the barrier to social intercourse with the outside" with the means of departing "often built into the physical plant," or where there are constraints or physical liabilities on departure such as death or imprisonment. Furthermore, in Goffman's view, although "a basic social arrangement in modern society is that the individual tends to sleep, play, and work in different places, with different co-participants, and without an overall rational plan," the preeminent characteristic of a total institution "can be described as a breakdown of the barriers ordinarily separating these spheres of life." Indeed, the institutional quality of military life (e.g., barracks, camps) can be readily counterpointed to that existing in the civilian sector. Thus Goffman claimed, in a total institutional framework (prisons, asylums, or military settings), socialization would occur as a result of deprivation, frustration, rejected status, and strict social control.[28]

Furthermore, in this context, the extent of socialization would depend upon the degree to which the individual involved has developed "positive" relationships before becoming enmeshed in the total institutional framework, in addition to the continuance of these relationships during this period. Research done on the socialization process in one total institutional setting—prison—has shown that the "culture" developed was not only dependent on values brought into the situation by the individuals themselves and those inculcated during the period, but it is also affected by expectations of the future. This result seems to resemble Robert Merton's anticipatory-socialization concept, in which the individual prepares himself for future roles, tasks, or positions, something that is at the basis of the military-socialization process, that is, the preparation for future possible combat roles and military task fulfillment.[29]

To sum up, as Lang observed, any formal military organization can be considered a total institution "in the sense that it is organized to protect the larger society against both internal and external dangers," whether real or perceived. Lang continued: "in addition to conducting military operations during periods of war (or national emergency requiring military skills), the military are responsible in peacetime for steps to put the armed forces in a state of adequate preparedness and to deploy them in strategically operational positions. Since neither the procurement of resources and manpower nor their advantageous deployment can occur on short notice, this function involves much long-run planning." All of this, of course, involves the inculcation of the notion that the military is distinctly different from civilian society both in concept and in function. This is accomplished by stress on the fulfillment of the mission of the military, which of necessity involves the performance of specific tasks in a closed or partly closed setting, not precluding civil-military interactions as such, but proscribing them to a significant degree, depending on the task to be fulfilled.[30]

A CRITIQUE OF THE FORMAL ORGANIZATIONAL AND REFERENCE-GROUP APPROACHES

In a seminal paper on "political systems and the role of the military," Roslyn Feldberg pointed out, in concise and lucid terms, a basic fault in both the formal organizational and reference-group models of military-societal relations and, in turn, the role of the military in modernization and national integration. According to her, most of the work dealing with these issues has been based on accounts of the internal characteristics of the military. Among these aspects have been (1) the degree of professionalism; (2) whether a specific status or ethnic group dominates the military; (3) whether the military is geared to be elite or embraces all segments of society; (4) military traditions; (5) the military's role in key events, for example, independence struggle; and (6) the military's position in the social structure and whether it is a vehicle for social mobility. Feldberg rightly contended, however, that:

The major problem with such explanations is that they use internal characteristics as independent variables and attempt to predict the role of the military in the larger society. This ignores the institutional framework in which the military and political organs of the society function. It neglects the extent to which the role of the military is determined by the changing national and international environment with which it interacts and to which it must adapt.[31]

Ann Willner also provided a cogent critique of both the formal organizational and reference-group models in terms of "projective fallacy." In an important review essay on "the underdeveloped study of political development" published in 1964, Willner first warned of the dangers involved in projecting attributes of the military organization from one setting to another, that is, from developed to developing countries. In her study on "military elites as rulers and wielders of power" published in 1970, Willner claimed that in contrast to those "theorists who have emphasized the unifying role of the military,"

It can be well argued that in a multi-ethnic society the internal cohesion of a ruling military establishment can exascerbate cleavages, if the military is largely recruited from one ethnic group and tends to favour that group in its policies.

But more importantly, what the "national-integration" theorists

failed to do, however, is to specify or elaborate the linkages between a unified or cohesive military establishment and increasing national integration. Even if we can assume that the attributes of a particular military establishment contribute to unification of its diverse personnel and that factionalism is absent from its leadership, what are the processes by which unity within the military contributes to unity within the polity?[32]

It is not my intention to attempt to answer the question Willner posed. Rather, I would prefer to suggest the possibility that a situation of projective fallacy—following from the straightforward and uncritical application of theories of systemic, institutional, and organizational behavior to interaction situations for which they may be unsuited—may have occurred with regard to the minority-military interaction in developed countries. I would attribute this to the inherent dichotomy between the military as a modernizing agent as against the national-integration function also usually attributed to it. As Wilson McWilliams noted:

There tends to be a major conflict between the image of the military as the spearhead of modernization and the image of the armed forces as a vehicle for national integration. "Modernization" tends to emphasize the control of the public by a comparatively small military; "integration" involves masses and presumes meeting their demands for reward and status, at least to some degree.[33]

Thus McWilliams continued, "efforts to achieve national integration through the military [often] tend to slide over into 'integral nationalism' of a quasi-totalitarian variety. Military education and techniques for influencing opinion are typically shaped by the desire to achieve control; at best, they skate on a thin layer of ice between education and manipulation.'' However, he continued, ''armies need not be supportive of integral nationalism . . . they can be supportive of political pluralism, and often they are. This result is likely if the military recruits most of its personnel from minority social strata or from ethnic groups which operate at a disadvantage in the political process.'' An alternate situation can result, on the other hand, if ''an 'advanced' minority uses a monopoly of military power to achieve rapid development despite the objections of traditionalists and others . . . [since] it is . . . precisely in these situations where national integration is minimal.''

Now, given that the developed countries were modernized by and during the process of urbanization and industrialization, one would think that the process of ''national integration'' and ''amalgamation'' could have been carried out by the military in such cases with a minimum of effort. In contrast to this, however, the existence of highly pluralistic societies in some developed countries attests to the fact that in these cases the military was either (a) not called upon, refused, or failed to fulfill a national-integration function; or (b) some groups toward whom such an effort was directed saw in military service a means of asserting their pluralistic tendencies and thus resisted these efforts accordingly. Thus the projection of the ''natural'' integrative characteristics of the military, stemming from both the formal organizational and reference-group approaches, may not be valid in the cases of minority groups and military service in developed countries. As Willner noted, ''in some armies, recruits of similar regional or ethnic background are dispersed throughout the various units . . . in others . . . army divisions may be specialized along regional and ethnic lines. In cases of the latter type, divisional rivalries may be reinforced by parochial attitudes, and subnational differences may be promoted rather than diminished by army experience.'' Militaries in developed countries corresponding to the former type may or may not have succeeded in promoting ''national integration,'' depending on case-specific characteristics.

Situations of the latter type seem to abound in both developed and underdeveloped countries, where the nature of national integration is expressed in terms of either "pluralism" or "segmented pluralism," the first referring to underdeveloped countries; the second, to developed countries.[34]

In any event, we can formulate "grounded" generalizations regarding the nature and characteristics of minority military participation from the case studies themselves, rather than attempting to analyze them within the rigid framework of the formal organizational and reference-group approaches.[35]

NOTES

1. See, for example, S. N. Eisenstadt, *The Political Systems of Empires* (Glencoe, Ill.: Free Press, 1963), pp. 130-131, 172-75. The concept of *mercenary* has been adequately defined by Anthony Mockler in his book *Mercenaries* (London: MacDonald, 1970), ch. 1, pp. 13-24. See also S. Andreski, *Military Organization and Society* (London: Routledge and Kegan Paul, 1954), pp. 45-46; F. A. Snowden, *Blacks in Antiquity* (Cambridge: Harvard University Press, 1971), pp. 130ff. and chs. 1-4; H. M. D. Parker, *The Roman Legions* (Oxford: Oxford University Press, 1928), ch. 6, pp. 169ff.

2. On these points, see G. Webster, *The Roman Imperial Army* (London: Black, 1969), pp. 143-44; G. R. Watson, *The Roman Soldier* (London: Thames and Hudson, 1969), p. 154; G. L. Cheesman, "The Auxilia of the Roman Imperial Army," *Studia Historica* (Rome) 59 (1968), p. 84; A. E. R. Boak, *Manpower Shortage and the Fall of the Roman Empire in the West* (Ann Arbor: University of Michigan Press, 1955), pp. 92-119; R. McMullen, *Soldier and Civilian in the Later Roman Empire* (Cambridge: Harvard University Press, 1963), pp. 12-19, 96-98; P. A. Brunt, *Italian Manpower: 225 B.C.-14 A.D.* (Oxford: Clarendon Press, 1971), pt. 4, pp. 391-509.

3. W. Kaegi, "Patterns of Political Activity in the Armies of the Byzantine Empire," in M. Janowitz and J. van Doorn, eds., *On Military Intervention* (Rotterdam: Rotterdam University Press, 1971), pp. 5ff.; S. Andreski, *Military Organization*, pp. 56-57, 201; and G. Mosca, *The Ruling Class* (New York: McGraw-Hill, 1939), p. 228.

4. See, for instance, E. Be'eri, *Army Officers in Arab Politics and Society* (London: Praeger, 1970), p. 297; A. Cohen, "The Army in

Palestine in the 18th Century," *Bulletin of the School of Oriental and African Studies* (University of London), 34, 1 (1971), pp. 46-53.

5. On these issues, see A. Vagts, *A History of Militarism* (London: Hollis and Carter, 1959), pp. 251-52; S. Cohen, *The Indian Army* (Berkeley: University of California Press, 1971); and idem, "The Untouchable Soldier: Caste, Politics, and the Indian Army," *Journal of Asian Studies* 28, 3(1969), pp. 453-68; A. Mockler, *Mercenaries*, ch. 4, pp. 74-104, gives a good account of Swiss mercenaries.

6. D. Thomson, *Europe Since Napoleon* (London: Penguin, 1972), p. 487; N. Pasic, "Factors in the Formation of Nations in the Balkans and among the South Slavs," *International Social Science Journal* 23, 3(1971), p. 420, n. 33; R. F. Inglehart and M. Woodward, "Language Conflicts and Political Community," *Comparative Studies in Society and History* 10, 1(1968), pp. 34-37.

7. On these and other African cases, see J.: Cardoso, "The Black Man as a Soldier," in J. Roucek and T. Kiernan, eds., *The Negro Impact on Western Civilization* (New York: Philosophical Library, 1970), pp. 347-52; M. G. Smith, *Government in Zazzau* (Oxford: Oxford University Press, 1960), p. 242. For the Arabian case, see R. Sanger, *The Arabian Peninsula* (Ithaca: Cornell University Press, 1956).

8. K. Tsurumi, *Social Change and the Individual: Japan Before and After Defeat in World War II* (Princeton: Princeton University Press, 1970), pp. 89-90.

9. R. H. Mitchell, *The Korean Minority in Japan* (Berkeley: University of California Press, 1967), pp. 71, 87; R. P. Dore, ed., *Aspects of Social Change in Modern Japan* (Princeton: Princeton University Press, 1967), especially ch. 11, pp. 337-72; G. De Vos and H. Wagatsuma, *Japan's Invisible Race* (Berkeley: University of California Press, 1966), p. 51. See also W. Newell, "Some Problems of Integrating Minorities into Japanese Society," *Journal of Asian and African Studies* 2, 3-4 (1967); J. Cornell, "Caste in Japanese Social Stratification," *Monumenta Nipponica* 25, 1-2 (1970); E. Norbeck, "Continuities in Japanese Social Stratification," in L. Plotnicov and E. Tuden, eds., *Essays in Comparative Social Stratification* (Pittsburgh: University of Pittsburgh Press, 1970).

10. S. Andreski, *Military Organization,* p. 201; L. McAlister, "The Military," in J. J. Johnson, ed., *Continuity and Change in Latin America* (Stanford: Stanford University Press, 1964), pp. 139-40; J. Johnson, *The Military and Society in Latin America* (Stanford: Stanford University Press, 1964), p. 238; T. L. Smith and Y. Fuji, *The Acculturation of Japanese Immigrants in Brazil* (Tampa: University of Florida Press, 1959);

G. Freyre, *Mansions and Shanties: The Making of Modern Brazil* (New York: Knopf, 1963), pp. 368ff.; J. Zamor, "Social Mobility of Negroes in Brazil," *Journal of Inter-American Studies* 12, 2 (1970), pp. 251-52.

11. R. Garthoff, "The Military as a Social Force," in C. E. Black, ed., *The Transformation of Russian Society* (Cambridge: Harvard University Press, 1960), p. 327.

12. M. Garder, *A History of the Soviet Army* (London: Pall Mall, 1966), p. 175; A. Nove, "History, Hierarchy, and Nationalities: Some Observations on the Soviet Social Structure," *Soviet Studies* 21, 1 (1969), pp. 83-84; V. G. Kiernan, "Conscription and Society in Europe Before the War of 1914-18," in M. R. D. Foot, ed., *War and Society* (London: Elek, 1973), pp. 152-53; D. White, *The Growth of the Red Army* (Princeton: Princeton University Press, 1944), pp. 272-73.

13. D. White, *The Growth of the Red Army*, pp. 360-61; M. Garder, *History of the Soviet Army*, p. 175; A. Benningsen and C. Lemercier-Quelquejay, *Islam in the Soviet Union* (London: Pall Mall, 1967), pp. 199-200; G. Wheeler, *Racial Problems in Soviet Muslim Asia* (Oxford: Oxford University Press, 1962), p. 47; T. Wolfe, "The Military," in A. Kassof, ed., *Prospects for Soviet Society* (London: Pall Mall, 1968), p. 126.

14. J. Cowan, *The Maoris in the Great War* (Wellington, N.Z.: Whitcombe and Tombs, 1926), pp. 4-7, 9-23; P. S. O'Connor, "The Recruitment of Maori Soldiers, 1914-18," *Political Science* (Wellington, N.Z.) 19, 2 (1967), pp. 48-59; M. Sorrenson, *Maori and European Since 1870* (Auckland, N.Z.: Heinemann, 1967), pp. 23ff.

15. P. S. O'Connor, "Recruitment of Maori Soldiers," pp. 60-83; J. F. Cody, *Official History of the Twenty-Eighth (Maori) Battalion in World War II* (Wellington, N.Z.: War History Branch, Dept. of Internal Affairs, 1956), pp. vi, 1-9; E. Schwimmer, "Why the Maoris Choose the Army," *Te Ao Hou* (New Zealand) 36 (September 1961), pp. 7-8; Statement of Mr. P. T. Watene, M.P., *Parliamentary Debates, New Zealand*, 34th Parliament, 1st Sess., 23 June 1964, p. 263; Letter to author from Col. F. H. Childs, Director of Training, New Zealand Ministry of Defence, 13 Oct. 1972 (50/8/8/DPRPS); Letter to author from R. D. Wilson, Assistant to the Secretary of State for Maori Affairs, New Zealand, 11 Dec. 1972 (19/1/239).

16. C. C. Moskos, "Minority Groups in Military Organizations," in R. W. Little, ed., *Handbook of Military Institutions* (Beverly Hills: Sage, 1971), p. 286.

17. Ibid., p. 276; C. C. Moskos, "The Emergent Military: Civil, Traditional or Plural," *Pacific Sociological Review* 16, 2 (1973), pp. 255-80.

18. M. Janowitz, *The Professional Soldier* (New York: Free Press, 1964), ch. 20; B. Barber, *Social Stratification* (New York: Harcourt, Brace, 1957), p. 34; S. Finer, *The Man on Horseback* (London: Pall Mall, 1967), p. 86. See also I. L. Horowitz, *Three Worlds of Development* (Oxford: Oxford University Press, 1966), pp. 276-79.

19. See notes 31 and 32 below.

20. E. Shils, "The Military in the Political Development of the New States," in J. J. Johnson, ed., *The Role of the Military in Underdeveloped Countries* (Princeton: Princeton University Press, 1962), p. 31; A. Perlmutter, "The Praetorian State and the Praetorian Army," *Comparative Politics* 1 (April 1969), p. 384; K. Lang, "Technology and Career Management in the Military Establishment," in M. Janowitz, ed., *The New Military* (New York: Sage, 1964), pp. 39-81.

21. M. Janowitz, "Military Organization," in R. W. Little, ed., *Handbook of Military Institutions,* p. 13; idem, "Armed Forces and Society in World Perspective," in *Transactions of the Sixth World Conference on Sociology* (Evian, France: International Sociological Association, 1967), p. 148; idem, *The Military in the Political Development of New Nations* (Chicago: University of Chicago Press, 1964); idem, *The Professional Soldier*, ch. 1.

22. M. Levy, *Modernization and the Structure of Societies,* vol. 2 (Princeton: Princeton University Press, 1966), p. 594.

23. E. Shils, "The Military in the Political Development of the New States," also in J. J. Johnson, ed., *The Role of the Military*, pp. 32-33.

24. M. Janowitz, *The Military in the Political Development of New Nations,* p. 53.

25. L. Pye, in "Armies in the Process of Political Modernization," J. J. Johnson, ed., *The Role of the Military,* pp. 82-83.

26. S. Stouffer et al., *The American Soldier* (Princeton University Press, 1949).

27. See, for example, H. Selvin, *The Effects of Leadership* (New York: Free Press, 1960); idem, "Adult Socialization," in *International Encyclopedia of the Social Sciences* (New York: Macmillan, 1968), pp. 559-60. See also D. Clemner, *The Prison Community* (New York: Rhinehart, 1958).

28. E. Goffman, *Asylums* (New York: Anchor, 1961), pp. 4-5. On the military as a total institution, see also K. Lang, "Military Organization," in J. G. March, ed., *Handbook of Social Organizations* (Chicago: Rand McNally, 1964), pp. 848ff.

29. S. Wheeler, "Socialization in Correctional Institutions," in L. Radinowicz and M. Wolfgang, eds., *The Criminal in Confinement* (New York: Basic Books, 1971), pp. 99ff.

30. K. Lang, in J. G. March, ed., *Handbook of Social Organizations,* pp. 838ff.

31. R. Feldberg, "Political Systems and the Role of the Military," *Sociological Quarterly* 11, 2 (1970), p. 207.

32. A. R. Willner, "The Underdeveloped Study of Political Development," *World Politics* 16, 3 (1964), pp. 468-82; "Perspective on Military Elites as Rulers and Wielders of Power," *Journal of Comparative Administration* 2, 3 (1970), pp. 263ff.; quotations from (1970), p. 263, 267.

33. W. McWillams, ed., *Garrisons and Government* (San Francisco: Chandler, 1967), pp. 22, 25.

34. A. Willner, "Perspectives on Military Elites," pp. 266-67.

35. On the concept of "grounded" generalizations, see B. Glaser and A. Strauss, *The Discovery of Grounded Theory: Strategies for Qualitative Research* (Chicago: Aldine, 1967). See also their critique of M. Janowitz's study *The Military in the Political Development of New Nations,* where they also suggested that he has fallen into "projective fallacy," pp. 134-35.

2

BELGIUM

DIMENSIONS OF THE BELGIAN SITUATION: SOCIETY, POLITY, AND MILITARY

In 1970 Val Lorwin, while discussing "linguistic pluralism and political tension in modern Belgium," wrote that "few people would die to break up the Belgian unitary state, just as few people would die to hold it together." Lorwin, a prominent observer of the Belgian situation, made this cogent point in describing the "temper and style" of the Belgians when dealing with their political conflicts. But this comment may be more significant than merely a description of Belgian political temperament. Indeed, before making this observation, Lorwin cited the words of one of the most important Flemish newspapers, which in 1964 claimed that "Belgium is not condemned, but it must prove its right to live." Of course, time has passed since those words were written, but the fundamental difficulties Belgium faces, including the question of whether it should continue in its present form, are still prevalent, dominating every facet of national existence. However, whether or not those "people" Lorwin talked about would willingly sacrifice themselves in defense of their country is a different matter, for history has shown that members of both major Belgian communities have made such an effort, although communal tensions have also found their way into this sphere of activity.[1]

Almost every aspect of Belgian life exhibits the characteristics of "plural minoriticity." This, of course, results from the fact that, at the same time, both main groups in the country—the Flemings and Walloons—are engaged in efforts to "improve" their situation in political, economic, and sociocultural affairs, each perceiving of itself as occupying a subordinate position vis-à-vis the other, in addition to efforts to defend their respective "patrimonies" and traditional spheres of influence and control.

In historical perspective, then, the Belgian situation can be divided into a number of periods. The first of these periods both precedes 1830, when as a result of independence the "communal problem" can be said to have begun, and continues up to World War I, with the period of the war itself and the time up to World War II deserving consideration in its own regard. The third period of World War II also merits specific consideration, with the postwar era dating to 1958 or 1959, when fundamental changes occurred in Belgian sociopolitical life. The period following 1959, therefore, is the fourth and final one dealt with here.

THE PRE-INDEPENDENCE AND POST-INDEPENDENCE ERA

Until 1830 no "communal problem" existed in Belgium. In the earliest period after the partition of Charlemagne's empire in 843 A.D., language had no political importance in Belgium, since the official language of the time was Latin. French gained in stature as time went by and was spoken by both the Walloons and the Flemish elite. Still, Flemish remained the tongue of the masses in Flanders and was also used for local administration. For the most part, however, language during these early years was not a rallying point around which political movements crystallized.[2]

Both Belgium and Holland passed into Spanish rule, and although the Dutch gained their independence after a war of liberation, Belgium remained under foreign rule, being passed on to Austria by Philip II of Spain. Under Spanish rule, French was the administrative and legal language overall, Flemish being used for local administrative purposes. Rule by Austria ended with the French invasion and the annexation of Belgium in 1794, with a subsequent "Frenchification" process being forced upon Flanders. This ended in 1815 with Napoleon's defeat and the action of William of Holland, who declared himself king of the "low countries," that is, Holland and Belgium. Belgian reaction to this, however, was that the Dutch were simply conquerors, and the union ended with a revolution in 1830. The outcome of the brief union with Holland, however, did prove to be significant, insofar as William's efforts to replace French with Dutch did revive Flemish cultural activities, especially among the intelligentsia. But his effort also proved counterproductive to the extent that the anticlerical Francophile Flemish bourgeoisie joined forces with both the Walloons and the religious Flemish Catholic masses in opposing Dutch rule, since the latter perceived the teaching of Dutch to be the forerunner of a Calvinist attack on their way of life, Holland being a Protestant country.[3]

When Flanders and Wallonia did secede from the Netherlands in 1830, then, there existed two distinguishable linguistic groups, the cleavage along center-periphery lines coincidental with the linguistic cleavage. But although French predominated not only as the administrative and cultural tongue but even as the language of the Flemish ruling elite, at the time of independence, Flemish speakers outnumbered Francophones by more than four to three. Previously, Flemish had been relegated to a peripheral status, being limited to those not participating in political affairs, that is, the Flemish peasants, workers, and lower middle class. The "nation builders" of the new Belgian state wanted to inbue a sense of national unity among both communities. Soon after independence therefore, French was declared to be the predominant language de jure, with laws published only in that tongue, being translated into the local Flemish dialects only if absolutely necessary. French, therefore, also became the only language used in all national institutions, that is, government, church, commerce, and the military. This occurred in spite of article 23 of the 1831 constitution, which contained the somewhat ambiguous clause that "the use of the languages spoken in Belgium is optional (faculatif); it may be regulated only for acts of the public authorities and for judicial affairs."[4]

Now, just as Flemish was a Dutch (that is, Germanic) dialect, so the tongues used in Wallonia—Walloon and Picard—were dialects of French. As a result of the adoption of French as a literary language in most of Europe, it was, of course, readily adopted by the Walloons, although Wallonia was situated outside the *political* boundaries of France, except from 1795 to 1815 (the notion of a state being based on nationality as defined by language was prevalent throughout the nineteenth century). Cooperation between the Walloons and the "Gallicized" Flemish bourgeoisie in support of French as the predominant language in Belgium could, therefore, exist only as long as the latter retained power in Flanders. Inasmuch as French was thought to be the "superior" tongue, language duality came to be symbolic of the structure of societal stratification, giving the Flemings a perception of first inferiority and then persecution. The efforts of William of Holland regarding language (from 1815 to 1830) described above also brought the linguistic question into the realm of education, besides reviving Flemish cultural and literary activities. The outcome of the combination of all of these factors, including the economic differences between the regions, was predictable. The Flemish movement began in earnest. Although this was, of course, a reaction to the efforts of the Walloons and Francophile Flemish bourgeoisie to defend French preeminence, its cultural element was contemporary to the revival of "national" literature among the Serbs, Magyars, Croats, and Czechs and thus can be said to have occurred in a "pan-European" context. But as Lorwin, James Dunn, and Derek Urwin noted, the Flemish movement initially proceeded slowly, partly due to the economic situation of the Flemish masses, partly to their disenfranchisement (until 1893 and even after, when plural voting tempered universal suffrage for men, resulting in Francophile Flemish overrepresentation), and partly to the fact that the Flemish activists during the early period were primarily Belgian nationalists and thus did not question French predominance as long as Flemish was recognized in Flanders.[5]

In any event, by 1840 a Flemish petition signed by 100,000 men was presented to the government, asking that (a) the official language of Flanders be made Dutch and that it be used in local and regional administration and the courts, (b) Dutch be used at the University of Ghent and in other government-financed educational institutions, and (c) an academy for Dutch literature be founded. In 1850 the first of a long series of school laws to attempt to establish parity between French and Flemish in education was passed, but it proved difficult to implement, and it wasn't until 1874 that there were enough university-trained Flemish teachers to enable the teaching of Dutch at the highest secondary-school levels. This was, of course, due to the fact that the language used in Flanders was basically an unwritten dialect, and most Flemings could not read "correct" Flemish, that is, standardized Dutch.[6]

In 1856 a commission was set up by the government to deal with the linguistic question. During its tenure, it examined the situation in other multilingual states such as Switzerland, where solutions had been found to similar problems. It also rejected the view that Belgian unity was dependent upon a "national" language, that is, French, and upheld the constitutional equality of Flemish. It dealt with the language situation at most stages of education, supporting the view that Flemish replace French and thereby become the only language of instruction in Flanders up to higher secondary and university levels. It also urged that at least courses involving medicine, law, and education given at the University of Ghent be conducted in Flemish. As for the institutional aspect of the linguistic issue, the commission proposed that (a) all official publications should be translated as a right into Flemish; (b) communications between central government and provinces of Flanders should be in Flemish, or in both languages, and not solely in French; (c) all laws and regulations should be translated into Flemish; (d) all higher diplomatic personnel should know Flemish so as to represent the "whole" of Belgium; and (e) the army should be divided into separate Flemish and French regiments. The government, however, upset at the scope of the reforms proposed, refused to publish the report, and it was published only in 1859 by private initiative.[7]

It is necessary to distinguish between the "Flemish *movement*" as such and "Flemish nationalism" as it emerged after 1919 (when true, that is, universal male suffrage was adopted), which is discussed in more detail below. The industrial revolution and its associated effects in the form of workers protest movements came to Belgium early, mainly affecting the South, that is, Wallonia, and produced characteristic radical syndicalism and anticlericalism. The church retained its grip on the populous and mainly agricultural Flanders, although there was a growing antagonism against the Francophile bourgeoisie among Flemish workers in the urban areas—mainly Antwerp and Gent—where, as Lorwin maintained, "most industrial workers were lost to the church." Still, Flanders, by and large, became, in G. A. Kelly's terms, "the bulwark of Catholicism and Catholic society," while Wallonia, except in rural areas, "turned on the curé and embraced the forms of the socialist anti-church." According to Kelly, then, for one, the Flemish *movement* was the outcome "of the forces of democracy and Catholicism," a strange combination, to say the least.[8]

In any case, a royal decree of November 1864 established, in Vernon Mallinson's words, a "parity of esteem" between Flemish and French, which enabled a series of acts over the next few decades to bring about the construction of a legal bilingual system. Thus in August 1873, a statute was enacted revising legal procedure in Flanders, with Dutch to be used in all Flemish courts, and in May 1878, Dutch was made the sole language for Flemish public affairs and administrative matters. In June 1883, Dutch was imposed as the sole language to be used in all secondary education, and in 1886, a Flemish Academy was founded. Finally, in April 1898, Dutch was legally adopted as the second official language of Belgium.[9]

But according to Mallinson, at least, the main reason for the reforms in favor of Flemish after 1884 was the assumption of power by the Catholic party from the Liberals. The Catholics, who, in fact, held power until 1919, recognized that they owed their victory to the Flemish electorate and attempted to build their own power base on this section of the population accordingly. Thus not only did the linguistic question become bound up with the religious split in the country, but it also became "politicized," especially since the Liberal-oriented Francophile-Flemish bourgeoisie became identified in the minds of the leaders of the Flemish movement and their followers with anti-Catholic and anti-Flemish interests, although the "Fransquillons," as they are still called, were anything but radical. As it became politicized, however, ideological differences emerged, and the Flemish movment itself split into Liberal, Catholic, and Socialist segments.[10]

The paramount issue remaining in the educational field that faced the Flemish movement after 1898 was the question of the "flamandisation" of the State University at Gent. This struggle is not recounted in detail here, but the issue continued to smoulder for three decades, with the Germans—in order to curry Flemish support and encourage separatism—opening a completely Flemish university during their occupation in 1916, which was immediately closed after the war. It was only in July 1923 that the university became bilingual and not until April 1930 that it received a charter for teaching in Flemish.[11]

The Flemish movement extended into every sphere of public life where French was predominant, and thus it also affected the situation in the Belgian army. As indicated above, French was adopted as the sole language used in the army after 1830. Obviously the "Flamingants" (Flemish-language activists) were resentful of the necessity for Flemings wanting to follow a career in the military to initially learn French. This condition, they maintained, prevented many Flemings from serving as NCOs and created difficulties for both officers and privates who were Flemish. The Grievance Commission of 1856 recognized these problems, as noted above, but until 1884 there was no improvement in the situation. In 1884 a bill was presented to the Chamber of Deputies (the lower house of the Belgian Parliament) stipulating that all officers should have a knowledge of Flemish. However, the bill was delayed in committee for three years. In 1887 the bill was finally debated and immediately opposed by Walloon representatives. Before it was eventually passed, the bill was revised three times, both in the lower house and the Senate, and in the end provided only that Flemish would be taught in the officers school and regimental schools, and after January 1892, Flemish would be acceptable in exam qualifications for entry into the officer corps. The amendments to the bill so altered it that most Flamingants considered its passage a defeat and not a victory for their cause.[12]

The situation in the militia was similar to that in the army, but by 1897 a law had been passed providing for military judicial proceedings to be held in Flemish and that it be used for instruction, administration, and command for all militia units in Flanders. As noted above, the situation in the military was not improved by the 1888 law, and additional reforms were thus sought by the Flamingants. The suggestion made by the 1856 commission regarding the creation of separate regiments was taken up by the Flamingants, but this was not successful, so the bill that finally passed in 1913 stipulated only that a knowledge of Flemish and French be required of students in the military school. This, however, did not alter the situation significantly, since it was not possible to teach Flemish to those officers already serving, so most officers spoke only French at the outbreak of war. Thus when compulsory service was instituted in 1913, those lower class Flemings without a knowledge of French were commanded in what was, to them, "a foreign language."[13]

Until now I have focused upon the movement for Flemish linguistic equality. After the 1912 elections, in which the Flemish-oriented Catholic party reinforced its 1884 victory margin, Walloon reaction became organized, with a Walloon congress held in Liege. At the congress, some delegates proposed the administrative division of the country. A permanent Walloon Assembly was set up, and, among its resolutions of October 1912 was one protesting the growing trend toward linguistic equality. The advent of war, however, interrupted the development of an organized Walloon movement, although Walloon journalistic activism continued even during the German occupation.[14]

In summary, contrary to other European "provincial" dialects, Flemish did not fade into a picturesque folk language. Rather, cognizant of the fact that Dutch was used as a "language of state" in the Netherlands, more and more of the Flemish populace came to support what became known as the Flemish movement. At first the movement was unorganized, but as time went on, and after the standardization of Flemish to the Dutch form, the movement developed a clear set of goals and proposals for reform. But as noted above, it became divided along party political lines, dissipating any political power it could have acquired among the three parties—Catholic, Liberal, and Socialist—and putting off the development of a Flemish "nationalist" party. Even after Flemish was declared to be Belgium's second official language in 1898, as Dunn noted, "this was more of a legal fiction than a linguistic reality: business as usual continued largely in French." Thus the distinguished parliamentarian Jules Destree was not far from wrong when, in describing the Belgian situation at the time to King Albert in 1912, he wrote, "There are no Belgians. . . . There are Flemings and Walloons, but there are no Belgians."[15]

WORLD WAR I AND THE PERIOD
BETWEEN THE WARS

The speed and route of the German offensive against Belgium in August 1914 resulted in the conquest of most of Wallonia within a very short time after the initial invasion. As a result, full mobilization occurred only in Flanders, and thus those elements of the Belgian army that engaged the Germans in the trench warfare that characterized the years after 1914 were mainly composed of Flemish soldiers. A number of observers have, in fact, placed these proportions at some 20 percent Walloon, most of whom were in the officers corps, and 80 percent Flemish, mostly in the ranks. Other factors also aggravated an already tense situation in the military, such as the fact that almost all officers were Francophone, and that since a 1913 statute providing for parity in language use was not implemented, French was almost exclusively used for orders and command in the trenches. In addition, when skilled workers were needed in French war industries, most of those withdrawn from the front line were, of necessity, Walloon.[16]

A number of serious incidents occurred due to the linguistic situation both in the trenches and in punishment camps. The situation on the "home front" also affected the Flemish soldiers in the trenches. A Flemish separatist movement was encouraged by the German occupation authorities, with actions occurring such as the establishment of a Flemish university in Gent, as noted above. A collaborationist Council of Flanders was organized in 1917 by a small number of Flemish activists, mostly literary and cultural figures, rather than political leaders, thereby further dividing a movement already fragmented along partisan political lines before the war, although it had, at least, been united regarding its general aspiration of linguistic parity. But this emboldened Flemish "activists" at the front, who, formulating the slogan "a Free Flanders in a Free Belgium," founded the Front party in the same year. This group adopted a defeatist attitude and the next year advocated surrender in case of a Belgian retreat in the face of a German counteroffensive. In the first elections held after the war in 1919, they ran as an independent political party, eventually calling themselves the Flemish Nationalist Front (VNV). Their strength grew, and the VNV had, by 1933, some 60,000 members actively engaged in a campaign for an autonomous Flemish state, if not a completely independent one; however, more about this below.[17]

Those Flemish civilian activists that had openly collaborated with the Germans were actively prosecuted after the war. The consequence of this, however, was a stiffening of Walloon opposition to renewed Flemish demands for linguistic reform, and Flemish perception that the Flemish movement as a whole was being put on trial along with the collaborators. In such an atmosphere, it is hardly surprising that the Flemish movement regained its prewar coherence of purpose only in the late 1920s. Of course, this can also be attributed to the fact that a Flemish-speaking elite oriented toward linguistic reform was absent until then, with new political leaders emerging who had, in Mallinson's terms, "outgrown the inferiority complex of their predecessors."[18]

In 1929 a Flemish congress sponsored by the Catholic party passed resolutions that were eventually incorporated in a series of linguistic laws that went into effect in late 1932. These new laws provided that (a) Dutch would be the only official language in Flanders; (b) Dutch would be the only language to be used in

Flemish courts; (c) there would be separate Flemish and French sections in all government departments; (d) all teaching in Flemish primary and secondary schools would be in Dutch only, although Francophones still living in Flanders would be accommodated; and finally, foreshadowing linguistic difficulties to come in the Brussels conurbation, (e) that educational authorities must assure that Flemish children living in Walloon areas would be taught in Flemish, and similarly for Walloon children. These laws, although only partially implemented—except in the judicial system, where sanctions were used to encourage compliance—in effect made both Flanders and Wallonia unilingual, leaving only the Brussels region as bilingual. But as Lorwin noted, although "the hopes for French as a national unifying factor had failed"—that is, the hopes of the Francophile-Flemish elite and the Walloons—"it continued in national economic life and in the higher ranks of public administration to hold a predominance which, diminishing and precarious as it was, roused the opposition of many Flemings," and thus the campaign of the Flemish movement continued.[19]

After the war, the attention of the Flemish movement again turned toward the linguistic situation in the army, and the Flamingants began to press for the division of the army into separate regiments for Flemish- and French-speaking soldiers. By 1928 a bill was proposed in parliament stipulating that (a) soldiers should be allocated to regiments or battalions where either the language of his native province or his mother tongue is used, (b) both languages be given equal status at the military academy, and (c) officers should speak the language of the soldiers in the units they command. This proposal, while arousing opposition in the Chamber of Deputies, finally became law in November 1928, and by 1932 a Flemish section of the military academy had been set up, and the army was made bilingual in that parallel but separate units came into being. However, as both Lorwin and Kelly noted, final "equality of language status in the armed forces" was attained only in July 1938.[20]

The emergence of Flemish nationalist parties as a political force after the institution of universal male suffrage in 1919 notwithstanding, the movement as a whole was still characterized by electoral weakness as a result of its fragmentation among the various political parties. Thus although it did serve as a pressure group on the Flemish segments of the "traditional" parties—and thereby on parliament and government—the Flemish nationalist parties per se were still unable to gain any significant political power for themselves. For example, these parties were never able to obtain more than 8 percent of the overall or 15 percent of the Flemish vote. The movement was, however, able to bring about a further law in July 1935 providing that any defendant facing judicial proceedings must be tried in his mother tongue, regardless of where he had committed the offense, and a commission sponsored by the movement not only stipulated that complete cultural autonomy be given to Flanders, but that both languages should have equal standing officially in their respective regions along the lines of the Swiss cantonal model. Finally, just before the outbreak of World War II, a de facto linguistic frontier dividing the country was established.[21]

An alternate hypothesis regarding the electoral failure of Flemish nationalism in the interwar years was proposed by André Simon. He maintained that over this period, the Flemish nationalist movement actually became alienated from the church as a result of the latter's concern for national unity, and that this, of necessity, implied the predominance of French. This, of course, is quite plausible, since it was only the lower clergy that were originally at the forefront of the Flemish movement, and the church hierarchy had been somewhat suspect of it from the beginning. In any case, with the rise of European fascism in the 1930s, similar trends also emerged in Belgium, both affecting the Flemish nationalist parties and catalyzing a home-grown fascist movement, Leon Degrelle's Rexists.[22]

With regard to the Rexist movement, only six months after it was founded, in the elections of 1936, it had obtained more than 15 percent of the total vote, winning twenty-one seats in the Chamber of Deputies. The movement, nationalist in orientation, originally appealed to the Catholics, and adopted both an anti-Marxist and anti-Semitic stance, becoming an outright fascist movement by 1939. As for the Flemish nationalist parties, they adopted a more separatist stance as time went on, with the largest of them, the

VNV, advocating Flemish autonomy with an authoritarian, corporatist approach borrowed from the Italians, in contrast to the earlier democratic, and even pacifist, outlook that characterized the Flemish movement's orientation. But as Urwin noted, it actually "performed a valuable function in preventing the Rexists and other right-wing groups from making inroads in Flanders" before the war, since the linguistic problem prevented the emergence of common ground between right-wing nationalist groups and Flemish separatists such as the VNV.[23]

To sum up, in the early stages of the Flemish movement, the objective had been bilingualism and linguistic parity. However, with their effort to defend their "patrimony" and their unwillingness to learn Flemish, the Walloons and Bruxellois-Francophones only reinforced the Flemish movement, which had, by now, changed its view to one that engendered Flemish autonomy, if not separatism. The Walloons and Bruxellois had now to abandon the "Fransquillons" (Francophile-Flemish) to their fate. Not only had the notion of French predominance as a unifying factor failed, so had *"integral"* bilingualism. Since both Flanders and Wallonia were to be unilingual, and only in the Brussels region was bilingualism to be practiced, as Lorwin wrote, "the principle was that of territorial, rather than personal choice." Thus it seemed that by the outset of war, there were no significant linguistic grievances to overcome and as Mallinson noted, observers felt that the aspirations of the Flemish separatists would come to nil. But as we shall see below, the *querelle linguistique* arose again, and with equal acrimony, soon after the end of World War II.[24]

The law of 30 July 1938 regarding the use of language in the Belgian armed forces forms the basic legislation affecting linguistic matters in the Belgian military until the present, being only slightly amended in 1953, 1963, and 1970, respectively. The law consists of four parts, dealing with (1) obligations imposed on officers and officer candidates, (2) obligations imposed on noncommissioned officers, (3) organization of educational and training establishments along linguistic lines, and (4) the use of language in reports of military authorities and in administrative matters.[25]

The initial part can be summed up as follows. The law

states that the unity of the officer corps should be maintained. To do this, it is essential that every officer can serve in units of any linguistic type. Thus an officer must know both national languages to the extent that he may fulfill the functions of his rank equally well in a Dutch-speaking or French-speaking unit. Every officer must undergo two examinations to test his knowledge of the second national language accordingly. The first is to be given to candidates for sublieutenant, to gauge their knowledge against that required of a junior officer. The second examination, which every candidate for major must undergo, is to see whether the individual has the linguistic competence required of a senior officer.[26]

The second part of the law provides that bilingualism is not required of noncommissioned officers. Thus the candidate for sergeant is not required to know both national languages, but in such a case, he would be assigned to a specific linguistic unit only. The third section of the law deals with the Royal Military Academy and other military schools, stipulating that they be organized in two sections—one Dutch- and one French-speaking. Every student would be assigned to his respective linguistic section, but he would also receive intensive instruction in the second language to help him prepare himself for the required examination. The same regulations would apply in all establishments charged with training officer candidates, and in every school, the uniformity of program and instruction would be the specific responsibility of the commander of the unilingual sections.[27]

The fourth part of the law stipulates that in all circumstances, the military authorities will use the language of the individual soldier or civilian with whom it is in communication. The law implicitly recognizes that although a parallel structure of military organization along linguistic lines may be desirable, there is the necessity, in specific instances, for "mixed units," and thus it provides for this by stating that soldiers of Dutch-language origin will be assigned to Dutch-language units in every case below company level, and officers with whom they come into contact will be required to conduct military training in Dutch accordingly. In a Dutch-language unit, therefore, Dutch will be the language used in reporting all military matters.[28]

WORLD WAR II AND THE POSTWAR PERIOD: 1939-1959

September 1939 found Belgium still preserving the neutrality it had declared in 1936. Eight months later, however, it fell to the German Blitzkreig of 10 May 1940 in only eighteen days, although this time, the Belgian army had been fully mobilized. As in 1914, Belgium again came under occupation. But this occupation was different, for it was total, and the country was not united to the extent it had been during occupation in World War I. Flemish extremist elements, Rexists, and opportunists supported the occupation. The "divide-and-rule" policy that had failed the Germans in World War I succeeded this time. One such move on their part was that Walloon prisoners taken during the hostilities of 10-28 May 1940 and after the surrender on May 28 were sent to Germany, whereas Flemish prisoners were liberated. The collaborationists, in fact, turned the four years of occupation into years of civil war, with executions of resistance members and deportations to Germany. They organized a large propaganda machine praising the "New Order," with both Rexists and Flemish extremists taking over the newspapers and calling for "a community of ideas and ideals." Indeed, their support for the occupation and the fascist cause extended to the formation of Flemish and Walloon legions that the Germans sent to the Russian front. By liberation in September 1944, deportations numbered some half-million, and German camps were filled with resistance members.[29]

After liberation, collaborators were brought to justice, but again, as after World War I, the Flemish were affected, both actually and psychologically, to a considerably greater extent than Walloons. Thus the Flemish movement reemerged only slowly, initially in the form of youth and cultural organizations. But by the 1950s, a Flemish party—the People's Union, or Volksunie—had gained some electoral support and, in the late 1950s, became, in electoral terms, the third largest party in Flanders, surpassing the strength of the Liberals. In the national elections of 1968, it received about 17 percent of the Flemish vote, greater than the highest vote (15 percent) for Flemish nationalist parties in the period between World Wars I and II.[30]

As for the Walloons, postwar censuses proved to be shocking for them. In late 1944, a preliminary census survey showed that 50.0 percent of the population lived in Flanders, 34.5 percent in Wallonia, and 15.5 percent in the Brussels conurbation. Three years later, in 1947, a linguistic census was conducted, revealing that 50.3 percent of the population spoke Dutch; 33.0 percent spoke French; 15.7 percent were "bilingual," that is, lived in the bilingual region of Brussels; and 1.0 percent spoke German. This, combined with the economic difficulties of Wallonia, started a process of "role reversal" that continued to the present, for now the Walloons *also* considered themselves to be in a "minority" situation. They perceived government favoritism toward Flanders—as regards the channeling of new investment—and their attitude against teaching Flemish as the second language in their schools hardened even more. A new tendency toward advocating some form of federalism or autonomy developed, and Walloon radicals even argued for independence or union with France.[31]

Two important national issues arose in the early postwar period that, at the same time, emphasized the duality of Belgian polity and society and inhibited discussion of the linguistic issue per se until the early 1960s. The first of these was the "Royal Question." Although this issue is not dealt with in detail here, it divided the nation on regional lines. After a long and heated debate that lasted for some five years, the issue was decided in March 1950 by referendum. Flanders voted for the continuance of Leopold as king, and Wallonia voted against his return to Belgium. But when Leopold did return, violence broke out, and he finally abdicated on 16 July 1951.[32]

The second issue—the "School Question"—emerged almost as soon as the "Royal Question" was settled. It involved the problem of government financial assistance to Catholic secondary schools. Again, as in the Royal Question, the conflict ran along party lines, with the Catholics pitted against the Liberals and Socialists, and due to the nature of support for these parties in the regions, a majority of Flemings opposed a majority of Walloons. What was at issue was not whether the Catholic schools *should* get aid, but its amount, since the Liberals and Socialists thought the large sums the Catholics were demanding meant that the state schools would suffer accordingly. The problem was finally resolved, however, in 1958 and 1959, with a "School Pact" negotiated in the aftermath of the 1958 elections, the effect of which was, in the view of Dunn and Lorwin, to "deconfessionalize" Belgian politics—that is, hasten the decline of party conflicts along strictly "religious" or ideological lines and the rise of politics based on specific immediate interests—and thereby enable the reemergence of issues related to the linguistic problem to again attain centrality in Belgian politics.[33]

After the war, linguistic difficulties also reemerged in the military. In 1946 a mixed commission was set up to review the linguistic law of July 1938 and to enable the chief of staff to adapt the organizational structure of the armed forces in light of (a) the changes in the technical nature of the armed forces and aspects of national defense; (b) the linguistic rights of national servicemen, that is, draftees; and (c) the necessity for officers from both linguistic groups to either know both languages or at least have an adequate knowledge of the second, to enable him to fulfill his service obligations and command responsibilities. On 28 February 1952, the minister of national defense had declared in the Belgian Senate his intention of setting up a mixed commission composed of parliamentarians, educators, and military officials to study the linguistic problems of the Belgian armed forces. By June the members of the commission had been appointed, and it met for the first time on June 17. Its general terms of reference, as set down in the Royal Decree creating it, were to study all problems relating to the application of the law of July 1938 concerning the use of languages in the military and to make any recommendations to the minister of national defense judged to be useful for the complete implementation of the law's provisions. But at the first meeting on June 17, the minister of defense made it clear that what was at issue was the defective application of the law as manifest in the unacceptable number of Flemish- relative to French-speaking officers.[34]

He stated that although as of 1 April 1951 unilingual brigades had been reinstated, according to the provisions of the 1938 law, the main linguistic problem could be resolved only by a significant augmentation in the number of Flemish officers. He claimed that there was a serious imbalance in the fact that while three-fifths of the national servicemen were Flemish, of some 5,300 officers overall—servicemen on active service and in the reserves—only 2,000 were Flemish, and that the numbers in the officer corps should be more in proportion to that overall. He then turned to the problem of Flemish entry into the Royal Military Academy and War College, stating that although there were Flemish sections in both institutions, he was unhappy about the numbers of Flemings in both institutions and especially about the number of Flemish candidates for entry into the former. Indeed, over the five-year period 1946-1950, the number of Flemish candidates entering the academy was, on average, less than 40 percent of total entries, although there was a slightly rising trend in both applications and admissions by 1952. He instructed the commandant of the Royal Military Academy, who was a committee member, to examine the situation and make suggestions for improvements.[35]

The president of the commission responded that it was indeed a violation of the spirit, if not the letter, of the law that such situations occurred, but he reminded the commission that although a dual linguistic structure for the military had been legislated in 1928, it was put into effect only by the 1938 law. Since then, he stated, it had simply been defectively applied, as evident in the statistics given by the minister himself. He concluded, therefore, that the three issues the commission should concentrate upon and make recommendations to correct were (1) the defective application of the 1938 law, (2) the disproportion between French- and Flemish-speaking officers, and (3) the difficulties surrounding Flemish entry into the Royal Military Academy.[36]

The commission met twenty-two times, holding its last session on 8 July 1953, almost fifteen years after the implementation of a dual linguistic structure in the Belgian armed forces. The report of the commission, published in 1953, ran along the lines of the original terms of reference, although it also turned its attention to the linguistic situation in the gendarmerie (State Militia). In the report, the commission dealt in detail with all three service branches and also with the situation in both the officer corps and ranks. It found that of *active* service officers in the army, only 17 percent were Flemish; in the air force, the figure was 20 percent; in the navy, it was some 45 percent; and overall, the percentage was only slightly more than 18 percent. As for reserve officers, however, the situation was much more favorable, about 60 percent being of Flemish origin in 1952, which was a complete reversal of the immediate postwar situation (1945-1947), when Flemish reserve officers were outnumbered by French-speaking reservists by almost three to one on average. Regarding noncommissioned officers, Walloons outnumbered Flemings 55 percent to 45 percent, and the commission pointed out that a serious effort had been made to recruit more Flemings accordingly. Table 1 illustrates the situation prevailing in 1952 among noncommissioned officers by using an "index of dissimilarity" between Flemish and Walloon rank distribution (the index represents the percentage of one of the groups that would have to change categories to obtain equality of rank distribution between the two groups).[37]

Table 1

Noncommissioned Officers in the Belgian Armed Forces, Rank Distribution by Linguistic Group, 1952

| | WALLOON | | FLEMISH | | |
Rank	Number	Percent	Number	Percent	Difference
Adjudant 1st class	286	5.1	96	2.1	− 3.0
Adjudant	825	14.5	394	8.6	− 5.9
Sgt.-maj. 1st class	1,184	21.0	777	17.0	− 4.0
Sgt. 1st class	1,267	22.5	1,020	22.5	—
Sgt.	2,081	36.9	2,272	49.8	+ 12.9
	5,643	100.0	4,559	100.0	

Note: Index of dissimilarity = 12.9

On the organizational level, the commission found that although a "unilingual" structure existed in the infantry up to the brigade level, the communications, ordnance, and quartermaster corps—in addition to the parachute and commando regiments—were "mixed." In the air force, however, due to its specific technical nature, most units except for airbase defense were mixed, but the technical language was, as in Holland, actually English. In the navy, due to the predominance of Flemish personnel, there were, in effect, no "mixed" units, but the commission in fact recommended its reorganization into unilingual units.

The main recommendation of the commission was that a permanent body be set up to review periodically the linguistic situation in the military and provide for day-to-day implementation of the linguistic laws, with powers to conduct active investigations to this end. Indeed, it recalled that the government had, as early as 1917, accepted the idea of such a body. It would be composed of nine members, six chosen from parliament and three from the military, serving for four years, with a secretarial staff provided by the Ministry of Defense. Other recommendations included the following:[38]

1. Although 60 percent of available places were reserved for Flemish candidates in the Royal Military Academy, and there were a good number of Flemish applicants for these places, not enough entries resulted. Thus to correct this chronic situation, a special campaign for information and preparation would be instituted in all middle and secondary schools in Flanders, and the examination system would be reviewed and revised accordingly.
2. Reforms would be instituted in linguistic examinations requiring officers to have a knowledge of both languages when passing out of the military academy, and periodic examinations would be held, with those candidates for major required to be fully bilingual.
3. Efforts would be made to encourage "cultural intercourse" between Flemish- and French-speaking personnel in the officer corps, with special emphasis on familiarizing Walloon officers with Flemish culture.
4. In mixed units, stress would be put on equality of language usage.
5. Special efforts would be made to increase the number of Flemish officers.

In his closing statement, the minister of defense complimented the commission on its work, noting that the number of bilingual officers was on the increase, and ended by saying that the fact that five of eleven colonels being considered for promotion to general were Flemish was a good sign that the language situation was improving.[39]

THE INSTITUTIONALIZATION OF CONFLICT: 1958-1959 ONWARDS

As noted above, during the early 1950s, Wallonia entered a period of sustained economic decline, while Flanders experienced significant economic growth. Thus after the contrast had become evident, a number of Walloon politicians began to maintain that Flemish politicians—who, in fact, formed a parliamentary majority—were exhibiting favoritism towards their region in terms of economic subsidies and investment distribution. The Walloon spokesmen advocated more autonomy for Wallonia so that its economic difficulties could be treated at the regional, and not governmental, level, since they perceived the latter to be dominated by the Flemish. The movement for "structural reform," in addition to the perception of Flemish domination of the central government, resulted in the creation of the Rassemblement Wallon, a federalist party founded in the mid-1960s.[40]

Lorwin, in writing about the new "Walloon problem" in 1966, noted that there had "never been a Walloon consciousness as strong as the Flemish consciousness," and in a more recent article on "linguistic pluralism and political tension in modern Belgium," he dealt with the reasons for this. In spite of their "prise de conscience," he claimed, the Walloons had never "had either the self-consciousness or the organization of the Flemish," since "the Flemish concept of *ons volk* has included all Flemish speakers, those of Brussels as well as those of Flanders, in a sentimental entity which—in part because of the century long struggle for linguistic equality—has reality beyond that linguistic bond."[41] Walloons, on the other hand, thought of themselves, for the most part, in local rather than in regional or linguistic terms, and thus as long as Francophones ran Belgium and Wallonia was prosperous, no "Walloon problem" existed. Indeed, Marion Coulon, writing in 1961 about cultural autonomy in Belgium, reported on the extension of the "querelle linguistique" to the Congo, with a proposal being put forward at one time to divide it into a Flemish-speaking region above the equator and a French-speaking region below. The Congolese, as Lorwin claimed, had, in fact, called the linguistic problem of their colonial masters "luttes tribales," that is, tribal struggles. [42]

But by the end of 1960, Belgium had lost the Congo, and because of the resulting economic upheaval, the Social Christian party (PSC, formerly the Catholic party) and Liberal coalition government passed an economic "retrenchment" bill. The outcome of this, however, was a general strike in December 1960 and January 1961 that lasted for thirty-four days, despite the fact that the majority of Socialists had opposed such action. Originally a protest against the government's new economic policy, the strike was turned into a protest against its policy toward Wallonia, with some Walloon radical socialist leaders advocating federalism and launching a new organization, the Mouvement Populaire Wallon, or MPW. As Lorwin noted, this not only aggravated the cleavage between Flemish and Walloon, but it actually divided the Belgian Socialist party (PSB), the leadership of which viewed the MPW as an electoral threat. [43]

Both Urwin and Dunn contended, therefore, that the trend of the early 1960s was toward confrontation between the communities and Belgian politics being dominated by linguistic polarization. One of the major issues polarizing the two communities was language usage in Brussels, since the nineteenth century saw the once-Flemish town become a city with a majority of Francophones. As noted above, not only was French stronger in cultural terms; knowledge of it was a requisite for upward mobility, and thus social pressure made it attractive on a personal level, while most local authorities in the Brussels conurbation discriminated against Flemish through administrative measures. They showed indifference to the requirements of the 1932 law, which provided for educational and administrative facilities, besides employment opportunities in local administration for Flemings. Furthermore, most business and cultural affairs were conducted in French. The growth of the Brussels population extended French influence into the Flemish Brabant province surrounding the city, and these people naturally asked for Francophone educational and other facilities.[44]

Flemish politicians now perceived the national capital—Brussels—to be a place where they, who formed a majority of Belgians, simply "did not feel at home," in Lorwin's terms, and also as "a domination to overcome; a terra irredenta to redeem; and an 'oil stain,' as they said, to hold back from inundating more 'Flemish soil.' " The Flemings, therefore, stepped up their cultural efforts in Brussels, with the new Flemish elite opposing the "francisation" of the capital.[45]

The election of 1961 brought a Catholic-Socialist coalition government to power that attempted to meet the growing linguistic polarization head on by legislative means. Three major laws were, therefore, enacted in 1962 and 1963 that attempted to remove linguistic problems from the political arena, but, in fact, as most observers contend, they had an opposite effect. In any case, the first of these laws actually revoked the language census clause of the 1932 law, which provided for changes in administrative and educational facilities according to changes in the linguistic composition of localities, ostensibly fixing the linguistic boundaries permanently and making all provinces, except for the Brussels region, homogeneous in linguistic terms. This, of course, had the effect of institutionalizing the bicommunal-state concept advocated by federalists in both linguistic groups. The second law dealt with language problems in the Brussels conurbation, protecting the linguistic "patrimonies" of *both* communities by (a) providing for better Flemish educational and cultural facilities, (b) stipulating that children could only be sent to the schools of their own language group, and (c) granting educational facilities in the French language for Francophones living in Flemish areas of the Brussels metropolitan region. The third law provided for the improvement of the Flemish position in municipal administration while also granting the Francophones concessions in a number of localities in Flemish areas in the suburbs of the city, while the government attempted to readjust the boundaries fixed only a year earlier. This, however, created a good deal of opposition among the Flemings and almost forced the government to resign. About the same time, the Ministry of Education and Culture was split into separate but parallel Flemish and French ministries at the behest of Flemish members of parliament.[46]

As noted above, in the opinion of most observers, the outcome of these laws was only to polarize the linguistic situation even more, since with every Flemish effort toward linguistic parity in Brussels or success in linguistic reform, the Walloons and Francophone-Bruxellois became more and more aware of their new position vis-à-vis the Flemings and thus demanded constitutional protection from Flemish "domination." To reassure the Walloons, the then prime minister promised that constitutional reform would occur, with special guarantees that would prevent "minorisation" of the Walloons. In his article on "parliamentary guarantees against minorisation and constitutional revision in Belgium," Ivo Rens both dealt with this issue and defined *minorisation* in the Belgian context. He claimed that the word—one constantly reoccurring in Belgian political terminology of the time—evoked a state of mind more than a real condition. It could be defined, therefore, in psychosocial terms "as a collective complex of frustration, or of grievances, either economic, social, cultural, or linguistic, not to mention purely nationalistic, which serve as an alibi for demonstrations of mistrust, isolation, or aggressiveness." In fact, as George Kelly noted, the linguistic animosity went so far as to have people in both groups advocating English, rather than Flemish or French, as the second language to be taught in their respective schools.[47]

The poor handling of the language issue by the PSC (Catholic) party resulted in a heavy electoral loss in Flemish areas to the Volksunie (Flemish Nationalist) party in the 1965 general election, with the latter winning twelve seats and even the two Walloon nationalist parties five seats in parliament. The Flemish nationalists almost doubled their vote compared to the 1961 election. The incoming prime minister, therefore, felt it necessary to formulate a program for increased regional cultural autonomy and institute commissions to improve "interregional" relations. He erred, however, in forming his cabinet, giving Francophones a majority

of one therein. This, combined with other issues, such as the
government's inability to deal with a strike threat by doctors,
forced the prime minister's resignation.[48]

A reversal of the strategy of meeting language issues directly was
then tried by a PSC-Liberal coalition in 1966. Declaring a "truce"
in the linguistic conflict, the then prime minister hoped that by
diverting the country's attention to economic issues, the problem
would recede in importance. The "truce," however, was broken in
1968 by the "University Question" regarding the Catholic
University in Louvain. The issues involved over language usage in
this case are not discussed in detail here, but they were serious
enough to have not only caused rioting and communal violence,
but to have brought down the PSC-Liberal government in early
1968, the first government, according to Mallinson, to have
"fallen over the language issue."[49]

Now, the 1965 election saw the successful electoral perfomance
of opposition linguistic parties due to the fact that the linguistic
problem was a key issue in the election, an outcome, as Andre
Philippart put it, of the "process of radicalization" that had
affected both communities. However, an additional factor affecting
the election, according to Philippart, was that not only had the
PSB (Socialists) unofficially split along regional lines, but middle-class
Walloons withdrew their support from the PSC (Catholics),
fearing the "Christian" trade unions, whose leaders and members
were mostly Flemish. In Philippart's view, therefore, "the
language question became another battleground for the opposition
of the social classes."[50]

The 1968 election, on the other hand, can be and has been
described as a "triumph of linguistic extremism." Although the
Socialists attempted to play down the language problem, this policy
failed as a result of the decision of their own Flemish section—just
before the election—to run its own slate in Brussels. The Liberals
also attempted to minimize the language problem, claiming
themselves to be the only party that opposed "regionalism."
But they also split into Walloon and Flemish sections just before
the election. The PSC (Catholics) focused on the Brussels region
during the campaign and also put themselves up as the party of

national unity, but it was also split into Flemish and Walloon sections. The outcome of the elections saw the Volksunie increase their number of seats in the lower house (Chamber of Deputies) from twelve (in 1965) to twenty, while the Walloon nationalist parties increased their representation from five seats (in 1965) to twelve, with the PSC and PSB losing eight and five seats, respectively. Together, the linguistic parties received almost 30 percent of the total vote, with the Volksunie outpolling the Liberals in Flanders, while the French-speaking nationalist parties collectively were almost matching the Socialist vote in Brussels. There were attempts to form a three-party coalition after the election, but this failed when the Liberals were unable to unite the sectional interests in their party. A government was finally formed combining the Flemish wing of the PSC and the PSB, which divided the cabinet between them, fourteen Walloon and fourteen Flemish ministers accordingly, with separate ministries for regional economic development also created.[51]

In July 1970, the PSC-PSB coalition had failed in its attempt at constitutional revision providing for cultural and economic councils that would give a degree of regional autonomy. By December 1970, however, the government had obtained enough support (that is, the necessary two-thirds parliamentary support) to initiate constitutional change and was able to attain such support again in the summer of 1971 for legislation to enable the changes to be implemented. The constitutional revisions are not discussed in detail here, but the "guarantees against minorisation" promised almost a decade before were instituted through (a) specific parliamentary devices designed to prevent a majority of one language group dominating the other in parliament; (b) linguistic parity in government and cabinet formation through the development of a linguistic "key" for allocation of ministries and seats in the cabinet; and (c) the operation of a new type of law, the nature of which superceded even a constitutional amendment, giving each of the communities power of veto over matters that would significantly alter relations between them. Regional cultural autonomy was also institutionalized by the constitutional revision, with the creation of regional cultural councils and a "Cultural

Pact''—along the lines of the earlier ''School Pact''—agreed on among most parties (with the exception of the Volksunie and Walloon nationalists) by early 1972. Special arrangements for the ''Brussels problem'' were also instituted, giving the Flemish areas around the city equal political weight to the Francophone center on governing bodies of the metropolitan region.[52]

A plan for economic decentralization—seen by the Walloons as quid pro quo for the cultural autonomy granted the Flemings—that was approved in December 1970 was postponed, due to a dispute over the necessity for constitutional amendment in this case. The part of the December 1970 plan, which recognized the existence of three national regions—Brussels, Flanders, and Wallonia—however, also became a constitutional issue and was thus left as a piece of legislative ''unfinished business.''[53]

In the election of November 1971, the revisions met their first test of communal public opinion. The outcome of the election saw the linguistic parties continue to gain electoral strength. The Volksunie increased its share of the Flemish vote to almost 19 percent while the nationalist Rassemblement Wallon received more than 20 percent of the vote in Wallonia, and the Francophone Nationalist party in Brussels, the FDF, got more than 30 percent of the votes there. Thus although the three major parties—PSC, PSB, and Liberals—still received about three-fourths of the total vote, their combined poll was the lowest percentage obtained since the 1936 election and the second lowest since 1919, when universal manhood suffrage was instituted.[54]

The 1971 election was followed by a prolonged governmental crisis that lasted for seventy-five days. Finally, on 20 January 1972, a PSC-PSB coalition was formed, but the Flemish wing of the PSC was still unhappy about the outcome of the election, making coalition negotiations difficult. Thus by the end of November 1972, a new crisis faced the government, brought on by the Flemish wing of the PSC over limitation of the Brussels region to prevent the spread of French influence, reciprocal autonomy for language enclaves in Wallonia and Flanders, and the powers of the regional cultural councils. The prime minister resigned, and negotiations began to bring the Liberals into the government, rather than hold a general election. The three "traditional" parties formed a coalition in January 1973—the first since 1945—with the specific aim of implementing "economic regionalization" and settling problems relating to linguistic enclaves. By October 1973, however, the Flemish Cultural Council implemented a new law that promised to affect Francophone workers employed in Flanders by making Flemish the only language for both verbal and written communication between management and employees, thereby again threatening to upset the delicate balance that had been achieved by the "grand coalition."[55]

A number of general attempts to describe the Belgian societal situation have been made. Arend Lijphart, for example, claimed that it exhibited "consociational" characteristics, and Lorwin developed the concept of "segmented pluralism" to describe it. Dunn applied the term *état communautaire*, that is, "communitarian state," to the Belgian case, maintaining that both Lijphart's model and Lorwin's concept—which, as he noted, is the "structural basis" for the "consociational" approach—are no longer applicable to the Belgian situation, since, in his view, "the severity of the language conflict in Belgium makes that country resemble a centrifugal as much as a consociational democracy."[56]

The terms *minority* and *majority* have also been used by these and other observers to describe the situation of one or another of the groups in the Belgian context. Lorwin, for example, in his study entitled "Belgium: Religion, Class, and Language in National Politics," noted that although "the Flemish still see themselves as oppressed, despite the political weight of their members, the progress in use of the Dutch language everywhere except in the Brussels area, and a recent economic growth in Flanders that is much more rapid than that of Wallonia," it is the Francophone-Belgians, both Bruxellois and Walloon, who "always a numerical minority, now fear that they will become a sociological minority." In fact, Lorwin continued, since "Bruxellois feel threatened between Flemish aggressiveness and Walloon indifference to their special interests," there actually exists in this case "one oppressed majority and two oppressed minorities." In a later article dealing with "linguistic pluralism and political tension in modern Belgium," Lorwin reiterated his statement, claiming that "the nation has become an amalgam of one oppressed majority and two oppressed minorities. . . . If the situation is new, it follows an old rule: many are oppressed, but no one oppresses," and ending the article by referring to the "impatience of the old sociological minority which was now a political majority," that is, continued Flemish dissatisfaction with their situation.[57]

This, Lorwin argued, may be due to "the reflexes" of both "underdogs" and "overdogs" and the memory they engender. Indeed, as Everett Hughes noted, one characteristic distinguishing between "majority" and "minority"—or between "insecure" and "secure" groups—may be the difference in their "time perspective." He maintained that "the insecure, subject to continuous threat, must take note of all that threatens them, and recent past and immediate future must be sharply defined." Thus Lorwin claimed that the Flemish perception of their subordinate position vis-à-vis the Walloons continues "far beyond the conditions that created them." The Walloons, for their part, "look backward too but only to contrast past security with fears for the future."[58]

George Kelly, writing about Belgium in terms of "new nationalism in an old world," noted that although the Flemish "are a numerical majority, they still have many of the attributes of a psychological minority. This is partly owing to the difficulty of competing against a world language." He claimed, in addition, that "the psychological superiority of the Francophones is often irritating." Pierre Bie, in comparing Flemish and French-Canadian nationalism, saw the Walloons as also exhibiting minority characteristics, "although," as Mallinson noted, "the Walloons still retain a tradition of cultural superiority and will not readily let the Flemings forget this." He observed that "the root cause of all the trouble is that the balance of power is still shifting from the Walloons to the Flemings," but "that inferiority complex still lingers with the Fleming and makes him nowadays even more frustrated and discontent." A. R. Van den Brande claimed that there are "three Belgian sociological minorities," that is, the Flemings, Walloons, and Bruxellois. However, I tend to agree with Urwin, who wrote that "what exists in Belgium today is a bi-national entity composed of two linguistic minorities, one social and psychological, the other demographic and economic," since this view parallels my claim that Belgium in fact exhibits the characteristics of "plural minoriticity" as outlined above.[59]

Now, in citing Dunn's view of the Belgian case, we see him using the term *centrifugal* to describe the communal situation. Lorwin also used this terminology in analyzing both recent trends in and future prospects for Belgian society. With regard to the recent situation, Lorwin observed that, "The national sentiment that might offset the centrifugal tendencies is weaker—for good or ill—than in any other European nation. . . . Except for the king, few national symbols have power to move or to hold. And the monarchy, though generally accepted, is far from universally popular." As for the future, he posed the question, "might Belgium offer the first significant experience of a federalism between only two (or two and a half) components; of a federalism created, not by centripetal forces bringing together disparate entities, but by centrifugal forces restructuring a unitary state?"[60]

But what of the "unifying power" of the other Belgian national symbol, that is, the military? Lorwin answered this bluntly, claiming that "the army suffers as a symbol from the antimilitarism traditional among the Flemish in general and among the Socialists in Wallonia." This, in addition to the formalized bifurcation of the military, which results from projection of the societal cleavage structure onto the system of military organization, has, of course, influenced recent patterns in communal military participation in Belgium and will probably continue to do so.[61]

RECENT TRENDS IN AND PARAMETERS OF MILITARY PARTICIPATION

In 1924 the periodical *La Belgique Militaire* published a tract addressed to "the friends of our Army" in which it attacked the introduction of the linguistic "pest" into military affairs through the separation of the army according to linguistic group. The periodical claimed that such action, from the military point of view, "would be disastrous." It maintained that "combat groups," under specific conditions, would be united through the circumstances of combat itself. Thus, in its view, the division of the military along linguistic lines would encourage separatist tendencies leading eventually to "Flemish and Walloon armies" and thereby endangering the very fabric of the country. It cited the Belgian national motto "L'Union fait La Force" in support of its view that the army should remain a "homogenous" (sic) institution, concluding that a "cohesive" army would maintain national unity, whereas linguistic separation would prepare the way for administrative division of the country and "national ruin."[62]

Although the predicted effects of the linguistic division of the Belgian armed forces did not materialize, the 1924 article does illustrate the degree to which feedback between the military and society in Belgium was perceived to exist even then.

In this section, I first briefly consider the system of military procurement and organization that exists in the Belgian armed forces. I then analyze various global parameters of communal military participation. Finally, I deal with the issue of national service and the introduction of a volunteer system parallel to it as a first step towards the establishment of an all-volunteer armed forces in Belgium.

Until the present, Belgium has had a compulsory national-service term of one year for all eighteen year olds (unless exempted). After induction, the new conscripts (*miliciens*) pass through a Recruitment and Selection Center for three days, where they are interviewed and given medical and psychotechnical tests for purposes of occupational and service branch assignment. After completing this battery of tests, they are assigned to a basic training unit for six weeks and then are posted to a permanent unit for the remainder of their national service.[63]

The projection of the sociolegal structure governing relationships between the two communities in civilian life onto the military manifests itself in the law of July 1938, which was amended and complemented by further legislation in July 1955, August 1963, and June 1970, setting up "linguistic juries" to replace earlier versions and a permanent commission for linguistic control and use as recommended in the 1953 report discussed previously. As noted above, the Belgian armed forces are divided, by statute, into parallel Flemish- and French-speaking elements, although mixed units do exist in specialized or technical service branches such as the air force or logistics. By law, conscripts must serve in a unit of their own language, but the two companies of conscripts usually procured from the small German-speaking section of the Belgian population living in the eastern part of the country—Liege and Luxembourg provinces—are incorporated into French battalions. Since the singular linguistic structure only applies to units higher than the company level, in some circumstances, Flemings may be commanded by Walloon officers, but these officers are, in any case, required by law to be bilingual since they would hold the rank of major or above. Still, some anomalies in the organization of the armed forces along linguistic lines remained until the early 1970s. For example, the 1938 law prevented, in effect, the entry of German-speaking Belgians into the Royal Military Academy, since it stipulated that the languages of the entrance exam and instruction were to be either French or Dutch, so the law had to be amended to allow German speakers in.[64]

Some indication of the direction in which communal military participation is proceeding can be obtained by reference to trends in global parameters such as those presented in tables 2 to 6, "F" indicating Walloons and "N" indicating Flemish.[65]

As can be read from the tables, the number of Flemish and Walloon miliciens has remained in proportion to the population of the respective linguistic group, that is, 60 percent Flemish, 40 percent Walloon. This is true for all services, including the navy, due to the strict adherence to the policy of proportional national-service quotas by linguistic group. This is not the case, however, as regards permanent party personnel in the Belgian armed forces. Thus although there is also an almost sixty-forty split by linguistic group among active service NCOs in the army and air force, the Flemings dominate the NCO ranks in the navy, by a ratio of 75 to 25 percent. This, of course, can be attributed to the geographical proximity of Flanders to the sea and the naval tradition of the Flemish.

Table 2

National Servicemen (Miliciens), Percentage Composition of Service Branch by Linguistic Group, Selected Years

	1952		1962		1972		1979	
Branch	*F*	*-%- N*	*F*	*-%- N*	*F*	*-%- N*	*F*	*-%- N*
Army	38	62	36	64	39	61	36	64
Air force	43	57	39	61	40	60	42	58
Navy	40	60	40	60	37	63	34	66
Overall	39	61	36	64	39	61	37	63

Table 3

Active Service NCOs, Percentage Composition of Service Branch by Linguistic Group, Selected Years

	1962		1972		1979	
Branch	*F*	*-%- N*	*F*	*-%- N*	*F*	*-%- N*
Army	43.7	56.3	41.2	58.8	39.9	60.1
Air force	43.2	56.8	42.4	57.6	41.1	58.9
Navy	24.9	75.1	26.6	73.4	26.6	73.4
Overall	42.5	57.5	40.5	59.5	39.6	60.4

Table 4

Active Service Officers, Percentage Composition of Service Branch by Linguistic Group, Selected Years

	1952		1962		1972		1979	
Branch	*F*	*-%- N*	*F*	*-%- N*	*F*	*-%- N*	*F*	*-%- N*
Army	83	17	68	32	55	45	n.a.	
Air force	80	20	61	39	47	53	n.a.	
Navy	55	45	41	59	29	71	n.a.	
Overall	82	18	65	35	52	48	42	58

Note: n.a. = not available.

Table 5

Gross Rank Distribution of Active Service Officers, Percentage Composition of Service Branch by Linguistic Group and Type of Rank, Selected Years

Branch and Rank	1962			1972			1979		
	F	-%-	N	F	-%-	N	F	-%-	N
Army									
Junior officers	61	39		49	51		*Overall*		
Senior officers	85	15		64	36		*Belgian*		
Generals	100	—		71	29		*Armed Forces*		
Air force									
Junior officers	55	45		42	58		40	60	
Senior officers	85	15		59	41		46	54	
Generals	86	14		70	30		49	51	
Navy									
Junior officers	35	65		22	78				
Senior officers	67	33		50	50				
Admirals	100	—		—	100				

Key: Junior officers—from sublieutenant to captain-commandant.
    Senior officers—from major to colonel.
    Generals—including major and lieutenant generals.

Table 6

Officers Commissioned (Sublieutenant), Percentage Composition of Service Branch by Linguistic Group, Selected Years

Branch	1952		1962		1972		1979	
	F	-%- N	F	-%- N	F	-%- N	F	-%- N
Army	57	43	35	65	49	51	40	60
Air force	60	40	22	78	56	44	44	56
Navy	—	100	31	69	40	60	50	50
Overall	57	43	33	67	50	50	42	58

With regard to the officer corps overall, between 1962 and 1972, there was a significant increase in the number of Flemish officers, to about one-half of the active service officers in the Belgian armed forces, and over one-half in the air force. In all services, including the navy, there was a considerable improvement over the situation in 1952, when Flemish officers were only less than 20 percent of the total in the Belgian military. Again, the Flemings dominate the naval officer corps, comprising more than 70 percent, and the large number of Flemish officers who entered military service in the early 1960s was felt in the 1970s. There has been a strong increase in Flemish junior officers and senior officers in all three services, and since the air force expanded most rapidly, Flemish officer entry into this service grew fastest at both junior and senior levels.

It is most interesting to note that differential entry rates into the officer corps in the early 1960s so affected the structure of rank distribution and overall percentages by linguistic group that in the early 1970s, the trend was reversed, so as not to completely imbalance the officer corps in favor of the Flemings. Thus in 1972 intake of officers into the air force and army reverted to the percentages of the 1950s.

The position regarding the general staff also changed over the period 1962-1972. Although there were no Flemish generals in 1962, by 1972 30 percent of the general staff in the army were Flemish. The same situation occurred in the air force, where the rapid increase in the number of Flemish officers required the appointment of Flemings to the general staff to administer the Flemish-language section of that service. In the navy, the situation completely reversed itself, and command of that service at the general-staff level passed completely to the Flemish.

Between 1972 and 1979, the percentage of Flemish NCOs in both the army and air force continued to grow. The proportion of Flemish active-service officers in the Belgian armed forces overall increased significantly over the period, as did the proportion of Flemish senior officers and generals, while the intake of Flemings into the officer corps also grew at a significant rate.

Of course, as in other countries in Western Europe, national service has not been and still is not popular among Belgian youth, notwithstanding the existence of student deferments, which enables university study before entering the military for the required one year of service. Indeed, proposals to abolish the deferment system led to mass student demonstrations in the late 1960s and early 1970s. Plans calling for the induction of only one son per family also led to marches by schoolchildren in 1973, since the young people saw this as unjust, and their parents saw it as a source of family tension. Thus in August 1974, the minister of defense introduced a plan that proposed what was, in effect, the first step toward an all-volunteer armed forces. The plan provided for a decrease in military service requirements over the period 1974-1978, with the transformation of the Belgian NATO contingent in Germany into a totally professional force, with all conscripts serving only in Belgium accordingly. The one-year term of conscription would be reduced by stages to six months in 1978. Reserve duties would also be cut from fourteen years to seven, but the proposal to limit military service to one son per family was included in the plan. Efforts toward recruiting women, who did not serve in the peacetime military, would be made, and although some increase in defense expenditure would be expected, the extra manpower released was expected to offset this.[66]

The plan divided the total of national servicemen serving at any time into three groups. The largest group would consist of those who, after a six-week basic training period, would be given a four-month training course in performing specific tasks for which they would be recalled in case of war. A second group would, after their basic training, be assigned to military occupations that paralleled their civilian jobs, if these were of a technical nature, such as mechanics and builders. The third group, consisting of about 3,000 youths at any time, would be employed in other public sectors during their term of national service. These jobs included working in police traffic safety programs, working in youth clubs run by the Ministry of Culture, working in environmental-protection programs, or assisting in social-service work with old-age pensioners, and so on. Insofar as only one son per family would be conscripted, a "national-solidarity tax" would also be levied, which would implicitly cover the additional expense of enlisting the extra 6,000 personnel a year needed over the period 1974-1978 to make up for the decrease in national servicemen. After 1978 only some 4,000 volunteer personnel a year, according to Ministry of Defense calculations, would be required to compensate for wastage of personnel and keep the troop level up to the 90,000 required.

In any event, on 13 July 1976, legislation establishing a mixed national-service-volunteer armed forces was adopted by the Belgian Parliament. By 1979 there were over 30,000 volunteer soldiers in the Belgian armed forces at the enlisted ranks level, of which one-third were long-term or "career" volunteers, and the other two-thirds were short-term, or "temporary" volunteers. The overall proportion of Flemish among total volunteers was 55 percent, and Walloons comprised 45 percent. Of the "career" volunteers, however, 62 percent were Flemish and 38 percent Walloons. Among the "temporary" volunteers, 51 percent were Flemish and 49 percent Walloons. Thus despite the lack of a military tradition in Belgium, which many observers thought would result in a volunteer-enlistment rate far below the figures projected by the government in 1974, the pecuniary benefits offered by the armed forces to volunteers, in addition to the opening up of opportunities for Flemings at both the NCO and officer levels, seems to have given impetus to the possibility of success in transforming the Belgian military into an all-volunteer armed forces.[67]

In contrast to the situation that prevailed in other colonial contexts, there existed only the most tenuous of links between "metropolitan" and "colonial" armies in the Belgian case.[68] As Jean-Claude Willame recounted, the "Force Publique"—founded by Royal Decree in 1888 for garrison duties in the Congo—was isolated from the metropolitan Belgian armed forces, with the separation, in his view, being "reinforced by the unbridled disdain of white officers in the Congo toward their counterparts in Belgium." Indeed, the military defeats suffered by the Belgian army and its evident lack of experience were held in sharp contrast to the success of the Force Publique in military operations. In fact, Willame observed, when units of the metropolitan army were sent to the Congo in the early 1950s, they were not welcomed by the commanders of the Force Publique who thought the use of such troops to be unwarranted and their presence to be interference in the Congo's internal problems.[69]

With regard to the characteristics of the Force Publique itself,

Willame cited a Congolese student manifesto of 1961 that claimed: "At the beginning of independence, there were two classes in the Congo, the *basenji*, or 'natives,' and the soldiers of the Force Publique. The soldiers were responsible for the subjugating of *basenji* to white rule." Originally, this task was undertaken by African troops from Zanzibar for the Eastern Congo and by Ivory Coast Hausa who were enlisted especially for the aim of exploring the colony's western part. The 1888 Royal Decree instituted a mixed civil and military rule in the Congo, whereby the administration of territorial districts was undertaken by military officers directly responsible to the governor-general who was also the Force Publique's commander-in-chief. Until 1891 recruitment to the Force Publique was voluntary; however, after its introduction, conscription became its main source of manpower. Although recruits were supposed to have been chosen through a lottery system, most were just dragooned into service by local chiefs and headmen who, as Willame claimed, "usually conscripted slaves, prisoners taken in intertribal wars, criminals, the chronically ill, and other marginal elements in the community." As late as 1954, this practice was common, for, as Willame noted, the annual report of the colony in that year stated that "surveys suggest that many recruits from urban centers were assigned to the army because of their undesirable traits. The territorial administration has often recruited these men into the Force Publique rather than send them back to their villages."

Colonial authorities also approached their manpower problems in terms of seeking recruits from "martial tribes," so a few groups came to dominate the Force Publique. After a serious tribal mutiny in 1896, however, the policy changed, and in order to prevent the repetition of such an event, both the conscription base and enlistment base was made more widespread and was applied—in principle, at least—to all tribes. The rationale for this, according to Willame, was that such a policy would so fragment the Force Publique in tribal terms that even the smallest unit would not become dominated by any one tribal element. Furthermore, under the new policy, troops were stationed away from their native territories. The isolation of the Force Publique from Congolese society and the attempt to alienate its members from their tribal origins was, according to Willame, emphasized in a very strong manner by the white officers who attempted to obtain from their Congolese troops loyalty to the Belgian crown in the person of the king and thereby instill them with an esprit-de-corps based upon such loyalty. The white officers thereby stressed the elite nature and position of the Force Publique, with the result that such attitudes continued in the postindependence Congolese Army, as shown by Willame, who cited a passage that appeared in that army's magazine, namely, "the best remedy for subversion and corruption in the army is the isolation of troops by inculcating a positive zealotry towards their craft and the nobility of military ideals [and by teaching them] to despise the masses, who lack military discipline."

Despite the fact that elements such as special privileges, esprit de corps, or professionalism are features of most armies in the post-World War II period, the Force Publique, according to Willame, was unique in that its structures and activities were strictly colonial in orientation, a factor that he claimed contrasts with Lucien Pye's assertion regarding the modernizing function of the military in developing countries that were formerly colonies. Although its leaders never admitted it, the true function of the Force Publique was not to defend the Congo against external threat, but to surpress all internal disorder. Although the Force Publique did take a small part in campaigns in both World Wars I and II, its major efforts were in the form of police actions directed against elements in the population that resisted penetration by the Europeans, including the Afro-Asian tradesmen and Mahdists of the eastern and northern Congo. The Force Publique was also active in supressing tribal rebellions, strikes, taking punitive measures for payment of taxation and conscription of forced labor, and implementing the population "resettlement" policies of the colonial administration.

As for the Force Publique's system of organization, although it opened a Military Academy in 1955, no Africans ever graduated. All officers were of European origin, and no Congolese could really hope to rise above the rank of sergeant. As a result of the politicization of all activities just before independence, a number of Congolese were, however, nominated as master sergeants. To sum up, the outcome of the complete isolation of the Force Publique manifested itself in the army mutinies that occurred in the Congo almost immediately after independence. The complete fragmentation of its successor—the Armee Nationale Congolaise (ANC)—into a number of "private armies" resulted not only from the demoralization of the military after the mutinies in 1960, but from its involvement in political activity, something the Belgians never allowed.

Now, as noted above, I have described Belgium as a case of plural minoriticity, focusing on the Flemings and Walloons, respectively, and only briefly mentioning the German-speaking group. This is due to the fact that although this group now numbers some 100,000, it still constitutes only 1 percent of the Belgian population, and, more importantly, the greater part of the German-speaking region exists as a part of Belgium only since 1920. Although the history of the region is not discussed in detail here, the following are some of its key points.[70]

The region first appeared as a principality in the early Middle Ages and was taken over, in turn, by the Duchy of Burgundy, Austria, Spain, and finally France in 1794. The Congress of Vienna divided the region, giving part to Holland and part to Prussia. After the foundation of Belgium in 1830, two German-speaking provinces were included in Belgian territory, but by 1839 Limburg province was returned to Holland.

As a result of the Versailles treaty, Germany ceded the German-speaking Malmedy border region to Belgium, and it was added to the province of Liege. During the 1930s, however, members of the German-speaking group started to advocate secession and reunion with Germany, and, in fact, the region was immediately incorporated into Germany after Belgium's capitulation in 1940. After Germany's defeat, however, the region was transferred back to Belgium.

As such, German, along with French and Flemish (Dutch), is recognized as the third official language in Belgium and is the principal language used for administrative, educational, and judicial purposes in these provinces. Finally, in military terms, German-speaking conscripts constitute some one-half of 1 percent of the annual number conscripted and are organized into small German-speaking units that are either incorporated into or brigaded with French-speaking battalions.

NOTES

1. V. R. Lorwin, "Linguistic Pluralism and Language Tensions in Modern Belgium," *Canadian Journal of History* 5 (1970), pp. 20-21.

2. A. Rabushka and K. A. Shepsle, *Politics in Plural Societies* (Columbus, Ohio: Merrill, 1972), pp. 106ff.; V. Mallinson, *Belgium* (London: Benn, 1969), pp. 176ff.; Adrien De Meeus, *History of the Belgians,* trans. G. Gordon (London: Thames and Hudson, 1962).

3. See note 2 and V. R. Lorwin, "Linguistic Pluralism," p. 2.

4. V. R. Lorwin, "Linguistic Pluralism," p. 3.

5. Ibid.; F. Rousseau, "The Walloon Movement," in S. Simpson, ed., *Belgium in Transition*, collection published in hardback volume of *Annals of the American Academy of Political and Social Science* 247 (Sept. 1946), p. 130; J. A. Dunn, "The Revision of the Constitution in Belgium: A Study in the Institutionalization of Ethnic Conflict," *Western Political Quarterly* 27, 1 (1974), pp. 144ff.; D. W. Urwin, "Social Cleavages and Political Parties in Belgium," *Political Studies* 18, 3 (1970), pp. 330ff.; V. Mallinson, *Belgium*, pp. 180ff.

6. E. R. C. van Bogaert, "Belgium: Two Clashing Cultures," in *Year Book of World Affairs* 23 (1969), p. 82; V. Mallinson, *Belgium*, pp. 181-82; idem, *Power and Politics in Belgian Education* (London: Heinemann, 1963), pp. 154ff.; V. R. Lorwin, "Linguistic Pluralism," p. 4.

7. E. R. C. van Bogaert, "Belgium: Two Clashing Cultures"; V. Mallinson, *Power and Politics*, pp. 155-56.

8. . R. Lorwin, "Linguistic Pluralism," p. 5; G. A. Kelly, "Biculturalism and Party Systems in Belgium and Canada," in J. D. Montgomery and A. O. Hirschman, eds., *Public Policy* (Cambridge: Harvard University Press, 1967), pp. 318-19.

9. V. Mallinson, *Belgium*, pp. 181-82. See also G. van Geyt, "The Flemish Movement," in S. Simpson, *Belgium in Transition*, p. 128.

10. V. Mallinson, *Belgium*; J. A. Dunn, "The Revision of the Constitution in Belgium," p. 145; V. R. Lorwin, "Linguistic Pluralism," pp. 6-7.

11. V. Mallinson, *Power and Politics*, pp. 160ff.

12. S. B. Clough, *A History of the Flemish Movement in Belgium* (New York: Smith, 1930), pp. 169-70. See also his article "The Flemish Movement," in J. A. Goris, ed., *Belgium* (Berkeley: University of California Press, 1945), pp. 114-15.

13. S. B. Clough, *A History of the Flemish Movement*, pp. 170-71.

14. F. Rousseau, "The Walloon Movement"; R. Gillouin, *De L'Alsace á la Flandre* (Paris: Promethée, 1930), pp. 177-83; A. Zolberg, "The Making of Flemings and Walloons: Belgium—1830-1914," *Journal of Interdisciplinary History* 22 (1974), pp. 178-235; E. R. C. van Bogaert, "Belgium: Two Clashing Cultures," p. 83.

15. J. A. Dunn, "The Revision of the Constitution in Belgium," p. 145; J. Destree, "Lettre au Roi sur la separation de la Wallonie et de la Flandre," *Revue de Belgique* (Aug. 15-Sept. 1, 1912), p. 740.

16. E. R. C. van Bogaert, "Belgium: Two Clashing Cultures," p. 83; *Annales Parliamentaires* (Bruxelles), 17 May 1919, speech of F. van Cauwelaert; V. R. Lorwin, "Linguistic Pluralism," p. 11; V. R. Lorwin, "Belgium: Religion, Class, and Language in National Politics," in R. A. Dahl, ed. *Political Oppositions in Western Democracies* (New Haven, Conn.: Yale University Press, 1966), p. 161.

17. S. B. Clough, "The Flemish Movement," p. 117; V. R. Lorwin, "Belgium: Religion, Class, and Language"; E. R. C. van Bogaert, "Belgium: Two Clashing Cultures," pp. 83-84; V. Mallinson, *Belgium,* p. 183.

18. E. R.C. van Bogaert, "Belgium: Two Clashing Cultures"; Mallinson, *Belgium*; V. R. Lorwin, "Linguistic Pluralism," p. 11.

19. V. Mallinson, *Belgium,* p. 184; E. R. C. Bogaert, "Belgium: Two Clashing Cultures," p. 84; V. R. Lorwin, "Belgium: Religion, Class, and Language," p. 164.

20. S. B. Clough, *A History of the Flemish Movement,* pp. 239-40; V. Mallinson, *Belgium;* V. R. Lorwin, "Linguistic Pluralism," p. 13; G. A. Kelly, "Belgium: New Nationalism in an Old World," *Comparative Politics* 1, 3 (1969), p. 348.

21. V. Mallinson, *Belgium*, p. 185; V. R. Lorwin, "Linguistic Pluralism"; idem, "Belgium: Religion, Class, and Language," p. 163; D. W. Urwin, "Social Cleavages and Political Parties in Belgium," p. 331; J. A. Dunn, "The Revision in the Constitution in Belgium," p. 146.

22. A. Simon, "L'influence de l'Eglise sur la vie politique dans l'entre deux guerres," *Res Publica* 4 (1962), pp. 387-96; V. R. Lorwin, "Linguistic Pluralism," p. 6.

23. V. R. Lorwin, "Linguistic Pluralism," p. 12; idem, "Belgium:

Religion, Class, and Language," p. 163; D. W. Urwin, "Social Cleavages and Political Parties in Belgium," pp. 332-33.

24. V. R. Lorwin, "Linguistic Pluralism," p. 13; V. Mallinson, *Belgium*, p. 185; J. A. Dunn, "The Revision of the Constitution in Belgium," p. 146.

25. The text of the law in abridged form is cited in *Rapport par la Commission Mixte du Probleme Linguistique au sein des Forces Armees* (Bruxelles: Ministere de la Defense Nationale, 1953), pp. 13-14, hereafter cited as *Rapport*.

26. 1938 Law, ch. 1, in *Rapport*, p. 13.

27. Ibid., pp. 13-14.

28. Ibid., p 14. The *Rapport* here refers to articles 19, 20, and 22 of the law.

29. A. De Meeus, *History of the Belgians*, pp. 370-71; G. A. Kelly, "Biculturalism and Party Systems," p. 319; G. A. Kelly, "Belgium: New Nationalism," pp. 359-60; V. R. Lorwin, "Linguistic Pluralism," p. 13.

30. E. R. K. van Bogaert, "Belgium: Two Clashing Cultures"; V. R. Lorwin, "Linguistic Pluralism," p. 13; J. A. Dunn, "The Revision of the Constitution in Belgium," p. 146.

31. E. R. C. van Bogaert, "Belgium: Two Clashing Cultures," p. 85; G. A. Kelly, "Biculturalism and Party Systems," p. 320; V. Mallinson, *Belgium*, pp. 185-86; V.R. Lorwin, "Linguistic Pluralism," pp. 14-15; F. Rousseau, "The Walloon Movement," p. 131.

32. A. De Meeus, *History of the Belgians,* pp. 373-74; J. A. Dunn, "The Revision of the Constitution in Belgium," p. 146; V. R. Lorwin, "Belgium: Religion, Class, and Language," pp. 168-69.

33. V. R. Lorwin, "Belgium: Religion, Class, and Language," pp. 169-70; J. A. Dunn, "The Revision of the Constitution in Belgium," p. 147.

34. *Rapport*, pp. 6, 9-10.

35. Ibid., pp. 9-10.

36. Ibid., pp. 10-11.

37. Ibid., pp. 15, 50-51.

38. Ibid., pp. 33-37, 53-56, 58.

39. Ibid., p. 60.

40. J. A. Dunn, "The Revision of the Constitution in Belgium," p. 148; V. Mallinson, *Belgium*, p. 186; V. R. Lorwin, "Linguistic Pluralism," p. 14.

41. V. R. Lorwin, "Linguistic Pluralism," pp. 15-16, 21; idem, "Belgium: Religion, Class, and Language," pp. 171-72.

42. M. Coulon, *L'Autonomie Culturelle en Belgique* (Paris: Plisner, 1961), p. 29.

43. V. R. Lorwin, "Belgium: Religion, Class and Language," p. 171-72.

44. Ibid.; D. W. Urwin, "Social Cleavages and Political Parties," p. 333; J. A. Dunn, "The Revision of the Constitution in Belgium," p. 148.

45. V. R. Lorwin, "Linguistic Pluralism," pp. 17-18.

46. A. Rabushka and K. A. Shepsle, *Politics in Plural Societies*, p. 115; V. R. Lorwin, "Belgium: Religion, Class, and Language," p. 173; idem, "Belgium: Religion, Class, and Language," p. 18; V. Mallinson, *Belgium*, pp. 186-87; J. A. Dunn, "The Revision of the Constitution in Belgium," pp. 148-49.

47. E. R. C. van Bogaert, "Belgium: Two Clashing Cultures," p. 86; Ivo Rens, "Les garanties parlementaires contre la minorisation et la revision constitutionnelle en Belgique," *Res Publica* 7, 3 (1965), pp. 189-221; G. A. Kelly, "Biculturalism and Party Systems," p. 335.

48. A. Rabushka and K. A. Shepsle, *Politics in Plural Societies*, pp. 116-17; J. A. Dunn, "The Revision of the Constitution in Belgium," pp. 149-50.

49. E. R. C. van Bogaert, "Belgium: Two Clashing Cultures," pp. 87-88; V. R. Lorwin, "Linguistic Pluralism," pp. 19-20; V. Mallinson, *Belgium*, pp. 173, 188-89.

50. A. Philippart, "Belgium: Language and Class Oppositions," *Government and Opposition* 1 (1966), pp. 70-72.

51. A. Rabushka and K. A. Shepsle, *Politics in Plural Societies*, pp. 117-19; J. A. Dunn, "The Revision of the Constitution in Belgium," pp. 150-51; V. R. Lorwin, "Linguistic Pluralism," p. 19.

52. A. Rabushka and K. A. Shepsle, *Politics in Plural Societies*, p. 119; J. A. Dunn, "The Revision of the Constitution in Belgium," pp. 152-59. See also idem, "Consociational Democracy and Language Conflict: A Comparison of the Belgian and Swiss Experiences," *Comparative Political Studies* 5, 1 (1972).

53. A. Rabushka and K. A. Shepsle, *Politics in Plural Societies*, p. 119; J. A. Dunn, "The Revision of the Constitution in Belgium," p. 159.

54. J. A. Dunn, "The Revision of the Constitution in Belgium," p. 161.

55. Ibid., p. 162. See also *International Herald Tribune* (hereafter cited as *IHT*), 21 Jan. 1972; *Times* (London), 22 Nov. 1972; *IHT* 23, 27 Nov. 1972; *IHT* 28 Sept. 1973.

56. A. Lijphart, "Consociational Democracy," *World Politics* 21 (1969), pp. 207-25; V. R. Lorwin, "Linguistic Pluralism," p. 8; J. A. Dunn, "The Revision of the Constitution in Belgium," p. 163; idem, "Consociational Democracy," p. 32. See also V. R. Lorwin, "Segmented Pluralism: Ideological Cleavage and Political Cohesion in the Smaller European Democracies," *Comparative Politics* 3 (1971), pp. 141-74.

57. V. R. Lorwin, "Belgium: Religion, Class, and Language," pp. 174-75; idem, "Linguistic Pluralism," pp. 15, 22.

58. V. R. Lorwin, "Belgium: Religion, Class, and Language," p. 175; Everett Hughes, *The Sociological Eye*, Selected Papers (Chicago: Aldine, 1971).

59. G. A. Kelly, "Belgium: New Nationalism," p. 348; P. Bie, *Le Fait Canadian Francais: Etude Comparative Des Nationalismes Flamand et Canadien Francais* (Louvain: University of Louvain Press, 1948), p. 9; V. Mallinson, *Belgium*, p. 189; A. van den Brande, "Elements for a Sociological Analysis of the Impact of the Main Conflicts on Belgian Political Life," *Res Publica* 9, 3 (1967), p. 422; D. W. Urwin, "Social Cleavages and Political Parties in Belgium," pp. 339-40.

60. J. A. Dunn, "Consociational Democracy," p. 32; V. R. Lorwin, "Belgium: Religion, Class, and Language," p. 176; idem, "Linguistic Pluralism," pp. 21-22.

61. V. R. Lorwin, "Belgium: Religion, Class, and Language," p. 176.

62. "Aux Amis de notre Armee," *La Belgique Militaire*, 19 Oct. 1924, pp. 3-8.

63. On these points, see, *Opinions de Miliciens sur leur passage au Centre de Recruitment et de Selection* (Bruxelles: Forces Armees Belges, Centre d'Etude Sociales, Avril 1963).

64. The Belgian Ministry of National Defense is required by law to present an annual report to the Parliament on the linguistic situation in the military. These reports are prepared in two versions: a detailed report for internal use, which contains complete statistics relating to the military participation of the respective linguistic group; and an edited version, which contains only summarized statistical data and is presented to parliament, usually in September. These reports are compiled by the ministry's Central Directorate for Judicial Affairs, and they survey the situation in the preceeding calendar year. The internal reports used here are cited below according to their file number by year, that is, ACJE/2118/year.

On these points, see also *Rapport*, which originally recommended the institution of an annual-report system. For details of the 1970 amendment, see ACJE/2118/1971.

65. The data for 1952 are compiled from *Rapport*, pp. 15, 16, 25. The 1962 data source is ACJE/2118/1963. The 1972 data source is ACJE/2118/1973. The 1979 data is from the edited version of ACJE/2118/1980 presented to the Belgian Parliament on 1 Sept. 1980 (*Document 634*, No. 1) and thus lacks detailed data on the linguistic distribution of officers by service branch.

66. See, for example, David Cross, "Belgium Plans Professional Defense Force," in the *Times* (London), 20 Aug. 1974. See also *Le Soir* (Bruxelles), 18 Sept. 1973, p. 2; *Times*, 1 Feb. 1973; *Guardian*

(London), 3 Feb. 1973.

67. Cross, "Belgium Plans Professional Defense Force." Information on this plan and other aspects of the Belgian armed forces was obtained during interviews and meetings with the secretary to the minister of national defense; the director of the Personnel Division, Belgian army; and his assistant, who were working on the "Van den Boeynants' Plan." The meetings and interviews were held in Bruxelles during January and August 1973 and January 1974. *Document 634*, No. 1, Sept. 1980, is the source for information and statistics regarding the extent of volunteers in the Belgian armed forces.

68. On this point, see E. W. Lefever, *Spear and Scepter* (Washington, D.C.: Brookings Institution, 1970), pp. 86-90.

69. On these points, see J. C. Willame, *Patrimonialism and Political Change in the Congo* (Stanford: Stanford University Press, 1972), ch. 4, pp. 58-65.

70. C. Amelunxen, "The History of the German Speaking Minority Group in Belgium," *Plural Societies* (The Hague) 2, 4 (1971), pp. 39-45.

3

CANADA

DIMENSIONS OF THE CANADIAN SITUATION: HISTORICAL, POLITICAL, MILITARY

In June 1962, Eugene Forsey, the newly elected president of the Canadian Political Science Association, entitled his inaugural lecture "Canada: Two Nations or One?" In answering the question he posed, Forsey concluded that as regards the Canadian identity, at least, "There are not two Canadian histories . . . one French and one British . . . but one history. . . . The History of Canada after 1760 [the British conquest] is only a continuation and extension of the history of Canada before 1760 [New France]." Over 120 years earlier, in his report of 1839 on the situation in Canada, Lord Durham wrote: "I expected to find a contest between a government and a people; I found two nations warring in the bosom of a single state: I found not a struggle of principles but of races." Durham had gone to Canada in the wake of the Rebellion of 1837-1838, which was the severest test to that date of British domination in Canada. Although armed conflict between English- and French-Canadians has occurred very few times since the British conquest in 1760, political conflict between French and English has been the predominant theme of Canadian affairs for more than two centuries and seems to be the prospect in the forseeable future.[1]

We have to analyze the military participation of French-Canadians, therefore, against the background of the ongoing rift between the two linguistic communities that, in turn, has structured French-Canadian attitudes toward the defense of Canada and Canadian defense obligations to a very significant degree. In historical perspective, we can distinguish four main periods in French-Canadian military participation: the first, between 1534 and 1760, from the establishment of "New France" to the British conquest of Canada; the second, from 1761 to 1913, the period of consolidation of British domination and Imperial defense; the third, between 1914 and 1945, encompassing the world wars and the interwar period; and the fourth, from 1946 onwards, the period of economic and political revitalization of Quebec and the reemergence of French-Canadian separatism.

FROM NEW FRANCE TO CONQUEST: 1534-1760

In 1534 Jacques Cartier received a commission from King François I to consolidate France's claim in North America—Nova Gallia, originally established by John Cabot some four decades earlier. Cartier charted the Gulf of St. Lawrence and the next year returned to explore the waterways of New France. The connection between France and North America during the next seventy years was mainly limited to isolated settlement efforts. During the first decade of the seventeenth century, there was a concentrated effort at colonization initiated by Champlain, but although the fur trade expanded rapidly and trading posts were established throughout Quebec, there were no permanent agricultural settlements per se in New France until the 1630s.[2]

The struggle for control of North America began, in fact, with British privateers capturing the first real colonization expedition to the St. Lawrence sent out by Richelieu's company of New France. About the same time, Champlain was forced to surrender Quebec, in July 1629, to other British-sponsored privateers. This conquest was only the first round in the second Hundred Years War between England and France, which eventually resulted in British domination of almost all of the North American continent. British control of Quebec, this time, lasted only until 1633. when under the terms of the treaty of St. Germain, Charles I traded New France and Acadia for the unpaid dowry of his French-born royal wife, Henrietta Maria.[3]

The Catholic church, rather than the French trading companies and the monarchy, was the bastion of support for the colony during its crucial formative period. This can be seen in the fact that in 1675, more than sixty years after Champlain's settlement at Montreal in 1611, there were only about 7,500 Europeans of French origin in Quebec and Acadia, hardly enough to implement France's claim to North America. Thus when the struggle between England and France for domination in North America began in earnest in 1689, only 10,000 French-Canadians were pitted against some 200,000 Anglo-Americans (that is, including those in the American colonies), and in 1756, when the final phase of the Seven Years War began, 70,000 French-Canadians were faced by 1,500,000 Anglo-Americans. It was the simple fact of relative population size, then, added to the sea power of Britain, that settled New France's fate and symbolized the Ancien Regime's attitude toward its North American colony, which, in Voltaire's words, was only "several acres of snow."[4]

In a recent paper on the social, economic, and political significance of the military establishment in New France, W. J. Eccles described the nature and role of the militarized society of the French colony in Canada. Eccles noted that in terms of its economic importance to New France, the military establishment was second only to the fur trade. Furthermore, the geopolitical role selected for the colony in the Imperial policy of France was to tie down large numbers of the enemy (that is, British) to prevent them from being used to counter French forces in other areas of conflict. According to Eccles, the combination of the emphasis on its military role and the importance of the military in the economic life of the colony resulted in the condition that "the whole fabric of (French) Canadian society was imbued with the military ethos . . . in remarkable contrast to the Anglo-American colonies."[5]

Indeed, almost immediately after settling at Quebec, the French became involved in persistent wars with the Iroquois. As a result, the first militia units were set up in 1651 on an ad hoc basis (both men and women participated), since the regular troops originally sent by the French crown proved unable to contain the Iroquois attacks. By 1662 the Iroquois threat to the colony became so great as to necessitate the intervention of the crown. Some 1,300 regular troops were sent from France over the next three years. During this period, the total civilian population reached only 2,500, and thus by 1665 the military comprised some 35 percent of the European population of New France. These additional forces were able to bring the Iroquois under control, and for some twenty years the colony enjoyed relative quiet.[6]

Although most of these soldiers were recalled in 1668, more than 400 chose to remain in New France, and an additional 400 soldier-settlers arrived the next year. A new system of administration organized along military lines, was imposed on the colony at the same time, so the government of New France became, essentially, a military one. A formal militia system encompassing all of the male population between the ages sixteen and sixty was organized in 1669 by order of the crown, with most officers appointed from among the settlers. These officers acted as both legal agents and police officers of the governor-general and local governors, and although unpaid, they enjoyed an elevated social status.[7]

The major importance of the formal militia system in New France was that the armed population could be quickly mobilized by its local officers, which gave it a significant advantage over the neighboring English colonies in time of war. When Iroquois attacks on the colony began again between 1683-1685, the crown responded by sending over 1,600 regular troops. The total population of the colony at this time was less than 11,000, and the new infusion of manpower was not only able to help put down the Iroquois uprising, but provided badly needed extra labor. After the end of hostilities, they remained in New France, the soldiers becoming either agricultural workers or tradesmen and their officers landowners, thus integrating well into the economic and social life of the colony.[8]

In all, there was only a half-century of relative quiet in New France in the century and a half between its establishment (1608) and its conquest by the British (1760). The longest uninterrupted period during which the militia was not engaged in action was the two decades between Iroquois uprisings (1666-1684). Thus, in effect, war was the norm rather than the exception in New France, and as a result, probably all men fit for militia duty were, at some time, engaged in combat.[9]

During the more than two centuries of French domination, war and the threat of war served as the mainstay of Canada's economy and imbued French-Canadian society with a military ethos. On the other hand, the eventual development of an effective militia system in French Canada lessened the military dependence of the colony on the mother country, except in time of overall conflict with either the Indians, English, or both. In fact, except for the linkage between the upper class and the Ancien Regime, the ties between the mass of French-Canadians and the mother country were linguistic, cultural, and religious—not political. Indeed, the majority of immigrants to Canada after the initial colonization efforts was composed of either young men from good families who had fallen into disgrace or deported poachers, smugglers, and counterfeiters—hardly a group who could be said to have held allegiance to the French crown.[10]

Thus although the French-Canadians saw themselves as abandoned by the mother country after the fall of Quebec, this abandonment was actually a part of French Imperial strategy, whose design was to burden England with Canada and foster Anglo-American tendencies toward independence. The stratagem proved successful, since British military expenditure in Canada grew steadily as time went on, and tension between England and the Anglo-American colonies increased, culminating in the war of American independence and the unsuccessful American invasion of Canada during the War of 1812.[11]

UNION, CONFEDERATION, AND IMPERIAL DEFENSE: 1761-1913

Between 1759—the fall of Quebec—and 1763—the treaty of Paris—control over Canada passed from France to Britain, during which time most of the bourgeoisie, colonial army officers, and administrative officials returned to France. However, the majority of the French-Canadian population, some 60,000-65,000—the peasants, clergy, merchants, traders, and artisans of New France—remained after the British conquest.[12]

The transition from French to British rule was singularly lacking in change as regards both the administrative and legal structure of the colony. There was a continuance of administrative districts, parish priests and militia captains remaining the central power's agents, as under the former regime, with the militia captains even taking on the role of both magistrate and policeman in the parishes. With regard to the military situation in their newly acquired colony, the British authorities neither totally disarmed the rural population nor dismantled the militia structure.[13]

In contrast to what one might expect—and despite Canada being governed under martial law from 1760 to 1764—the British attitude toward the newly acquired subject population was, in fact, positive. Thus after an initial period of tension in 1763, when it was proclaimed that French-Canadians would be assimilated into an "English colony," the British authorities granted a considerable number of concessions to the indigenous French-Canadian population. The Quebec Act of 1774 both confirmed and expanded four principles that may have ensured French-Canadian survival during the transition period from French to British rule. These consisted of (1) French-language usage in government and the courts, (2) the continued validity and application of French civil law to property and personal-status matters, (3) freedom of religion regarding Catholicism and the right of Catholics to hold office, and (4) government via the preconquest institutions such as the Superior Council. However, the Quebec Act was passed in the British Parliament on the eve of the American Revolution. This was, as Mason Wade noted, a British attempt to strengthen their hold upon that part of North America that was in fact to remain under their control "by allowing it to remain French and Catholic." In addition to this, the act was, in fact, more beneficial to the French-Canadian elite—both lay and clergy—than it was to the masses, since it reestablished their control via its negation of representative government.[14]

In any event, the historical significance of the Quebec Act can best be summed up in the words of Wade, who wrote that "the real importance of the Act was for the future, and its effect was not confined to Canada. A new principle of empire was laid down when it was conceded that the French-Canadians could be British without becoming English. A precedent was thus established for the creation of multi-national empires."[15]

The first test of French-Canadian attitudes toward the new regime in Canada came with the American Revolution. The opening of hostilities between the American colonies and Great Britain in 1775 found the French-Canadians facing a dilemma. Initial American victories in the border area and along the traditional invasion route into Canada in May of that year caused the British governor, Carleton, to mobilize the militia, after having requested the support of the bishop of Quebec, who duly called the "habitants" to the defense of the colony. Faced with the choice of going against the wishes of their prelate, or joining the Americans against the British, the majority of French-Canadians chose to remain neutral, refusing to serve in the militia in some cases and strongly resisting the overzealous mobilization efforts of local militia captains in other cases.[16]

With the onset of spring 1777, a Militia Act was passed by the newly appointed Legislative Council. The act imposed a service on all French-Canadians between sixteen and sixty years of age. This act was much resented by the French-Canadian populace, who had been free from compulsory military service from the onset of British rule in Canada. One astute observer of French-Canadian history even claimed that "in the enforcement of this law upon an unwilling people may be found a basis of the lasting French-Canadian dislike for compulsory military service." Despite the heavy penalties threatened against those who did not comply, the British governor succeeded in raising only some 300 French-Canadian militiamen for the British invasion force against the American colonies, and corvees were imposed to obtain the additional men needed for support and construction.[17]

Without a doubt, the American Revolution had a decisive influence on the future of Quebec. It not only indirectly settled the fate of the Ancien Regime in France, but it caused a split between the masses and elite in Quebec regarding attitudes toward America, and it introduced into Canada about 6,000 pro-British refugees from the American colonies, who were to form the core of the English-Canadian community. These American Tories did not settle for the most part among the French-Canadians but in uninhabited Upper Canada. The effect of this new influx of population, according to Mason Wade, "clinched Wolfe's victory; Canada was not to be French, but French and English." The political manifestation of the binational character of Canada, and the beginning of the political separation of British North America, came in 1791, when not only were parliamentary institutions granted, but the colony was divided into two parts. Lower Canada comprised the region settled by the French, and Upper Canada consisted of the area settled by the English and American loyalist refugees.[18]

The period of the French Revolution and the Napoleonic Wars found the French-Canadian elite, at least, expressing support for the British side both politically and financially. Refugees from France, both clergy and members of the upper class, found their way to Quebec and their influence was immediately felt, especially in cultural and educational matters. Their coming strengthened French culture in Quebec, and they took an active part in the revival of formal education in the province.[19]

The latent anti-Americanism and anti-Republicanism of the French-Canadians during this period came to a head at the end of the Napoleonic Wars, when a new Franco-American alliance was in the offing, and the French-Canadians were incensed at both American immigration and Jefferson's implicit threat to invade Canada. Feeling against Napoleon also ran high; the Quebec press referred to him as the "lawless leader of France," and the French defeat at Trafalgar was even celebrated by the French-Canadians. When a new Militia Act was passed in early 1812, 6,000 French-Canadians were enlisted without problems, and the representative Assembly allocated $1,000,000 (Canadian) for military spending, which was passed almost unopposed. Just before the outbreak of war with the United States, Lt. Col. Charles de Salaberry, a French-Canadian soldier long under the patronage of the duke of Kent, raised the first regular French-Canadian regiment, whose ranks he was able to fill almost immediately.[20]

The War of 1812 between the British and Americans was fought mostly in Upper Canada. American forces attempted invasions of Lower Canada twice, the first time reaching only the border, the second time being routed by a much smaller Canadian force that included de Salaberry's French-Canadian regiment. Canadian forces led by British regulars then invaded the United States, but were stopped at Lake Champlain when their ships were destroyed by the Americans. British military successes in the Ohio River valley were due, in large part, to the Canadian forces, but the gains were bargained away—in the view of the English merchants of Montreal, at least—by British diplomatic folly in the treaty of Ghent. The British loyalty of the English in Canada was actually weakened by the outcome of the war, while French-Canadian loyalty was demonstrated to a much greater extent than in 1775. In fact, a new Canadian spirit was beginning to develop among both peoples, whose common effort to repel invasion had begun to dispel their doubts about one another. The Canadianism that started to develop as a result of the emergence of a common interest against British misrule was to manifest itself in the future collaboration of members of both groups toward attaining self-government for Canada.[21]

During the first quarter of the nineteenth century, a new elite developed in French Canada made up, for the most part, of lawyers, doctors, and other members of the liberal professions. This new elite took upon itself the responsibility for representing the French-Canadian people and elaborated a political ideology for the people to follow, which defined the French-Canadians as a nation that should and would gain political independence eventually. The nature of representative government in Canada during this period, however, was as unsuccessful as it had been in the former American colonies. Although the representatives were elected on a popular base, they were unable to exert control over the executive branch, that is, the governor and crown agents. Reformers and reform schemes were opposed by the colonial executives, who were able to override reform influence in the Assembly by exercising their power and patronage, going so far as bribery and intimidation if this failed.

The failure of reform measures to improve the position of the

French-Canadian rural population vis-à-vis the banks, merchants, and land companies led to agrarian uprisings by the middle 1830s that culminated in the Rebellion of 1837. During this episode, there was fighting between French-Canadian extremists and English-Canadian loyalist reactionaries, and the rebellion was put down somewhat heavy-handedly by the British army garrison, with a not insignificant number of French-Canadian casualties and damage to property in both Lower and Upper Canada. The events of 1837-1838 brought about Lord Durham's *Report* on Canada, which was to affect the course of Canadian history for the next century.[22]

The main features of Durham's *Report* may be summarized as follows. First, he noted that the conflict between the two peoples in Canada extended throughout all phases of life in the country, being, in his words, "the origin or essence of every dispute which divides the community," so a clash between them was inevitable. The growing influx of English-speaking settlers into Quebec was, in French-Canadian eyes, a threat to their way of life, and they began to use their majority in the representative Assembly to initiate legislation that would protect their interests and maintain the status quo. Durham, however, regarded French Canada as an anachronistic remnant of the Old World in the New, being "the remains of an ancient colonization and . . . ever must be isolated in the midst of an Anglo-Saxon World." He also considered the Quebec Act and its guarantees to French Canada as a policy mistake, since it had effectively protected and preserved a culture he thought inferior and backward compared to Anglo-Saxon culture.[23]

Even in the event of eventual political independence, Durham claimed, the French-Canadians were surrounded by English-speaking peoples—the United States to the South, Upper Canada to the North—so he predicted they would briefly experience only "a wretched semblance of independence which would expose them more than ever to the intrusion of the surrounding population." Thus Durham saw no future for French Canada as such and believed French-Canadians would be better off if they were anglicized and assimilated. Durham cited the case of the Franco-

Americans in Louisiana and the Dutch in New York as examples of successful assimilation. He further suggested that the process could and should be duplicated in the French-Canadian case. This was to be based on the principle of developing loyalty to a centralized state that would both override attachment to its cultural values and speed up the breakdown of the "feudal and rural nature" of French Canada.

Thus Durham concluded:

I entertain no doubt of the national character which must be given to Lower Canada; it must be that of the British Empire; it must be that of the great race which must, in the lapse of no long period of time, be predominant over the whole North American continent. . . . It must be the first and steady purpose of the British Government to establish an English population, with English laws and language in this province (Quebec), and to trust its government to none but a decidedly English legislature.

To achieve this aim, Durham proposed the formation of a British North American Union encompassing Upper and Lower Canada and the Maritime Provinces.[24]

The British government implemented Durham's recommendation in the form of the Union Act of 1840, which amalgamated Quebec (Lower Canada) and Ontario (Upper Canada) into one state. The outcome of the Union Act, according to one astute observer of Canadian history, was the loss of French-Canadian hope and confidence regarding their future. In addition to this, some intellectual leaders among the French-Canadians began to see their people as a minority group whose most vital aim was to preserve its culture: "In fighting assimilation and anglicization, they turned more and more to their past for guidance and inspiration. Their Golden Age lay no more in their future independence but in their French past. To salvage their cultural heritage, they idealized the kind of society they had become." Not all French-Canadian leaders, however, adopted an ultranationalist ideology. The majority actually advocated cooperation with those reform politicians of Upper Canada who would support the survival of French Canada's customs, institutions, laws, and language.[25]

A new influx of population that was to affect the future cooperation between Francophone and Anglophone liberal leaders came in the form of 100,000 Irish immigrants who arrived in Canada by 1847. Indeed, the British governor-general of the country thought the Irish to be a potentially more dangerous element and threat to continued British rule than the French-Canadians, that is, if they were to join in political activities with their "kith and kin" across the border in the United States. In the context of veiled threats of annexation in the American press at the time, along with the issues raised by the Oregon question, and with "manifest destiny" being unsatisfied by the American takeover of Texas and California from Mexico, the governor-general, Elgin, refused to reduce the English garrison and convinced the Assembly to take a larger share of the defense burden upon the country it was there to defend.[26]

Internal affairs, however, still dominated the political scene during the two decades following the Union Act. The most significant development during the period was the controversy and crisis brought about by the passage of an act that compensated French-Canadians for property losses suffered during the 1837-1838 rebellion. The Tory party had previously pushed such an act regarding Upper Canada through the Assembly, but they most strongly opposed a similar bill regarding Lower Canada now passed in the Assembly by the coalition of French- and English-Canadian reformers. Indeed, the debate on this act and its aftermath was one of the most bitter periods in Canadian history. The parliamentary recriminations of the 1837-1838 period spilt onto the streets of Montreal, resulting in the sacking and burning of the Assembly building and the homes of leading reform politicians by an English-Canadian mob and mob rule in Montreal until the British army garrison restored order. In any event, the bill was ratified by the British governor-general despite the vehement protests of the Tories.[27]

When the Union Act was implemented, and despite the fact that the population of Lower Canada numbered 600,000 compared with 400,000 in Upper Canada, both provinces were given equal representation in the Assembly. The overall number of Anglophones in Canada quickly increased as a result of the influx of immigrants from the British Isles. Their numbers grew to the extent that by 1852 the population of Upper Canada surpassed that of Lower Canada, and according to the census of 1861, there were 300,000 more people in Upper than in Lower Canada. This stimulated agitation for representation by population among the English-Canadians, who had strongly disapproved of such a system in 1840, much to the dissatisfaction of French-Canadians. The emerging English-Canadian attitude toward their Francophone counterparts was expressed by the leader of the reactionary wing of the Upper Canada Liberal party, who claimed that "the Negroes are the great difficulty of the States and the French-Canadians of Canada."[28]

The French-Canadian political leadership now strongly opposed representation according to relative population size and was successful in resisting the effort made by the Upper Canadian Liberal party to change the basis of parliamentary representation in Canada. The government of the day, led by the French-Canadian Cartier, was, however, unable to overcome the opposition of its own members in the Assembly to reorganize the militia system and increase defense expenditures in the face of a threat from the Union army during the American Civil War resulting from the Trent incident between Britain and the United States in 1861. A measure to increase the militia to 50,000 men at a cost of $1,000,000 (Canadian) was defeated by a slim majority, with thirty-seven out of fifty-eight MPs from Lower Canada voting against the government.[29]

The breakdown of the political system imposed by the Union Act was imminent, with four governments falling between 1862 and the end of 1864. Two general elections were held, but no party was able to maintain a working majority in parliament. The constitutional crisis was now accompanied by a real threat from the Northern forces, since both Britain and Canada had openly sympathized with the Confederacy, Canada even allowing a Southern military contingent to raid a Vermont border town from a Montreal base late in the war. This aroused great resentment in the North and spurred the northern annexationist newspaper, the *New York Herald,* to call for the American annexation of Canada after the defeat of the South "peacibly if possible, forcibly if necessary The seriousness of the crisis forged political cooperation between the leaders of Upper and Lower Canada and brought about the implementation of a Confederation of all Canadian provinces—that is, Quebec, Ontario, and the Maritimes—to replace the broken-down "double-majority" system of the Union Act.[30]

At the time of the Confederation in 1867, French Canada found itself in a situation that brought about a more accelerated development of national consciousness than had existed previously. The French-Canadians now numbered only one-third of the overall population of Canada. In Quebec itself, they accounted for more than three-fourths of the population, but their influence predominated only in the rural areas. The French-Canadians lacked power in the cities of Quebec, where the English had gained the upper hand by initiating trade and industry and then concentrating their control over these activities, with the French-Canadians supplying the labor force. Thus Quebec became a province of Canada where the French-Canadians were the majority, but since they were the minority in Canada overall and were dominated economically in their own region, they readily developed minority-group attitudes and behavior. This became manifest in the defensive posture adopted by the French-Canadian populace and political leadership alike. Despite the guarantees provided French Canada via fixed federal representation and the establishment of a Quebec legislature, the fear of assimilation became overwhelming. A reactionary spirit accordingly developed among the French-Canadians, which was reinforced by English-Canadian infringements of the rights and privileges guaranteed French-Canadians throughout Canada under the Confederation.[31]

With regard to military affairs of the period, before Confederation, the British maintained a substantial garrison in Canada. This was supplemented, in times of tension or war, by the Canadian militia, which provided manpower for the British regiments or was formed into ad hoc units to support the regular forces. Service in the Canadian militia was universal and compulsory for all males aged eighteen to sixty-five. In principle, at least, this should have resulted in a reflection of the composition of Canada's population, but in practice, French-Canadians were channeled into the reserve militia rather than the active militia, which was dominated by the English-Canadians. With Confederation, Canada was forced to provide for her own defense, and British troops were withdrawn in 1870-1871. A small, permanent Canadian army was then set up, mainly for instructing the volunteer active and reserve militia. To enable French-Canadians to serve in the active militia if they wished, regulations and orders were translated into French. The incentive for French-Canadians to enter active militia service was minimal, however, and even less so for joining the permanent army. In spite of this, French-Canadians did take militia service seriously, and although it is not well known, they took an important part in military activities during the period. In fact, Richard Preston, in a paper on the transfer of British military institutions to Canada in the nineteenth century, claimed that "there seems to have been a conspiracy of silence among Canadian historians of both languages to hide the fact that French-Canadians also played a part" in the development of the Canadian armed forces. According to Preston, between 1862 (the threat of American invasion) and 1871 (the withdrawal of the British garrison), at least nine French-Canadian militia battalions and two full regiments were organized. In addition to this, French-Canadian cadets attended the Royal Military College.[32]

The militia saw active service in Canada only once between 1870 and 1900, being called out to put down the Northwest Rebellions and the Indian uprising of 1885. This was the first military effort made by a purely Canadian military force, since no regular British troops participated. A third of the troops from the eastern provinces were supplied by Quebec, where patriotic feeling initially outweighed any sympathy with the plight of the half-breed Metis (of mixed French-Indian origin) and Indians who were in revolt against English-Canadian excesses in the Northwest territories. Although French-Canadian units actively participated in the fighting and won high praise for their ability and courage from their English-Canadian commander, the chief of staff of the militia overlooked their contribution and praised only the English-Canadian troops. The surrender, subsequent trial, and execution of Riel, the leader of the Northwest Rebellions, brought out the latent antagonism between linguistic groups that had been put to one side while English- and French-Canadian troops fought together. The basic issue in conflict was the linguistic and educational rights of Francophone-Canadians outside Quebec and especially in the western territories, something that had not been specifically guaranteed under Confederation and thus had been bargained away by a series of political compromises, despite the constitutional guarantees regarding the French language and schools written into the Manitoba Act.[33]

A year before the Northwest Rebellions, Lord Melgund, the military secretary to the British governor-general, organized—with the help of the Canadian minister of militia—a contingent of mostly French-Canadian volunteers that was dispatched to the Sudan as part of the Gordon Relief Expedition. Later in the same year, Melgund raised a Canadian force that served in Egypt, at London's suggestion, as an Imperial force rather than as a contingent of the Canadian militia. This was the beginning of Canada's contribution to "Imperial defense," something that was to generate a severe rift between English- and French-Canadians in the years to come.[34]

As the Transvaal crisis deepened and war approached, English-Canadian patriotic feelings rose, while those of their French-Canadian counterparts were unaffected. The delay of the government—headed by Laurier, the first French-Canadian prime minister, elected in 1896—and its initial reticence to send a Canadian contingent was attacked by English-Canadian politicians and aroused anti-French sentiments among the English-Canadians. In response, one French-Canadian newspaper wrote, for example, "We French-Canadians belong to one country, Canada. Canada is for us the whole world; but the English-Canadians have two countries, one here and one across the sea." This expressed the fundamental French-Canadian objection to participation in foreign (that is, British) wars, something that was to bring about two additional major crises in Canadian national life in the future. However, although Laurier, like most French-Canadians, was sympathetic to the Boer cause, he eventually yielded to the combined pressure of the

British government and English-Canadians regarding the dispatch of Canadian troops to South Africa.[35]

Canada did not, however, send an official contingent; rather, at Laurier's insistence, an order-in-council was passed authorizing the dispatch of a volunteer force. The initial contingent of Canadian volunteers included a French-Canadian company, which was raised, however, only with difficulty. The Canadian troops were kept as a separate unit, again, at Laurier's behest, and were not attached to British regiments, as was the case, for example, of Australian troops. Additional contingents were dispatched to South Africa with British military setbacks, and in total, Canada supplied about 7,300 men for the British war effort, of which two-thirds were volunteers and only one-third were sent in the form of militia contingents late in the war. As the war dragged on, ill feelings between English- and French-Canadian activists rose, culminating in street riots in Montreal between prowar English- and antiwar French-Canadian university students. Verbal violence in both parliament and the press brought about the development of a new nationalist movement in Quebec led by Henri Bourassa. After the end of the war, Bourassa's outspoken opposition to Canadian participation in it and future Imperial defense responsibilities forced Laurier into withdrawing his support of the establishment of an "Imperial Council," in contrast to the idea's acceptance by all other British dominions. As time went on, more and more French-Canadians actively supported his views, and Bourassa established himself as the new leader of French-Canadian nationalism.[36]

With the end of the Boer War, Canada reorganized its standing army and militia system. This led to an increasing trend toward English unilingualism in the militia, since only one infantry school gave instruction in French. The growth in size of the standing army before 1914 led to a decline in French-Canadian influence in both the militia and permanent force, so by the outbreak of World War I, the Canadian army was, in effect, unilingual. The Canadian navy came into being only in 1910 as a direct result of the increasing naval buildup in Europe. The new service was established as a permanent force with a reserve along militia lines, but on a wholly voluntary basis. Although the day-to-day running of the navy was the responsibility of the Canadian government, the original Naval Service Bill specified that in time of war, it could be put under Imperial control with the assent of the Canadian Parliament. This bill was strongly opposed by Bourassa and the French-Canadian nationalists, who accused Laurier of reversing his original position against participation in Imperial defense not directly involving Canadian security. The considerable debate and controversy in both parliament and the press over the establishment of the navy further widened the split between English- and French-Canadians on the issue of Canada's participation in Imperial defense. The outcome of the growing cleavage between the linguistic communities in Canada regarding issues of military participation was to be seen in French-Canadian opposition to compulsory military service during World War I and later during World War II.[37]

In contrast to the charged atmosphere in Ontario on the eve of World War I, Quebec was more anxious about the situation of French-Canadians living in the western territories than the prospect of a European war. Since they did not share the enthusiasm for nation building of their English-Canadian compatriots, there was no great French-Canadian migration to western Canada. Those that did migrate were treated as foreigners and aliens by the already established English-Canadian settlers, and, in addition, French was not recognized as an official language. The problems of French-Canadians in the western provinces were to play a major part in the formation of French Canada's attitudes toward participation in the coming war effort.[38]

THE GREAT WARS AND THE INTERWAR PERIOD: 1914-1945

The outbreak of war in August 1914 came as something of an anticlimax in comparison to the tense atmosphere of the Balkan crisis of 1912. Canada's preoccupation with its own domestic affairs caused its leaders to pay only passing attention to the Sarajevo incident in June 1914, and they were also unaware, until the eve of war, of Britain's commitment to France in case of German attack. The French-Canadian leadership, for their part, were vacationing in Europe itself, as was the custom of the day. At first, most of French Canada responded with sympathy toward Belgium and France and enthusiasm toward the Allied cause. Even though Bourassa was still in Europe, some discordant notes were sounded, however, by French-Canadian nationalist activists. They raised the school and linguistic issues when voicing their objections to direct Canadian military participation in the war, with one nationalist leader even saying, "if we are asked to go and fight for England, we reply: let us have our schools in the Western provinces and Ontario."[39]

The French-Canadian press, except for Bourassa's nationalist daily *Le Devoir*, supported the recruitment of men for voluntary military service, with one paper even suggesting that separate French-Canadian battalions be formed and dispatched directly to France. The nationalists strongly objected to this and again raised the connection between the situation in Europe and that in Canada, stressing especially the educational problem of French-Canadians living in neighboring Ontario province. The situation resulted from the severe limitation on the use of French in teaching in Ontario—Regulation 17, as it was called. Due to the federal structure of Canada, the central government in Ottawa could not intervene directly to remedy the situation and private representations of even the prime minister of the day were rebuffed by the local authorities. The deputy-leader of the nationalists in parliament made the connection between the schools issue and military participation of French-Canadians clear when he wrote, "Whatever be the gravity of European events and the problems they raise for us, that does not give us the right to shut our eyes on the longstanding injustice in Ontario." He also predicted the necessity of conscription due to the eventual lack of volunteers, since, as Mason Wade observed, "French-Canadian recruiting did not match the French-Canadian press' enthusiasm for the war."[40]

There were three main reasons for the weak French-Canadian response to calls for voluntary military participation. First, as we noted above, the Canadian army was almost wholly anglicized by 1914, preference being given to English-Canadian officers over their French-Canadian counterparts, and English was the sole language of command. The number of French-Canadian officers and men among permanent army personnel was, correspondingly, low. In fact, less than 5 percent of graduates of the Royal Military College between 1876 and 1900 were French-Canadians, thus severely limiting the number of French-Canadian officers eligible for senior command positions. Second, the old local French-Canadian militia units were disbanded, and Sam Hughes, the English-Canadian minister of militia, well known for his anti-Quebec position, refused to form new separate French-Canadian battalions and regiments at the beginning of the war. The largest French-Canadian units agreed to by the English-Canadian military authorities were of company-size only, and these units were amalgamated within Anglophone battalions. Hughes's insensitivity to French-Canadian feelings even went so far as his appointment of a Protestant clergyman as supervisor of recruitment in Quebec. Third, Henri Bourassa, who narrowly escaped being interned by the Germans at the outbreak of war during a European trip, returned to Canada. Bourassa had initially supported Canadian participation while still in France, even when his supporters in Canada were questioning it, but after his return he changed his views and openly questioned Canada's role in the conflict; this, after also observing the rabid prowar enthusiasm that had gripped English Canada.[41]

At the same time, the prowar element among the French-Canadian lay and clerical leadership was engaged in a campaign for the formation of a separate French-Canadian regiment, with the aged Laurier even writing the English-Canadian prime minister, Borden, to express his support for the effort and pointing out that "the [British] War Office at all times has taken advantage of the force of race sentiment in the formation of the army." The government reluctantly agreed to the formation of the Twenty-second French Canadian Regiment of the First Canadian Division, so as not to alienate public opinion totally in Quebec and to ensure further support for the raising of an additional Canadian division. At a mass public recruiting meeting where the moderate French-Canadian leadership supported enlistment, Laurier urged French-Canadians to answer the call to arms, claiming that "if some Canadians were frightened by the monster of conscription in the past, they must now recognize this monster as a myth"—words that had a hollow ring some three years afterwards. Bourassa, however, did not appear at the meeting, calling it an "explosion of empty and sterile chauvinism."[42]

The constantly increasing manpower pressures on the Canadian government led to the formation of ten additional French-Canadian battalions, only half of which met their recruiting quotas. The lack of French-Canadian response to the recruiting effort led to open hostility on the part of most English-Canadians, who accused them of shirking their responsibility and of being unpatriotic. The French-Canadians, however, were reluctant to serve in an army where English was the only language used for command and where their chances of advancement were limited. In fact, the English-Canadian minister, Hughes, personally intervened to promote his friends to senior officer positions, even relieving one French-Canadian colonel, the son of a political enemy, of his command in the process. In addition, French-Canadians were still more concerned with the problems of the Franco-Ontarians. As Bourassa put it, "The whole problem of the French language and of French survival is being raised in Ontario. For Canada, for all America, it is not on the battlefields of Europe that this survival will be maintained or extinguished . . . let no mistake be made—if we let the Ontario minority be crushed, it will soon be the turn of other French groups in English Canada." Bourassa's nationalists also demanded that French take priority in the public services and in business in Quebec.[43]

The attitude taken by the English-Canadian leadership to the school and linguistic problem only exacerbated the situation. The nationalist position was that French-Canadians would not go willingly to fight in Europe until the Ontario problem was solved. Bourassa's deputy, Lavergne, claimed "if we must conquer our liberties, it is here we should stay. It is not in the trenches of Flanders that we shall win the right to speak French in Ontario, if we have not been able to obtain it here." The English response was, as Mason Wade put it, "enlist first and then we shall see."[44]

Manpower pressures grew even more as the war continued, and after heavy Canadian casualties in 1915 and 1916, there was a significant drop in enlistment in both English and French Canada. As a result, the military authorities initiated parliamentary discussion on a plan for national registration for the purpose of conscription. The figures presented in parliament showed that although French-Canadians comprised some 30.0 percent of the populace, only 4.5 percent of all recruits were French speaking. Now, besides the reasons cited previously for the low French-Canadian response to calls for enlistment, the large-scale transfer of personnel from French- to English-Canadian units also caused difficulties and demoralization among the French-Canadian recruits, who reported back to their civilian counterparts. The rate of desertion grew, and disturbances occurred in some French-Canadian battalions, leading to the dismissal of officers of two battalions and the court-martial and imprisonment of the commander of one of them, who was found guilty of inciting his men to aid deserters and oppose conscription.

As the call for conscription grew louder in English Canada, French-Canadian opposition to it grew also. The French-Canadian press, while recognizing a gap in recruitment between French and English Canada, cited the fact that most French-Canadians joined combat battalions, while many of their English-Canadian counter-parts enlisted in service and support units. In addition, the French-Canadian press claimed, if one left out the British-born recruits and compared the responses of native Canadians from the various provinces, the difference was not that great. The English-Canadian press countered with accusations that Quebec was shirking its responsibility and that the French-Canadians "enlist in retail and desert in wholesale." The lack of official recruiting figures by linguistic group only served to make matters worse.[45]

The Canadian government finally decided to introduce the Military Service Act (conscription) in June 1917. Both the French-Canadian nationalist and traditional leadership were opposed to the act, including Laurier, who demanded a referendum or an election on the issue; this, even though the act did not specifically assign conscripts to combat units. The government forces in both the lower and upper houses of parliament, however, prevailed, and the law passed in late July 1917. To stress the necessity of the act, the military presented statistics that confirmed the low recruitment rate in Quebec compared to the rest of Canada. The split between English and French Canada over the issue was brought to its height by the rhetoric of the French press, with *Le Devoir*—the nationalist organ—censuring parliament and claiming the French-Canadians were being forced to fight for the British in the same way "the Senegalese were being forced to fight for France." The Catholic church in Quebec also opposed the new law, since it did not exempt lay brothers and theological students.[46]

Feelings grew as nationalist leaders such as Lavergne, Bourassa's deputy, urged disobedience and even armed resistance to the act. Anticonscription rallies were held in French Canada throughout the period of parliamentary debate, and disturbances mounted in August, with crowds marching through downtown Montreal and damaging business premises. French-Canadian extremists dynamited the home of the publisher of the English-Canadian *Montreal Star*, which strongly supported conscription. At a later trial of the offenders, their plans were revealed. These included further attacks on the offices of English-Canadian newspapers, bombings of clubs and politicians' homes, and the assassination of the English-Canadian prime minister and other English-Canadian leaders who backed conscription.[47]

The disturbances started to become violent when the police tried to break up the street rallies against conscription in late August, but quieted down upon appeals for calm from the church and the French-Canadian traditionalist leaders. The atmosphere in French Canada remained tense during the first few months of 1918, and the enforcement of the new law proved to be difficult in Quebec. Many French-Canadian conscripts claimed exemptions, and when agreed to by local tribunals made up of French-Canadians, the military appealed, and the conscripts were inducted. Thus by the end of February 1918, only 10 percent of more than 20,000 men conscripted originated from Quebec, and by the end of March, only 31,000 men overall had been ordered to induction centers, of which 5,000 men didn't comply—again, mostly from Quebec.[48]

The authorities expected antidraft riots in Montreal when the police were given orders to arrest draft evaders. Riots unexpectedly broke out in Quebec City in late March 1918, when a French-Canadian was arrested by the police and when a mob subsequently burnt down the police station in which he was being held. The police asked for military assistance, but this was initially turned down. Two newspaper offices were then sacked, but still the military did not intervene. It was only the following day, when the office of the registrar of the Military Service Act was attacked, that the government ordered the military to intervene, and a Toronto battalion, which had been on stand-by alert, was brought in to reinforce the federal police protecting the building. The troops advanced with fixed bayonets, and a riot erupted that led to bloodshed. The rioters faced the military on Easter Sunday, 1918, despite military orders to the citizens to remain in their homes, and were driven back by cavalry charges. The next day, the rioters returned, but this time some were armed, and extremists opened fire on the troops, who returned the fire with rifles and automatic weapons. The cavalry unit attacked the crowds with swords drawn, and snipers exchanged fire with troops throughout the night. Order was restored only the next day; this, after five soldiers had been seriously wounded, four civilians killed, and many others wounded and arrested. The government temporarily suspended habeas corpus and implemented immediate conscription of many of the rioters arrested. Some English-Canadian leaders called for imposing martial law in Quebec and internment, but this was rejected by the government, which preferred to calm the situation, rather than aggravate it. The government appealed for the support of the church and moderate French-Canadian leaders to quiet the highly charged atmosphere in Quebec, especially after it was forced to cancel all draft exemptions due to the German breakthrough in late March, when Canadian troops were called in to reinforce British units.[49]

Laurier and the church hierarchy answered the government appeal, and Borden, the prime minister, responded in kind by asserting his support for the formation of a French-Canadian brigade, which moderate Quebec leaders had wanted since the war started. Borden also discussed plans to form other new, separate French-Canadian units with moderate French-Canadian leaders, but he claimed that the government thought mixed units—that is, small French-Canadian units attached to larger English-Canadian ones—to be better than separate units, a statement that raised nationalist French-Canadian suspicions that the government sought to anglicize French-Canadians via military service. The Canadian army chief of staff visited Quebec, stated his support for separate French-Canadian units commanded by Francophone officers within larger, divisional-sized units, and admitted that the minister of militia's order to break up the old militia units had harmed the recruiting effort.[50]

The military pressed the application of the Conscription Act due to a new German offensive that threatened the Channel Ports, and an amnesty for defaulters was instituted, during which 10,000 men registered for the draft. Between August and November 1918, the Canadian Expeditionary Force in Europe saw constant action after the Allied breakthrough at Amiens and suffered more than 30,000 casualties. The Twenty-second French-Canadian Regiment was a key unit in the Allied offensive, and its officers and men distinguished themselves in action, with two members winning VCs and its senior officers being promoted to brigadiers. By November 1918, some 15,000 French-Canadians had seen service at the front, another 15,000 were in training in Canada and England, and between 4,000 and 5,000 had served in the Canadian navy and merchant marine.[51]

With regard to the role of French-Canadians in naval service and in the fledgling Royal Canadian Air Force (RCAF), the Royal Canadian Navy (RCN) was established only in 1910. As such, the influence of the British Royal Navy on the organization, personnel structure, and cultural milieu of the RCN was overwhelming. The result was that those French-Canadian recruits and conscripts who entered the navy had to adapt to a completely Anglophone environment, giving rise to a tradition of aversion to naval service among French-Canadians that was to last for over half a century. The same situation held in the RCAF, which was essentially part of the British Royal Air Force (RAF) until after World War II.[52]

All told, about 35,000 French-Canadians served in the armed forces and merchant marine during World War I, but this is only an estimate, since no official figures were issued after March 1918, so as to lower the intergroup tensions over perceived differential participation rates. It was generally acknowledged, however, in both English and French Canada, that conscription was a failure, since at considerable economic cost, it actually supplied fewer men per month than the volunteer system; the default rate was high, even in English Canada; and it stirred intergroup divisions. Although the feelings in English Canada soon cooled down regarding the perceived low participation rate of Quebec, the French-Canadians have never forgotten the 1917-1918 period, since, in the words of one observer: "To French-Canadians, 1917 (conscription) was the climax of a long history of defeat; once again, a brutal and insensitive majority had violated the tolerant principles of Confederation and imposed its will upon a helpless minority."[53] Although this may overstate what actually happened, the psychological effects of the imposition of conscription during World War I extended over a quarter century and reverberated in the conscription crisis that again deeply divided French and English Canada during the last phase of World War II.

The period between the wars was characterized by the further development of French-Canadian nationalism, which was also accompanied by the emergence of an extremist movement along European fascist lines. Although even the aging Bourassa criticized the rise of "clerical fascism" in Quebec, the movement found support in the towns and cities of the province among students, intellectuals, and some nationalist leaders.[54]

The reasons for the strengthening of the nationalist-separatist trend during this period were as follows. First, despite their high birthrate, French-Canadians comprised only a bit more than 25 percent of the overall population of Canada. The population of Quebec itself had grown some 18 percent in the decade 1911-1921, compared with 22 percent in Canada as a whole. Quebec's proportion of overall population had declined instead of growing from 1867 onwards due to French-Canadian emigration to the United States and English Canada (the western provinces and Ontario), and a large influx of immigrants into English Canada itself from Great Britain and Ireland. Within Quebec Province, the population had become urbanized and the rate of industrialization due to the war was rapid. The immediate postwar depression did not affect Quebec as much as the rest of Canada, but although its economy prospered, the fruits of this prosperity did not reach the French-Canadian masses. English-Canadian and American business almost entirely controlled Quebec's commerce and industry, with the French-Canadians only supplying the labor force. The nationalist press began to protest the "economic invasion" and "foreign exploitation" of Quebec's natural resources. The effects of the Great Depression lasted in Canada until 1939, heightening tensions between English- and French-Canadians and increasing the economic aspect of French-Canadian nationalism.[55]

With regard to military developments and attitudes toward foreign affairs during the interwar period, French Canada was, for the most part, either unconcerned or isolationist. After World War I, the French-Canadian Twenty-second Regiment was upgraded and given permanent force status, but the majority of military installations were set up outside Quebec. Thus Francophone soldiers had to spend most of their careers away from their home province. The interwar period was, in fact, one of the most British-oriented periods in the history of the Canadian armed forces. French Canada was preoccupied with its own affairs as European rearmament accelerated. Most French-Canadian politicians—both nationalist and moderate—opposed increasing defense expenditure. In addition, an antiwar group of French-Canadian Liberal MPs supported by the nationalists crystallized in the federal parliament to oppose the "Imperialist" tendencies of the Conservative government, which held office until 1936. Quebec remained deeply isolationist throughout the period and sought to avoid taking part in the future wars of Britain and the empire.[56]

Canada declared war on Germany in mid-September 1939, and

two weeks later elections were held in Quebec for the provincial parliament. The elections were called by Maurice Duplessis, the head of the Quebec nationalist party L'Union Nationale. The party had come to power in Quebec after defeating the Liberals in 1936. In its first three years of office, the extravagance of the Duplessis administration doubled the provincial debt, thus offending the French-Canadian sense of moderation, and had also alienated the labor movement in the province by its autocratic methods of government. The French-Canadian Liberal party leaders in the federal parliament had joined the government of Mackenzie King after the Liberal victory in the 1936 national election, and they now attacked Duplessis's antiwar stand and threatened resignation if Quebec didn't "clean house" and support the Liberal's moderate war policy, which promised no conscription. Quebec responded by deposing Duplessis, which was greeted by the English-Canadian press and political leadership with high praise, since his party had been associated with the prewar fascist movement. The prime minister, King, claimed that "nothing since Confederation . . . contributed more to national unity" than the removal of Duplessis from office. The English-Canadians were further heartened by French Canada's response in the federal elections of May 1940, when the Liberal party took all but one seat in Quebec.[57]

Quebec had decided to go along with the Liberal party during the "phony war" period, which lasted until the spring of 1940, since it saw few dangers from the Liberal's "pay-as-you-go" policy. When a Canadian division was dispatched to England in December 1939, there was no protest in French Canada. In fact, although the rate of recruitment in Quebec during 1939 was slower than in English Canada, the French-Canadians did enlist in reserve units in considerable numbers and some French-Canadian units were among the first to attain full strength. Many English-Canadians criticized the high French-Canadian enlistment rate in reserve army units rather than in regular units that were destined for overseas service. According to one astute observer of Canadian history, the English-Canadians simply forgot, however, that for many French-Canadians—who had never been out of their home province—service in British Columbia, the Maritime provinces, Greenland, or the Yukon Territory was actually "foreign service." In addition, French-Canadians had always preferred service in Canada to "overseas adventures" and, until the United States entered the war in late 1941, were not actually convinced that the defense of Canada began in Europe.[58]

The Allied setbacks, which started with the fall of Norway in April and ended with the defeat of France in June 1940, brought the war closer to Quebec and Canada as a whole. The British retreat at Dunkirk and subsequent position of Britain alone in the face of the Nazi onslaught brought on a wave of English-Canadian loyalism. This even extended to criticism of the Liberal government's war effort as being too little and King's leadership too cautious. The Quebec press and political leadership urged French-Canadians to continue the French tradition now that France itself had fallen and support the Canadian defense effort. French-Canadian morale was boosted by the prime minister's message to Quebec on the province's national holiday, when he declared that French Canada now had "the duty of upholding French culture, civilization, and love of liberty."[59]

Quebec and its moderate leadership, both lay and clerical, even accepted the imposition of limited conscription for home defense—the National Resources Mobilization Act (NRMA) of June 1940—without much protest, since the measure did not require service outside of Canada itself. The nationalist press and nationalist politicians tried to stir up opposition to the act, but the attempt failed, and an antimobilization act sponsored by nationalists and the Union Nationale party was defeated by a large majority in the Quebec legislature. One leading nationalist figure—Houde, the mayor of Montreal—was, however, interned by the government when he urged French-Canadians not to register under the act, but the French-Canadian press disapproved of his actions and claimed that the government had acted in accordance with the law and, in view of the wartime situation, was justified in its action. French Canada's acceptance of limited conscription and its support for the government's war policy led both English-Canadian politicians and military leaders to believe that Quebec would be willing to come to terms with conscription for overseas service if this became necessary. This, however, was a misconception that was to cause much consternation when such a measure was eventually instituted late in the war.[60]

In any event, by January 1941 some 50,000 French-Canadians had enlisted in both regular and reserve units, and a French-Canadian battalion was the first in the army to fulfill its overseas volunteer quota. French-Canadians also enlisted in the Royal Canadian Navy and Merchant Marine—where they comprised some 30 percent of the personnel—and even joined the Royal Canadian Air Force, although this organization was still part of the British RAF and thus completely Anglophone. The army high command was very aware of the problem of French-Canadian participation, and as the official army historian of the period put it, "no question commanded more urgent attention . . . than that of French-speaking (sic) representation in the Army." Thus at the outset of the war, the army formed regionally based French-Canadian units, and, in addition, a number of bilingual officer's training schools were established. The other services later adopted similar measures to encourage French-Canadian enlistment, but only at the prodding of the civilian defense officials and politicians.[61]

Specific problems arose, however, regarding French-Canadian participation in the technical branches of the army and in the navy and air force, where "English-only" was the rule. A 1941 report compiled by the army on the recruiting problem in Quebec cited the lack of technical education and background as limiting the number of French-Canadians who were eligible for service in technical units. As for the other services, although the army could maintain Francophone units, they preferred to give English training to Francophone recruits, since their operational language was solely English. Even the army, however, retained English as the language of command, thus limiting the career prospects of unilingual French-Canadian NCOs and officers. All services claimed that efficiency was the only reason for this, but studies conducted after the war showed that both the navy and RCAF also barred French-Canadian unilingual recruits in the prewar period and at the beginning of World War II on the basis of "tradition." As the official naval historian wrote, "in the interest of operational efficiency the RCN had to employ a common language, and since the great majority of its members were English-speaking and its traditions were British, that language was English." No attempt was made during the war to man ships with totally Francophone crews, since the naval authorities considered this to be "administratively . . . difficult, almost to the point of impossibility."[62]

With regard to the air force, the RCAF cited its necessity to adhere to the RAF example and regulations and thus to maintain its unilingual training and operational tradition. No provision was made for training French-Canadian recruits before the war in any case, since not only was English the sole language of training, but no course in remedial English was organized for those French-Canadian recruits that did join the RCAF before 1939. It was only a year after the war began that the RCAF established a manning depot in Quebec—the first RCAF installation in French Canada. The base was set up to give unilingual French-Canadian recruits intensive courses in English before their technical training. The RCAF, in contrast to the navy, stepped up its recruiting program in French Canada after 1940, and by the end of 1941, a separate course for Francophone mechanics was organized. A French-Canadian fighter squadron was formed in June 1942, which was attached to RAF Bomber Command and saw action in the European theatre. Recruiting facilities in Quebec were also expanded, and school visits by bilingual RCAF officers were instituted. No official figures on overall French-Canadian participation in the RCAF during World War II are available, however, since that service "did not keep records according to the ethnic origin of its personnel." In RCAF units overseas, it is estimated that French-Canadians comprised some 4 percent of the officers and 11 percent of the ranks and in total composed some 11 percent of RCAF personnel.[63]

In contrast to the RCAF, the Royal Canadian Navy made no special effort during the war to attract French-Canadian recruits or train them, and the problem of retaining French-Canadian personnel per se was recognized only late in the war. Although

French-Canadians were recruited, there was a high failure rate among them due to inadequate English language skills. The RCN finally opened a special language school in July 1943 to give a three-month English-language course to French-Canadian recruits before their basic training. If at the end of the course his English was judged still deficient, the recruit was sent to a base in English Canada for shore duties for an additional three months to "assimilate more English." At the end of this period, if he failed an English-language test, the recruit was discharged. So as not to lose the manpower, however, the navy proposed that French-Canadian recruits unable to meet its English-language standards be channeled into the Free French Forces. When the Canadian prime minister learned of this, he strongly criticized navy policy as being "indefensible" and ordered its thorough revision. The RCN, however, instructed its recruiting officers only in 1943 that no French-Canadian recruit was to be turned away because he was unilingual or understood and spoke English with difficulty. In the same year, it also finally instituted recruiting in Quebec by bilingual RCN officers. The result of the RCN policy toward French-Canadian participation is reflected in the naval enlistment rate in Quebec during World War II, which was the lowest of all the provinces.[64]

Manpower considerations and political pressure from the Conservative opposition led the Liberal government in late April 1942 to propose a plebiscite on the amendment of the NRMA to provide for the possibility of conscription for overseas service. This measure split Canada and destroyed national unity in the war effort. The French-Canadian Liberals initially supported the measure and urged the people of French Canada to support it also. As a result of the efforts of the nationalists, however, the response in Quebec was a 72 percent "No" as against 80 percent "Yes" in all other provinces. An amendment was introduced in parliament but was altered under pressure from English-Canadian Liberal Cabinet members, who saw their chance to neutralize the French-Canadian Liberals' influence on the prime minister. A cabinet crisis resulted, and Mackenzie King gave in to the English-Canadian faction, which proposed action by order-in-council and subsequent parliamentary approval, rather than parliamentary debate on the issue. The Quebec Liberals felt betrayed, and their leader resigned from the Cabinet. The nationalists strongly attacked the bill to amend the NRMA, and when the vote was taken, the measure passed, but parliament divided along ethnic and not party lines.[65]

By the end of 1942, French-Canadian support for the war effort had markedly deteriorated, despite the heroic action of French-Canadian troops during the furtive Dieppe raid. The cabinet had also decided in the meantime to dispatch NRMA conscripts to Greenland and Alaska under orders-in-council and without parliamentary debate. The growing antiwar feeling in Quebec crystallized politically around the former Liberal and now nationalist MP Maxime Raymond, who formed a new party, the Bloc Populaire Canadien, which grew rapidly in strength. In fact, a poll conducted in April 1943 revealed that the Bloc had almost approached the strength of the Liberal party in Quebec, with 37 percent supporting it, 39 percent supporting the Liberals, and the rest undecided. Public opinion in French Canada was also aroused by reports of a disturbance at a training camp between French- and English-Canadian troops, which resulted in one soldier's death. The Quebec press viewed the incident as typical of the contemptuous English-Canadian attitude toward French-Canadian conscripts, who were even called "Zombies" by one English-Canadian newspaper.[66]

Despite the participation of a French-Canadian battalion in the joint American-Canadian invasion of the Japanese-held Aleutian Islands, Quebec's attitude toward the war effort did not change. The dispatch of French-Canadian NRMA conscripts to British Guiana, Bermuda, and the Bahamas did not improve the situation, and a public opinion poll taken at the time showed two-thirds of French-Canadians to be in favor of conscripts remaining in Canada and 60 percent of English-Canadians wanting them sent abroad. On the eve of the battle for Europe, then, Quebec was almost totally at odds with the rest of Canada.

After the initial enthusiasm for the Normandy invasion had receded, the differences between French- and English-Canadians once more were highlighted by street clashes between civilians, soldiers, and even schoolchildren of both groups in Montreal. This was brought on by the increasingly heavy losses of the Canadian forces in Europe and the growing feeling among English-Canadians that Quebec was not doing its fair share. The inequality of casualties issue was clouded by the government's unwillingness to supply enlistment figures by linguistic group. It was generally felt by English-Canadians, however, that they bore the brunt of the casualties, since with their smaller families and higher percentage of overseas volunteers, their losses were more evident.[67]

Political agitation for overseas conscription mounted as reports of a possible reinforcement shortage became common. The Conservative opposition and the proconscription English-Canadian press led the campaign against the Liberal's policy of keeping NRMA conscripts, for the most part, in Canada. The army chief of staff (COS) proposed that navy and air force recruiting be halted and volunteers channeled into the army to make up a growing shortage in the infantry. When it became apparent that the Germans were not going to collapse before the Allied offensive in October 1944, the Army COS recommended that trained NRMA troops should provide the needed reinforcements. Pressure on the government also grew from within its own ranks, and the prime minister finally yielded to a group of proconscriptionist English-Canadian Cabinet ministers after they threatened to bring the issue before a caucus of the Liberal party. By that time, the new defense minister, who had replaced the former proconscriptionist one who was fired by the prime minister, also came to the conclusion that the volunteer system would not succeed in generating the manpower required and recommended conscription for overseas service. The prime minister, foreseeing the consequences of such a measure, reluctantly went along with the decision, and the government passed an order-in-council accordingly.[68]

The order, which authorized the dispatch overseas of 16,000 NRMA conscripts for reinforcement purposes, was presented for parliamentary approval. The Conservative opposition criticized the government action as being too little, too late, and a heated debate ensued, the likeness of which was only surpassed by that over conscription during World War I. The prime minister asked for a vote of confidence in his war policy during the debate and after the resignation of his own air minister from the Cabinet, who thought conscription for overseas service to be unnecessary and likely to provoke "a national scission." The motion, as a vote of confidence, passed by a two to one majority, although all French-Canadian MPs voted against it. During the debate in parliament, feeling in Quebec ran high. Disturbances took place in Montreal and Quebec City after Bloc Populaire protest meetings, and some government offices and business premises were damaged, but marches on English-Canadian newspaper offices were dispersed by the local police. The government ordered the police to deal with the disturbances, rather than order troops in, and after appeals for calm from moderate French-Canadian leaders and from the church, they ended without bloodshed.[69]

The overseas conscription order brought about a considerable number of desertions as the conscripts were moved to embarkation camps and given their last leave. Of the 14,500 men eventually ordered to report for embarkation, 4,100 did not show up, of which 2,400 men (some 59 percent) were from Quebec. In total, some 2,400 (some 23 percent) were actually from Quebec. This figure is not surprising since at the beginning of the overseas conscription debate, the government had announced that the number of NRMA men from Quebec was some 23,000 out of a total of 60,000, and thus French-Canadian NRMA participation was more or less in proportion to its population.[70]

In fact, during World War II, the policy of the Canadian government was the maintenance of a fixed proportion of French- and English-Canadians in overseas army service as far as this was possible. Some forty French-Canadian battalions were eventually formed, mostly infantry and artillery, with some support units also established. There were virtually no French-Canadian technical units, since, as noted, English was the army's operational language, and French was used only in training, administration, and tactical control of French-Canadian units. A plan to organize a French-Canadian brigade was shelved due to the shortage of Francophone officers, and, in fact, unilingual French-Canadian officers were not to be found in higher command positions. With regard to military participation, figures published at the end of the war confirmed the lower participation rate of Quebec, but a postwar army study of manpower problems during World War II cited three reasons for the low French-Canadian enlistment rate. First, there were not enough Francophone militia units before 1939. Second, there were not enough French-Canadian technical units, and service in technical units was limited to bilingual personnel. Third, there was a widespread feeling in Quebec that French-Canadians would be assigned only to the infantry.

In any event, the military authorities had considerably over-estimated the casualty rate in the closing months of the war and thereby the need for reinforcements. Although they became aware of the lower rates at the time of the parliamentary debate, they still insisted on the necessity of overseas conscription. Put another way, Canada nearly split itself in two over a situation that never materialized. In the words of Mason Wade, "the reinforcement crisis of 1944 was in great measure an artificial one," caused by political opportunism and military errors of judgment. World War II ended, therefore, with Canada more deeply divided than it had been when it entered the war.[71]

THE POST-WORLD WAR II PERIOD: AFTER 1946

The policy of maintaining a fixed proportion of French-Canadian personnel in the army and Francophone units was carried over into the postwar period. After some deliberation, the army authorities decided to set a quota of 30 percent French-Canadian personnel for infantry service and 15 percent in other branches. The army started a French-language program in 1946 for Anglophone officers and NCOs, and French-langauge instruction was also introduced by the Army COS for headquarters personnel. Since English was the army's operational language, French-Canadian officers and soldiers were unable to compete on equal terms with their English-Canadian counterparts. Although low-level exami-nations and basic training could be in French—something that was at the time denied to Francophones in other armed services—once the French-Canadian soldier advanced beyond the lower ranks, he was at a distinct disadvantage. Most technical training and advanced courses were given in English only, and English was the language of instruction in the training establishments and staff colleges for officers.[72]

In 1950 a committee was set up by the army to study its bilingual problem and to determine how a more equitable distribution of French-Canadian personnel could be attained in service arms besides the infantry. The army's effort permitting French-Canadians to undergo training in French was noted, and it was agreed that knowledge of English was essential only at the level of NCO technical specialist. This decision was taken to enable a greater number of unilingual French-Canadians to enter technical units and attain English fluency as they advanced in rank.

The acute shortage of Francophone officers was also evident as Canadian units were dispatched to aid the United Nations forces in Korea, and at one point, it became necessary to transfer Anglophone officers to French-Canadian units. To remedy the situation, a Francophone equivalent of the Royal Canadian Military College was set up in late 1952 and expanded in 1953 to take in 400 cadets a year. Despite this effort, the shortage of French-Canadian officers continued, and by 1958 Francophone personnel comprised only 15 percent of all lieutenants, 12 percent of all captains and majors, 9 percent of all lieutenant colonels, and only 8 percent of all with the rank of colonel and above.[73]

With regard to the Royal Canadian Navy, the wartime practice of implicit exclusion carried over into the postwar period. As one French-Canadian MP put it in a parliamentary debate in late 1946: "Always there are very high obstacles to cross before a French-Canadian is admitted. . . . It seems to me that the high officials (in the Navy Ministry) do not want a single French-Canadian to get on board the ships." The rank structure of the RCN in the early 1950s attests to the outcome of the traditional exclusion of French-Canadians from this service. Francophone personnel comprised only 9.8 percent of naval ratings (leading seaman and above). In the officer corps, the situation was more obvious, since only some 7.8 percent of all officers (including cadets) were French-Canadian. No French-Canadian had risen above the rank of naval captain (equivalent to army colonel), and of captains,

Francophones comprised less than 5 percent, while less than 15 percent of commanders (lieutenant colonels) were French-Canadian. Given the overall situation of French-Canadians in the navy, it is not surprising that recruiting of Francophones in the early post-World War II period lagged far behind English-Canadian enlistment.[74]

As a reaction to the manpower shortage brought about by the Korean conflict, in 1951 the navy decided to study the problem of French-Canadian participation. A French-Canadian naval commander, Marcel Jette, was designated to prepare a report on the specific reasons for the low rate of French-Canadian enlistment and to make recommendations for remedying the shortfall in recruitment. His report cited six main reasons underlying the lack of French-Canadian enthusiasm for naval service. According to Jette, the French-Canadians felt (1) that the RCN was more British than Canadian; (2) that the RCN did not want them; (3) that all concessions had to come from them because the RCN was unwilling to compromise; (4) that there was favoritism toward English- and discrimination against French-Canadians; (5) that entrance exams were not suited to French-Canadian recruits; and finally, (6) that the navy's real attitude was evident in the fact that there were seven recruiting posts in Ontario and only two in Quebec.

Jette's main recommendation was the establishment of an English-language school in Quebec City for the purpose of instructing Francophone sailors—both recruits and regulars—in English, mathematics, and seamanship. Such a school was set up, and in 1952 a French-language course for naval officers was also offered. When one officer suggested in 1959 that such a course be offered to Anglophone ratings, this was rejected by the naval authorities, as was a request from Anglophone officers to attend Laval University's French-language course. The reasons given were a lack of bilingual instructors in the former instances and budgetary considerations in the latter case. According to one astute observer of the Canadian defense establishment, however, the real reason for these decisions was a "shortage of imagination . . . a commodity which in the RCN was seldom in over-supply."[75]

Despite its wartime overtures to French-Canadians, the post-

World War II Royal Canadian Air Force continued its strong Anglophone orientation, but with the RAF's influence being increasingly replaced by that of the United States Air Force. The exclusive operational language of the RCAF remained English, in which all personnel were required to be proficient. Although a small number of Francophone officers had attained wing commander status (2.5 percent) by 1951, no French-Canadian advanced beyond this rank. In the words of one observer, "the RCAF was run by Anglo-Canadians largely as if Canada were an Anglo-Canadian nation." In fact, only in 1950, after being ordered to do so by the defense minister, did the RCAF start to use French in their correspondence with Francophone individuals, municipal authorities, and the government of Quebec. In contrast to postwar army practice, there was no program in the RCAF that allowed Francophone personnel to use French-language materials for study purposes, since no RCAF technical manuals were even translated. French-Canadian recruits whose knowledge of English was below RCAF standards were sent to an RCAF English school located in Ontario, which was moved to Quebec only in 1951.[76]

In addition, in 1951 RCAF orders and regulations were published for the first time in both English and French, again only after instructions from the Defense Ministry. This was the extent to which French was formally used by the RCAF. In fact, as late as 1963, the RCAF stipulated that all of its personnel had to be able to converse in English. Although French-Canadian recruits were given English-language courses, all training was conducted in English, and it was used exclusively for examination purposes at both the officer level and in the ranks. The RCAF justified its postwar policies on the grounds of operational effectiveness and the necessity for coordinating its deterrent activities with the U.S. Air Force. It argued that if French were elevated to operational language status, this could have resulted in communications difficulties with a high cost—in terms of potential casualties—in case of an attack on North America. In the view of James Eayrs, for one, the cost of retaining a unilingual RCAF in terms of national unity may have proven greater.

For the first time in Canada's history, a French-Canadian,

Gen. Jean Allard, was appointed defense chief of staff in 1966. His appointment was strongly opposed by some English-Canadian senior naval officers—both active and retired. This led to the dismissal and replacement of two rear admirals by Defense Minister Hellyer and subsequent bitter parliamentary debate. A Defense White Paper on the reorganization, integration, and eventual unification of the Canadian armed forces had been published two years earlier, in 1964. But although the early stages of unification went smoothly, after its principle was accepted by the traditionalists in the navy, the parliamentary debate on unification in 1967 was accompanied by sharp questions from Quebec MPs regarding its effects on French-Canadian members of the armed forces. They were not satisfied, however, by the defense minister's answers, since up to that point, English was still regarded as the only official language in the military, and some armed forces personnel had taken this quite literally, prohibiting the use of French in some cases.

The Canadian armed forces were unified in May 1967, and their operational roles divided into six functional commands. In the same year, a limited number of steps were initiated to remedy the French-Canadian situation in the military. The results of extensive research on the problem were presented to the Defense Ministry, and a bilingual secretariat was created at Canadian Forces Headquarters that was charged with the translation and editing of training manuals and the updating of French military terminology for the purpose of publishing a bilingual dictionary—the last having appeared in 1945. In addition, a number of positions that required bilingual personnel were established in both recruiting and training, the first to enable contact with the public in both official languages and the second to assist French-Canadians who found it difficult to follow training courses given in English. A Canadian forces language school was also set up in late 1967, centralizing English-language instruction for Francophone recruits and offering courses in French for Anglophone personnel.[77]

The outcome of effective unilingualism in the Canadian armed forces during the 1950s and early 1960s was that although enlistments from Quebec were in proportion to its population, the military was faced with a very low reenlistment and retention rate among French-Canadians. This is attested to by the fact that during the 1950s, the average length of army service for Francophone soldiers and NCOs was only three and one-half years, as against five and one-half years for Anglophones. With regard to officers, the difference was even greater, with Anglophone officers averaging twenty-one years of service, while Francophone officers averaged only eleven years of service.[78]

The manpower shortages created by a low reenlistment rate in the Canadian forces overall in the 1960s eventually led the defense authorities to the conclusion that something had to be done regarding both French-Canadian enlistment and retention. Thus in the early part of 1968, special allowances were granted to married Francophone soldiers serving in English Canada for their children's education. The more significant and extensive program, however, was introduced in April 1968 when the defense minister presented a plan drawn up by his French-Canadian deputy, Cadieux. The Cadieux plan provided for specific units and bases in all Canadian forces commands (land, sea, and air) to have a majority of French-Canadian personnel, and that French would be used as the language of *work* accordingly. To encourage bilingualism, Francophones would comprise 20 percent of personnel in all Anglophone units at a minimum, and similarly for Anglophones. This applied to all units and bases throughout Canada. A number of units and bases were designated as predominantly Francophone, including one destroyer, an air force fighter squadron, and more importantly, one of the five Canadian Mobile Forces (army) combat divisions. This division—to be based in Quebec—included the three infantry battalions of the Royal Twenty-second Regiment, one of which usually served with the British Army on the Rhine (BAOR), artillery and armored regiments, signals and engineering squadrons, and support units. In addition to this, an Anglophone airborne commando regiment was to be composed of 30 percent Francophone soldiers.

With regard to training, it was proposed that all French-Canadian basic training be conducted in Quebec and that for Anglophones be held in Nova Scotia. Recruits who were to serve in the Francophone division were not to be given any training in English, while those recruits for air and sea commands were to be given an English course only after completing their basic training, which was to be conducted in French. Before this, as noted, Francophone recruits for the navy and air force had to undergo basic training in English, and this, only after having to take a preliminary course in English if deemed necessary. A special program for regulating French-Canadian basic training was set up a year later.[79]

The English-Canadian press and politicians reacted quietly to the Cadieux plan, except for one Toronto paper that published an article criticizing the setting up of a Francophone ship by one of those retired navy rear admirals who had been involved in the earlier controversy over the appointment of a French-Canadian chief of defense staff. The French-Canadian press was pleased with the new program and thought it could bring about a change in the armed forces, which, in their view, had been "une ecole d'anglicisation."[80]

Developments in Quebec itself after World War II can be divided into three intervals, "catching up" between 1945 and 1960; a "quiet revolution," which took place between 1960 and 1966; and the development of a new nationalism and separatism from 1966 onwards, culminating in the electoral victory of the separatist Parti Quebeçois in the provincial elections of 1976. Quebec had undergone an intensive process of modernization during World War II that transformed it from a semirural agriculturally based region to the most urbanized and industrialized province in Canada. In the century between 1839 and 1939, the number employed in manufacturing in Quebec increased by some 200,000. In the decade between 1939 and 1950, manufacturing employment rose by the same amount. Quebec's industrial growth during the years 1939-1950 increased ten times as much as during the hundred years preceding this period and was higher than the growth in the rest of Canada. The traditionalism of Quebec—which defined the province as rural, agricultural, Catholic, and French—was upset by the new economic and demographic trends. It was only displaced politically, however, in 1960, when the autocratic Duplessis regime and nationalist-conservative Union Nationale party was replaced by the Liberal party led by Jean Lesage.

The sense of political dynamism and change brought on by the "quiet revolution," however, went further than bringing Quebec to political maturity. In 1967 a number of French-Canadian politicians, led by René Levesque, left the Liberal party to establish a new movement—the Parti Quebeçois—that sought to unify all nationalist elements in Quebec and bring about eventual independence for the province. Despite this, a year later, the Federal Liberal party, led by the French-Canadian Pierre Trudeau, won the national parliamentary elections with large majorities in both Quebec and in Canada as a whole. The "new nationalism," however, developed steadily, successfully absorbing the smaller Quebec separatist blocs. The Parti Quebeçois was, however, also pushed into adopting less and less moderate positions on the question of Quebec's relations with the federal government by the activities of the more extremist separatists in the province, the Front de Liberation Quebeçois (FLQ).[81]

As early as the spring of 1963, the FLQ had organized and undertaken terrorist actions. In what was more or less a measure to "put out the fire" in Quebec, the Quebec Liberal party pressured the Canadian prime minister into establishing a Royal Commission on Bilingualism and Biculturalism later that year. The commission's preliminary general report was published in 1965 and was received coolly by Quebec's political leadership, since they were now becoming more interested in unilingualism in their province, and some by then had lost hope of attaining bilingualism in Canada. A conservative reaction had also set in against the wide-ranging reforms of the Lesage administration, and in 1966 the Quebec Liberals were defeated in the provincial parliamentary elections by a combination of the younger leaders of the Union Nationale party and the two smaller separatist blocs, which were subsequently amalgamated into the Parti Quebeçois.

As noted above, after its formation in 1967, the Parti Quebeçois took a more active part in the politics of Quebec. Extremist separatist elements, however, represented by the FLQ, also resumed activity in that year. FLQ terrorism increased and reached its climax in 1970, when the British consul in Quebec was kidnapped and Quebec's minister of justice, a French-Canadian, was kidnapped and murdered. The federal government applied the

War Measures Act during October-November 1970, and for the first time since the conscription crisis of 1917-1918, the army was brought into Quebec to restore public order, and habeas corpus was suspended. Some 450 people were arrested and detained, with 435 later released and the rest charged with various offenses and conspiracy.[82]

RECENT TRENDS IN AND PARAMETERS OF
FRENCH-CANADIAN MILITARY PARTICIPATION

The possible negative impact on recruiting in Quebec resulting from the use of the army during the emergency in late 1970 was foreseen by the Canadian military authorities. In early 1971, they introduced a program that was to give top priority to implementing bilingualism in the Canadian forces by considerably increasing the number of Francophone officers and men. The aim of the plan, which was drawn up by the chief of defense staff, General Sharp, was to increase to 40 percent the number of bilingual officers above the rank of lieutenant colonel by April 1976 and raise this to 60 percent by April 1980.[83]

The program was, in effect, the culmination of deliberations within the defense establishment over the recommendations made by the Royal Commission on Bilingualism's final report published in late 1969. The report outlined measures for both implementing bilingualism and improving the conditions of Francophone personnel in the Canadian forces. In its report, the commission dealt with all aspects of French-Canadian military service, ranging from rank and occupational structure to the problem of education of children of Francophone personnel, and it went considerably beyond the Cadieux plan in the scope of its recommendations. In a series of seventeen policy measures, the commission outlined ways of making the Canadian armed forces a totally bilingual organization.

To this end, four measures, which went further than all previous government plans, were suggested to ensure bilingualism at the *operational* level by officially recognizing the equality of the two languages. This involved amending the National

Defense Act, so that all regulations, administrative orders, directives, notices, forms, and so on would be drafted and issued in both languages simultaneously, rather than being translated from English into French. With regard to disciplinary procedures and appeals and complaints and grievances, the commission suggested that the proceedings be held in the language of the individual involved. The commission also outlined a solution to the educational problem of children of Francophone personnel serving outside Quebec, which involved cooperating with provincial authorities for organizing Francophone schools on or near the military base, rather than sending the children to school in Quebec and separating them from their parents. Another two recommendations dealt with linguistic and cultural equality in all activities of the Department of National Defense and Canadian forces and in their relations with both the public at large and other institutions such as municipal and provincial authorities.

The main body of recommendations—ten in all—made by the commission dealt with measures restructuring the Canadian forces and its system of training. The most important of these went further than any other government program and included recommendations: (a) that a Francophone military sector be established, extending over all commands—mobile, air, and maritime—including bases and other support installations; (b) that the Francophone units and bases be situated in Francophone areas; (c) that each unit and base in the respective Canadian forces commands be designated as either Francophone or Anglophone; (d) that communications between formations be conducted in the language of either of the respective language sectors or that designated by the receiver of the communication; (e) that positions requiring bilingual personnel be formally designated; (f) that there be adjustment of rank and promotion quotas to accelerate the advancement of bilingual and especially Francophone officers; and (g) that all personnel serving in the Francophone sector be competent in French.

As for training officers and men, the commission recommended the translation of all military texts, manuals, and teaching materials required; that Francophone recruits intending to serve in the

Francophone sector not be required to take courses in English unless their military occupational specialty required this; and most importantly, that the Francophone Royal Military College in Quebec be placed on equal footing with its Anglophone counterpart in Ontario, enabling it to grant degrees and offer identical curricula, and that strong emphasis be placed on teaching of the other sector's language in the respective institutions to generate bilingualism among the officer corps in the future. Finally, the commission recommended the establishment of Francophone units at the Ministry of Defense and Canadian Forces Headquarters, including setting up a language bureau as the fifth headquarters branch, responsible for the organizational planning, coordination, and implementation of the commission's recommendations.[84]

Some indicators of the nature and extent of Francophone participation in the Canadian armed forces in the period before and following the Royal Commission's report are presented in tables 7 through 10. These tables illustrate a number of differential effects as regards Francophone participation in the Canadian armed forces. First, although low French-Canadian participation in the navy at all levels is clearly seen, the rate of growth of Francophone entry into the navy—that is, at the officer cadet, junior officer, and other rank level—is the highest of all services. At the same time, however, the number of Francophone senior naval officers and NCOs decreased, for the most part probably due to the retirement of French-Canadian personnel who had entered the navy in the early 1950s. Second, although the degree of French-Canadian participation and entry into the army and RCAF at the other ranks level is about the same, the number of French-Canadian officers in the RCAF lags behind the army. This may continue due to the proportion of Francophone RCAF cadets, which is similar to that in the army. At the same time, however, the proportion of French-Canadians in the RCAF overall has increased to a level almost identical with that in the army. Third, although there is an increase in the proportion of Francophone officers in all three services, significant growth of French-Canadian entry into both the senior officer and cadet category was achieved only in the army.

Table 7

*Anglophone and Francophone Participation, Overall
and by Service Branch*

		1966			1972		
		A	*-%-*	*F*	*A*	*-%-*	*F*
Canadian forces:	Total	84.0		16.0	81.6		18.4
	Officers	89.7		10.3	86.7		13.3
	Ranks	83.0		17.0	80.5		19.5
Army:	Total	81.3		18.7	79.9		20.1
	Officers	85.4		14.6	82.9		17.1
	Ranks	80.8		19.2	79.3		20.7
Navy:	Total	90.8		9.2	86.9		13.1
	Officers	94.6		5.4	90.5		9.5
	Ranks	90.3		9.7	86.1		13.9
RCAF:	Total	83.8		16.2	80.9		19.1
	Officers	91.2		8.8	87.7		12.3
	Ranks	82.3		17.7	79.1		20.9

Key: A = Anglophone, F = Francophone.

With regard to officers, then, although some progress in French-Canadian participation has been made in the navy and RCAF, these services still lag behind the army. As regards other ranks, on the other hand, the growth of Francophone entry into the army has been the slowest of all services. It seems, therefore, that although Francophone personnel are advancing faster in the army, new Francophone recruits at the other ranks level are more attracted to the other services due to the expansion of opportunities resulting from the creation of a French-language sector encompassing all Canadian forces. The efforts made by the Canadian defense authorities to increase Francophone entry into the officer corps, for its part, has borne fruit in the case of the army and navy. The slow growth in the proportion of French-Canadian air force

Table 8

Gross Rank Distribution of Active Service Officers,
Percentage Composition of Service Branch by
Linguistic Group and Type of Rank

		1966			1972		
		A	-%-	*F*	*A*	-%-	*F*
Branch and Rank,							
Canadian forces:	S.O.	93.7		6.3	92.1		7.9
	J.O.	89.3		10.7	88.5		11.5
Army:	S.O.	88.1		11.9	84.0		16.0
	J.O.	85.1		14.9	84.4		15.6
Navy:	S.O.	96.5		3.5	98.2		1.8
	J.O.	94.3		5.7	92.8		7.2
RCAF:	S.O.	97.1		2.9	95.3		4.7
	J.O.	90.6		9.4	89.6		10.4

Key: S.O. = senior officers, lieutenant colonel-general.
J.O. = junior officers, second lieutenant-major.

Table 9

Gross Rank Distribution of NCOs and Other Ranks,
Percentage Composition of Service Branch by
Linguistic Group and Type of Rank

		1966			1972		
		A	-%-	*F*	*A*	-%-	*F*
Branch and rank,							
Canadian forces:	NCO	88.3		11.7	89.0		11.0
	E.M.	81.3		18.7	77.4		22.6
Army:	NCO	86.8		13.2	86.3		13.7
	E.M.	78.8		21.2	76.6		23.4
Navy:	NCO	91.7		8.3	95.4		4.6
	E.M.	89.5		10.5	81.6		18.4
RCAF:	NCO	87.9		12.1	88.0		12.0
	E.M.	80.8		19.2	76.5		23.5

Key: NCO = sergeant through chief warrant officer;
E.M. = private and corporal.

Table 10

Percentage Distribution of Officers and Officer Cadets by Linguistic Group, Overall and by Service Branch

		1966		1972	
		A -%- F		A -%- F	
Canadian forces:	Officers	89.7	10.3	86.7	13.3
	Cadets	76.7	23.3	71.6	29.4
Army:	Officers	85.4	14.6	82.9	17.1
	Cadets	77.4	22.6	71.3	28.7
Navy:	Officers	94.6	5.4	90.5	9.5
	Cadets	85.0	15.0	70.0	30.0
RCAF:	Officers	91.2	8.8	87.7	12.3
	Cadets	72.3	27.7	70.4	29.6

cadets, however, may reflect increasing competition from the civilian sector for Francophones with skills that would qualify them for RCAF cadetship.[85]

To sum up, whether Canada will remain a bilingual-bicultural entity is up to the French-Canadians. With the coming to power of the separatist Parti Quebeçois in Quebec, however, the future does not look as promising as it did when the federalist French-Canadian Pierre Trudeau initially became the prime minister of Canada in 1968. If the words of René Levesque, the prime minister of Quebec, are taken as representative of French-Canadian sentiment, Canada still faces the prospect of eventual cleavage between Quebec and the rest of the country. In 1963, when Levesque was Quebec's minister for natural resources in Lesage's Liberal administration, he said, "I know that Quebec is my country, I'm not quite convinced Canada is." Despite the outcome of the 1980 referendum in which Quebec decided, for the time being, to remain a part of Canada, and no matter what the outcome of constitutional revision regarding the relationship between the federal government and Quebec, whether Levesque and other French-Canadians finally decide to remain Canadians and not become independent Quebeçois seems to depend on the extent to which they are convinced that remaining part of Canada serves their own best interests.[86]

Even an autonomous Quebec, however, would still be linked to Canada by economic ties and, more importantly, the existence of French-Canadians in other regions of the country. In addition, as regards the foreign relations of an autonomous Quebec, for example, with France, this would also prove problematic. Notwithstanding de Gaulle's "vivre Quebec libre" position, subsequent French governments have allowed economic relations to base themselves only on the trend toward Quebec's eventual autonomy, while playing down the possibility of complete independence and substantive political linkage with and dependence upon France. It is important to note, however, that Levesque has argued that the 1,400,000 French-Canadians residing outside Quebec were already "lost," and that the Parti Quebeçois could "save" only those living in Quebec itself. As for relations with France, Levesque had always looked on this in economic rather than political terms, and even during his tenure as a Liberal provincial minister, he engineered large capital investment in Quebec by French banks and industry.[87]

An autonomous Quebec would mean a large cut in potential and actual manpower for the Canadian armed forces, and the transition period could prove difficult for both Canada and Quebec itself. Whether an independent Quebec could or would maintain a standing army, or even its own economic viability, are difficult questions to answer. If it did choose to exhibit its independence by maintaining an army, however, the relations between the Quebec military and the Canadian military would be problematic, but not insurmountable, as the Quebec forces could be "leased" to Canada, or could be allied—as in NATO—to the Canadian forces. If on the other hand, Quebec chose to remain neutral in the East-West confrontation— as France has done—it could follow the Scandinavian model and donate the services of its army to the United Nations. In any event, what is clear is that both Canada and Quebec face a difficult period ahead.

NOTES

1. E. Forsey, "Canada: Two Nations or One?" *Canadian Journal of Economics and Political Science* 28, 4 (1962). Durham quote cited from M. Wade, *The French-Canadians 1760-1967,* rev. ed. (Toronto: Macmillan, 1968), p. 197.

2. M. Wade, *The French-Canadians,* pp. 6-14.

3. Ibid., p. 14.

4. Ibid., pp. 3, 14-20.

5. W. Eccles, "The Social, Economic, and Political Significance of the Military Establishment in New France," *Canadian Historical Review* 52, 1 (1971), p. 1.

6. Ibid., p. 2.

7. Ibid., pp. 3-4.

8. Ibid., pp. 5-6.

9. Ibid., p. 7. Also see M. Wade, *The French-Canadians,* p. 29.

10. M. Wade, *The French-Canadians*, p. 30.

11. W. Eccles, "The Social, Economic, and Political Significance," pp. 20-21.

12. M. Wade, *The French-Canadians*, p. 50.

13. Ibid., pp. 50, 61.

14. J. Mallory, "The Canadian Dilemma: French and English," *Political Quarterly* 41, 3 (1970), pp. 281-82; M. Wade, *The French-Canadians,* p. 63.

15. M. Wade, *The French-Canadians*, pp. 65-67.

16. Ibid., pp. 68-69.

17. Ibid., pp. 72-73.

18. Ibid., pp. 74-75; J. Mallory, "The Canadian Dilemma," p. 282.

19. M. Wade, *The French-Canadians*, p. 100.

20. Ibid., p. 122.

21. Ibid., pp. 122-23.

22. W. Ormsby, "Lord Durham and the Assimilation of French Canada," in N. Penlington, ed., *On Canada* (Toronto: University of Toronto Press, 1971), ch. 3.; J. Mallory, "The Canadian Dilemma," pp. 282-83; M. Wade, "The French Canadians," ch. 4.

23. W. Ormsby, "Lord Durham," pp. 39ff.

24. Ibid., pp. 40-45; M. Wade, *The French-Canadians*, p. 208.

25. J. Mallory, "The Canadian Dilemma," p. 283; M. Rioux, "Quebec: From Minority Complex to Majority Behavior," in H. Tobias and C. Woodhouse, eds., *Minorities and Politics* (Santa Fe: University of New Mexico Press, 1969), p. 41.

26. M. Wade, *The French-Canadians*, pp. 264-265.

27. Ibid., pp. 269-71.

28. Ibid., pp. 283, 317-18.

29. Ibid., p. 318.

30. Ibid., pp. 319ff.

31. M. Rioux, "Quebec," p. 42; M. Wade, *The French-Canadians,* pp. 331-33.

32. H. Forbell, *Armed Forces Histories, Part 2: The Canadian Army,* in

Studies Prepared for the Royal Commission on Bilingualism and Biculturalism, Division 4, Report No. 20 (Ottawa: National Library, 1969); R. A. Preston, "The Transfer of British Military Institutions to Canada in the 19th Century," in W. Hamilton, ed., *The Transfer of Institutions* (Durham, N.C.: Duke University Press, 1964), pp. 94-95.

33. M. Wade, *The French-Canadians*, pp. 410-40; J. Mallory, "The Canadian Dilemma," p. 285.

34. M. Wade, *The French-Canadians*, p. 476.

35. Ibid., pp. 477-79; J. Saywell, "French Canada in the 1890s," in J. Careless and R. Brown, eds., *The Canadians 1867-1967* (Toronto: Macmillan, 1967), ch. 4.

36. M. Wade, *The French-Canadians*, pp. 479-512; M. Rioux, "Quebec," p. 43.

37. H. Forbell, *Armed Forces Histories, Part 2*, p. 62; M. Wade, *The French-Canadians*, pp. 567-85.

38. M. Wade, *The French-Canadians*, pp. 639-41; H. B. Newby, "The New Century," in J. Careless and R. Brown, eds., *The Canadians*, pp. 159-62.

39. M. Wade, *The French-Canadians*, 642-44; J. Granatstein, *Conscription* (Toronto: Ryerson Press, 1969), p. 2.

40. M. Wade, *The French-Canadians*, pp. 644-48.

41. Ibid., pp. 648-49; J. Eayrs, *The Art of the Possible* (Toronto: University of Toronto Press, 1961), p. 72; H. Forbell, *Armed Forces Histories*, Part 2.

42. M. Wade, *The French-Canadians*, pp. 650-58; C. Berger, ed., *Conscription 1917* (Toronto: University of Toronto Press, 1969), p. 1; Granatstein, *Conscription*, p. 5.

43. M. Wade, *The French-Canadians*, pp. 658-71; Roger Graham, "Through the First World War," in J. Careless and R. Brown, eds., *The Canadians*, ch. 4, pp. 184-86.

44. Cited in Wade, *The French-Canadians*, pp. 657, 687.

45. Ibid., pp. 693, 708-9, 723-24.

46. Ibid., pp. 740-45; D. Morton, *French Canada and the War* (Toronto: Erindale, 1970); R. Graham, "Through the First World War," pp. 188ff.

47. M. Wade, *The French-Canadians*, p. 747.

48. Ibid., pp. 763-64.

49. Ibid., pp. 764-66.

50. Ibid., pp. 766-67.

51. Ibid., pp. 767-78; H. Forbell, *Armed Forces Histories, Part 1*.

52. J. Eayrs, *In Defense of Canada* (Toronto: University of Toronto Press, 1972), pp. 127-28, 130.

53. M. Wade, *The French-Canadians*, pp. 768-69; C. Berger, *Conscription 1917*, p. 8.

54. M. Rioux, "Quebec," p. 44.

55. M. Wade, *The French-Canadians*, pp. 862-63.

56. H. Forbell, *Armed Forces Histories, Part 2*, pp. 64, 81; J. Eayrs, *In Defense of Canada*, p. 128; M. Wade, *The French-Canadians*, pp. 845-912; idem, *The French-Canadians*, p. 865.

57. M. Wade, *The French-Canadians*, pp. 930-31; F. Wilson, "French-Canadian Separatism," *Western Political Quarterly* 20 (1967), p. 120.

58. M. Wade, *The French-Canadians*, pp. 931-35; C. P. Stacey, "Through the Second World War," in J. Careless and R. Brown, eds., *The Canadians*, ch. 9, pp. 280ff.

59. M. Wade, *The French-Canadians*, pp. 931-32.

60. Ibid., pp. 932-34; H. Quinn, *The Union Nationale: A Study in Quebec Nationalism* (Toronto: University of Toronto Press, 1963).

61. M. Wade, *The French-Canadians*, p. 935; C. P. Stacey, *Arms, Men and Governments: The War Policies of Canada 1939-45* (Ottawa: Dept. of National Defence, Queen's Printer, 1970), p. 420. The RAF, however, did have some non-Anglophone units, for example, Polish, Czech, and Free French.

62. C. P. Stacey, *Arms, Men and Governments*, p. 420; J. Granatstein, *Conscription*, p. 32; G. N. Tucker, *The Naval Service of Canada: Its Official History* (Ottawa: Dept. of National Defence, Queen's Printer, 1952), pp. 154, 275-77.

63. M. Wade, *The French-Canadians*, p. 935; J. Eayrs, *In Defense of Canada*, p. 128; H. Forbell, *Armed Forces Histories*, Part 3: *Royal Canadian Air Force*, pp. 16, 31, 36.

64. J. Eayrs, *In Defense of Canada*, pp. 130-31; H. Forbell, *Armed Forces Histories, Part 1: Royal Canadian Navy*, p. 9; G. N. Tucker, *The Naval Service of Canada*, p. 275.

65. M. Wade, *The French-Canadians*, pp. 936-45, 950-52; H. Forbell, *Armed Forces History, Part 2*, pp. 50-51; F. Wilson, "French-Canadian Separatism," pp. 117-18.

66. M. Wade, *The French-Canadians*, pp. 952-60.

67. Ibid., pp. 966, 994-95.

68. Ibid., pp. 1022-39.

69. Ibid., pp. 1039-73.

70. Ibid., pp. 1074-75.

71. Ibid., pp. 1075-76; J. Eayrs, *In Defense of Canada*, pp. 133-34; H. Forbell, *Armed Forces Histories, Part 2*, p. 49.

72. H. Forbell, *Armed Forces Histories, Part 2*, p. 52; J. Eayrs, *In Defense of Canada*, p. 134.

73. H. Forbell, *Armed Forces Histories, Part 2*, p. 57; J. Eayrs, *In Defense of Canada*, pp. 69, 136.

74. J. Eayrs, *In Defense of Canada*, pp. 131-32; H. Forbell, *Armed Forces Histories, Part 1*, p. 14.

75. J. Eayrs, *In Defense of Canada*, pp. 132-33; H. Forbell, *Armed Forces Histories, Part 1*, p. 11.

76. H. Forbell, *Armed Forces Histories, Part 3*, pp. 30, 33, 39; J. Eayrs, *In Defense of Canada*, p. 129.

77. J. Eayrs, *In Defense of Canada; Studies Prepared for the Royal Commission on Bilingualism and Biculturalism* (hereafter cited as *RCBB*), Final Report—Documents, Book 3A, Part2: "The Work World," ch. 11, "Canadian Forces" (Ottawa: Queen's Printer, 19 Sept. 1969), pp. 298-300; House of Commons, *Debates*, vol. 9, 1st session, 20 Oct. 1966, p. 8890 (Ottawa, 1966).

78. House of Commons, *Debates*, vol. 14, 1st session, 4 April 1967, p. 14501; M. Chaput, "Les Canadiens Français dans l'Armee," *J'ai choisi de me battre* (Montreal: Club du Livre du Quebec, 1965), pp. 45-47.

79. J. Saywell, ed., *Canadian Annual Review* (Toronto: University of Toronto Press, 1969), p. 280; *RCBB*, Final Report, Book 3A, part 2, pp. 300-301.

80. J. Saywell, ed., *Canadian Annual Review*, p. 281.

81. M. Rioux, "Quebec," pp. 44-45; G. Spry, "Canada: Notes on Two Ideas of Nation in Confrontation," *Journal of Contemporary History* 6, 1 (1971), pp. 178ff.; G. Rutan, "Two Views of the Concept of Sovereignty: Canadian-Canadien," *Western Political Quarterly* 24, 3 (1971), pp. 461ff.; F. Wilson, "French-Canadian Separatism," pp. 120ff.; E. Corbett, *Quebec Confronts Canada* (Baltimore: Johns Hopkins University Press, 1968), pp. 333ff.

82. M. Rioux, "Quebec," pp. 45-49; F. Wilson, "French-Canadian Separatism," pp. 116-17; House of Commons, *Debates*, 4 Feb. 1971, p. 3065.

83. UPI Press Release, Ottawa, 1 March 1971.

84. *RCBB*, Final Report, Book 3A, Part 2, pp. 340-47.

85. Compiled from *Canadian Armed Forces: Effective Strength Personnel Report (PPFAGA)—1972*, Provided by L.A. Bourgeois, director-general, information, Department of National Defence, Ottawa, January 1973 (Ref. 1350-500/DIS). The 1966 data are from P. Coulombe, "Social and Cultural Composition of the Canadian Armed Forces," in H. Massey, ed., *The Canadian Military: A Profile* (Montreal: Copp-Clark, 1972), ch. 5, table 4, pp. 148-49.

86. M. Rioux, "Quebec," pp. 51-52; *Le Devoir*, 5 July 1963, p. 4.

87. *Economist Survey* (Canada), 12 Feb. 1977, pp. 5-10, 48-50; *Economist*, 7 May 1977, p. 72.

4

BRITAIN

DIMENSIONS OF THE BRITISH SITUATION: HISTORICAL, DEMOGRAPHIC, MILITARY

"Neither kith nor kin" well describes the situation of the "new" commonwealth communities in the United Kingdom, for in the historico-demographic sense they are, of course, not related to the indigenous British population. Be this as it may, there has still been a significant interaction between "new" commonwealth peoples and the British military for some three and one-half centuries, both in a colonial context and, more recently, between "new" commonwealth immigrants to the United Kingdom and H.M. Forces.

It is important to understand the specific demographic factors that differentiate among the groups involved and their military participation, past, present, and future. Three main groupings of new commonwealth peoples may be distinguished in this regard, West Indian, African, and Asian, although the latter category could be further subdivided into Indians and Pakistanis. In demographic terms, however, it is only the West Indians and Asians that have had sustained contact with *both* the military establishment and the indigenous population in the United Kingdom.

Over seventy years ago, in the July 1907 issue of the *North American Review*, W. P. Livingstone noted the better state of relations between the races in the West Indies as against the United States, but concluded that this was "not to be attributed altogether to the higher ethical principles dominating the actions of the British." He pointed out that this was, in fact, a result of the geographical distance separating "the West Indian Negroes . . . from the main body of British whites, and neither comes in direct contact and competition with the other." If conditions were to change, and significant contact developed, Livingstone maintained that "we should find a different state of things. Despite altruistic considerations, the whites would probably be much less tolerant of the Negro and more averse to his social advancement. The development of the British Empire has already furnished minor illustrations of what happens in such circumstances." Livinstone's insights are, however, not that remarkable, considering that initial contacts between Britain and "colored" peoples had occurred almost three centuries previously.[1]

In any event, we can still distinguish four main "phases" in the interaction under consideration: the early; middle; late; and postcolonial, or neocolonial, periods. The early colonial period corresponds, temporally, to the initial "contact" and "subjugation" phase in the case of the Indian subcontinent, "British" Africa, and the West Indies, dating from about the end of the Elizabethan era to the reign of Victoria. The middle colonial period corresponds to the Victorian era itself, and the late colonial period covers the Edwardian era through World Wars I and II. The postcolonial, or neocolonial, phase, then, corresponds to the period since the end of World War II and the large-scale new commonwealth or "colored" immigration to the United Kingdom.

We have used the term *large-scale* deliberately, for there has, in fact, been a "colored" presence in both the United Kingdom armed forces and the United Kingdom itself since the seventeenth century. However, those "colored" soldiers that did serve in the British armed forces (including colonial militias and forces in Asia and Africa) were almost always *nonresident* in the United Kingdom. In the West Indies, for example, manumitted or fugitive slaves were directly recruited into the militia, the West India Regiment, or the navy, and Indian, Punjabi and Bengali, and African soldiers were all recruited in their native regions. There were no significant communities of new commonwealth peoples in Britain until World War II and the start of large-scale immigration of these groups. In spite of the nonresidence factor, however, new commonwealth soldiers were nonetheless used and, as is shown below, proved crucial in some instances to Britain's military capacity.

A second factor also emerges here in the form of "interdependence" between the British military and members of these groups. As is also seen below, military service did, in certain cases, provide a vehicle for social mobility, and the military, in turn, depended to some extent upon these groups to provide manpower. (These and related issues are considered in more detail below.) Until now I have not used the term *minority* in describing the position of the groups mentioned above in the historical context of their military service to the British Empire. In the case of the British Indian Army, for example, it cannot be said that the Indians were a minority with regard to the power that recruited them; rather, they constituted a minority as regards their position within the broader framework of the British Raj. A similar situation existed in the African case, where, as Gutteridge noted, "It is no accident that African forces in Commonwealth countries also bear the marks of British Indian influence," since "the British military personnel operating in the two areas had almost everything in common and were frequently even the same men at different stages in their careers. Recruitment was, therefore, seen in the first place in terms of the imperial situation."[2]

THE EARLY COLONIAL PERIOD

During the early colonial period, British colonial expansion in Asia, Africa, and the West Indies was realized to some degree with the assistance of new commonwealth troops. In the West Indies, notwithstanding even the fears of the planter assemblies about the implications of arming the Negroes, no less than twelve Negro regiments existed by 1799. But the element of interdependence also emerges, in view of the fact that manumitted slaves were actively recruited throughout the period, in addition to those West Africans rescued from slavery who were directly enlisted after the Napoleonic Wars. The first black regiments, however, were formed during the French Revolutionary War itself when, due to heavy losses among British troops in the Lesser Antilles, resulting mainly from the climate (although some heavy fighting against the French did take place), there was hope that such Negro regiments would prove better suited to the tropics. In 1826, due to recruitment difficulties after the Napoleonic Wars, a company of the West Indies Regiment was, in fact, sent to Sierra Leone, to recruit manumitted slaves, leading eventually to the utilization of the West Indies Regiment in West Africa.[3]

As for the situation regarding the Indian subcontinent, while the French first used these "exotic" troops, the British established their position in India and all of South Asia by using the indigenous "martial races." Indeed, one observer has even maintained that in the Indian case, the British would never have succeeded in their conquest without the assistance of the Sepoys. There was, in fact, an interdependent element in this relationship also, as attested to by the mobility attained by some of those who did serve in the British Indian Army, although the degree of mobility was still limited, as is shown below. Interestingly, during this period of initial contact, conquest, and subjugation, missionary activity was prohibited in India, the ban being maintained, in fact, up to 1813. It is only in the next period—the middle colonial era—that both missionary activity and "evangelical" army officers appear on the scene, with a Colonel Wheeler of the Thirty-fourth Native Infantry, for one, maintaining that he had "endeavoured to convert Sepoys and others to Christianity."[4]

Even during this early period, some Indian regiments showed more unity of purpose with British colonization efforts than their British counterparts. For example, one can cite the incident at Bharatpur in 1805, where British troops under Lord Lake refused to advance, so the Indian battalions accompanying them took the initiative and attacked the fortress alone, suffering high casualties and eventually failing in their attempt. Such actions on the part of the Indian regiments, however, were more "a matter of honor" than anything else, as Philip Mason brilliantly showed in his book, *A Matter of Honour.*[5]

Despite the strict caste system that existed at the time, in the Bombay Army, at least, soldiers were recruited without reference to their caste, and they were taught to disregard caste while "in the ranks." Thus before being transformed into a grenadier regiment, some units of the Bombay Army had low-caste Mahars among their soldiers. However, after only three years of becoming a grenadier regiment, recruitment of Mahars ended, and the regiment began to recruit Rajputs, the traditional warrior caste. This was totally due to "sociosomatic" considerations, as expressed in the view that Mahars were simply "unsuitable" for a grenadier regiment. But such an attitude proved to be more and more prevalent as regards the peoples of southern India and their suitability for military service in general. According to Mason, this was, in fact, the beginning of the "drift to the North," that is, recruiting among the "martial" races; while William Gutteridge is even more explicit, claiming that there existed "a clearly defined recruitment policy" in India, where "British officers generally preferred the volunteer mercenary native soldier, especially if he happened to be both a Moslem and illiterate."[6]

THE MIDDLE COLONIAL ERA

The middle colonial period was characterized by the consolidation of British power and rule in all three new commonwealth areas—Asia, Africa, and the West Indies—and the growing dependence upon "native" forces to maintain it. For example, the West India Regiment served in suppressing rebellions in British Guiana and Jamaica and later took part in the Ashanti War (1872-1873). Indeed, the manpower situation of the British military establishment became so "tight" in the 1880s that the idea of a "black phalanx"—to be made up of regiments from the West Indies—was proposed but never implemented, in contrast to the successful use of the French "Force Noir" in both colonial garrison duties and, later, in World War I. The West Indies regiments did provide, however, most of the troops used in the area itself for garrison duties.[7]

In the Indian case, a peculiar situation arose. During the early colonial period, the Sepoys—being employed as mercenaries— had aided British conquest and received their reward, in booty and loot, accordingly. However, during the middle colonial period, their prospects became worse. They were subjected to slow promotion, and Indian officers (viceroy's commission) could not advance beyond regimental status and were, in addition, subordinate even to the most junior British officer. Although they could be considered "professional" soldiers, they still kept their village ties. Often, being of high caste—especially in the Bombay Army—although this did not necessarily imply wealth, their "aspirations" simply exceeded their "expectations," with the result that, as M. E. Chamberlain noted, "it was not beyond the bounds of possibility that the native army might look for a new and more accommodating master."[8]

Thus for two years, from 1857 to 1859, the Sepoys mutinied, and although ostensibly it was for religious reasons, the mobility aspects did play a part. The outcome of the mutiny affected the composition of the British Indian Army, however, from that time onwards. In any event, reliance on the British Indian Army was only marginally affected by the rebellion, for after changing its recruiting base to the "martial races," there were no further major difficulties. Indeed, the Sikhs, who had been conquered by the assistance of the Bengal Sepoys only ten years before, now actively participated in putting down the revolt and, after 1859, provided a key source of manpower. By the end of the period, then, as a result of the mutiny and the shift of the recruiting base from the South to the North, there were, in fact, rules set down regarding the "classes" eligible and suitable for recruitment, specifying caste, religion, and district of origin accordingly. Specific procedures and special recruiting officers for the Gurkas, Dogras, Sikhs, Punjabi Moslems, Jats, Ranghurs, and certain classes of Pathans—who were recruited in that order of preference—existed, and the written rules were fairly strictly adhered to; so much so that, as Mason noted, caste, an "Indian institution," had now "been taken over by the British."[9]

Now, the British military establishment had always realized that it was only through losing the loyalty of their native army that they might lose India itself. Indeed, as early as 1819, Lord Elphinstone wrote, "I think the seed of its [the Indian Empire's] ruin will be found in the native army—a delicate and dangerous machine which a little mismanagement may easily turn against us." In this context, it must be remembered that there were, in effect, two military forces in India at the time of the mutiny, the native army—numbering over 233,000 in 1857—and contingents of the British army itself, slightly over 45,000 in the same year. Thus after the rebellion was quelled, the most important problem facing the British was reconstructing the army, with the Bengal Army requiring a complete rebuilding. The emphasis, then, had to be on both a closer association between the native troops in the future and the British military establishment and precautions against any further possibilities of mutiny.[10]

As such, "company troops" were disbanded, and hereafter all British troops belonged to the regular army. Another measure taken was to mix European troops in equal numbers with Indians in Bengal, and British and Indian battalions were to serve together in mixed regiments. However, only European officers could hold commissions from the queen. Indians could be commissioned only by the viceroy, and despite the fact that upper class Indians objected to this—believing that any of the queen's subjects were entitled to hold her commission and even obtaining Lord Salisbury's support for their position—the restriction remained, limiting, to a certain extent, Indian mobility through military service. Another temporary measure taken was mixing Moslems and Hindus and those of different caste in the battalions, such that none could take on any specific sectarian character. Thus when, at the time of their intervention in Egypt in 1882, London wanted Moslem soldiers from India specifically to participate, it was told that such troops could not be provided, since the Indian Army was not—deliberately—organized in such a manner. As Mason noted, however, in the 1880s, this policy was reversed, and by 1892 the basis of recruitment again returned to religion and caste.[11]

It is interesting that only *after* the mutiny was the distinction between "martial" and "nonmartial" races stressed. Gurkas, Sikhs, and Punjabis were certainly "martial races," but it was still suspected that this distinction was only a convenient way of separating those who were loyal from those who could no longer be trusted. The professionalization of the Indian Army after the mutiny, as a result of reforms, however, did result in its nonparticipation in politics for some time. An additional factor is that India itself was responsible for the financing of the British army there. This was, of course, more and more resented as time went on. Besides its current operating expenses, India had to finance both internal campaigns, such as the Sikh Wars in the 1840s; border campaigns, such as those in Burma and Afghanistan; and even overseas campaigns, such as that in Egypt in 1882. In fact, the theme of excessive Indian military expenditure and its implications for the internal development of the country arose in the first Indian National Congress as early as 1885. It was only two years later that the Congress asked that the highest appointments in the military be open to Indians. Another point regarding this period is that during its latter decades, the first stirrings of Indian nationalism arose. By the 1870s, Irish nationalism had inspired its Indian counterpart to the degree that in 1866 Dufferin had complained to Kimberly, the secretary of state for India, that the art of Irish-style agitation had arrived in India. Such was the effect of the Irish movement on the Indian nationalists that in 1876, Banerjea, one of the founders of the Congress, said, "Let us have political associations on the model of the Catholic associations of Daniel O'Connell."[12]

There is, therefore, an interesting contrast to be drawn between the participation of new commonwealth, or colored, personnel in the British army and that of the Irish and Scots. During this middle colonial era, for example, Irish soldiers comprised a large proportion of the army—almost 40 percent in 1840—although by the advent of the late colonial period, their numbers had declined to only some 12 percent. Indeed, the high proportion of Irish in the army gave rise to fears that a significant section of the army was potentially disloyal and therefore unsuitable for use in Ireland itself. This was partially borne out by Fenian infiltration during 1865-1867 and the subsequent courts-martial of their supporters. But as H. J. Hanham noted in his study of "Religion and Nationality in the Mid-Victorian Army," the large proportion of Irish in the army was not due to their patriotism; rather, "Ireland was simply like good recruiting districts in England, where men were encouraged to enlist by want of alternative employment." The Scots, on the other hand, were never as numerous in the army as the Irish, although their reputation as soldiers was quite high, the Scottish regiments having an excellent combat record in the Crimea, during the Indian mutiny, in Egypt, and so on. The proportion of Scottish soldiers decreased from 13.5 percent in 1830 to 10.0 percent in 1870, and it was about 8.0 percent going into the late colonial era. As Hanham noted, they were overrepresented, in relation to their proportion of the United Kingdom population, in the middle colonial period and underrepresented in the late colonial era. In fact, the number of Scottish soldiers wasn't even enough to supply the nominally Scottish regiments, let alone to enable their service outside these regiments.[13]

Indeed, enlistment in Scotland was unable to meet the demand. Although the Highland regiments were able to recruit more than those in the Lowlands, even they found difficulty, due to a permanent narrowing of the recruitment base as a result of depopulation and weakened feudal ties that had secured recruitment during the early colonial period. As for the situation in the Lowlands, there was working-class prejudice against military service, and the army also faced competition from industry and emigration agents from America and Canada. As noted above, however, despite fears of possible disloyalty, Ireland was thought of as a prime manpower pool, and as a result, the Irish were to be found throughout the army—in the ranks, as NCOs, and as officers—in proportion to their percentage in the population of the United Kingdom (which included Ireland at the time), making, as Hanham observed, things easy for Fenian recruits who were, in fact, "able to build up a substantial body of supporters in nominally English or Scottish regiments, as well as in the predominantly Irish Royal Irish Fusiliers."[14]

The difference between colored military participation and that of the Irish and Scottish, however, may be illustrated by the effect of, in Hanham's words, "a substantial shift in the social function of the army" during the middle colonial period. One element in this shift, in Hanham's view, was a change in army attitudes toward the "common soldiers." Although Wellington thought of the army, according the Hanham, "as little better than cannon fodder: a mixture of Irish and Scottish mercenaries and the scum of English society,'' the common soldier—after the Indian mutiny at least—came to be thought of as simply another worker who was engaged in a special type of occupation. A second factor accounting for new army attitudes was the recognition among civilians that the maintenance of the empire was dependent as much on the army as it was on the navy, an outcome of both the need to defend the Indian sea route and of the growth, after 1870, of other European armies, in addition to the increasing sympathetic attitude of the public toward the "Tommy." In fact, Hanham concluded, by the advent of the late colonial era:

> The army was no longer seen as a militaristic threat to individual liberties or an authoritarian anachronism. Rather, it seemed to stand for the voluntary acceptance of a common purpose, a common discipline and, if necessary, a common sacrifice. During the South African War, the army attracted a degree of popular sympathy out of all proportion to its achievements . . . the army which came into being after the Haldane reforms was thus able to draw upon a measure of popular sympathy and understanding such as no British army had enjoyed before. The soldier was now a patriot, not a wastrel.[15]

However, although the Irish and Scots were included in this basic change in attitude both on the part of the army toward its own common soldiers and on the part of civilians toward the soldier, colored colonial troops were not.

THE LATE COLONIAL PERIOD

The late colonial period was probably the most crucial for the new commonwealth peoples, both as regards their military participation and the effect of the conflicts in which they became involved on the future course of events affecting them. From the turn of the century onwards, the military role of new commonwealth peoples in British Imperial defense became more and more important, although it still must be said that, in quantitative terms at least, this applied mainly to those from the Indian subcontinent. In fact, the contribution of the British Indian Army in the world wars was significant, in both combat and service roles. Regiments recruited in Africa and the West Indies did see limited action in World War I, but they were used, for the most part, as labor battalions or for garrison duty. Still, these units did enable Britain to concentrate most of her own indigenous forces in Europe in World War I, rather than having to allocate troops for action against the Germans in Africa.[16]

The overall effect of World War I on the new commonwealth peoples varies from case to case. In South Asia, although not *catalyzing* the Indian nationalist movement as such—indeed, Ghandi himself and the leaders of the Congress party supported the war effort—it still provided the movement with the argument of "self-determination." In the other two new commonwealth areas, however, the war had little or no effect on this *level*. On the level of the direct interaction between new commonwealth servicemen and the British military establishment, however, there were a number of incidents that foreshadowed the shape of things to come. For example, the treatment of West Indian soldiers did give rise to protest and the politicization of participation, but again, only to a limited extent as as a result of the residence factor. The residence factor was also noted by Michael Banton as affecting the social position of the small immigrant communities before World War I when he wrote on the changing position of the Negro in Britain in 1953 and cited the 1910 parliamentary committee that inquired into the situation of "distressed colonial and Indian subjects" in the United Kingdom.[17]

Although the resident Negro community in the United Kindom remained small and thereby relatively unaffected by the war, there was still hostility against them, and they were "visible" enough to be the focus of the 1919 race riots that occurred in Liverpool, Cardiff, and Manchester. Thus although increasing contact can be cited as a factor either in the increase or decrease of discrimination, racist attitudes that are socially acceptable usually "tilt" the argument in favor of that claiming an increase in discriminatory practices. In the British case, then, even such a prestigious paper as the *Times* could, in justifying the violence against Negroes in the 1919 riots, claim that Negro "fondness for white women" was the basic cause of hostility among the whites, accusing, in effect, the resident Negro of bringing his predicament upon himself and disregarding the economic factors such as unemployment and job competition in the depressed areas that resulted from the slowdown after the war.[18]

The nature of participation of the West Indians especially deserves attention, since it highlights the complexity of the relationship between this group and the British military establishment. First, in the British case, the regimental structure of the army resulted in the existence of separate West Indies regiments, and thus black West Indian troops were not integrated into existing regiments during World War I. Although this has recently been described as discrimination by one observer, it is probably closer to the truth that the West Indians themselves would have objected to serving in "English" regiments, since they perceived their regiments as representing the West Indies in the same way as British regiments represented their counties or regions. Objections did occur, however, regarding segregation of facilities and amenities according to color during World War I, such as cases where segregated hospitals caused death, and where friction between white and colored troops resulted from separate recreational facilities and restrictions on their use by the latter.[19]

In purely military terms, on the other hand, the British military establishment did tend to adopt discriminatory measures outright against the West Indian regiments, relegating them either to garrison duties in areas away from the front, in the case of the West India Regiment, or to labor battalions, as in the case of the West Indies Regiment. Thus, despite its distinguished combat record, the West India Regiment was kept "out of the way" during the war, as one observer put it, "the 1st Battalion in Jamaica and the 2nd in East Africa where it saw only limited engagement." When asked about its attitude toward changing the method of using the West Indies Regiment, which was then in Europe, the Army Council answered that it was agreeable only to the "formation of a 'combatant' battalion composed of colored men of higher social standing than were usually enlisted in the Regiment," thereby wasting the training and expertise of the unit, as exhibited by the distinguished record compiled by its elements that *were* engaged at the front.[20]

Black African military participation during World War I also provides an interesting case for consideration. The West African Frontier Force (WAFF), the nucleus of which was formed from the Lagos Hausa Battalion, the West African Regiment, recruited in Sierra Leone, and the King's African Rifles, raised in East Africa, participated in campaigns against the Germans in East Africa, the Cameroons, and Togoland. During the war itself, proposals for using the "massive" military potential of black African manpower in other areas, that is, in Europe, emerged. In October 1916, for example, Major Darnley-Stuart Stephens published an article in the *English Review* entitled "Our Million Black Army." In the article, Stephens (a former commander of the Lagos Battalion in 1882) claimed that he personally would be willing to undertake recruiting in West Africa, maintaining that he could raise a force of some 20,000 in only two months. Stephens went on to praise the military prowess of both the West African and the South African black "warriors," claiming that "between South Africa and West and West Central Africa [the western Sudan] half a million men could be raised and thrown on to the Western Front" in about nine months. Stephens was proposing their use *in Europe* and against the Germans *in combat*. Despite this, as C. L. Joseph and James Walvin related, the British War Office was reluctant to allow non-Europeans, that is, blacks, to fight against white Europeans, that is, Germans. Indeed, in contrast to the French use of their "Force Noir" and North African troops against the Germans, the British never effectively used either the African or West Indian manpower available to them. Some indication of the reason for this may be found, however, in the reaction of the British to French use of their black troops for garrison duties in Germany after the end of the war—a reaction racist in tone, for the most part, and highly critical of the French for inflicting a "horror" of this magnitude on a white population.[21]

The difference between the participation of "exotic" troops in the British and French armies is indeed an interesting aspect of the British attitude toward the military service of "colored" peoples. Alfred Vagts noted in his book *A History of Militarism* that the French were the first among the modern European nation-states to use such soldiers, although the British soon realized the potential of these troops. France saw its African territories as a manpower "reservoir," using them for conquest in the sub-Sahara and also using them outside the continent. Britain, on the other hand, used its native soldiers as an instrument of colonial administration for the most part and did not train officers from among their colonial troops, except in the Indian case, where the Indian officer held the viceroy's, rather than the crown's, commission. But although the French applied the theory of "the nation in arms" to their overseas territories with regard to conscription, as Richard Challener noted, "the idea of colonial conscription contained no egalitarianism, and almost the entire emphasis was upon the possibility of obtaining more soldiers," with the Republicans arguing against giving citizenship and civic rights to the conscripts just because they served in the army. "Thus," Challener concluded, "the familiar republican theory that citizenship and conscription were inextricably bound together formed no part of the case for compulsory service in French colonies." Shelby C. Davis, in his history of the "Force Noir," noted that the French use of native troops was actively modeled on the British use of Indian Sepoys. In fact, before 1836 the Africans served alongside Europeans in the colonial army in Senegal, for example, but it was then decided that they should be grouped separately to encourage interunit "competition." However, Davis, in both his history of the "Force Noir" and his later study of the French army as a whole, observed that although there were black NCOs, the officer cadre were Europeans.[22]

Still, as Robin Bidwell argued in his book on French North Africa, some locally recruited soldiers, especially those of North African origin, could rise to high rank in the French colonial army. More importantly, the French trained numerous officers from among their Moroccan troops, especially after restrictions were lifted on their becoming officers in World War I. By the 1920s, some elements of the colonial army—such as most Moroccan troops—were incorporated into the French army itself, giving the soldiers pension rights. The French thought they could demand the assistance of their colonial subjects in defense, since they claimed that, in contrast to all other colonial powers, their subjects were treated both benevolently and generously. Although this does exaggerate the basic facts, there is some element of truth in it. For example, as Martin Lewis recounted in his article on "the 'assimilation' theory in French colonial policy," the French advocated the policy of "assimilation," in theory at least, from the late nineteenth century onwards, reaching its climax in the creation of the ill-fated French Union after World War II, whose peoples were supposed to have become, in the words of those who advocated it, "one hundred million citizens and free men" of France.[23]

Indeed, in an interview with Andre Malraux in 1974, a question was asked about why the people of former French African colonies did not have the same complex about their colonial past as those in former English colonies. Malraux cited the heritiage of the Revolution, noting that the colonial peoples were made citizens of France by the 1792 Convention, but the implementation of full civic rights was effectively blocked by Napoleon, who vetoed the idea of colonial "emancipation" introduced earlier by the convention. Thus Malraux concluded, Senghor, the distinguished Francophone poet and Senegalese president, could claim that he was "French" before the citizens of, say, Alsace or Nice, which were incorporated into France only in the nineteenth century.[24]

In contrast to Britain, the French thought of their "black phalanx" as a source of manpower for *home defense*, so that during World War I, these soldiers made a quite significant contribution, with some 180,000 Senegalese, 175,000 Algerians, 50,000 Tunisians, 40,000 Malagaches, 34,000 Moroccans, and 2,000 Somalis serving. All in all, as Vagts wrote, France drew almost 545,000 troops and over 220,000 laborers, mostly from Senegal, from all of her colonies and protectorates. The magnitude of their contribution may be seen in that the death rate of these troops equalled that of the United States and Belgium combined.[25]

Thus a situation such as that which Norman Angell reported in the *Contemporary Review* of February 1922 emerged, whereby at the meetings of the Pan-African Congress in Paris in September 1921, the Anglophone Africans spoke of themselves as "we

Negroes,'' and the Francophones described themselves as "we Frenchmen.'' In fact, instead of objecting to conscription, as Angell observed, the Francophone African reaction to it was favorable, with their attitude based on arguments such as "we are Frenchmen. If Frenchmen in Normandy and Provence are subject to conscription, should Frenchmen of Guadeloupe or Senegal be exempted? You say those men don't understand the causes of the War. Do all the Normandy peasants? But they are prepared to stand with their fellow-citizens, be guided by their leaders; so in Senegal.'' In fact, the French, appreciating the military significance of their Force Noir in the post-World War I period, introduced limited compulsory military service in other West and Equatorial African colonies. In 1928, for example, the French army was composed of some 415,000 personnel from France itself, 16,500 Foreign Legionnaires, and 103,500 North African troops, in addition to 100,000 colonial troops—native, regular and irregular, and auxiliaries.[26]

At the end of the war, in the issue of February-November 1918, devoted to the British army after the war, the *Journal of the Royal United Services Institution* published a paper by Capt. J. F. W. Allen entitled "An African Army: Some Possibilities.'' In this paper, Allen dealt with the feasibility of a "black phalanx'' of African troops, listing a series of concrete proposals, but also criticizing those who had thought that such a force could have been raised during the war in the same proportion to the African population under British rule as the military participation ratio in Great Britain itself. The reason for this, according to Allen, was the fact that "nearly every trained African soldier was desperately needed in the firing line, and officers and NCOs competent to train recruits, and who could be spared for the work, were very few and far between.'' But "as to the future, there is no doubt we could raise and maintain from Africa a standing army of considerably larger size than we now have.'' Allen objected, however, to the idea of sending such troops to Europe in the event of a future war. What the employment of more African troops would do, according to him, was "to release a larger number of white troops'' from garrison duty. He also went on to propose a reserve of African troops, but added, "it would not be necessary to pay the men highly," although he proposed a minimum service term of six years.

Finally, Allen turned to the question of officers and NCOs for the postwar African army. He first posed the question of permanent officer assignment, as existed in the Indian case, or secondment from British regiments for a specified period, as was the practice up to then. He then questioned whether there would be white NCOs, as was the situation then, or only officers, as was the case in India. With regard to both officers and NCOs, he suggested that secondment should be the answer. As for the method of NCO utilization, Allen maintained that

Africans require a larger proportion of white men than Indian troops, and the only men who are educated enough to do clerk's work generally come from the coast, and in most cases do not get on well with the tribes from which the rank and file would be recruited. If they were employed, they would be used merely as clerks and not as NCO's. One or two good white NCO's to a company make an extraordinary difference, both on service and in peace time, and in addition they act as a 'white reserve' to fall back on.

This conclusion followed, of course, from his original premise, which was that "practically every European nation produces good fighting men when the raw material has been subjected to discipline and training—many African and Indian races can never produce fighting men, partly because of their lack of any martial qualities and also because of the very low level of their intelligence."[27]

In spite of Allen's negative comment regarding their "intelligence" and "prowess," the Indian Army still contributed significantly to the war effort, in manpower terms at least. Philip Mason, for example, recalled that although before the war, the Indian Army numbered only 150,000 men, it expanded *without conscription* to almost 1,500,000 in World War I and to over 2,500,000 in World War II, again without conscription, becoming the largest nonconscript army ever recruited. He recounted that "The newspapers were full of stories about the gallantry of Indian troops. India sent one army corps to France; Britain in 1914 sent two—tiny beside the French forces, but they plugged the gap, one-third were Indian. Australia and Canada had nothing ready until much later."[28]

The enormity of the Indian contribution can be measured in both manpower and money terms. As for manpower, only a few months after the war had begun, over 200,000 Indian soldiers had been shipped to various theatres of war, whereas previously, India's manpower contribution to overseas campaigns had never exceeded 18,000. By autumn 1914 the Indian troops arrived in Europe, Egypt, Mesopotamia, the Persian Gulf, Mauritius, and West and East Africa, their use in the latter area being quite significant, as will be seen below. Among the communities contributing to the almost million and a half men recruited by the war's end, the participation of Punjabi Moslems and Sikhs was the highest, the Moslems contributing some 136,000 and the Sikhs 88,000 men, respectively. Indeed, insofar as Indian casualties numbered over 100,000, it was said that India's contribution to the war effort in manpower terms was quite significant. In money terms, India's contribution, in spite of its low level of income per capita, was even more impressive, her financial contribution far exceeding her capacity to bear the burden for all Indian troop costs overseas, which she *voluntarily* assumed.[29]

An interesting, and until recently little recalled, aspect of Indian participation in World War I is the fact that Indian leaders advocated that, when conquered, German East Africa should both be given as a mandate to the Indian government and reserved for Indian colonization. Already, there were significant Indian communities throughout East Africa, an outcome of, in Hugh Tinker's view, "the export of Indian labour" by the British from the mid-nineteenth century onwards. This population movement came about with the abolition of slavery in the British Empire and the need to compensate for the loss of slave labor and, later, to meet labor shortages. Hundreds of thousands of landless Indians were recruited as indentured laborers and sent to Mauritus, the West Indies, Malaya, Uganda, South Africa, among other places.[30]

The significant contribution of Indian troops to the British war effort, therefore, only reinforced Indian claims to territory in East

Africa, especially as they were extensively engaged in the East African theatre itself. In fact, Indian troops were needed in this theatre at the very beginning of the war, and the first contingents arrived there by 1 September 1914. But they began to suffer reverses only a month after arrival. Defeat followed defeat, but finally the tide turned, and by the beginning of 1916, the British forces started to conquer German territory. By the start of 1917, they were defeated and driven from their territory, with German East Africa being declared a protectorate by the Allies in December 1917, so Indian troops began to be withdrawn and sent to other theatres, being replaced by conscripted Africans.[31]

However, after the war, the Indian defense role and contribution to the conquest of German East Africa became a contentious subject, with many Europeans belittling it and criticizing the local Indians especially. As for the Indian troops, one observer claimed that not only had some deserted, but that they were not reliable unless commanded by a European, in addition to the fact that they were "unfit" for the climate. Others cited the string of defeats the Indian troops suffered at the beginning of the campaign as illustrating their uselessness. With regard to the local Indian community in East Africa, only some 1,400 out of 20,000 adult males served in the armed forces, and only some 375 of them served in combat, the rest serving in noncombatant roles. Furthermore, most of those who served did so only since, as they were employed by the Uganda Railway, they were conscripted by law. As for casualties, although some 46,000 Africans who served in the Carrier Corps became fatal casualties, no local Indians were killed or wounded, but eight were found guilty of treason, with five executed.[32]

According to a 1923 memorandum on the claims of East African Indians, "the local Indian during the war was notorious for his efforts to avoid military service." After denouncing the war efforts of the local Indians during World War I, Lord Cranworth, in his book *Kenya Chronicles*, continued, echoing Allen's contention cited above, "but of course between the fighting races of India and the Hindu there remains a gap so immeasurable that we cannot see a period of time in which it will be bridged." The Indians and their supporters accused the Europeans of ingratitude and defended the Indian military contribution accordingly. The April 1920 issue of the London magazine *India*, for example, stated that the Indian military contribution "saved East Africa from destruction as a British possession during the war," and a month later, the Mombassa Indian weekly *Democrat* claimed that "Indian soldiers, Indian blood, and Indian resources saved East Africa for the British Empire, while the Indian community in the Protectorate was being subjected to the most invidious treatment."[33]

In any case, Robert Gregory, when dealing with the question in depth, summed the issues up in the following terms: "Although the local Indian's effort will always be somewhat questionable, the contribution from India to the Allied endeavour in East Africa was very important. . . . The presence of Indian troops in East Africa not only enabled forces from the United Kingdom to concentrate on the European theatre, but also permitted local European settlers to tend their farms."[34] During the period of the war, some 47,000 Indians served in the East Africa campaign, with some 5,000 fatalities due to wounds or sickness.

As for Indian territorial claims on German East Africa, which developed during the war itself, one observer commented, "it was regarded as certain by everyone who fought that India would receive generous consideration at the hands of Great Britain at the end of the war." Gregory, in fact, claimed that the idea that England would keep the territory, preserving it for Indian colonization or give it to India "was a logical inference not only because of the Indian's role in the war but also because of the large number of Indians settled in German East Africa." However, as Gregory related, the long effort to secure the territory as an Indian colony did not succeed, since the movement was opposed by many organizations and individuals in both England and India on the grounds that Indian efforts were "misdirected" since in their view more effort should have been directed toward attaining some semblance of self-rule in India itself.[35]

In a recent study entitled "War and the Colonial Relationship: Britain, India, and the War of 1914-18," Judith M. Brown made the cogent point that during the war, although in the superficial sense the association between Britain and India "seemed as stable as a rock," the war was, in fact, "a motor of change"—at least in ideological or perceptual terms—since it affected both the Indian and Briton. One Indian observer even claimed that "the war has changed us very much. It has changed the angle of vision in India as well [as] in England. I venture to say that the war has put the clock of time fifty years forward." But Brown continued, although "the 1914-18 war left deep and permanent marks in Indian society . . . It would be fair to conclude that the war did not shatter the acquiescence of the vast majority of Indians which helped to make the raj viable."[36]

As for Indian military service, Brown maintained that "while there were isolated instances of trouble among them . . . Indian soldiers played a significant role in many theatres of the war and in India itself their loyalty was the more important as British troops were removed" to serve in Europe. She concluded by observing that "in restrospect, during the First World War, the colonial relationship appeared to hold firm in India. . . . However, in responding to the challenge of war, the *raj* started the process of *adaptation* which finally broke the imperial bonds tying India to Britain." Still, as Chamberlain wrote, in view of the clashes that occurred in the previous decade, "when war broke out in 1914 India responded with a loyalty to the British crown that took many British commentators by surprise." Ghandi, for his part, returned to India from South Africa in 1914, raised an ambulance unit, and encouraged Indian volunteers to join the army. It was only as a result of incidents after the war that he became a fierce opponent of the *Raj*.[37]

In comparative perspective, then, the role of the British Indian Army in World War I was far more significant than either the Caribbean or African regiments. Indeed, although before the war the Indian Army was, by design, to be used only in the subcontinent, and there was little or no talk regarding its possible use outside India, by the end of the war, close to 1,000,000 Indians were dispatched to the expeditionary forces in Mesopotamia, Egypt, and France. But despite their willing response to the calls to defend "king and empire," wage discrimination was prevalent in the Indian, African, and West Indian cases during the war. As for entry into the officer corps during this period, new commonwealth, that is, colored, personnel were barred from commission in H. M. Forces by a statutory "color bar," the Army Council opposing commission of those "who are not of unmixed European blood." Thus the officers of the West Indian regiments, the African forces, and the Indian Army were "white," except in the case of the viceroy's commissioned officer in India.

In his seminal paper on the "Indianisation of the Indian Army, 1918-45," William Gutteridge dealt with the issues surrounding the "localization" of the officer corps in the case of India. The two-tier structure that characterized the officer corps of the British Indian Army—the king's or queen's commission, the higher form, and the lower form of commission given by the governor-general or viceroy—inevitably caused difficulties as regards the process of localization. The VCOs were, in effect, warrant officers who served as intermediaries between the Indian soldiers and the British officers. The VCOs functioned as platoon commanders, thus effectively reducing the proportion of British officers of comparable size. Although some Indians held the higher form of commission in the East India Company's army before the 1857 mutiny, higher commissions in the British Indian Army were given to British officers only until 1919, when the localization process was initiated. During the period until 1945, both British and Indian officers were given the higher form of commission, and it was only after October 1945 that new regular commissions were given only to Indian personnel. Although a special type of king's commission was introduced in 1904 for Indian officers, in response to the pressure of the Congress party, this only enabled Indian officers to command Indian soldiers and limited them to squadron or company officer level.

Over the decade 1919-1929, the issue of localization of the officer corps had polarized those involved in the process into two camps: the existing expatriate officer corps, the members of which opposed such a change, and the Congress party and other nationalist elements in the Legislative Assembly who demanded full Indianization. Three prominent opponents of the localization process were General Sir O'Moore Creagh, a former commander-in-chief of the British Indian Army; Sir Valentine Chirol; and Sir Reginald Craddock.

Creagh, in his volume on India published in 1919, claimed that "Indian soldiers much prefer serving under British officers, for they refuse to believe those of one Indian race will, or possibly can, deal out even handed justice to those of another. . . . The weakening in leadership caused by giving King's commissions to Indians must be reduced by being limited to people of warlike classes. . . . It will preclude British officers from serving in the Indian Army and on them its efficiency depends almost entirely."[38] Creagh did acknowledge, however, the advantage Indian VCOs had vis-à-vis their understanding of Indian soldiers and thus advocated the localization of some units based on class-caste-regiment considerations rather than take in officer candidates from "nonmartial" groups due to what he saw as political expediency. Chirol, writing on India in 1926, cited the opposition to the localization process as focusing on "the strong racial objections of British officers to being placed in the position of ever having to take orders from Indian officers." Craddock, in his book entitled *The Dilemma of India* published in 1929, maintained that without British leadership, the Indian Army would simply fall apart, each racial, caste, or communal group backing their own leaders.

On the eve of World War II, then, there were only some 400 Indian officers with the king's commission out of a total officer corps of over 4,400. In the period between 1939 and 1945, however, this ratio had declined to four to one, so when the Indian government announced on 22 October 1945 that only Indian personnel would be eligible for regular commissions, there were over 8,300 Indian officers, not including the medical corps, the most senior of whom had attained the rank of brigadier, which comprised the core of the future officer corps of India and Pakistan.[39]

The effect of World War II on the relationship between the new commonwealth peoples and Great Britain was, however, of fundamental importance, both in terms of their interaction with the British military establishment and the political and demographic transitions that came about in the postwar period. After World War I, there was a natural decrease in enthusiasm for both defense expenditure and Imperial solidarity in defense matters. As

William Golant wrote, it was the overall "lack of purpose in defense" that was to prove to be disastrous for Britain at the beginning of World War II. In Golant's view, "the Second World War alone did not destroy the old British Empire, it merely revealed what had been the latent weakness of Britain as a world power: to rule was too burdensome, to reform was too expensive, to secure the lasting cooperation of politicians outside Britain to the idea of an Imperial Commonwealth too impractical." Nowhere more did this apply than in the Indian case, for unpreparedness for war extended even to this "outpost." The Indian Army's equipment was obsolete and in ill-repair. Although the army numbered about 180,000 in 1939, its role was supposed to be limited to controlling frontier "disturbances" or for "internal pacification" duties. In case of invasion, its role would be to "contain" the enemy forces until the arrival of "Imperial reinforcements." Thus the situation in the Indian Army at this point is best reflected in the words of one observer, who wrote that before the war, personnel from H. M. Forces in Britain had, upon arriving in India, "to be retrained in the use of obsolete weapons and outworn tactical methods, while British units on leaving India have to be taught afresh before they can take their place in British field formations." But, again, despite all of its prewar shortcomings, the Indian Army, in Mason's words, and true to its battle traditions, "showed in Africa and in Italy that they could beat the Germans, and in Burma that they could beat the Japanese."[40]

On the other hand, as regards the general relationship between Britain and India, World War II can be said to have brought things "to a head," since, as Golant noted, "the World War, while changing the context in which Britain demanded obedience from Indians—for now Indians were asked to identify themselves with the Allied effort against totalitarianism—required of them a slavish submission to British authority which they resented." However, despite the concessions offered to placate Indian hostility—such as promises made in 1940 of full dominion status, self-government, and the right to secede from the commonwealth if and when independence was granted—after the failure of the Cripps mission in 1942, the Congress party rejected any compromise regarding its basic demands. As the Indians saw it, "the British desire our help only as slaves." A combination of the anger generated by the Cripps affair and British military setbacks gave impetus to Ghandi and the Congress party in their preparation of a mass campaign of civil disobedience and the adoption of a resolution calling on Britain, described as "India's immediate aggressor," to "Quit India." But the day the resolution was passed, 8 August 1942, both Ghandi and the leaders of the Congress party were arrested. The outcome of this was all too predictable. Even the viceroy was worried and surprised by the passion and intensity of the Indian reaction, reporting to London in the following words: "I am engaged here in meeting by far the most serious rebellion since that of 1857, the gravity and extent of which we have so far concealed from the world for reasons of military security. Mob violence remains rampant over large tracts of the countryside and I am by no means confident that we may not see in September (1942) a formidable attempt to renew this widespread sabotage of our war effort." All in all, before it was quelled, over 1,000 people were killed and over 60,000 arrested.[41]

In the African case, both East and West African soldiers actively participated in the British war effort, but mostly in the Asian and Middle Eastern theatre. As A. R. Haywood and F. A. S. Clarke recounted in their book on the history of the West African Frontier Force, even the Japanese acknowledged their contribution and, in a captured diary, the following entry was found: "The enemy soldiers are not from Britain but from Africa. Because of their belief they are not afraid to die, so even if their comrades have fallen they keep on advancing as if nothing had happened. They have an excellent physique and are very brave, so fighting against these soldiers is somewhat troublesome." The African contribution was also acknowledged in a number of postwar articles that appeared in Britain itself. In the *National Review* of January 1946, for example, Gen. William Platt dealt with "The East African Soldier," concluding that "The East African has proved his worth in battle. Numerically they are sufficiently large to offer an opportunity for reducing the burden on the already hard-pressed white man power of the Empire.'' In the *Army Quarterly* of October 1947, Brig. F. A. S. Clarke dealt with ''the development of the West African Frontier Force (WAFF) in World War II,'' citing the ''vital importance of West Africa to the war effort'' and the ''excellent record of the two WAFF divisions who served in Burma.'' This view was supported by the WAFF commander, Gen. Hugh Stockwell, who praised the WAFF's ''most valuable part in the Burma campaign.''[42]

The long-run effect of the war on Africa and the Africans was foreshadowed, however, in a letter cited in A. G. Russell's book *Colour, Race, and Empire*, published in London in 1944. The letter, referring to the situation in Tanganyika, stated that

there are some indications of anti-European feeling among Africans in this territory, and I think that two effects of the experience of the Africans serving in the forces are (a) they are learning of their man-power as men in a mass, and (b) they no longer consider the white man as ''on a pedestal.'' In my view, the period immediately following the disbanding of the African soldiers will be one of acute difficulty. In the economic sphere there will have to be racial adjustments. . . . I shall not be surprised if there are not within the next few years African Trade Unions and even Returned Soldier's Associations, to speak and fight for what they consider their rights.[43]

C. R. A. Swynnerton, writing in the *Army Quarterly* of January 1951, confirmed this when he tried to explain the events leading up to the disturbances in West Africa in which ex-servicemen demanded bonuses for their war service, which they claimed was promised to them when they enlisted during the war. He counterpointed the efforts of ex-servicemen's organizations that were affiliated with the British Empire Service League and that did ''a great deal to improve the lot of the ex-soldier'' to the activities of unofficial organizations in both the Gold Coast and Nigeria, which became involved in violent protest and riots over the bonus issue.[44]

With regard to the Caribbean region, the West Indies Regiment was disbanded following World War I, and by 1928 the West India Regiment was also disbanded. Thus at the outset of World

War II, there were no units from this area for the employment
of West Indians, and many came to Britain independently, to
serve in H. M. Forces, since until 1944 official recruitment in
the Caribbean was deferred, excepting forces for local defense.
Then a very interesting and still unexplained incident took
place that, according to one observer at least, resulted from the
fact that "War Office files became sadly mixed":

Instead of reforming the West India Regiment with its valuable traditions,
confusion with the less meritorious British West Indies Regiment led to
a decision to form a new regiment composed of contingents from no less
than ten different colonies. Known as the Caribbean Regiment, it was
an interesting touring exhibition of West Indian people but it never was
given the chance to develop into an efficient fighting unit—the war
ended before it saw action.[45]

Those West Indians that did serve in H. M. Forces after enlisting
in Britain were, at the beginning of the war, still barred from
holding a commission. But by this time, there was, in fact, an
organized "black" community in Britain that was eventually
able to bring enough pressure to bear to have the restriction
lifted, a result of the efforts, in the main, of Harold Moody and
the League of Coloured Peoples that he headed. Still, as late
as 1944, we see appeals, such as that in the *Yorkshire Evening
News* of May 9, for a less discriminatory attitude toward soldiers
of West Indian origin, some 8,000 of whom served in H. M. Forces
(mostly in the RAF) during the war.[46]

Now, interpretations of the effect of West Indian war service
differ, but observers agree that it did have a significant impact on
West Indian attitude formation and perceptions, the outcome of
which was to be seen in the postwar period. Dorothy Glass,
for example, wrote that stories regarding West Indian service
"became well known at home. A number of these people reached
commissioned rank, and all those who served were greatly
impressed not only by the absence of discrimination in the armed
services, but also by their introduction to an advanced industrialized
economy. Some of them remained in Britain after the war." She
recounted the story of a West Indian veteran who had just been

demobilized and, when he turned up at the Labour Exchange, noticed by chance that his file was marked "Coloured." In his own words: "I went mad. I got out my Air Force pay book and threw it at the clerk. 'This isn't marked coloured,' I shouted; No one in the Air Force cared whether I was coloured or not, why should you?" But even Glass must admit that,

Both before and after the second world war, many employers refused to recruit coloured workers. Such barriers were then well known; they caused considerable difficulties, particularly in the resettlement of West Indians who had been brought to this country under an official war time scheme for essential work in industry or for service in the armed forces. All was well so long as the Ministry of Labour had the powers to control the direction of labour. But as soon as these regulations were relaxed, and recruitment was again entirely at the discretion of the employers, many West Indians who had been doing vital, often skilled, war work found that they were no longer wanted. Most of the doors were now closed to them.[47]

Or in the words of one West Indian quoted by Ruth Landes in the September 1952 issue of *Man*:

Yeah, there's freedom in Britain, but a man don't have a chance. In the States there's Jim Crow, sure. Only certain jobs and so on. But he gets any job he goes after. Here, the job disappears with a black face. With the Yanks you know where you are. Here you don't. But you learn this much: You can have what the Englishman don't want. You can get the room he won't live in, the job he won't take, and the woman he throws out.[48]

To sum up, during World War II, there was, in fact, active recruitment of the new commonwealth peoples into the industrial war effort and the military. By 1947, however, most of the West Indian industrial workers and servicemen had been "repatriated," but encountered fairly bad economic conditions and prospects at home. Hence, favorable experiences in wartime Britain did mean that a considerable proportion of those who found it difficult to reintegrate themselves into West Indian economic life began to think of returning to the United Kingdom. Thus there began a "steadily mounting influx of peacetime immigrant workers, reaching its peak in the late 1950's and early 1960's," or, in other words, "the war of 1939-45 constituted . . . the beginning of the intrusion of the particular components of race and colour into [British] national life." In fact, in the West Indian case, "previous migration . . . had been almost entirely confined to the middle and upper classes. War service for the first time brought working class and lower middle class West Indians to Britain."[49]

THE POSTCOLONIAL ERA

Independence and immigration are the main themes characterizing the postcolonial period. But a number of issues emanating from new commonwealth military service still remained on the eve of independence. With regard to Indian partition, for example, in the words of one observer, "Britain placed its hopes in unity because it was simpler, in other words more likely to lead to a smooth transition in government departments, the police, and the armed forces." He continued:

The latter were especially important. Partition of the services was opposed by the Viceroy and the C-in-C, Field Marshal Auchinleck, because it was impractical and potentially dangerous. In a divided India, Muslims would not likely obey Hindu officers; by ending the present structure of command, service morale and efficiency would be threatened. Disgruntled servicemen could become a revolutionary force. The practical problems were also formidable. It was estimated to take at least a year to divide men and equipment, during which time the military units would be anything but an effective defence force.[50]

As for the West Indies, when the federation was created in 1958, the decision was made to reconstitute the West India Regiment, but the regiment failed along with the political union it was supposed to defend. Thus after independence, each ex-colony formed its own defense force, so the last British regiment was withdrawn from Jamaica by 1962. The African case is well documented and thus is not discussed here. However, despite a strong tendency for *political* anticolonialism, the "colonial legacy" of "military dependence," as Chester Crocker put it, remains to the present.[51]

To return to the demographic transition resulting from the process of immigration, in 1957 Sydney Collins noted that the main reasons for both Asian and West Indian migration was "response to the call for war service, economic hardship in the home country, and a desire for social advancement . . . [however] in most cases, these migrations are but a culmination and acceleration of processes of social change operating in the migrants' society." In the West Indian case, for example, Ken Hill, former mayor of Kingston and later a member of the Jamaican senate, claimed that, "Emigration has helped the Jamaican economy by reducing the high level of unemployment. . . . It is estimated that about 100,000 out of the island's 800,000 labour force are out of work . . . as such we find that immigration is the best form of economic assistance that Britain can give us." Furthermore, as Sheila Allen and Christopher Smith noted, the West Indians have moved, for the most part, into low-skilled jobs, so their children, upon leaving school, comprise an unskilled and semiskilled labor pool that, in recessionary times, forms, in turn, a core of unemployed with, according to the 1971 census, a rate over two times that of the comparable unemployment rate of white youth in England and Wales.[52]

Residential segregation has also occurred in the West Indian case in Britain, according to Ceri Peach, as a result of four main factors. First, West Indian migration to the United Kingdom occurred as a result of labor demand at the "lowest end of the occupational ladder," and thus it was to be expected that they would also become "concentrated at the lowest end of the residential ladder." The outcome of this can be seen in the concentration of West Indians in the older and less desirable housing in areas close to town centers. Second, the immigration process from the West Indies took place along family and residential lines, and thus groups from one family, village, or town would concentrate in specific areas, this being reinforced by the extended family structure characterizing the West Indian case. Third, in Peach's view, "the greater the contrast in social and economic environment between the homeland and the new area, the greater the probable degree of clustering." Thus it would be expected that a higher degree of clustering would occur among West Indians than among, say, British immigrants in Australia. Fourth, clustering may have occurred as a result of the relatively short period in which mass West Indian immigration took place. Additional problems that may affect the residential distribution of West Indians is the fact that there is still not a large enough number of persons who are able, as a result of residence and registration factors, to move to council estates or with a sufficient amount of money to be able to move into middle-class neighborhoods. Furthermore, when West Indians are given housing by local councils, they are occasionally channeled into the older and poorer, and not the newer, ones. Estate agents also attempt to divert West Indians from buying houses in middle-class areas so as not to affect house prices in those areas.[53]

Peach analyzed these elements in "color-caste" terms peculiar to the British case. He started from the observation that British society is, in fact, "very highly segregated," in residential terms, "along class lines," continuing: "Even the most cursory examination of British towns reveals areas which are clearly middle class and areas which are clearly working class. Yet segregation along class is not generally considered a social problem while segregation along colour lines is." He explained this in terms of the presence of "a negative element of compulsion preventing the dispersal of individuals from a class area like a council estate." He concluded that "from a geographical point of view, the importance of colour or caste is that it is a largely inflexible line and that, in the same way as there is a barrier to the movement from lower caste to upper caste, there is a barrier to the movement from lower caste areas to upper caste areas," and thus "the fundamental difference between caste and class areas is that while both experience positive pressures towards clustering, only caste areas experience negative forces preventing dispersal," such as those affecting West Indians.[54]

In the Indian case, some of the impetus to immigration can be seen as the delayed impact of the 1947 partition of the Punjab.

The forced migration of Sikhs resulted in considerable social upheaval. Many of them found it difficult to resettle, and the combination of this and reports of the progress of those Sikhs that had previously migrated to the United Kingdom, in addition to their perception of an abundance of employment opportunities in Britain, made migration an attractive prospect. However, the Asian immigrants in Britain originate from relatively limited areas of India and Pakistan and, aside from the Sikhs, hardly represent the "martial races" of the Raj; but more about this below. In retrospect, then, until the introduction of legislation and controls regarding immigration, and as a result of extending the option of United Kingdom citizenship to residents of every commonwealth nation, "push-pull" factors such as those outlined above resulted in the fact that, as C. Eric Lincoln observed in 1965, "for the first time in modern history," Britain had "an influx of non-whites in sufficiently large numbers to become conspicuous in London, Birmingham, Manchester, Bradford, Sheffield, and half a dozen other cities and towns."[55]

With regard to the Sikhs, as A. G. James related, there is little sign of a mixed Anglo-Asian culture developing among their young people, in contrast to the Anglo-Caribbean culture that has developed among West Indian youth. This is due to the fact that Sikhs are more likely to stay within an all-Sikh peer group, with its own sense of group identity based on traditional symbols and culture. James actually sees the prospect of British Sikh youth identifying with the external symbols of their group as an act of defiance directed against a hostile host community, such as the reluctance to wear safety helmets over their turbans recently manifested among those Sikh youth owning motorbikes and cycles. James considered this analogous to the development of black power symbols among West Indian youths. In fact, James distinguished between the Indian nationalism evident among groups and organizations such as the Indian Workers Association and the *lack* of United Kingdom nationalism among members of *all* Asian communities, including the Sikhs, living in Britain; this, of course, affecting Asian military participation in the United Kingdom armed forces.[56]

As for the Pakistanis, their migration to Britain differed from both the Sikh and West Indian experiences. In the early period, there were high ratios of males to females, which still affects the age and sex composition of the Pakistani community in the United Kingdom. As for their social organization, there was a fundamental division between Bangladeshis and West Pakistanis themselves; furthermore, there were differences between Punjabis and Pathans. All were Muslims, but the Pakistani community was still fragmented, although in the view of the host community, they formed one group.[57]

As early as 1947, K. L. Little argued that the new commonwealth immigrants were seen by the British as representing the "natives" of the empire. More recently, John Rex stated that the new commonwealth immigrant "cannot expect with confidence that his children or grandchildren will have been accepted into the stratification system of the host society," and Katrin Fitzherbert claimed that "however English in outlook, as they grow up they will still be classed as 'coloured,' as belonging with other coloured people." Even so, there are still intercommunal differences that must be taken into account in this regard, as noted above. Although white Britons find it convenient to see all Asians or West Indians as a single, alien community, as Kramer observed,

regardless of the number of non-whites in the population during the coming decades, the average colored Briton will be likely to consider himself not as a "non-white," but as a member of a much smaller, and thus weaker group, e.g. Jamaican, Trinidadian, Sikh, Pakistani, etc. The differences among the various segments of the immigrant population are perhaps even more spectacular than those separating some of these sectors from their "hosts," which means that it will be very difficult indeed for the ordinary immigrant to consider himself as belonging to a relatively large class labeled "colored" Englishmen. He certainly does not view himself in this light now, as is testified to by the absence of any broadly-based organization which even purports to defend the rights of *all* coloured people.

But on the other hand, a continued rejection of these communities could lead to a situation where "more and more . . . the immigrant [would see] himself less a West Indian or Sikh in English society, and more as a black man in white society."[58]

However, in more general terms, it is the Asian community that tends to avoid all contacts with the "host" community other than in work relationships and is self-segregating to a degree that was, before their arrival, seen only among the Chinese community. Their original intentions of avoidance and return to the subcontinent are becoming increasingly hard to fulfill due to the arrival of whole families and young children especially, who become "exposed" to the assimilationist pressures in the schools of the host society. This is in contrast to the West Indians, who, as Lincoln noted, generally intend to remain in the United Kingdom, perceiving themselves as "black Englishmen" or "black British." This manifests itself, as Glass wrote, in "the overt patriotic feeling shown by West Indians toward Britain . . . often greater than that shown by 'native' British people," or as Rex and Moore confirmed, in the popular notion that West Indians come to England as to their "mother country." As such, they are "imbued with a deep sense of English tradition of fair play, they expect equal treatment and no colour discrimination. These beliefs and hopes are almost universally destroyed after a few weeks in England." They added that, "there appears to be a greater desire among West Indians than immigrants from Pakistan and India to be integrated with the British community."[59]

To sum up, then, as Glass wrote, "Britain's colonial and colour problems have been abroad, and to most citizens they have been very remote. There has been and still is a dichotomy between attitudes towards 'colour' in the U.K. itself and in its territories overseas," but on the other hand, as Leonard Bloom recently observed, "the imperial-colonial relationship is not without significance for the contemporary host-immigrant situation. Racism in Britain today may be reinforced by the arrogance of the colonial period and the racist theory that was often developed to rationalize it." Thus, as Richard Schermerhorn wrote: "In most cases of voluntary migration, racial labels or assigned statuses are not imposed upon the newcomers. However, where the host society has a previous history of slavery or colonization, with concomitant racial ideologies, these may carry over to color the perception of the immigrant who is then defined in social terms."[60]

Now, in dealing with the interaction between the new commonwealth peoples and the British military establishment, I may have given the impression that the relationship was one-sided, that is, Britain dependent upon the manpower provided by the colonies. As indicated above, however, there was also an element of limited upward social mobility involved in military service, especially for those of low socioeconomic origins. In the African case, for example, we can see the difference between the military wage and the civilian wage by reviewing a further passage from the letter referred to earlier regarding the situation in Tanganyika during World War II. The writer noted that "the *askari* [African soldier] . . . in addition to being well fed and clothed receives 20 shillings or 30 shillings a month [and] will not readily work on a plantation for 8 shillings or 10 shillings and very much less acceptable food." It wasn't that the military was so good, however. The basic situation of the African was terrible at that time. In both the West Indian and Indian cases, as in the African one, a military career was, at least, a steady job. Thus the relationship may be characterized as one of *interdependence*. But it must also be noted that this interdependence was functionally determined, to the extent that there was a tendency for new commonwealth participation and "propensity" to participate to change, both with shifts in their mobility prospects and changes in the military need for manpower. We obtain, therefore, the situation where concomitant with the fourth, postcolonial phase, there was also a decline in the role of the British military establishment worldwide and thereby a decline in the new commonwealth military participation in H. M. Forces. Even so, Anthony Richmond could report in 1954 that "it is estimated that about ⅓ of the original volunteers are still living in Britain, or are attached to the forces or the merchant navy," and an analysis of 1951 census figures shows that the proportion of servicemen of "Caribbean" origin resident in the United Kingdom was over twice the proportion of those of "Caribbean" origin in the population as a whole.[61]

In a candid survey of "Recruitment and Army Careers in the

Seventies," the director of British army recruiting, Brig. A. J. Wilson, made the cogent point that from 1815 onwards, the British army had, in fact, been a colonial force for the most part, with the majority of its engagements, until 1914, being outside Europe, so, for over 150 years, its experience as a European force was limited to the world wars. But Wilson continued, "in neither case are regular regimental officers' memories of European soldiering particularly happy or successful." Wilson recalled that although in 1914 the regular army was deployed successfully alongside the French, it was almost totally wiped out by early 1915 after Ypres and other battles. After this, the new British forces were composed, for the most part, of nonregular personnel, with regular officers playing only a small part other than those at the level of the high command or staff. Similarly, in World War II, most of the officer cadre used at the regimental level were nonregular, with the regular officers, aside from those in higher command or those who entered the army just before the war, "relegated" to staff or training roles. Wilson concluded, therefore:[62]

Small wonder that after each major European conflict the Army's regular officers should have welcomed a return to "proper soldiering," conveniently provided in the twenties and thirties by the stylized operations on the Northwest Frontier of India and after World War II, by the successive problems of decolonization, Malaya, Kenya, Cyprus....

Anthony Verrier, in writing about the role of the British army in the 1960s, earlier recalled "the fact that manpower, and especially local forces, has been the cement of the Imperial system." Besides the dominant place of the Indian Army in this scheme, and its massive contribution in both World Wars I and II, local forces from Africa were depended upon in both World Wars I and II also and, as in the case of the King's African Rifles, later in Malaya. Indeed, Verrier reported that in the mid-1960s some members of the British Parliament had, in fact, suggested recruiting more Gurkas and establishing more Gurka battalions to make up for manpower shortfalls in the British army. But

Verrier went on, "the suggestion, although understandable, is as impracticable as filling the British Army with West Indians and Fijians."[63]

In the British case, then, although military service did have some effect on the social standing of the resident Negro community and did bring contact with future residents—in the form of West Indian servicemen who were stationed and demobilized in Britain in World War II—no large-scale "colored" communities existed in Britain, so none could "benefit" in sociopolitical terms from their military participation. The social standing of "colored" commonwealth citizens was little aided by their participation in service to the empire, if we limit consideration to the dimension of how that service affected the British view of the large-scale immigration of "colored" people, as against their view of the linkage between the war service of Australians, New Zealanders, and even British South Africans and the "inherent" rights of these groups to immigrate to the United Kingdom. Still, although there are strong bases for the "kith and kin" argument, one should also recognize that West Indians, Indians, Pakistanis, West and East Africans, and even Fijians also fought in defense of what some of them, at least then, perceived as their "mother country."[64]

Although a number of disturbing features of race relations and institutional discrimination in H. M. Forces during and since World War I have been recounted above, such as wage discrimination and segregation of facilities, the problem of constraint on the participation of new commonwealth servicemen in the postcolonial period is much better documented than outright racial discrimination as such. Although there was and still is supposed to be no discrimination or restriction upon the basis of color in H. M. Forces, there have been consistent reports of quotas and exclusion regarding colored servicemen. Indeed, it seems that by the beginning of the 1960s, the number of colored personnel in the services had reached such a level so as to necessitate public consideration and debate over service policies toward colored recruits in the context of the overall emerging social problem of immigrant-community relations.

Thus in 1961 the *Times* (July 19) reported the statement of a War Office spokesman, who said that the army was operating a policy of 2 percent colored men among total recruitment. The army later qualified this statement by noting that there was no legal "ceiling" as such, and thus the 2 percent figure was used as a working yardstick that could be altered "at any time." The *Guardian* reported in 1966 (October 29) that the then minister of defence for the army, Gerry Reynolds, had "ordered the withdrawal of all remaining obstacles to the recruitment of suitably qualified coloured soldiers," this, following a *Guardian* disclosure of a confidential War Office memorandum of 1964, excluding colored men from the Foot Guards, the Household Cavalry, the Highland and Lowland regiments, the Military Police, the Military Prisons Service, the Army Education Corps, the Intelligence Corps, and the Army Physical Training Corps.[65]

Notwithstanding Reynolds' orders, a *Times* inquiry in 1967 (May 8) found that the army was still operating a quota, this time a ceiling of 4 percent colored participation in most units. Allegations of exclusion from certain cavalry units, the Guards, and some Highland regiments continued even after Reynolds' orders, at least according to a *Nottingham Evening Post* report of 1 December 1966. As for occupational exclusion, the *Times* inquiry found that "coloured servicemen are not usually found in units dealing with 'sensitive' matters such as communications, intelligence, or advanced weapons."[66]

At the end of 1968 (Dec. 6), the *Daily Express* disclosed that the army had set a 3 percent quota for colored recruits. The secretary of state for defence, when questioned on this point, replied that "no coloured men had ever been turned away as a result of this quota." Six days after the *Express* disclosure, the *Times* (Dec. 12) reported that the secretary had "in view of the change in circumstances . . . decided that there was no longer any need for this type of limitation." Healy's parliamentary statement is cited below in full:

A percentage limitation on coloured personnel in the Army was authorized in 1961 at a time when operational circumstances often required units to be stationed in overseas theatres to which it was not customary to send coloured troops. The percentage was increased in April 1964. No coloured man has ever been turned away as a result. In the light of the changes in Defence policy introduced since that date, with its increased emphasis on the Army's role in Europe, I have decided that there is now no need for this type of limitation. Should the need ever arise, it would, of course, be open to the Army, as to any other organization, to secure or preserve a reasonable balance of persons of different racial groups, in accordance with the Race Relations Act, 1968.[67]

As for the Royal Navy and the RAF, both have failed to produce statistics on their colored personnel, although only the latter has denied the existence of a quota. Now, section 95 of the Army Act of 1881 stated that there could not be more than one alien to every fifty British subjects in any corps or regiment, and they could not rise above the rank of NCO or warrant officer. British subjects born outside the commonwealth are excluded from the navy and the RAF unless the secretary of state makes a rare exception. They can join the army, but only as private soldiers. In this regard, Sheila Patterson noted in 1969 that "curiously, until 1955 the Army Act of 1881 discriminated in favour of coloured aliens against white aliens. . . . Negroes and other persons of colour, although aliens, were . . . excepted" from the provisions limiting their service as put forth in the 1881 act "and when enlisted, were entitled to all the privileges of a natural-born British subject." This limitation was reinforced by section 21 of the Army and Air Force Acts of 1955, which restricted the number of "aliens" at any one time serving in H. M. Forces, whether as officers or ordinary servicemen, to one-fiftieth of the total number in the service. In this case, however, "positive discrimination" in favor of "colored" aliens did not occur; rather, it seems that the restriction formed the basis for the quota on colored servicemen overall and by unit.[68]

Indeed, at this point whether or not Healy's qualification of a possible army quota on colored personnel in case of personnel imbalance applies is not known. Some indication of the orientation of the Ministry of Defence toward the problem, however, emerges from a reply of the minister of state for defence, Lord

Balniel, to the then under-secretary of state for immigration and race relations at the Home Office, David Lane, dated 31 October 1972. Balniel, in speaking of the problem of conducting research on the racial composition of H. M. Forces, said, "The Services themselves have no wish or requirement to distinguish between servicemen of different races, *even where the law permits them to do so. . . .*" I therefore suspect that some form of de facto quota, at least, is operating, even at present, with regard to those of new commonwealth origin.[69]

TRENDS IN AND PARAMETERS OF NEW COMMONWEALTH MILITARY PARTICIPATION

As for the "propensity" of new commonwealth immigrants to participate in H. M. Forces, a number of observations can be made. The unemployment rate of West Indian youths, according to the 1966 census, was 4.9 percent, over twice the rate of all young people aged fifteen to twenty-four, and it was 14.8 percent, according to the 1971 census, again, over twice that of all youth. The rate of unemployment among West Indians aged fifteen to twenty was over 16.0 percent, double that of the overall rate for their age group in the population as a whole and almost triple that of Indian and Pakistani youths of comparable age, again, according to the 1971 census. This may account for an increase in black faces in H. M. Forces. However, as Sheila Patterson noted in 1965, regarding the West Indian at least, military service or the choice of the military as a career was not appealing due to the "low rate of pay and strict routine." Above, it was also noted that most Asian migrants, except for the Sikhs, do not originate from the "martial races," that is, from northern India, and thus should not have any "natural" affinity, at least, for military service. This phenomenon was noted by the United Kingdom Ministry of Defence when, in 1967, W. V. Webb of the Manpower Section observed that in the future, both the immigrants' "rate of application to join the armed forces and their ability to pass the various acceptance tests may be different from the corresponding factors for the indigenous population." In examining in more detail the developments in "colored" participation, note that the empirical data presented below relate to the situation as regards the participation of colored personnel in the late 1960s. In a letter to me dated 3 September 1980, the British Ministry of Defence claimed that, "The Army no longer maintains statistics on numbers of coloured personnel. . . . The Royal Navy and Royal Air Force have never maintained such information. *The Army stopped keeping records early in the 1970s because as coloured soldiers are treated no differently from any others in the Army there seemed no point in continuing the exercise.*"[70]

In global terms, census figures published for 1966 and data supplied by the Ministry of Defence (army) in 1968-1969 showed that the army, at least, was growing in popularity among colored males in the 1960s. The figures for the 1951 and 1966 censuses show an almost fourfold increase in the number of colored servicemen. Of the 2,087 colored male soldiers in the army in 1968, 28.7 percent had less than three years' service, 27.8 percent between three and six years', 34.8 percent between six and nine years', and only 8.7 percent more than nine years' service. Now, a cursory treatment of the original data provided by the army proved to be misleading to those who originally analyzed the figures and presented them in the 1969 study entitled *Colour and Citizenship*. The interpretation by E. J. B. Rose was made on the basis of the statistics supplied to him in a letter of 11 September 1968. Rose stated that,

the progress made by coloured soldiers (No information was available concerning officers) is described by Army authorities as encouraging and the figures would seem to confirm the statement that "The coloured soldier had every prospect of getting a real square deal in the Army." [Cf. letter to him from Ministry of Defence.]

Rose continued:

In view of the very marked reluctance of private industry to promote coloureds to positions of authority over white workers, the fact that over 40% of coloureds are NCO's is quite striking. Some 60% of all coloured soldiers are tradesmen, which is another interesting comment on private industry's assessment of coloured worker's skills. As far as distribution is concerned, every single major arm or corps of the Army had coloured NCO's of the rank of Sgt. or above. The lower percentage of coloured soldiers in the higher NCO ranks seems to be almost entirely due to shorter length of service. This is borne out by an examination of the figures for coloured soldiers with nine or more years of service, of whom half hold the rank of Sgt. or above.[71]

Whether Rose's interpretation of the data is correct, however, may be questioned. One may refer to the statistics themselves to answer the question about whether the colored soldier in the army really did get a square deal up to 1968. First, the fact that "over 40.0 percent"—to be more exact, 41.2 percent—"of coloured soldiers are NCO's " is, in fact, not as "striking" as Rose thought. This is due to the somewhat arbitrary approach taken by both Rose and the army with regard to the rank breakdown of colored personnel and its implications. For example, they defined *NCO* in this case to include ranks up from lance-corporal inclusive. Breaking down the data into junior ranks and senior NCOs would have been much more appropriate here. Furthermore, a comparison between "colored" and overall rank distribution data and information regarding rank mobility would have given a much different picture than that which emerged in the original table presented by Rose, This comparison is made in Tables 11-15 below.[72]

Table 11

Rank Distribution of Colored Male Soldiers in the Army and Distribution by Length of Service, 1968 (in Percentages)

RANK	LESS THAN 3	3+, LESS THAN 6	6+, LESS THAN 9	9+	% TOTAL	% EXPECTED	DIFF.
W.O. I	—	—	—	2.8	0.3	1.6	−1.3
W.O.II	—	—	—	8.2	0.7	3.9	−3.2
Staff sergeant	—	—	—	12.7	1.1	4.2	−3.1
Sergeant	0.2	0.6	4.7	27.4	4.2	9.9	−5.7
Corporal	1.5	10.7	31.1	31.3	16.9	16.2	+0.7
Lance-corporal	6.8	20.5	28.2	8.8	18.0	14.2	+3.8
Private	92.5	68.2	36.0	8.8	58.8	50.0	+8.8
	100.0	100.0	100.0	100.0	100.0	100.0	
Number:	(599)	(580)	(726)	(182)	(2087)		
Percentage:	28.7%	27.8%	34.8%	8.7%	100.0%		

Table 12

*Typical Career Pattern of Army Servicemen versus Colored
Attainment of Expected Rank Level, 1968*

YEARS OF SERVICE	EXPECTED RANK AT BEGINNING OF PERIOD	PERCENTAGE COLORED WHO ACHIEVED EXPECTED RANK
Less than 3	Private	100.0%
3 + , less than 6	Corporal	11.3
6 + , less than 9	Sergeant	4.7
9 +	Staff sergeant	23.7 [a]

[a]But note, absolute number is small.

Table 13

*Expected versus Actual Rank Distribution of Colored Male Soldiers
in Army, 1968*

CATEGORY	EXPECTED	ACTUAL	DIFFERENCE
Senior NCO (sergeant and up)	19.6%	6.3%	− 13.3
Junior ranks	80.4	93.7	+ 13.3

Table 14

*Occupational Distribution of Colored Male Personnel in
Army by Military Occupational Specialty, 1968*

OCCUPATIONAL CATEGORY	PERCENTAGE OF COLORED PERSONNEL
Infantry, gun crews, and Allied specialties	49.2%
Electronics equipment, communications, and intelligence specialists	9.7
Medical and dental specialists	6.2
Other technical and Allied specialists	8.0

Table 14 (continued)

OCCUPATIONAL CATEGORY	PERCENTAGE OF COLORED PERSONNEL
Administrative specialists and clerks	1.0
Electrical-mechanical equipment repairmen and craftsmen	6.3
Service and supply handlers	19.6
	100.0%

Table 15

Rank Distribution Data, Infantry and REME, Overall and Colored Male Servicemen, 1968

	OVERALL		COLORED		
Infantry Rank	*Number*	*Percent*	*Number*	*Percent*	*Difference*
W.O. I	331	0.8	—	—	− 0.8
W.O. II	960	2.2	1	0.2	− 2.0
Staff sergeant	973	2.2	2	0.3	− 1.9
Sergeant	3,131	7.1	12	1.9	− 5.2
Corporal	5,420	12.3	86	13.9	+ 1.6
Lance-corporal	5,896	13.4	98	15.8	+ 2.4
Private	27,294	62.0	420	67.9	+ 5.9
REME Rank					
W.O. I	471	2.9	1	0.8	− 2.1
W.O. II	980	6.1	4	3.0	− 3.1
Staff sergeant	1,015	6.3	4	3.0	− 3.3
Sergeant	2,437	15.1	11	8.3	− 6.8
Corporal	3,394	21.1	38	28.8	+ 7.7
Lance-corporal	2,319	14.4	29	22.0	+ 7.6
Private	5,486	34.1	45	34.1	—

Rose's claim that the reason for the lower percentage of colored soldiers in the higher NCO ranks is their shorter length of service is not supported by calculations based on the original data. Thus although by 1968 only 8.7 percent of the colored soldiers had served nine or more years, 48.9 percent were still in the junior ranks, and 8.8 percent were still privates. Crude rank mobility data also show that of these men, only 23.7 percent attained the rank expected after nine years or more in the army. More importantly, however, although in 1968, 34.8 percent of all colored soldiers had served six or more years, almost all were still in the junior ranks, 36.0 percent still being privates, and only 4.7 percent reached the expected rank (sergeant). Projecting forward on the basis of this situation, it is reasonable to assume that little improvement in colored representation among the senior NCO ranks is now taking place. Rather, we would expect that the 1968 situation, as regards rank distribution of those colored soldiers who had served nine or more years in 1968, is being replicated; although we should expect that some of the fifty-seven soldiers who had served for more than nine years (31.3 percent of all with more than nine years of service) and who were only corporals in 1968 should have been promoted by now to sergeant. It should still be noted that there was some improvement between 1968 and 1969, when the percentage of those who were lance-corporals or in higher ranks increased from 41.2 percent to 46.0 percent. But this was still less than the expected figure of 50.0 percent. In any case, it seems that, as regards rank, the transition point from corporal to sergeant, or, in other words, from junior rank to senior NCO status, was the barrier that colored personnel were unable to breach.[73]

Table 14 presents the occupational distribution of colored personnel in the British army in 1968 by military occupational speciality.[74] This table seems to contradict Rose's contention regarding the percentage of colored soldiers who are "tradesmen," for almost 50 percent are in low-skill, combat-related occupations, and another 20 percent are engaged in "labor-intensive" occupations also requiring only a low-skill level and providing only minimal trade training.

Finally, consider the 1968 rank distribution figures—overall and "colored"—in the infantry and the Royal Electrical and Mechanical Engineers (REME), two army corps that are functionally distinct, to see whether the "conventional wisdom" of military sociology deals adequately with the "social facts" of the situation as it existed in 1968. Now, the conventional wisdom tells us that we should expect that (a) both the overall and colored rank distribution in the infantry should reflect a "pyramid" shape, and the REME distribution should be slightly skewed above the lowest ranks, and (b) under the assumption of equiproportionality, overall and colored rank distribution should be similar in both the infantry and REME, unless some factor is intervening to prevent this from occurring. In fact, the equiproportionality in rank distribution in REME for colored personnel would result from the technical nature of that service branch, which involves a more "bureaucraticlike" rank structure, that is, opening up more middle-ranking positions, and thus more opportunities for colored personnel to fill them. The actual and colored rank distribution patterns for both infantry and REME are presented in table 15, which also gives the difference between the actual and colored percentages and that which would have been expected under the equiproportionality assumption.[75]

As can be read from the table itself, there are differences between expected and actual rank distribution figures for colored personnel in both cases, but they are more significant in REME, in spite of the conventional wisdom that indicated in this case, they would have more chances for advancement, all things being equal. But since only 6.3 percent of colored personnel were in REME in 1968, this in itself reflects a situation where all things may not have been that "equal."[76]

Racial tension in the British army and discrimination against colored soldiers is documented in a number of reports in both the press and official publications. On 21 November 1972, for example, the London *Daily Mail* reported that friction between white and colored soldiers caused a brawl outside the Post Exchange (NAAFI) at the Tidworth military camp—one of the largest in England—in which a number of men were injured and seven colored soldiers of the Queen's Regiment arrested and charged. The defense correspondent of the *Daily Mail* cited the fact that the British army was very worried about the situation of race relations in the army in general and was also concerned about the fact that the disturbance involved members of the Queen's Regiment, which had the largest "black contingent" in British army regiments, numbering more than 100 colored soldiers out of a total of 1,800, or 8 percent of the regiment. The *Mail* report, which was entitled "The Colour Clash That Shook the Army," also cited the fact that some regiments, like the Queen's, were "blacker" than others, since they recruited from areas of high immigrant concentration. With regard to discrimination against colored soldiers in uniform, the *Bulletin of the British Race Relations Board* reported the case of one Private Seaforth of the Royal Green Jackets Regiment, who, while undergoing training before being posted to Ulster, found himself with a free evening in April 1973 and decided to have a "night out" at the Hammersmith Dance Palais. Seaforth, who was born in the West Indies, but had lived in the United Kingdom since the age of eleven, got as far as the door, but according to the *Race Relations Board* "was allowed no further." Colored soldiers, it seems, were fit for service in Ulster, but not for dancing in Hammersmith. In any event, even the presence of colored soldiers side by side with white soldiers in the British army in Ulster, where they are targets of the mobs in particular, has not improved the image the British have of colored immigrants in general.[77]

The words of Enoch Powell at Eastbourne in 1968 seem to reflect the feeling that even the new generation of black British are neither "kith nor kin": "The West Indian or Asian does not by being born in England become an Englishman. In law he becomes a United Kingdom citizen by birth; in fact he is a West Indian or Asian still." If this is the case, one shouldn't expect the new commonwealth immigrants or their children to "queue up" in large numbers in the future to join the H. M. Forces. Indeed, as C. Eric Lincoln noted fifteen years ago in writing about the color problem in Britain, the overriding issue that may affect their future military participation "is whether the Anglo-Saxon with all his social and political sophistication can learn to live comfortably with diversity.''[78]

NOTES

1. For a good history of the "black presence" in the United Kingdom, see J. Walvin, *Black and White: The Negro and English Society* (London: Allen Lane, 1973). On the problem of enumeration distinctions, see, for example, D. Kramer, "White versus Colored in Britain," *Social Research*, 36, 4 (1969).

2. On these points, see Walvin, *Black and White*; A. B. Ellis, *History of the First West India Regiment* (London: Chapman and Hall, 1885); J. E. Caulfield, *One Hundred Years History of the Second Battallion of the West India Regiment* (London: Forster Groom and Co., 1899); C. Lloyd, *The British Seaman: 1200-1860* (London: Collins, 1968), p. 165; C. L. Joseph, "The British West Indies Regiment: 1914-18," *Journal of Caribbean History* 2 (1971); W. F. Elkins, "A Source of Black Nationalism in the Caribbean: The Revolt of the British West Indies Regiment at Taranto, Italy," *Science and Society* 34, 1 (1970); M. Crowder, "West Africa and the 1914-18 War," *Bulletin de l'Institute Francaise Afrique Noir* 30, 1 (1968). As for the Indian case, see S. Cohen, *The Indian Army* (Berkeley: University of California Press, 1971); and J. Fortescue, *History of the British Army* (London: Macmillan, 1899-1927); idem, *Military History* (Cambridge: Cambridge University Press, 1914). See also E. E. Sabben-Clare, "African Troops in Asia," *African Affairs* 44, 177 (1945); and D. H. Barber, *Africans in Khaki* (London: Edinburgh House Press, 1948), pp. 19-20, 33; W. Gutteridge, *Military Institutions and Power in the New States* (London: Pall Mall, 1964), p. 75.

3. C. Hamshere, *The British in the Caribbean* (London: Wiedenfeld and Nicholson, 1972), p. 199, and references cited above.

4. M. E. Chamberlain, *Britain and India: The Interaction of Two Peoples* (London: David and Charles, 1974), pp. 81, 90. See also S. Cohen, *The Indian Army*.

5. P. Mason, *A Matter of Honour* (London: Cape, 1974). See also his transcribed talk on the Indian Army as published in *The Listener*, 20 June 1974, pp. 805-6.

6. P. Mason, *A Matter of Honour;* and idem, *The Listener;* W. Gutteridge, *Military Institutions,* p. 71.

7. C. Hamshere, *The British in the Caribbean;* Ellis, *History of the First*

West India Regiment, pp. 1-25. See also S. C. Davis, *Reservoirs of Men: A History of the Black Troops in French West Africa* (Geneva: Kundig, 1934).

8. M. E. Chamberlain, *Britain and India*, pp. 90ff.

9. P. Mason, *A Matter of Honour*; S. Cohen, *The Indian Army*; W. Gutteridge, *Military Institutions*, p. 72.

10. M. E. Chamberlain, *Britain and India*, pp. 89-90ff.

11. Ibid., pp. 159-60; P. Mason, *A Matter of Honour.*

12. M. E. Chamberlain, *Britain and India,* pp. 128-30, 170-71.

13. H. J. Hanham, "Religion and Nationality in the Mid-Victorian Army," in M. R. D. Foot, ed., *War and Society* (London: Paul Elek, 1973), pp. 159-81.

14. Ibid., pp. 165-66.

15. Ibid., pp. 174-75.

16. C. L. Joseph, "The British West Indies Regiment."

17. W. Golant, *The Long Afternoon: British India, 1601-1947* (London: Hamish Hamilton, 1975), pp. 105, 155; M. Banton, "The Changing Position of the Negro in Britain," *Phylon* 14, 1 (1953), p. 78; C. L. Joseph, "The British West Indies Regiment"; J. Walvin, *Black and White*, ch. 13.

18. J. Walvin, *Black and White*, pp. 206-7.

19. C. L. Joseph, "The British West Indies Regiment"; W. F. Elkins, "A Source of Black Nationalism in the Caribbean"; J. Walvin, *Black and White,* p. 205.

20. C. L. Joseph, "The British West Indies Regiment," pp. 104, 118-19; J. Walvin, *Black and White.*

21. D. S. Stephens, "Our Million Black Army," *The English Review* 22 (Oct. 1916), pp. 353-60; C. L. Joseph, "The British West Indies Regiment," pp. 122-23; J. Walvin, *Black and White*; S. C. Davis, *Reservoirs of Men.*

22. A. Vagts, *A History of Militarism* (London: Hollis and Carter, 1959); R. Challener, *The French Theory of the Nation in Arms* (New York: Columbia University Press, 1955), p. 80; S. C. Davis, *Reservoirs of Men*; and idem, *The French War Machine* (London: Allen and Unwin, 1937).

23. R. Bidwell, *Morocco under Colonial Rule* (London: Cass, 1973), pp. 294ff.; M. D. Lewis, "One Hundred Million Frenchmen: The 'Assimilation' Theory in French Colonial Policy," *Comparative Studies in Society and History* 4, 2 (1961), pp. 129ff.

24. *Sunday Times Magazine*, 17 March 1974, p. 34.

25. A. Vagts, *A History of Militarism,* p. 252.

26. N. Angell, "France and the Black Power," *Contemporary Review*

121 (1922), pp. 226-29; L. H. Gann and P. Duignan, *Burden of Empire* (London: Pall Mall, 1968), p. 213.

27. J. F. W. Allen, "An African Army: Some Possibilities," *Journal of the Royal United Services Institution* 58 (1918), pp. 657-63.

28. P. Mason, *A Matter of Honour.*

29. For a discussion of the pattern of recruiting in 1914-1918, see *Times History of World War I* (London). See also R. G. Gregory *India and East Africa: A History of Race Relations within the British Empire, 1890-1939* (Oxford: Oxford University Press, 1971), ch. 5, pp. 148ff. However, the number of Indians killed in action and wounded was considerably less, in both relative and absolute terms, than the respective casualty rates in both the Canadian and Australian cases. In addition, the degree to which Indian war finance was indeed "voluntary" is dependent upon whether contributions by individuals or, for that matter, government appropriations are considered as having been freely given when the country itself was not even self-governing at the time.

30. H. Tinker, *A New System of Slavery: The Export of Indian Labour Overseas* (Oxford University Press, 1974).

31. R. G. Gregory, *India and East Africa*, pp. 148-50.

32. Ibid., pp. 150-51.

33. Ibid., p. 151.

34. Ibid., p. 155.

35. Ibid., pp. 156, 176.

36. J. M. Brown, "War and the Colonial Relationship: Britain, India, and the War of 1914-1918," in M. R. D. Foot, ed., *War and Society* (London: Paul Elek, 1973), pp. 85-106.

37. Ibid.; M. E. Chamberlain, *Britain and India,* p. 185; W. Golant, *The Long Afternoon*, p. 105.

38. O'Moore Creagh, *Indian Studies* (London: Hutchinson, 1919), pp. 274, 276.

39. See S. Cohen, *The Indian Army*; C. L. Joseph, "The British West Indies Regiment," pp. 103, 112-13, 119; M. Crowder, "West Africa and the 1914-18 War," p. 228; A. B. Ellis, *History of the First West India Regiment*; W. Golant, *The Long Afternoon,* p. 154; W. Gutteridge, "The Indianisation of the Indian Army 1918-45," *Race* 4, 2 (1963); V. Chirol, *India* (London: Ernest Benn, 1926), pp. 277-78; R. Craddock, *The Dilemma in India* (London: Constable, 1929). See also W. Gutteridge, *Military Institutions,* pp. 94-95.

40. W. Golant, *The Long Afternoon*, pp. 200ff.; P. Mason, *A Matter of Honour.*

41. W. Golant, *The Long Afternoon,* pp. 203ff., 211-12.

42. A. Haywood and F. A. S. Clarke, *History of the West African Frontier Force* (London: Gale and Polden, 1964), p. 470; W. Platt, "The East African Soldier," *The National Review* 126, 755 (1946), pp. 41-49; F. A. S. Clarke, "The West African Frontier Force," *Army Quarterly* 55, 1 (1947), pp. 58-73.

43. A. G. Russell, *Colour, Race, and Empire* (London: Kennikat Press, 1944/1973), p. 81.

44. C. R. A. Swynnerton, Commentary, *Army Quarterly* 61, 2 (Jan. 1951), pp. 234-35.

45. C. Hamshere, *The British in the Caribbean*, pp. 200-201.

46. J. Walvin, *Black and White*, p. 212; R. J. Macdonald, "Dr. H. A. Moody and the League of Coloured Peoples," *Race* 14, 3 (1973), pp. 300-301.

47. D. Glass, *London's Newcomers: The West Indian Migrants* (Cambridge: Harvard University Press, 1961), pp. 87, 105-6.

48. "Jim Crow" refers to the legal system of segregation prevalent in the United States before the 1960s.

49. On these points, see G. K. Lewis, "An Introductory Note to the Study of Race Relations in Britain," *Caribbean Studies* 11, 1 (1971), p. 5; A. H. Richmond, *Colour Prejudice in Britain* (London: Routledge and Kegan Paul, 1954); pp. 16, 20, 23; E. J. B. Rose et al., *Colour and Citizenship* (Oxford: Oxford University Press, 1969), p. 66; K. L. Little, *Negroes in Britain* (London: Routledge and Kegan Paul, 1947), p. 56.

50. W. Golant, *The Long Afternoon,* pp. 234-35.

51. C. Hamshere, *The British in the Caribbean,* pp. 200-201; C. A. Crocker, "Military Dependence: The Colonial Legacy," *Journal of Modern African Studies* 12, 2 (1974).

52. S. Collins, *Coloured Minorities* (London: Butterworth, 1957), p. 12; S. Allen and C. Smith, "Race and Ethnicity in Class Formation: A Comparison of West Indian and Asian Workers," in F. Parkin, ed., *The Social Analysis of Class Structure* (London: Tavistock, 1974), pp. 45-46ff. See also the *Times*, 21 Dec. 1968.

53. C. Peach, *West Indian Migration to Britain: A Social Geography* (Oxford: Oxford University Press, 1968), pp. 84-85.

54. Ibid.

55. See, for example, D. Hiro, *The Indian Family in Britain* (London: Community Relations Commission, 1967), p. 6; A. G. James, *Sikh Children in Britain* (Oxford: Oxford University Press, 1974); C. E. Lincoln, "The British Say They Aren't Prejudiced," *New York Times Magazine* 14 Nov. 1965.

56. A. G. James, *Sikh Children in Britain,* pp. 100-102.

57. B. Dahya, "Pakistanis in Britain: Transients or Settlers?" *Race* 14, 3 (1973), pp. 244ff.

58. K. L. Little, *Negroes in Britain*, p. 232; J. Rex and R. Moore, *Race, Community and Conflict* (Oxford: Oxford University Press, 1967), p. 109; K. Fitzherbert, *West Indian Children in London* (London: Bell, 1967), p. 52; D. Kramer, "White versus Coloured in Britain," pp. 589-90; G. K. Lewis, "Protest among the Immigrants: The Dilemma of Minority Culture," in B. Crick and W. Robson, eds., *Protest and Discontent* (London: Penguin, 1970), p. 89.

59. S. Patterson, *Immigration and Race Relations* (Oxford: Oxford University Press, 1969), p. 7; B. Davidson, *Black British* (Oxford: Oxford University Press, 1966), p. 31; E. J. B. Rose, *Colour and Citizenship*, p. 440; C. E. Lincoln, "The British Say They Aren't Prejudiced"; D. Glass, *London's Newcomers*, p. 4; J. Rex and R. Moore, *Race, Community and Conflict*, pp. 100, 156.

60. D. Glass, *London's Newcomers*, p. 109; L. Bloom, *The Social Psychology of Race Relations* (London: Allen and Unwin, 1971), p. 115; R. A. Schermerhorn, *Comparative Ethnic Relations* (New York: Random House, 1970), p. 113.

61. A. G. Russell, *Colour, Race, and Empire*. See also R. Fane, "The Return of the Soldier: East Africa," *Journal of Royal African Society* (1944); A. H. Richmond, *Colour Prejudice in Britain*, p. 24. *Caribbean* defined as British Guiana, Trinidad and Tobago, Jamaica, and other territories in "British Caribbean," *Census*, 1951 (England and Wales) (London: Her Majesty's Stationary Office, 1956); general tables 32, 33; occupation tables 1, 26 (1956).

62. A. J. Wilson, "Recruitment and Army Careers in the 1970's," *Brassey's Annual* (Defence Review) (1969), ch. 19, pp. 260-61ff.

63. A. Verrier, *An Army for the 1960's: A Study in National Policy* (London: Secker and Warburg, 1966), pp. 106-8.

64. On these points, see J. Walvin, *Black and White*, ch. 13; K. L. Little, *Negroes in Britain*, p. 56.

65. On instances of prejudice and discrimination, see, for example, K. K. Ghosh, *The Indian National Army* (Meerut: Asia Pub., 1969); C. L. Joseph, "The British West Indies Regiment." See also E. J. B. Rose, *Colour and Citizenship*, p. 305; B. Hepple, *Race, Jobs and the Law* (London: Penguin, 1968), p. 180.

66. The *Times* inquiry is supported by the 1968 occupational distribution of colored troops presented below.

67. Note that Healy referred to the ability of the Ministry of Defence "to

secure or *preserve* a *reasonable* balance of persons of different racial groups.'' What ''reasonable'' means, however, is a moot point in this context. On this issue, see the discussion below.

68. B. Hepple, *Race, Jobs and the Law*, p. 180, n. 4; E. J. Rose, *Colour and Citizenship*, p. 305; S. Patterson, *Immigration and Race Relations*, p. 189; A. Lester and G. Bindman, *Race and Law* (London: Longmans, 1972), p. 221.

69. Balniel to Lane, D/MIN/RB/1742, in my possession (original), dated 31 October 1972.

70. See, for example, the *Times*, 17 Nov. 1972; S. Patterson, *Dark Strangers* (London: Penguin, 1965), p. 82; W. V. Webb, ''A Model of Defence Manpower Availability,'' in I. M. B. Wilson, *Manpower Research* (London: English Universities Press, 1969), p. 164; Letter from John Pitt-Brooke, Defence Secretariat 14 (D/DS14/102/2/VI) 3 Sept. 1980. Brooke stated that the figures provided to me in December 1972 by the then head of DS14, D. H. Bennison, ''are among the last such records produced in this Department,'' and therefore the Ministry of Defence cannot provide ''any further information on this topic.''

71. The RAF and navy did not collect such figures; E. J. B. Rose, *Colour and Citizensip*, pp. 305-6.

72. The tables are calculated from figures provided to me by the Ministry of Defence, in a letter of 18 Dec. 1972 from D. H. Bennison, Head of Defence Secretariat 14 (D/DS14/122/12). In the case of ''% Expected,'' this is the equivalent percentage of noncolored by rank. As for the ''Expected Rank at Beginning of Period,'' this is adapted from J. C. M. Baynes, *The Soldier in Modern Society* (London: Eyre Methuen, 1972), pp. 151-52.

73. See, for example, N. Deakin, *Colour, Citizenship, and British Society* (London: Panther, 1970), p. 201.

74. Compiled from Ministry of Defence figures cited above. Occupational categories have been listed according to U.S. Department of Defense ''one-digit'' military occupational specialty-occupational work areas for military personnel. Due to the fact that British data provided only arm/corps of ''colored'' personnel in the army, the following adaptation was made: infantry, gun crews, and so on includes those in the infantry, Pioneer Corps, Armoured Corps, and Royal Artillery; electronics equipment, communications, and intelligence specialists includes those in the Royal Signals and Intelligence Corps; medical and dental specialists include those in the Royal Army Medical Corps; other technical specialists and so on includes those in the Royal Engineers; administrative specialists

includes those in the Royal Army Pay Corps; electrical/mechanical equipment repairmen and craftsmen include those in the Royal Electrical and Mechanical Engineers; service and supply handlers includes those in the Army Catering Corps, Royal Ordnance, and Corps of Transport. Note that colored personnel were to be found *only* in the arm/corps listed above, and thus no other branches are included in the work-area adaptation. The British army, however, makes the distinction between "tradesman" and "nontradesman." In this case, 59 percent of "colored" personnel were tradesmen, as against 41 percent who were "nontradesmen."

75. For the "conventional wisdom," see, for example, M. Janowitz, *The Professional Soldier* (New York: Free Press, 1964); K. Lang, "Technology and Career Management in the Military Establishment," in M. Janowitz, ed., *The New Military* (New York: Sage, 1964).

76. See discussion on occupational "channeling" above.

77. *Daily Mail*, 21 November 1972, p. 6; *Race Relations,* Winter 1974.

78. C. E. Lincoln, "The British Say They Aren't Prejudiced."

5

UNITED STATES

DIMENSIONS OF THE UNITED STATES SITUATION: HISTORICAL, DEMOGRAPHIC, MILITARY

In his West India emancipation speech in 1857, Frederick Douglass, the noted United States Negro publicist and orator, declared that,

The whole history of the progress of human liberty shows that all concessions yet made to her august claims have been born of earnest struggle. . . . Power concedes nothing without a demand. It never did and it never will. Find out just what any people will quietly submit to and you have found out the exact measure of injustice and wrong which will be imposed upon them, and these will continue till they are resisted with either words or blows, or both. The limits of tyrants are prescribed by the endurance of those whom they oppress.[1]

One hundred years later, his descendants were still engaged in a struggle to achieve both equal justice and equal opportunity, to share in the American dream and power structure. In only a few spheres of American institutional life were opportunities open to the Negro. One of these was the military. Whether one walks through the Kassernes of West Germany or the camp towns of the southern United States, one readily notices large number of "blacks" in khaki. If one can say that since 1945, at least, the black community in the United States has taken its history into its own hands, then, insofar as blacks have participated in all wars America ever fought, serving even before independence, it could also be said that one of the most crucial facets of this history has been, and still is, military participation.

We can distinguish four main phases in the relationship between the Negro and the American military. The first of these phases encompasses the period of independence and civil war, extending through the era of expansion and "manifest destiny." The second phase sees America's emergence as a "world power" in World War I and the period between the wars. The third phase includes United States participation in World War II and Korea, when its global role is firmly established. The fourth phase deals with the post-Korean situation, intervention in Vietnam, and its aftermath as seen in the introduction of a volunteer army.

FROM INDEPENDENCE TO MANIFEST DESTINY

Negro military participation, and exclusion, in North America did not begin with the Revolution. Even before this, Negroes served in, and were then excluded from, various colonial militias. The earliest use of Negro manpower actually occurred in Virginia, when after 1619 Negroes helped in defense against Indian attacks. By 1636, however, they were exempted from service there, but were required, in the same year, to enlist in the Massachusetts militia. The Dutch also used Negro manpower against the Indians, but fears of slave uprisings in Virginia and cooperation between "armed" Negroes and Indians in Connecticut caused their exclusion from the militia there. In other states, however, such as Rhode Island and even South Carolina, slaves were trained and armed. As for free Negroes, the colonists feared their possible instigation of slave uprisings, and thus they were relegated to noncombat positions in the militia, such as labor or service roles.[2]

With the increasing conflict between France and England, manpower pressures also increased on the colonies, which were required to fill quotas set by the British, and thus the use of Negro manpower was necessitated. The Negroes welcomed this as an opportunity to improve their position, either as a chance to gain freedom, if they were slaves, or as an extension of citizenship for the free Negro, and they were not hesitant to join the militias. Negroes thus participated in all "colonial wars" fought in North

America between 1689 and 1763, playing a significant role in the French and Indian War (1755-1763) on the British side on both land and sea. In the course of their participation, there was no segregation or differential treatment. The Negroes fought alongside whites and received equal pay, and slaves who distinguished themselves in military service were usually manumitted.[3]

Although during the first few weeks of the Revolution Negroes were used, by the end of 1775, black soldiers were excluded from both state militias and the "continental" army. However, manpower pressures grew on both state and continental forces, so that by 1777-1778 Negroes were again enlisted by both state and continental armies, generally being inducted into the latter. At first, the southern states did not enlist Negroes; however, they were requested to use their slaves as soldiers when the manpower situation became grave in 1779. The British also saw the slaves as a potential source of manpower and invited them to leave their American masters and join the British forces. There was a large response among slaves in the South, alarming the Americans, who took steps to prevent slaves from joining the British.[4]

These measures succeeded only partially, and large numbers of slaves made their way to British lines, serving as laborers for the most part. At the end of the war, when the British were preparing their evacuation, those Negroes who had gone over to the British intended leaving with them. The Americans demanded the return of their slaves, but the British objected, and the former slaves eventually left with them. Of the 8,000 to 10,000 Negroes who served in the American Continental Army, some 5,000 saw combat, participating in most major battles of the war and also serving as pilots in the navy of the new United States.[5]

However, the United States was considered by its inhabitants to be a "white man's country," and congressional legislation during this period confirmed this popular notion. Congress passed a law in 1790, for example, limiting alien naturalization to whites, and in 1792 it restricted militia enrollment to whites; in 1810 it even restricted carrying the mail to whites only. In addition, states whose constitutions limited the legal rights of Negroes were repeatedly admitted to the Union. As Leon Litwack noted, "on the basis of such legislation, it would appear that Congress had resolved to treat Negroes neither as citizens nor as aliens." The anomalous legal position of the Negro also extended to military participation. Thus although Negroes were barred from the militia, there were no legal barriers to their service in the army, navy, or marines early in the period. For example, the 1792 Militia Act had the effect of barring Negro military participation, although the 1790 Army Act did not restrict Negro voluntary enlistment—if they were "freedmen"—in the regular army. But since military organization was based mainly on the militia system, Negroes were effectively prevented from participating in the military. In addition, as Mary Berry observed, since all able-bodied male citizens were compelled to do service in the militia, such a policy "indicated the non-recognition of the Negro's right to be regarded as a citizen and a human being." The 1792 act, it should be noted, was not repealed until 1862.[6]

By 1798, however, directives were issued prohibiting Negroes from enlisting in the marines or serving in the navy. Again, manpower needs prevailed, and Negroes in both the navy and marines during the period of naval confrontation with France (1798-1800) and the war of 1812 served with distinction. Indeed, one-quarter of the men who served under the noted American naval commander Perry in the 1812 war were Negro, and Perry even wrote, "I have yet to learn that the colour of a man's skin . . . can affect a man's qualifications or usefulness." Most naval commanders were well satisfied with their Negro seamen, since, in Perry's words, they were "absolutely insensible to danger." On the land, a manpower shortage forced Andrew Jackson to call for black recruits, appealing to their patriotism and promising equal wages and land bounties, but proposing their formation into a separate battalion or regiment. Still, Negroes willingly volunteered and served in Jackson's forces against the British at the Battle of New Orleans. In 1820, however, a general order was issued that stated, "No Negro or Mulatto will be received as a recruit of the Army."[7]

A number of issues were raised by Negro military participation during this period, the most important of which involved the question of whether Negroes could qualify for the land bounties that were promised to veterans of the 1812 war. The attorney-general ruled in 1823 that they were entitled to land grants, but he added that "it was not the intention of Congress to incorporate Negroes and people of Color with the Army any more than with the militia of the United States." By 1842 the southern senator Calhoun attempted to "clarify" the policy toward Negro military participation, and the United States Senate passed a measure excluding Negroes from both the army and the navy, but a similar bill was not passed by the House of Representatives. In any case, as T. D. Philips noted, before the Civil War, the regimental structure of the U.S. Army enabled prospective servicemen to enlist directly into the regiment of their choice, but this did not apply to Negroes, since by law whites couldn't be assigned to colored regiments and vice-versa.[8]

At the very beginning of the Civil War, Negroes were not accepted by the Union for military service, although the statutes governing the regular army did not restrict their enlistment. War Department policy, however, was one of Negro exclusion. A number of other considerations also entered the equation, such as Lincoln's desire not to alienate the white population in the "border states" and the opposition of many federal officers to the use of colored troops. Thus although Negroes strongly wanted to participate in the war effort, feeling that the war could provide the chance to eliminate slavery and discrimination, they were turned away. Manpower pressures soon changed Northern attitudes, along with the realization that while the South was using black labor in agriculture and other sectors, freeing whites to fight, the North was not efficiently using its black manpower.[9]

After an initial high rate of volunteer enlistment, and a reluctance to implement general conscription, manpower shortages built up, and the Militia Act of 1862 was passed, which also provided for the use of Negro troops in the states' militia, the act having the effect of a draft, if a state's quota was not voluntarily filled. However, even this policy was unsuccessful due to the inefficiency of state procurement machinery, and national conscription was introduced in 1863.[10]

The outcome of the national conscription act was, in fact, the general induction of Negroes and a more effective claim, on their part, to recognition as citizens, while Lincoln's Emancipation Proclamation explicitly sanctioned military levies on Negroes. The response of hard-pressed governors of Northern states, who found it hard to fill the quotas, was immediate since, due to the fact that the Negro population of the North was small relative to that of the South, they had to send recruiting agents to those territories in the South captured by the Union. But the state agents found themselves in competition with recruiting agents of the federal government. In March 1863, the secretary of war authorized the recruitment of Negro brigades in the Mississippi Valley. Finally, in May 1863, the "Bureau of Colored Troops" was set up to organize Negro units and examine officer candidates for them.[11]

With the signing of the Conscription Act in March 1863, Lincoln fully committed himself to the use of Negro troops in all capacities and not just in static defense roles. He even referred to this "great available and yet unavailed force for restoring the Union." Of course, it was obvious to Lincoln that if the administration expected the white population to accept compulsory military service, Negroes would also have to be drafted. In fact, when the draft actually began in the summer of 1863, a number of serious riots directed against Negroes occurred. These incidents were the result of the opposition of white northerners to a war to emancipate black slaves who might then come North and compete for their jobs.[12]

Although Negroes who had tried to enlist were rejected at the start of the war, now that the war was for Negro freedom, they would, in fact, be compelled to serve. This was indicated by the lack of a racial clause in the conscription act showing the government's intention to use every available source of manpower. What was important for the Negro, however, was that the act's implementation provided them with a greater claim to citizenship rights. This was due to the fact that, as Berry noted, the provisions of the act referred to "able bodied citizens, and if Negroes were drafted under its provisions, then no one could deny that they were citizens." Although the Negro was now eligible to serve in the Union army and, as noted above, was actively recruited by both state and federal authorities, an unequal pay policy had a serious effect on Negro morale. When they enlisted, they were promised equal treatment, for, as Berry observed, "they enlisted in the first place because men were called for, and because the government signified its willingness to accept them as men." In truth, the 1862 Militia Act enabled the War Department to pay Negroes less, since it specifically referred to the use of Negro troops in garrisons and labor battalions, and thus no "combat" bonus was paid to Negroes when they enlisted. This, however, should have applied only to militia service and not to the regular army. Efforts made to equalize pay, therefore, may be seen as a method by which to recruit more Negroes, in the place of whites. Negro soldiers' protests regarding unequal pay were supported by a number of prominent Northerners, but it wasn't until the Army Appropriation Act of 1864 that pay equalization was legislated.[13]

As a result of the passage of the Confiscation Act in July 1862, slaves from the border states were also drafted, since the act stipulated that all Negroes between the ages of twenty and twenty-five were to be considered as liable to the draft and part of the national manpower pool. One incentive to increase the enlistment of slaves in the border states was the passage of a bill, before the Emancipation Proclamation, providing for the freeing of their relatives. Still, the feeling was prevalent that manumitted slaves could not be turned into good soldiers, since they couldn't be subjected to the discipline necessary in the military. General Sherman thought Negroes to be unequal to whites, advocating their use only as pioneers, servants, or for garrison duties, and thus he did not use them for skirmishes and picket duty since, in his view, this would involve individual initiative, and Sherman stated, "Negroes are not equal to this."[14]

Now, of the 186,000 colored troops in the northern army, only 2,500 were killed or died of their wounds. In commenting on their role in the Civil War, Francis Lord stated that "the employment of Negroes was a political measure, but their presence was resented by both sides, while their contribution on the battlefield was of little value." In fact, federal Negro troops who were captured by the South while their contribution on the battlefield was of little value." In fact, federal Negro troops who were captured by the South received much harsher treatment than their white counterparts. The southerners justified this differential treatment by claiming that Negroes were captured property, and not prisoners of war, or that those federal Negro soldiers who were former slaves were in a state of rebellion against their southern masters and thus would be dealt with as rebels. This policy was reflected in the massacre of Northern black soldiers and civilians—including women and children—by Confederate forces at Fort Pillow. The massacre was eventually condemned by an official inquiry, but no measures were ever taken against the officers responsible.[15]

In the South, manpower pressures had resulted in calls for Negro "freedmen" to serve in the Southern ranks as early as March 1862, especially in Louisiana, where there was a significant community of "free" Negroes, who, in fact, responded enthusiastically, at least according to Southern accounts. As for the slaves, they were used both in labor gangs or impressed into military construction projects, with due payments to their owners, and were also regarded as the "Army of the Soil," whose task it was to grow and harvest the food for feeding the Confederate army. By 1864 the South's manpower problem was so great that calls developed within the military itself for the arming of the Negro slaves. This was, however, turned down by the Confederate high command.[16]

But in February 1865 Lee himself had decided that it would be necessary to use even the slaves as soldiers, and he thus proposed the freeing of those so employed. The Confederate Congress eventually passed legislation to this effect, even suggesting equal pay and rations for black and white troops. It was, however, a completely futile effort, for within two months of Lee's original proposal, the South had capitulated. It may be interesting to recall here the reaction of one Confederate officer to the original 1864 idea of arming the slaves: "I will not attempt to describe my feelings on being confronted with a proposal so startling in its character, so revolting to Southern sentiment, Southern pride and Southern honor. . . . If this thing is once openly proposed to the Army, the disintegration of the Army will follow in a fortnight."[17]

All in all, some 186,000 Negroes served in the Union army as combat troops, with more than 200,000 participating in service units. Some 100,000 of the combat troops were drafted by the Federal government, with the rest coming through states' militias. Over 45,000 Negro troops were obtained from captured Southern territories. Negroes also comprised some 25 percent of the Union navy, and Negro troops participated in some 200 battles and skirmishes during the war. As many observers have noted, however, the relationship between the military and the Negro here was not one-sided, since service in the Union army, at least, did result, in some cases, in basic literacy training being obtained by the black soldier recruited in the North or the newly freed slave.[18]

After the Civil War, Congress authorized the retention of Negro soldiers in four segregated regiments only, two infantry and two cavalry. Negroes served throughout the frontier conflicts with the Indians subsequent to 1865 and, in fact, participated in the last skirmish between the U.S. Army and renegade Indians in January 1918. Over the period of service in the West, Negroes participated in both combat roles and labor-construction services, but mostly were engaged in garrison and escort duty.[19]

The attitude of the black community during the American "quest for empire" at the end of the nineteenth century was, at first, as it had been during the Civil War, that is, a mixture of both patriotism and self-interest, approaching the problem mainly in terms of justice toward their own people. During the Spanish-American War, Negroes served in both the Cuban and Philippine campaigns, although in segregated regiments and subject to segregated facilities en route. Indeed, as Willard Gatewood noted, the War Department thought Negro troops to be especially suitable for Caribbean service since they were more "immune" to diseases of the tropics than whites.[20]

But despite the fears expressed by some Negroes that they would bear the brunt of losses during the war, the response that prevailed among both the Negro community and Negro servicemen was positive, at least initially, toward this, the first chance for the Negro to obtain recognition of their military contribution and prove their loyalty since obtaining citizenship by means of the Fourteenth Amendment to the Constitution in 1868. Indeed, in Gatewood's view, "For the black man to oppose either the war or territorial expansion was likely to play into the hands of those bent on nullifying the 14th and 15th (equal rights) amendments. Hence many black Americans rationalized that the loyalty and patriotism of their race were on trial."[21]

Politicization of participation in this instance concerned the issue of black officers for the separate Negro regiments. In addition, the stationing of Negro soldiers in military camps in the South aroused southern resentment and gave rise to numerous racial incidents and a number of riots. As for their combat service in Cuba, opinions differed. Theodore Roosevelt claimed that black soldiers had a tendency to "drift to the war," but many others praised their contribution, especially after the battle of Santiago. However, according to Gatewood:

Even before the signing of the treaty ending the war with Spain, black Americans had begun to alter their view regarding expansion. . . . The war had multiplied the black man's grievances rather than, as some predicted, overcoming them. Few Negroes were misled by the patronizing praise lavished upon black troops in the wake of the Santiago campaign. Such praise was both brief and illusory; it became readily obvious that the black man's role in the war had done little to eradicate prejudice at home.[22]

The effort of the United States to put down the Philippine insurrection that followed about a year after the American conquest was, however, opposed by many Negroes, who saw it as an independence movement paralleling their own struggle for equal rights. According to Gatewood, Negro opposition to United States policy in the Philippines was so intense that the War Department was unsure whether to send black volunteers there. However, they didn't doubt that Negro regular army regiments, since they were, it seems, better indoctrinated and trained than their civilian based counterparts. All four regular Negro regiments were shipped to the Philippines, and in 1899 President McKinley, to appease hostile attitudes in the Negro community, authorized that in the two volunteer units that were to be formed, the officers should be obtained from among Negroes who had served with distinction in

Cuba. The response to McKinley's efforts, however, was only "lukewarm," although the regiments were eventually formed and shipped to the Philippines. The effect of the anti-imperialist attitudes of the Negro community, however, was reflected in the unusually high black desertion rate from these units.[23]

The presidential election campaign of 1900 saw the Negro community split between supporting the imperialist policies of McKinley's Republican party, on the one hand—which most Negroes had supported from the time voting rights were granted to them by the Fifteenth Amendment to the Constitution, since it was Lincoln's party—or backing the ostensibly anti-imperialist Democrat William Jennings Bryan. Some in the Negro community were also incensed at the vice-presidential candidate on the Republican side, Theodore Roosevelt, who, as noted above, had deprecated the Negroes' military contribution in Cuba. But despite this, most Negroes voted Republican, since they were not willing or able to vote for a Democratic party also composed of a large segment of Southern racist politicians. After McKinley's reelection, the volume of Negro protest against United States policy in the Philippines quieted, with their attention now being directed at the increase in racial incidents and violence directed against Negroes in the United States itself.[24]

In the period between the Spanish-American War and World War I, two incidents occurred that were to affect the future course of Negro military participation. The first of these incidents took place during an action against Mexican bandits, when black troopers of the Tenth Cavalry Regiment panicked and fled while under attack. The official unsatisfactory judgement of their performance was, however, to be further reinforced by certain incidents that occurred during World War I itself. The second, and more serious, incident took place in 1906, when black soldiers became involved in large-scale racial conflict. The details of the "Brownsville incident" are not discussed here, but the incident took place as a direct result of discriminatory behavior on the part of both the townspeople and police in the Texas town and the violent reaction to it on the part of black soldiers. When the offenders' counterparts refused to turn them over to the military police, all members of their companies—167 men in all, including officers—were dishonorably discharged, forfeiting all benefits

and pension rights automatically. But the memory of Brownsville lingered on, in both the army's collective view of Negro
soldiers and in the mind of the black community. The men
were only officially cleared of wrongdoing by the army sixty-five
years later, in 1971.[25]

WORLD WAR I AND THE PERIOD BETWEEN THE WARS

The large-scale movement of Negroes from the rural South, and
agricultural employment, into the urban, industrial North that
started at the turn of the century had already led to both Negro
concentration in urban areas, and the start of ghettos, on the one
hand, and an increase in political power, on the other hand. Early
in this period, some Negroes saw even the segregated military
as a way out of rural squalor or urban blight. Thus, as Lee noted,
"The Negro regiments were filled to capacity—and remained so.
Re-enlistments on the day following discharge, or within 20 days
for non-commissioned officers, were regularly high. The Negro
units lost few men through normal discharges. Even before World
War I these regiments had a high percentage of career soldiers;
during the period of reductions nearly all men of these regiments
were professional soldiers. Vacancies (and promotions) became
rarities in most Negro units."[26]

At the outbreak of war in Europe in 1914, the Negro community
was, in the main, indifferent, although Negro intellectuals were
favorably disposed towards the French cause, but only due to the
liberal French attitude as regards color problems. By 1917,
however, most blacks sympathized with the Allied cause, but,
again, they saw the war in broader terms, that is, relating to
their own problem. Thus, W.E.B. Du Bois claimed that, "This
war is an End, and, also a Beginning. Never again will darker
people of the world occupy just the place they have before." In
fact, most Negro leaders backed the feelings expressed by the
annual report for 1916 of the NAACP, which stated that, "If
thousands of American black men do fight in this world
war . . . then who can hold from them the freedom that
should be theirs in the end?" But as Jane and Harry Scheiber

observed, "throughout the war, [President] Wilson was unwilling to make any formal statement that would seem to ally him with black leaders—perhaps because to do so would identify him with their demands for racial equality as *quid pro quo* for their wartime efforts." The war did lift certain restrictions on the Negro in the civilian sector, but for the most part, segregation remained the rule.[27]

In military terms, the manpower aspect of the relationship between the military establishment and the Negro may be seen in the global statistics of Negro participation during the war. Although they constituted only 10.7 percent of the United States population, 13.1 percent of all draftees were Negroes. All told, some 350,000 Negroes served during the war, half went to France and 40,000 belonged to units that served at the front. On the other hand, Negro units formed 106 of the 213 labor battalions extant. In short, Negroes, who comprised one-tenth of the United States population, constituted one-eighth of its military strength during the war, one-third of the military laborers, but only one-thirtieth of its combat forces.[28]

In addition, when the United States entered the war, there was no officer training program for Negroes. However, after a good deal of protest from both the NAACP and Negro colleges, a training program was instituted. The War Department expected it to fail, but it didn't. Still, during the war there were only some 1,400 Negro officers, comprising only 0.7 percent of the total officer corps. This resulted, in fact, from a restriction placed on the number of Negro officers to be commissioned at field rank. Furthermore, in the Negro regiments themselves, many Negro officers were removed and replaced by whites, the reason being that the military thought Negroes would respond more readily and be better commanded by white officers. Thus all senior officers in both "all-Negro" divisions, the Ninety-second and Ninety-third, were white. As for these divisions themselves, they were never trained or sent on maneuvers as complete units, and the Ninety-third was never fully assembled; rather, its component regiments were transferred to the French army, under the aegis of which they compiled a distinguished combat record that was, however, never officially recognized by the United States military establishment.[29]

The Negro's move northwards, resulting from the demand for labor in the war industries, also brought in its wake increased racial conflict in the North. The summer of 1917 saw a series of racial clashes in many major northern cities, with the worst incident taking place in East St. Louis, Illinois. Racial tensions developed during 1916 as a result of labor troubles and the use of black migrants in strikebreaking. In May of 1917, mob violence directed against the Negro community erupted, lasting four days and resulting in many deaths and injuries, with over $3,000,000 in property damages suffered by the black community. The response of the black community was both shock and anger, but it also manifested itself a month afterwards, when black soldiers rioted in Houston, Texas.[30]

The riot erupted when soldiers of the Twenty-fourth Infantry Regiment, a "regular" black unit, resented the tight enforcement of "Jim Crow" laws by Houston residents and police, insisting that dignity be accorded to them as members of the U.S. Army. Arrests of black soldiers followed, and in late August, when a black soldier attempted to stop a policeman from assaulting a Negro woman, he was also beaten and arrested. When a member of the regiment's military police arrived to inquire about the soldier's whereabouts, his manner was found "offensive" by the police, and he was also beaten and arrested. Although he was released soon afterwards, a rumor spread throught the regiment's camp that he had been killed. That evening, soldiers from one company broke into an ammunition tent, stole guns, and marched on the city. On the way, they met some whites and clashed with them. By the time they reached the town, armed civilians and police were waiting. There was an exchange of fire, and two blacks were killed, but seventeen whites, among them five policemen, were also killed. White soldiers were immediately sent to the city, and the regiment's men were disarmed.

Over the next month 156 men were court-martialed for "mutiny." At the first trial, which occurred in December 1917, 63 soldiers were tried. Thirteen were given the death sentence, 41 were given life imprisonment, 4 were sentenced to shorter terms, and only 5 were acquitted. The 13 were hung one week after sentencing, before an appeal could be made on their behalf to the army's judge advocate general. In later trials, 16 more blacks were condemned to death, with many more given life sentences. Because of the swift execution of the original 13 the black community reacted strongly, with the result that the army provost marshal declared that no future death sentence could be carried out until after review and presidential approval. Thus in 1918 President Wilson, acting on the recommendation of the secretary of war, commuted the death sentence of 10 of the men, but the other 6 were executed. However, even the secretary of war had to advise the president that Houston's strict enforcement of "Jim Crow" laws was the real reason for the incident.[31]

The performance of Negro troops overseas was affected to a great extent by the conflict between the white commander of the "all-Negro" Ninety-second Division and his direct commander, who was in charge of the American Second Army, of which the division was a part. This was recently revealed in the study of black American troops in World War I entitled *The Unknown Soldiers*, by Arthur Barbeau and Florette Henri. Lt. Gen. R. L. Bullard, the commander of the Second Army, was a Southerner and in the view of all observers, a racist, this being reflected in both his attitude toward the Ninety-second Division and the blatantly racist reports regarding its behavior that he submitted to the War Department. Maj. Gen. C. C. Ballou, the commander of the Ninety-second Division, on the other hand, although favorably oriented toward the idea of using Negro troops, was still affected by the prevalent racial attitudes and policies of the War Department and eventually lost the confidence of the men that served under him. After the war, upon the request of the War Department, Ballou submitted a report on the performance of his division. As a result of various incidents of poor combat performance on the part of some Negro troops, the outcome of poorer leadership of their white officers and, in the worst such case, the panic and hysteria of one white officer in particular, he wrote, "I forgot that the average Negro is a rank coward in the dark, and I subsequently realized to the full how worthless this trait renders him in the service of security and information." The War Department, by the time of receiving Ballou's report in 1920, was almost convinced that the use of Negro troops was of dubious military value, and with Ballou's report, their "self-fulfilling" prophecy was confirmed, as the report was deemed to be the considered judgment of one who had been in direct command of Negro troops and thus had observed their performance closely.[32]

Finally, then, it is interesting to observe the attitude change that occurred in the black community from the time of the "Close Ranks" editorial written by W. E. B. du Bois in the NAACP's journal *Crisis*, which supported the Allied cause and the Negro's participation in the war effort, urging him to take part actively, and the editorial he wrote after the parade of returning Negro soldiers up New York's Fifth Avenue. In his "Close Ranks" editorial, he wrote:

We of the colored race have no ordinary interest in the outcome. That which the German power represents today spells death to the aspirations of Negroes and all darker peoples for equality, freedom, and democracy. Let us not hesitate. Let us, while this war lasts, forget our special grievances and close out ranks shoulder to shoulder with our own white fellow citizens and the allied nations that are fighting for democracy. We make no ordinary sacrifice, but we make it gladly and willingly with our eyes lifted to the hills.[33]

This appeared in the *Crisis* issue of July 1918. By May 1919, however, du Bois had changed his views, writing, in his editorial "Returning Soldiers,"

We return. We return from fighting. We return fighting. Make way for Democracy! We saved it in France, and by the Great Jehovah, we will save it in the United States of America, or know the reason why.

Almost immediately after the war, the army staff began to formulate a definite policy regarding Negro manpower, since many in the military establishment thought the lack of one was the main reason for the difficulties encountered during the war with regard to procurement and utilization. Although there was to be no change in the policy of segregation and job exclusion, the army planners still had the use of Negro manpower in wartime very much in mind. They were, in fact, faced with a problem. On the one hand, they thought the Negro troops to be unreliable under combat conditions. But on the other hand, on the basis of past experience, if combat losses were to be as high in any future conflict, and borne *exclusively* by whites, there would be much resentment among the families of those killed or injured. However, although long-range military manpower planning was initiated by the army at this time, the army planners proved to be both poor historians and economic forecasters. They both forgot the demand of the war industries for labor at the close of World War I and failed to foresee the manpower demands of another *global* war, as their forecasts later showed. For example, a study made for the army chief of staff in November 1922 "concluded that Negroes must be used in combat as well as in service units . . . that Negro officers should be used, but no Negro officer should be put in a position where he could command white troops."[34]

On 30 October 1925, however, a document was submitted to the army's chief of staff by the Army War College. This was entitled "The Use of Negro Manpower in War." It was considered the most complete study made on the issue. It was, however, based largely on questionnaires given to the white officers of Negro troops. No additional study, however, was made regarding the opinions of the Negro soldiers regarding their white officers. The study, made by field-grade officers, many of whom were to play leading roles in World War II, was in the opinion of all observers since then one of the most racist documents ever to be submitted to the military establishment, since most of its authors were southerners. In any event, its recommendations were to become army policy for the next fifteen years. Among its conclusions were that, "As an individual the Negro is . . . careless, shiftless, irresponsible, and secretive, unmoral, untruthful, and his sense of right doing is relatively inferior." In the light of such an assessment, it is hardly surprising that the imposition of quotas, restrictions, and even exclusion from military service followed. In effect, then, what resulted from the chain of reports starting with Ballou and ending with the War College document was the propagation and constant repetition of a racial mythology, directly influencing the attitudes of officers with little or no combat experience themselves and determining all policy and future practices of the army.[35]

Thus the situation in the interval between the wars was one of continued racial prejudice culminating in the decision of the War Department on 17 June 1931 officially to prohibit enlistment, reenlistment, or promotion of Negroes in the army. Before this decision, the army had followed the policy originally formulated in July 1866, that is, quota and fixed units. For three years, then, the existing Negro regiments were maintained at minimal strength. Even after enlistments were resumed in 1934, there was little room in the Negro regiments for new recruits, since enlistments could be accepted only if a vacancy occurred, so a Negro who wanted to enlist could not simply appear at a recruiting station and be taken in. He had to find out where Negro units were stationed and where vacancies existed, apply to the officer in charge of the unit where he wanted to serve, and present himself at the post at his own expense after enlistment was approved. The reason the army gave for adopting this policy was that it had no money to transport Negroes from, say, the East Coast to Arizona, where the Twenty-fifth Infantry, for example, was stationed. Thus few Negroes went beyond initial inquiries at the local recruiting station. With regard to the status of Negro strength in the regular army, there was little change. The total strength of the army and National Guard in 1937 was 360,000, of whom Negroes totaled 6,500, or about 1.8 percent.[36]

On the eve of World War II, the position of the War Department regarding the use of Negro troops was, then, basically, that they would be mobilized in proportion to their percentage of the national manpower of military age; that they would be mobilized earlier than whites to be able to train them adequately, since their training, in the War Department's view, would take a longer than normal period; and that their numbers in the military should be about 9 percent. This quota limit was, as seen above, never reached in the interwar period and only slightly exceeded during World War II itself. This resulted, in the main, from the objections of officers commanding arms and services in the military who opposed Negro entry into their branches. These objections can be traced to World War I and its legacy, as manifest in the chain of negatively oriented reports on Negro soldiers.[37]

WORLD WAR II AND KOREA

Differences in opinion in the military regarding the utilization of Negro manpower appeared before American entry into World War II. Ulysses Lee, for example, noted the refusal of the Signal Corps to accept Negroes on the grounds that there were no "properly qualified" Negroes to be found. Although the Organization and Training Division (G-3) agreed with the exclusion of Negro trainees in both the Air and Signal Corps, the Personnel Division (G-1) disagreed, noting that "the use of Negroes . . . must be predicated upon the actual availability of personnel with the required qualifications rather than upon any arbitrary elimination of the Negro as a whole on the grounds of lack of technical capacity." But the army establishment alone wasn't guilty of blatant racist attitudes and thought. Secretary of War Henry L. Stimson (in charge of the army) noted Negro demands for the "right to fight," in return for their political support for Roosevelt, in his diary entry of 22 October 1940, as follows: "The Negroes are taking advantage of this period just before (the) election to try everything they can in the way of recognition from the Army." Although Stimson himself emphasized his Northern-conservative-abolitionist "moral strength" in approaching the problems of the relationship between the army and the Negro, it was his statements and policy decisions that reinforced those of the hard-core racist officers below him, if they weren't, out of Stimson's lack of interest in the subject, prepared by those officers themselves. For example, later in the war, in February 1944, when Congressman Hamilton Fish—who himself was in command of Negro soldiers during World War I—asked Stimson about reports that the fully trained and equipped Negro Twenty-fourth Infantry was engaged in only labor duties in the South Pacific for almost two years, Stimson replied, in a letter actually drafted and sent by his military assistants, in the following terms: "It so happens that a relatively large percentage of the Negroes inducted by the Army have fallen within lower educational qualifications, and many Negro units accordingly have been unable to master efficiently the techniques of modern weapons." Richard Dalfiume cited Stimson as an example of the extent to which "racist assumptions existed within the Army and dictated its Negro policy."[38]

Channeling, in the form of job exclusion, was planned for use regarding Negro troops throughout World War II by the army general staff. Dalfiume, for example, noted mobilization plans that "provided for the exclusive use of coloured troops in labor units" and showed the thinking from which such plans resulted: "There is general consensus of opinion that coloured units are inferior to the performance of white troops except for service duties . . . due to the inherent psychology of the colored race and their need for leadership." This memo was, in fact, from the then assistant chief of staff of the army, Eisenhower, to the army chief of staff.[39]

Differences in army intelligence test (AGCT) scores were also used to justify job exclusion. The AGCT was supposedly designed to "indicate the ability to absorb training." The grade categories ran from 1 (highest) to 5 (lowest), with the expected percentage distribution pattern following a normal population distribution curve, with its midpoint at grade 3. Grades 1, 2, and 3 were expected to produce leadership cadre, technicians, and specialists, and grades 4 and 5 were expected to produce laborers and semiskilled soldiers. Scores of white inductees generally fit the expected pattern, and those of Negroes were skewed towards grades 4 and 5, with over 80 percent of them falling within those grades. Now, although lower AGCT scores were concentrated among Negroes, it was the policy of segregation that concentrated Negroes of low AGCT scores. Thus although military planners had set a limit of 10 percent grade 5 men per unit, because beyond this they deemed it impossible for the unit to operate effectively, Negro units were in trouble from the start, since between 80 and 90 percent of their troops fell in AGCT categories 4 and 5. It was well known that most of the Negroes who scored low on the AGCT, as well as most of the whites, were from the South. This, of course, only resulted from conditions in the region. Eli Ginzburg and Douglas Bray noted in their book *The Uneducated* that not only did this region allocate relatively less of its expenditure for education as compared to other areas in the United States, but these funds were also maldistributed by the existence of a segregated educational system, and that there was a significant correlation between expenditures on education and rejection from military service. Dalfiume observed, however, that this was not taken into account by the army when interpreting AGCT scores, and that it was prevalent in the army to refer to them as intelligence indices, although they actually measured educational background. In fact, Negroes and whites of similar educational background achieved similar scores. Thus, as Dalfiume continued, from this mistaken interpretation, the postulate was derived

that *all* Negroes were innately inferior in intelligence, and this allowed Army planners to use the unfavourable scores to justify restrictive practices in the use of Negro manpower. For example, in late 1941, the Army had adopted more rigid literacy standards "mainly" to reduce the number of Negroes the Army had to induct. But, Secretary Stimson saw this as "reacting badly in preventing us from getting some very good and illiterate (white) recruits from Southern mountain states." White illiterates, it was somehow reasoned, were superior to Negro illiterates.[40]

The belief that "white illiterates" from the South made better soldiers derived, of course, from the Confederate military mystique.

The concentration of low AGCT personnel in Negro units due to segregation resulted in the emergence of self-fulfilling hypotheses. The legacy of World War I reports and the belief in Negro inferiority closed the vicious circle. Again, units of the "all-Negro" Ninety-second Division came under attack for "melting away in panic in the face of the enemy" during the Italian campaign in June 1944. Warman Welliver, however, in his 1946 "Report on the Negro Soldier" in *Harper's Magazine*, cited the observations of a former white officer in the Ninety-second Division. The officer remarked that most of his colleagues believed that "colored troops cannot fight . . . they are all or almost all cowards, or inept, or both." The echo of white officers in World War I was still quite strong. The Fahy Committee, which recommended the desegregation of the army in 1948, noted the gap between army policy and practice regarding Negro troops. It stated that although "every study of Negro manpower utilization which was conducted by the Army War College between the wars recommended that the Army never again form Negro units of divisional size" (that is, concentrate Negroes of low AGCT scores), "despite these recommendations and contrary to the assurance which the Army gave to the Selective Service that Negro divisions would not be formed, the 92nd and 93rd divisions were reactivated in World War II." The Ninety-second and Ninety-third divisions were, as noted above, "all Negro," except for most of their officers.

In two important articles in the *Journal of American History* dealing with Negro protest, race relations, and interracial conflict during World War II, both Harvard Sitkoff and Lee Finkle dealt with the developments leading to the 1943 racial disturbances in both the civilian sector, where they reached major proportions, and the military itself. Sitkoff actually claimed that the war itself "stimulated racial militancy, which in turn led to increased interracial violence that culminated in the bloody summer of 1943." Directives issued by the War Department regarding *on-base* desegregation of certain facilities such as post exchanges (PXs), transportation, and motion picture theatres, regardless of local custom, especially in the South, served to lessen tensions somewhat; however, the continuing discrimination that affected black soldiers in the South still resulted in riots such as those at Camp Van Dorn and Camp Stewart, among many other incidents. In the navy, racial disturbances also occurred in San Francisco and Guam. The magnitude of disturbances in the civilian sector in New York and especially Detroit during the summer of 1943 was the outcome of growing interracial tension that had started with the residual effects of the Depression and the competition between black and white workers for housing and other amenities in the areas of concentration of war industries and had proceeded through the "zoot-suit" riot in Los Angeles, which occurred in June 1943—only a week before the Detroit race riot. The sordid details of the Detroit riot are not analyzed here, but according to Sitkoff, the final toll of this riot was 34 people killed, 25 of whom were Negroes, with more than 700 people injured. In addition, over $2,000,000 worth of property was damaged and, perhaps more important, some 100 million hours of war production were lost.[41]

Still, manpower needs during the war did cause some policy changes. From recommending that "Negro troops be dispatched to an active theater of operations at an early date" in July 1943 since "in the opinion of the McCloy Committee, such action would be the most effective means of reducing tension among Negro troops," Assistant Secretary of War John J. McCloy "experienced a change of thinking on the Negro problem," stating on 29 February 1944 that "it is a vital national policy to make a military asset out of that part of the population." The manpower needs created by the German offensive at Bastogne even caused a senior military officer, Lt. Gen. John Lee, Eisenhower's commander of service forces, to propose that Negro volunteers be trained to fight in white units, assigning them "without regard to color or race to the units where assistance is most needed," adding, in a circular letter to be sent to Negro troops, "and give you the opportunity of fighting shoulder to shoulder to bring about victory." However, this proposal evoked strong protest from other military officers such as that of Eisenhower's chief of staff, Lt. Gen. Walter Bedell Smith, who advised Eisenhower that,

Although I am somewhat out of touch with the War Department's Negro policy, I did, as you know, handle this during the time I was with Gen. Marshall (Army Chief of Staff). Unless there has been a radical change, the sentence which I have marked in the above circular will place the War Department in very grave difficulties. It is inevitable that this statement will get out, and equally inevitable that every Negro organization, pressure group, and newspaper will take the attitude that, while the War Department segregates colored troops into organizations of their own against the desires of all the Negro race, the Army is perfectly willing to put them in units with white soldiers when an emergency arises.[42]

The document General Lee prepared was never circulated. Eisenhower was persuaded by Smith, but the manpower crisis still resulted in the fact that some military commanders pledged Negro volunteers for other organizational needs. However, by early March 1944, both Stimson and McCloy had decided that "we must settle on a policy which will use this great asset of colored men of the nation in a more effective way," so by the Battle of Bastogne, the two Negro divisions were ready for combat assignments, which they duly received.[43]

Thus, as Dalfiume suggested, "from viewing the Negro as a problem, some had come to recognition that Negro manpower was an asset that had not been fully realized." As John McCloy put it in a letter of 22 August 1945 to the then secretary of the navy (and future secretary of defense), Forrestal, "it had always seemed to me that we never put enough thought into the matter of making a real military asset out of the very large cadres of Negro personnel we receive from the country." Notwithstanding the successful combat performance of Negro air combat units such as the 332nd Fighter Wing, as noted above, questions about the performance of Negro troops in combat were again raised during World War II. The Negro, in fact, was only "proven in combat" when he served in "integrated" units at the very end of the war, when small Negro squads were attached to larger white units after the Battle of the Bulge, although this time, the World War II experience was soon forgotten after the war's end.[44]

Despite the liberal direction of the New Deal, for example, in the form of the Fair Employment Practices Commission (FEPC), and even Roosevelt's position vis-à-vis civil rights, it was Malcolm X who best summarized the position of the Negro in the World War II period both eloquently and succinctly:

Around that time, 1939, or '40, or '41, they weren't drafting Negroes in the Army or the Navy. . . . They wouldn't take a black man in the Navy except to make him a cook . . . this is what they thought of you and me in those days. . . .

When the Negro leaders saw all the white fellows being drafted and taken into the Army and dying on the battlefield, and no Negroes were dying because they weren't being drafted, the Negro leaders came up and said "We've got to die too. We want to be drafted too, and we demand that you take us in there and let us die for our country too. . . ."

So they started drafting Negro soldiers then, and started letting Negroes get into the Navy. . . . But not until Hitler and Tojo . . . were strong enough to put pressure on this country, so that it had its back to the wall and needed us, (did) they let us work in factories; I'm talking about the North as well as the South.[45]

After World War II, the "manpower approach" was not only advocated by bureaucrats such as McCloy. The fall 1947 *Journal of Social Issues* contained articles by Arnold Rose on "Army Policies Towards Negro Soldiers: A Report on a Success and a Failure" and Roy K. Davenport on "The Negro in the Army: A Subject of Research," which the editor of the journal claimed "should properly be considered a pair. Though separated in space, certainly out of communication, both are unmistakably interested in a question of policy, the maximal utilization of the nation's manpower resources, and both are concerned about the welfare of minority group members in the Army." Rose put it more succinctly: "one may say that the Army cannot be expected to solve a problem which the nation itself cannot solve. But the Army's problem is far simpler than the nation's; it is only to make the most effective use of manpower." Davenport, as the editor of the *Journal* noted above, echoed this feeling. Rose collaborated with Gunnar Myrdal on the 1944 work *An American Dilemma*, the most important work published on race relations in the United States until then, and is the author of later significant works such as *The Negro's Morale*, a direct "spin-off" of the earlier work. Arguments by "liberals" such as Rose based on the "manpower approach," however, did not seem to affect army thinking very much at the time. It was only a "forcing of the Army's hand" by the Fahy committee combined with the manpower needs of the Korean War, both coming about within a changing civil-military relationship in the form of the emergence of the Department of Defense, that changed army policy.[46]

Although the process of rapid demobilization in the immediate post-World War II period affected servicemen of both races, the Negro was somewhat less eager to return to civilian life than his white counterpart. As Samuel Stouffer noted in *The American Soldier*,

perhaps the most compelling indication that Negroes believed that life in the Army was not so bad for colored men in comparison with civilian life lies in the statistics of volunteer enlistments at the end of the war. In the first six months after the war's close (Sept. 1945-Feb. 1946), over 17% of the men who signed up voluntarily were Negroes, although Negroes constituted under 11% of the male population 18 to 37. This proportion continued to rise and at one time, in July 1946, it was announced in the press that persuant to Army policy of including Negro troops in about their population proportion, Negro enlistments were being temporarily halted.[47]

The military services were still segregated, although some advances in on-base living conditions for Negro servicemen had been made during the war, involving some desegregation of on-base facilites. However, the very fact that the Negro saw even the segregated military as providing him with better opportunities and economic security was not a reflection on the merits of the military but of the failures of American society as a whole.[48]

Although the Fahy Committee, which was set up at the behest of Truman to investigate the possibility of military desegregation and eventually provided the basis on which the Truman Desegregation Order of 1948 was predicated, also persuaded the army to abolish its racial quota by April 1950, there was constant pressure from the army general staff to have it reinstated due to the big increase in Negro enlistments. Dalfiume noted that these had been only 8.2 percent of the total in March 1950, but when the quota was abolished, they increased to 22.0 percent the next month. Now, the problem was that the Negro units in the army were geared only to take a maximum of 10 percent overall Negro manpower. Thus the only way the army was able to keep segregation with an increased number of Negro soldiers was to maintain Negro units at overstrength, that is, placing more Negroes in "Negro" units than was required in the organizational table for the respective unit. However, this answer was difficult to justify in view of the white units that were short of personnel at the time. To solve the problem, the Personnel Division (G-1) of the army general staff asked that the quota be reimposed in September 1950, with more Negro units being established to absorb Negro overstrength. This was, however, subsequently denied by the army secretary who, by then, was subordinate to the secretary of defense.[49]

The implementation of the Truman desegregation order became the responsibility of Louis Johnson, the second secretary of defense. This occurred only a short time after the final amalgamation of the service departments into the National Military Establishment as manifest in the Department of Defense. The individual secretaries of the services, who had previously been members of the president's cabinet, were now subordinate to the defense secretary, who was the only cabinet representative of the new department. Johnson was convinced by the arguments of the Fahy Committee report and intended to implement the Desegregation Order in full, but also realized that it would take time for the integration process itself, as against the ending of the segregation policy, due to "bureacratic inertia." Thus he ordered a "gradual" ending of racial separation. But even these orders were not initially implemented, since they had to pass through the hands of the army secretary, Kenneth Royall, who adhered to the view of the army chief of staff, Bradley, that they were too radical. Royall proposed even more watered down plans, but Johnson turned them down. Royall was then replaced as army secretary, being succeeded by Gordon Gray. Gray was successful in getting the army to propose an integration plan on 1 October 1949 that was acceptable to both Johnson and the Fahy Committee, which was still meeting. It was surprising, to some observers, that the Fahy Committee and Johnson accepted them; however, Gray wasn't even able to carry out these limited measures, since later that month, he discovered an army general staff order countermanding his proposals. Thus in November he restated the same order, this time making sure that they weren't rescinded by the generals. In summary, then, Gray, as Royall before him, found the generals' racialist views to prevail over the army department rather than being subservient to the policy of the civilians who were supposed to be in control.[50]

Outside the military, armed forces integration did little to change American society, although Kenneth Clark, for example, did use the military experience to support his writings advocating desegregation in the schools that were used in the arguments producing the *Brown* vs. *Board of Education* decision of the Supreme Court eventually ending "separate but equal" in education. Thomas Pettigrew pointed out that in the South, white veterans tended to show more tolerance regarding race than southern white civilians. But all in all, the consequences of the complete integration of the armed forces by the end of the Korean War, although improving the lot of the Negro in military service, hardly affected his condition outside of it.[51]

In February 1951, however, a board of three generals was set up with the aim of considering what would be the most effective way of using Negro manpower in light of the process of integration that was then taking place in Korea. The board (later called after its chairman, Lieutenant General Chamberlin) accepted statements obtained from integrated combat units indicating that the integration policy was proceeding successfully and that Negro-white tension was actually decreasing. They had reservations, however, regarding the continuing absence of a racial quota and the concomitant increasing number of Negroes in the army. They were afraid that the increasing number of Negroes in the army could not be absorbed successfully and that the increasing number of poorly educated blacks could significantly affect the operational effectiveness of combat units, reducing their combat efficiency accordingly. The board concluded, therefore, that the racial quota should be reimposed and that those units still segregated should remain so. By the end of the Korean War, however, the quota issue had disappeared, inasmuch as the army accepted the conclusions of Project CLEAR, which assessed the results of the integration experience in Korea as significantly positive. This indicated that where integration was tried, army units were shown to be able to be composed of between 15 and 20 percent Negro personnel without any loss in efficiency; rather, the opposite was the case: the more integrated the Negro soldier, the better he performed his task, and so on regarding Negro units mixed with white units in a de facto form of integration, justifying the complete integration of the army's organizational structure.[52]

Before the reluctant acceptance by the army of the Fahy Committee proposals for effective desegregation of that organization, the job exclusion practices noted above remained, even after Executive Order 9981 was issued in 1948. For example, as Dalfiume noted,

Under the prevailing procedures . . . a Negro soldier could enroll in an Army school course only if there was an opening waiting for his specialty in a black unit. Since only a comparatively small number of all-Negro units existed and they were of a limited type, many qualified Negro soldiers were not allowed to pursue their interests or aptitudes. Of 106 Army courses open to recruits in April 1949, only 21 were open to Negroes.[53]

By the end of the Korean war, as noted above, the army had made progress to virtual integration. On 1 January 1954, only some 10,000 Negroes out of a total of 250,000 were serving in segregated units. The Pentagon Civil Rights Counselor, James Evans, however, was able to announce that no all-Negro units remained only on 31 October 1954.[54]

THE POST-KOREAN ERA AND VIETNAM

With the complete integration of the military and elimination of job exclusion by 1954, the beginning of a trend had been set. Negro first term reenlistment rates tended to increase until, by the 1960s, they were almost double that of white servicemen. Both the desire for economic security and widening career opppportunities strengthened the trend. The Negro community was hit relatively harder than the white community in the recurrent periods of economic recession over the Eisenhower administration. Although the economic situation of the Negro improved over the 1950s, in general, equal employment opportunity was denied to him. The once productive and intellectually fruitful black neighborhoods turned into poverty-ridden and neglected ghettos. The relationship between the black community and the white community deteriorated as the gap between Negro aspiration and expectation widened. In the same year that the complete integration of the military was implemented, the landmark *Brown* vs. *Topeka* decision was handed down by the Supreme Court. The anti-Jim Crow demonstrations in Montgomery in 1955, the rise of the Black Muslim movement from 1956 onwards, and the Little Rock riots in 1957 gave further impetus to the struggle for equal rights in the civilian sector. The quickened pace of violent demonstrations in Mississippi and Alabama in late 1962 and 1963 accelerated action on civil rights programs in the military, where problems regarding off-base segregation began to emerge. Thus President Kennedy appointed a committee in mid-1962 to deal with these and related issues, which affected equal opportunity of Negro military personnel. The committee's terms of reference also included personnel problems in the military itself, and it made recommendations along these lines accordingly.[55]

The Gesell Committee report, submitted in 1963, directed that it was the responsibility of local military commanders to ensure that equal opportunity in housing off-base was provided to all servicemen and their families, in addition to the provision of equality in all off-base facilities approved for the use of servicemen. Kennedy was impressed by the conclusions of the report and, in a letter to then Secretary of Defense McNamara, wrote:

As the report emphasizes, a serious morale problem is created for Negro military personnel when various forms of segregation and discrimination exist in communities neighboring military bases. Discriminatory practices are morally wrong wherever they occur—they are especially inequitable and iniquitous when they inconvenience and embarrass those serving in the Armed Services and their families. Responsible citizens of all races in these communities should work together to open up public accommodations and housing for Negro military personnel and their dependents. This effort is required by interests of our national defense, national policy, and basic considerations of human decency.[56]

Within a month, McNamara made a strongly worded policy statement supporting the president, which was sent to commanders of every military installation:

Our military effectiveness is unquestionably reduced as a result of civilian racial discrimination against men in uniform. The Committee Report has made this point with great clarity. With equal clarity it demonstrates that the Department of Defense has in the past only imperfectly recognized the harm flowing from off-base discrimination. That imperfect recognition has in turn meant the lack of a program giving rise to the conditions giving rise to the harm.[57]

McNamara told the base commanders that detailed directives were under preparation that made clear that they were responsible regarding the provision of equal opportunity for their servicemen off-base. He also hinted that, if necessary, sanctions would be taken against local accommodation facilities that discriminated against Negro personnel, saying that "certainly, the damage to military effectiveness from off-base discrimination is not less than that caused by off-base vice, as to which the off-limits sanction is quite customary." To oversee the new Department of Defense policy, a new office was created, that of the deputy assistant secretary for civil rights and industrial relations, which was also supposed to implement policy set down during the Eisenhower administration regarding discrimination by industrial suppliers of the defense department.[58]

The defense department acted quickly after this, issuing orders to base commanders, directing them to assist families of servicemen in their units to enter nonsegregated schools. Other directives ordered commanders to cooperate with private citizens groups seeking open occupancy and adequate housing for the families of Negro personnel, not to take part in educational programs at segregated schools, and to prohibit military personnel and units from participating in segregated events, such as fairs and displays. This followed from the conclusions of the Gesell report regarding the role of the local military commander in implementing equal opportunity programs:

The record of base commanders in dealing with such problems has not been impressive. Their failure in this regard stems from a number of causes. . . . As a group they do not believe that problems of racial discrimination in the local community should be their concern. . . . Base commanders express this view in various ways: That the authority of the base commander ends at the gate, that it is not part of his job to rearrange the social order, that it is not part of the military mission to change community attitudes, that any pressure would be misunderstood and merely stir up trouble, that questions of this kind should be left to the courts, that military personnel are traditionally non-political and should not involve themselves in controversial questions. . . . Thus, a different concept of the base commander's functions in the racial field must be evolved.[59]

The Johnson administration continued to press for the implementation of McNamara's directives, which, by then, were also supported by the enactment of the 1964 Civil Rights Act, and with the escalation of the Vietnam War in 1965, manpower needs grew to the extent that Negroes were being drafted out of proportion to their percentage of the population. They also began to suffer disproportionate combat casualties and deaths. Increased tension in the civilian sector affected the attitude of the Negro community toward black participation in the Vietnam War, but black servicemen still continued to reenlist at rates far greater than whites. New programs were instituted such as Project 100,000, which provided for basic education of badly needed manpower that had to be procured from draftees who were previously rejected due to their low level of education or illiteracy, the majority of whom were Negroes.[60]

Now, it is the consensus of most observers that the effect of integration in the United States armed forces has been significant. The manpower aspect of the integration process has shown that "the military," *at the enlisted level, at least*, "has become a major avenue of career mobility for many Negro men." Although the enlistment rates for qualified Negroes and whites were about equal, the difference in their first-term reenlistment rates—with Negroes, until recently, reenlisting at about twice the rate for whites—had led the U.S. Civil Rights Commission to conclude by 1963 that "Negro servicemen believe on balance that the armed forces offer them greater career opportunities than they can find in the civilian economy . . . (as) Negro enlisted men enjoy relatively better opportunities in the Armed Forces than in the civilian economy in every clerical, technical, and skilled field for which the data permit comparison." Career opportunity was not all, however; economic security motivated and still may motivate the high rate of Negro reenlistment. In the critical age group of twenty to twenty-four year olds, Negro unemployment has consistently been almost twice that of whites, reflecting the overall two to one Negro-white unemployment ratio that has characterized the post-Korean War era, since, in 1954, the post-World War II "boom" seemingly ended for Negroes, the very year in which the Supreme Court overturned "separate but equal" in education and in which the armed forces completed their integration. Seen in terms of dollars and cents, then, the bonus for a first-term reenlistment or even airborne hazardous duty pay would be appealing to a youth who had nothing to look forward to when he got out of service. Thus the overrepresentation of blacks in the marines and airborne enlisted and NCO ranks from the early Vietnam period until the end of that conflict is not surprising.[61]

RECENT TRENDS IN AND PARAMETERS OF NEGRO MILITARY PARTICIPATION

The degree to which upward mobility has actually been attained by Negroes, both in and as a result of military service, must be assessed in light of recent studies that show wide gaps between perception and relative mobility patterns by race. Defense department data show, for example, fundamental differences in white-black promotion patterns among enlisted men in general and NCOs in particular, even, in the former case, when controlling for those factors that would tend to influence promotion patterns (for example, length of service, military occupation, AFQT scores [aptitude tests]). Interestingly enough, although the NCO data are based on 1969 personnel records, a survey undertaken in 1969 independent of defense department sponsorship showed that Negro NCOs recognize inequities in promotion patterns whereas their white counterparts (and some outside observers) do not.[62]

Furthermore, although some may argue that military service and technical training obtained during service contributes to upward mobility in general and mobility for Negroes in particular, again, recent studies show that this is not necessarily the case. What these studies do show is that although some mobility is attained in the first instance by Negroes after release from first-term active duty, for example, the skills they have acquired are not sufficient to maintain any sustained degree of upward mobility in terms of occupation and income level achieved over both the medium term and the long run, if they are able to use military acquired skills at all. Thus the appeal of a service career to one "resocialized" in a military setting, where to some degree, one is at least "treated like a person" and not a "Negro" as such, cannot be overlooked; the argument being that in the civilian sector of the United States, the black has been socialized into "Negritude."[63]

In effect, then, the process model is as follows: Negroes can and have attained a degree of upward mobility while in military service. Inability to translate service experiences into mobility in the civilian sector, however, may be due to either (a) general labor-market discrimination and general economic and employment conditions (for example, the "last hired-first fired" phenomenon, recession, or unemployment), or (b) failure to convert or transfer military acquired skills and thus "slot into" the civilian job market, due to either the nature of the skills acquired (for example, combat occupations) or supply-demand factors influencing the market for those skills in the presence of the general factors mentioned in (a), thus resulting in little or no mobility in occupational or income terms that can be attributable to military service itself or training received while in service. What this implies is that long-term mobility prospects for Negroes are either static or downwards directed upon leaving military service, whereas the opposite is true if the Negro remains in service, provided his on-the-job performance is adequate, or, in other words, at the enlisted level at least, once "in," it may pay to "stay in."[64]

On the other hand, if mobility can be and has been attained by Negroes in military service, why has a "race-relations crisis" developed in the United States armed forces, an institution that had prided itself, after a complete attitude reversal on its part, on being in "advance" of the civilian sector in racial matters? Could this be because in "fighting on two fronts" again during the most recent conflict, the Vietnam War, the "home front" proved to be much more relevant to the Negro community than the outcome of the war itself? (This, in addition to the opposition to the war on the part of both the established black leaders such as Martin Luther King, Malcolm X, and many others and the radical black leadership.) Developments in race relations in American society in general and in the new "all-volunteer" armed forces in particular should answer these questions in due course. However, Negro objections to fighting "white men's wars" abroad while being subject to racism at home are inexorably bound up with a developing attitude that it is not that the military is "so good" but that the job prospects in civilian society are "so bad" that it makes the military "look good" in comparison—the result of a survey undertaken among Negro servicemen recently. In other words, the attitude is now being taken by a growing number of Negroes that, how, in the final analysis, can one serve in defense of a society when that society still denies equal opportunity for all?[65]

Now, the issues of (a) Negro officers, (b) the effect of the introduction of an "all-volunteer" armed forces (that is, Volunteer Army—*VOLAR*—and elimination of the draft system and "draft pressure") on the nature and extent of minority-group participation in military service, and (c) the role of Negro women in the armed forces must also be dealt with. With regard to (a), consider again the point made above, that "the military," *at the enlisted ranks*, "has become a major avenue of career mobility for many

Negro men." This idea deserves more emphasis than was given by its author, Charles Moskos, a prominent observer of the race problem and the United States military in general. Although the Negro enlisted man, if he is not job channeled, does to some degree compete with his white counterpart on "equal" footing (the preponderance of Negro servicemen find themselves in combat occupations, due to their low level of educational achievement, that is, they are "channeled" into combat-related jobs), the Negro officer faces special problems, both as regards his advancement within the military and his transition to civilian employment after retirement or separation from military service (similar problems are also faced, however, by the retiring or separated Negro career enlisted man). As another observer noted, "the emphasis on academic education for officer careers effectively limits most Negro opportunity to the enlisted levels," not to mention the problems faced by the Negro officer already commissioned. Some of these problems include, for example, assignment to service schools, war colleges, and staff commands. This observer noted, furthermore, that "admission of Negroes on an equal basis with whites is of recent origin, so that most Negroes lack the seniority for advancement." Now, if the seniority system also holds for assignment to the service schools and war colleges, and if "attending these schools is important not merely for the education received there but because it is here that one meets contemporaries who may sit on future promotion boards, the social experience rather than the learning aspects" making Negro acceptance to these schools important for their military advancement, another vicious circle is completed. The Negro officer does not have the required seniority; therefore he is passed over for attendance at the service schools and war colleges and assignment to staff commands; as career advancement hinges on these factors, the Negro officer simply "stays" where he is.[66]

As for the participation of Negro women, table 18 shows their growing participation in all service branches at all levels. Data on their occupational distribution show a high concentration in nursing and allied health fields, that is, medical and dental specialties. (Tables 16-21 show various aspects of Negro participation in the armed forces.)

Table 16

*Negroes in the Armed Forces and Each Service as a
Percentage of Total Personnel, Selected Years*

YEAR	TOTAL ARMED FORCES	ARMY	AIR FORCE	NAVY	MARINE CORPS
1949	5.9%	8.6%	4.5%	4.0%	1.9%
1954	7.9	11.3	7.5	3.2	5.9
1962	8.3	11.3	7.8	4.7	7.0
1966	9.1	11.3	9.1	4.6	8.7
1970	9.8	12.1	10.0	4.8	10.2
1972	11.9	15.6	11.1	6.5	14.2
1976	14.8	21.3	12.6	7.2	15.7
1980	19.3	29.3	13.9	10.0	19.9

Table 17

*Negroes as a Percentage of Officer and Enlisted Personnel for Each
Service, Selected Years*

	1945	1949	1954	1962	1966	1970	1972	1976	1980[a]
Officers									
Army } Air force }	0.7%	1.9% 0.6	2.9% 1.1	3.3% 1.2	3.5% 1.2	3.4% 1.7	3.9% 1.8	5.2% 2.8	7.2% 4.4
Navy	b	b	0.1	0.3	0.3	0.7	1.0	1.6	2.4
Marines	n.a.	b	0.1	0.2	0.6	1.3	1.7	3.4	3.9
Enlisted Personnel									
Army } Air force }	10.3%	11.1% 6.1	12.3% 8.6	12.3% 9.2	12.4% 10.4	13.5% 11.7	17.5% 13.0	23.7% 14.7	32.5% 15.9
Navy	4.8	4.4	3.6	5.2	5.1	5.4	7.2	8.0	11.0
Marines	n.a.	2.5	6.5	7.7	9.4	11.2	15.8	17.0	21.7

Note: n.a. = not available.
[a] March 1980.
[b] Less than 0.5 percent.

The VOLAR problem has been the subject of much ongoing
controversy in the United States, and a review of the arguments
still produces no consensus. The views range from the creation of
a "mercenary army" composed of a high proportion of blacks, to

Table 18

Female Negro Participation in the Armed Forces, Percentage of Total Female Personnel by Service, Selected Years

SERVICE	1966	1970	1976	1980[a]
Army				
Total	10.7%	13.7%	20.5%	34.0%
Officer	4.8	3.3	5.4	11.6
Enlisted	13.8	18.2	22.1	36.7
Navy				
Total	3.9	5.3	8.9	12.4
Officer	0.9	1.4	3.2	4.3
Enlisted	5.6	7.3	10.0	13.7
Marines				
Total	7.1	14.0	16.6	20.7
Officer	0.0	1.7	4.4	3.6
Enlisted	8.3	15.8	18.1	22.1
Air Force				
Total	9.4	9.2	15.5	16.8
Officer	4.6	3.8	6.5	10.3
Enlisted	13.5	11.8	17.1	17.7
All Services				
Total	8.5	10.6	16.4	23.0
Officer	3.7	3.1	5.2	9.2
Enlisted	11.2	13.9	18.0	24.9

[a]March 1980.

the view that although short-term imbalance in black-white accessions will occur, in the long run, both demographic constraints and expansion of economic opportunities in the civilian sector will compete with the "attractiveness" of the new volunteer army, thus setting an upper "limit" in the long run on Negro participation. The key point to recognize here is just what constitutes an "unacceptable" or "undesirable" level of Negro participation in

Table 19

Negroes as a Percentage of Total Enlisted Personnel in the Army,
by Rank, Selected Years

RANK	1964	1968	1972	1976	1980[a]	KEY
E9	3.3	5.5	8.6	14.8	28.1	Sgt. major
E8	5.8	10.6	14.4	18.3	25.0	1st sgt.
E7	7.9	15.7	19.9	23.1	24.6	Sgt. 1st class
E6	12.2	20.6	23.9	21.0	23.7	Staff sgt.
E5	14.8	11.6	16.9	20.1	30.2	Sgt.
E5-E9	12.7	14.5	19.4	20.7	26.8	Total NCOs
E4	12.5	11.1	14.1	25.2	36.1	Corporal
E3	11.9	12.4	16.7	24.0	39.0	Priv. 1st class
E3-E4	12.2	11.6	15.0	24.7	37.1	Squad leaders
E2	11.6	13.0	18.5	25.3	38.6	Private
E1	6.4	10.7	18.4	27.5	30.0	Recruit
E1-E2	9.2	11.8	18.5	26.2	34.1	Total priv.-rec.

[a]March 1980.

the armed forces. The argument is tempered, however, by the significant interservice differentials in participation, as can be seen in the tables presented above. Thus Pentagon proposals for limiting intake into the "new" all-volunteer armed forces to high school graduates may even limit Negro participation in the army and marine corps, besides limiting participation in more "technological" services, that is, the air force and navy. The end result, therefore, projecting a continuing overall two to one reenlistment rate, could be a heavier concentration of Negroes in the senior NCO ranks as time goes on or, in other words, participation developing along the lines of a "Sepoy" model of a predominantly black NCO cadre rather than an "all-black" armed forces as such.[67]

Table 20

Overall and Negro Rank Distribution in the Army, Selected Years

	(Percentages)						
	1962		**1972**		**1980**[a]		
	Overall	*Negro*	*Overall*	*Negro*	*Overall*	*Negro*	*Key*
Officers							
07 & up	0.5	—	0.5	0.2	0.5	0.4	Generals
06	4.9	0.2	5.4	2.1	5.6	3.3	Colonel
05	11.7	3.7	11.9	16.2	13.2	9.2	Lt. col.
04	16.6	13.4	19.2	25.1	19.6	12.1	Major
03	31.2	48.7	37.4	37.3	32.2	32.2	Captain
02〕 01〕	35.1	34.0	25.6	19.1	28.9	42.8	Lieutenants
Enlisted men							
E9	0.2	0.2	0.6	0.3	0.6	0.3	Sgt. major
E8	1.0	1.5	1.8	1.5	1.9	1.5	1st sgt.
E7	4.0	7.3	6.8	7.7	6.8	5.1	Sgt. 1st class
E6	8.4	16.1	11.0	15.0	11.4	8.3	Staff sgt.
E5	14.6	16.6	16.1	15.5	17.5	16.3	Sgt.
E5-E9	28.8	41.7	36.3	40.0	38.2	31.5	
E4	21.5	27.7	23.6	19.0	25.3	28.1	Corporal
E3	24.4	14.1	11.7	11.1	14.1	16.9	Priv. 1st class
E3-E4	45.9	41.8	35.3	30.1	39.4	45.0	
E2	11.7	9.6	13.7	14.5	10.6	12.6	Private
E1	14.1	6.8	14.7	15.4	11.8	10.9	Recruit
E1-E2	25.8	16.4	28.4	29.9	22.4	23.5	

[a]March 1980

With regard to Negro participation in the United States armed forces overall, by 1980 almost one-fifth of personnel in the military were black. This figure is significant, considering that upon the

Table 21
*Occupational Distribution of Negro Enlisted Personnel
in the Army: Enlisted Men, Selected Years*

			(Percentages)		
OCCUPATION	**1964**	**1968**	**1972**	**1976**	**1980**[a]
Infantry, gun crews, etc.	29.9	32.5	40.0	25.5	26.9
Electronics specialists	5.9	5.3	3.4	3.3	3.4
Communications and intell. specs.	6.9	5.1	4.3	8.0	9.5
Medical and dental	6.3	4.7	4.7	3.4	4.5
Other tech. specs.	1.7	1.3	1.0	1.0	1.5
Admin. specs.	15.3	19.2	19.4	18.4	18.3
Elect./mech. repair	11.4	13.7	10.9	11.3	14.3
Craftsmen	2.9	3.5	2.2	1.9	2.0
Service and supply and misc.	19.7	14.7	14.1	27.2	19.6

[a] June 1980.

introduction of an all-volunteer armed forces in 1972-1973 the percentage of Negroes in the United States military—about 12 percent—was proportional to their percentage in the population in the same period. The largest proportion of Negroes, almost 30 percent in 1980, is concentrated in the U.S. Army, and some 20 percent of the marine corps is composed of black personnel. Negroes are still underrepresented in the navy. In 1980 their proportion in that service reached only 10 percent of personnel. Negro participation in the air force did not grow at the same rate between 1972 and 1980 as in the other service branches, including the navy, so their proportion of total air force personnel in 1980 is only 14 percent. As for their service in the army, as early as 1954, there was a significant number of Negroes in that branch of the United States armed forces, but Negro participation in the Navy, on the other hand, was limited as a result of traditional patterns of discrimination (the Truman desegregation order was implemented by that year). The percentage of Negroes in both the air force and marine corps did not reach a point of proportionality to their population until the Vietnam expansion of those branches of the United States military during the late-1960s.

Although the percentage of Negro officers in all branches of the United States armed forces has increased since World War II, it is still very low, considering the rapid growth in the number of Negroes serving in the enlisted ranks and as NCOs. Again, interservice differentials are quite obvious, with the army having the highest percentage of Negro officers, followed by the air force. The Vietnam expansion of the marine corps, and the maintenance of its combat readiness throughout the 1970s, however, gave strong impetus to the proportion of Negro officers in that service, which increased almost sevenfold over the period 1966-1980. The navy lags behind all other service branches, with the number of Negro officers reaching only 2.4 percent of the total in 1980, although this represents an eightfold increase over the percentage in 1966.

The percentage of Negro enlisted personnel in the U.S. Army rose from some 11 percent in 1949, a year after the Truman desegregation order, to almost 33 percent in 1980. This is a very significant development, and a continuation of this trend may indeed lead in the direction of the "Sepoy model" proposed above, especially as Negroes comprised some 27 percent of army NCOs in 1980. The increase in the percentage of Negro enlisted personnel in the marine corps is also significant, rising from less than 3 percent in 1949 to almost 22 percent in 1980. Again, the turning point can be found in the mid-1960s, with the expansion of this service due to the Vietnam War. The percentage of Negro enlisted personnel in the air force constantly grew during the period 1949-1970 to a point of proportionality with the Negro population, but during the decade between 1970 and 1980, the increase in black enlisted personnel in that service was, in fact, the lowest of all the armed forces, including the navy. Again, the navy lags behind all other branches of the United States military, and the percentage of Negro enlisted men in the navy is only half of that in the marine corps and a third of the percentage in the army.

The changing pattern of Negro rank distribution in the U.S. Army can be taken as representative of what has happened in other branches of the United States armed forces. In the early 1960s, about half of the Negro officers were captains, but only some 17 percent had attained the rank of major or above. When compared to the overall rank structure of the officer corps in the U.S. Army, the Negro officer rank structure was then clearly skewed toward the lower rank levels. By 1972, however, the situation had almost reversed itself, with some 45 percent of Negro officers having attained the rank of major or above, as against 37 percent overall. The percentage of Negro captains in both 1972 and 1980 is identical. What is significant, however, is the high percentage of Negro second and first lieutenants compared with the overall percentage in 1980 and compared to the situation in 1972. This may indicate that by 1980 Negroes who qualify for entry into the officer corps, for example, those with higher education and so on, have once again turned to the military for career development and mobility.

With regard to the rank structure of Negro enlisted personnel in the U.S. Army, as early as 1962, this was skewed toward the NCO levels, with more than 40 percent of Negro personnel holding the rank of sergeant or above, as against less than 30 percent of enlisted personnel overall. By 1972 the enlisted rank distribution pattern of Negroes and that overall were more or less similar, with a significant increase in Negro entry into the enlisted ranks below NCO. The continued large-scale intake of Negro enlisted personnel between 1972 and 1980, almost doubling in terms of participation percentage, has affected, somewhat, the rank structure of Negroes in the army as against the overall structure, with more Negroes at the level of squad leaders and so on. However, the percentage of Negro NCOs still rose at an astounding rate between 1972 and 1980, especially at the senior NCO level, with over a threefold increase in the proportion of Negro sergeant majors, reaching some 28 percent of the total in the U.S. Army in 1980.

The occupational distribution of Negro enlisted men in the U.S.

Army attests that the percentage of Negro combat personnel increased at the same time the proportion of Negro technical specialists decreased over the period 1964-1972. Thus although the percentage of Negro NCOs remained the same over the period, it seems that more and more new NCOs were being channeled into combat occupations, along with new enlisted personnel. This could be attributed to the Vietnam War. However, considering that the overall rank structure and that of Negro enlisted men were almost identical in 1972, it seems that although opportunities were indeed expanded for Negro personnel at the NCO level, due to the changing organizational structure of the U.S. Army as a result of new military technology and sustained conflict or near-conflict situations, Negro personnel at both the NCO and enlisted ranks level were actually being channeled away from more technical occupations and toward combat and related occupations. This situation continued over the period 1972-1980, when, with the winding down and end of the Vietnam War, black enlisted men were once again channeled into service and supply occupations, in addition to combat occupations. There was some slight improvement with regard to Negro participation in a limited number of technical specialties, but almost half of all Negro enlisted men were concentrated in combat and service-supply occupations in 1980, a situation that had not changed since 1964.

In his paper "Assessing Black Enlisted Participation in the Army," John Butler analyzed trend data on the rank distribution of Negroes and their assignment to military occupations using rank-order correlation techniques. He found that although the unequal distribution of Negroes across ranks decreased during the period 1962-1972, they were significantly underrepresented in the technical occupations, even when their mental group level (AFQT) was controlled, and that this situation did not improve over the period. Thus reports regarding race relations in the United States armed forces and studies of black and white servicemen's attitudes toward equality of treatment and opportunity by and in the military have pointed increasingly toward black dissatisfaction both with the military policies and practices and with opportunities in the military itself. On the other hand, there is a continuing trend in enlistment-reenlistment behavior that shows up in an overall black reenlistment rate of almost twice that for whites. Again, the determining factor may be that the military isn't so good, but civilian job prospects are even worse for those Negroes who do decide to enlist and stay in the armed forces.[68]

Of course, changes in the attitude of United States blacks toward military service has resulted from both the societal effect of the Vietnam War and the growth of the black power movement; however, as Morris Janowitz and Charles Moskos noted in their paper assessing "Five Years of the All Volunteer Force: 1973-78" in the United States,

the rising percentage of blacks in the all-volunteer force operates, in part, independently of the end of conscription and can be attributed to a degree to the large increase in the proportion of blacks eligible for military service, specifically, the increasing number of black high school graduates and the larger percentage of blacks placing in the upper levels of the mental aptitude tests required for service entry. . . . The military, it can be added, will continue to draw disproportionately from young blacks as long as they are the victims of certain structural problems in the national economy—specifically, the steady flow of manufacturing jobs away from cities where so many poor blacks are trapped.[69]

In any event, Frederick Douglass accounted for the somewhat problematic attitude exhibited by the Negro as regards military service. In 1863, in attempting to answer the question posed by whites about "why the black man has been so persistent in pressing for military service," he said:

Let the black man get upon his person the brass letters U.S., let him get an eagle on his buttons and a musket on his shoulder, and bullets in his pocket, and there is no power on the earth which can deny that he has earned the right to citizenship.[70]

There was one power, however, that did deny this to the Negro, and that was the United States itself.

NOTES

1. Cited from F. Douglas, *Two Speeches by Frederick Douglass* (New York: Rochester, 1857).

2. See, for example, L. Greene, "The Negro in the Armed Forces of the U.S.," *Negro History Bulletin* 14, 6 (1951), p. 123.

3. Ibid., p. 124. See also L. Greene, *The Negro in Colonial New England* (New York: Columbia University Press, 1942).

4. See, on these points, "Black Servicemen and the Military Establishment," in H. A Plonski and E. Kaiser, eds., *The Negro Almanac* (New York: Bellwether, 1971), pp. 552ff.

5. L. Greene, "The Negro in the Armed Forces of the U.S.," pp. 124ff. See also G. Williams, *A History of Negro Troops in the War of Rebellion* (New York: Krauss Reprint, 1888), who outlined the early Negro contribution.

6. L. Litwack, *The Negro in the Free States* (Chicago: University of Chicago Press, 1961), pp. 31-32; M. F. Berry, "The Negro Soldier Movement and the Adoption of National Conscription: 1652-1865" (Ph.D. diss., University of Michigan, 1966), ch. 2, pp. 20-22.

7. L. Litwack, *The Negro,* p. 32; H. A. Plonski and E. Kaiser, eds., *The Negro Almanac,* pp. 553-56.

8. L. Litwack, *The Negro,* pp. 32-33; T. D. Phillips, "Black Regulars— Negro Soldiers in the U.S. Army, 1866-91" (Ph.D. diss., University of Wisconsin, 1966), pp. 50, 68.

9. M. F. Berry, "The Negro Soldier Movement and the Adoption of National Conscription," ch. 3; F. A. Lord, "The Federal Volunteer Soldier in the American Civil War" (Ph.D. diss., University of Michigan, 1949); H. A. Plonski and E. Kaiser, *The Negro Almanac,* pp. 557ff.

10. M. F. Berry, "The Negro Soldier Movement and the Adoption of National Conscription," pp. 50-60.

11. On these points, see J. Wilson, *The Black Phalanx* (Hartford, Conn.: Connecticut Historical Society, 1890); J. Blassingame, "Recruitment of Negro Troops in Missouri during the Civil War," *Missouri Historical Review* 57 (1964), pp. 326-38; M. F. Berry, "The Negro Soldier Movement and the Adoption of National Conscription," ch. 5.

12. M. F. Berry, "The Negro Soldier Movement and the Adoption of National Conscription," pp. 92ff. See also T. W. Higginson, *Army Life in a Black Regiment* (East Lansing: Michigan State University Press, 1960); L. H. Fishel and B. Quarles, *The Black American: A Documentary History* (New York: Morrow, 1970), pp. 220ff.; J. McPherson, *The Negro's Civil War* (New York: Random House, 1965).

13. M. F. Berry, "The Negro Soldier Movement and the Adoption of National Conscription," pp. 99ff.; ch. 7, pp. 134ff.; H. A. Plonski and E. Kaiser, *The Negro Almanac,* p. 561.

14. M. F. Berry, "The Negro Soldier Movement and the Adoption of National Conscription," ch. 9; "Major General Sherman on Recruiting Negroes," *Army and Navy Journal* 2, 27 (August 1864), p. 7; F. A. Lord, "The Federal Volunteer Soldier in the American Civil War," pp. 426ff.

15. F. A. Lord, "The Federal Volunteer Soldier in the American Civil War," pp. 520ff.; H. A. Plonski and E. Kaiser, *The Negro Almanac*, p. 561. See also G. Williams, *A History of Negro Troops in the War of Rebellion*, p. 266; B. Dyer, "Treatment of Colored Union Troops by the Confederates," *Journal of Negro History* 20 (1935), pp. 273ff.

16. H. A. Plonski and E. Kaiser, *The Negro Almanac*, pp. 562ff. See also N. W. Stephenson, "The Question of Arming the Slaves," *American Historical Review* 18 (1913), pp. 295ff.; C. Wesley, "The Employment of Negroes as Soldiers in the Confederate Army," *Journal of Negro History* 4 (1919), pp. 239ff.; B. G. Reid, "Confederate Opponents of Arming the Slaves," *Journal of Mississippi History* 22 (1960), pp. 249ff.

17. L. H. Fishel and B. Quarles, *The Black American*, pp. 247-48; H. A. Plonski and E. Kaiser, *The Negro Almanac*, p. 562.

18. H. A. Plonski and E. Kaiser, *The Negro Almanac*, pp. 561-62; J. McPherson, *The Negro's Civil War*.

19. H. A. Plonski and E. Kaiser, *The Negro Almanac*, pp. 568ff.; T. D. Philips, "Black Regulars—Negro Soldiers in the U.S. Army."

20. H. A. Plonski and E. Kaiser, *The Negro Almanac*, pp. 570ff. See also W. B. Gatewood, "Black Americans and the Quest for Empire," *Journal of Southern History* 38, 4 (1972), pp. 545ff.

21. W. B. Gatewood, "Black Americans," pp. 547-48.

22. H. A. Plonski and E. Kaiser, *The Negro Almanac*, p. 571; W. B. Gatewood, "Black Americans," p. 555.

23. W. B. Gatewood, "Black Americans," pp. 560-61.

24. Ibid., pp. 562ff.

25. A. Barbeau and F. Henri, *The Unknown Soldiers* (Philadelphia: Temple University Press, 1974), pp. 16-17.

26. See, for example, A. Spear, "The Origins of the Urban Ghetto," and M. Kilson, "Political Change in the Negro Ghetto 1900-1940's," both in M. Kilson, ed., *Key Issues in the Afro-American Experience* (New York: Harcourt, Brace, 1971); T. L. Smith, "The Redistribution of the Negro Population of the U.S.," *Journal of Negro History* 51, 3 (1966); U. Lee, *The Employment of Negro Troops in World War II* (Washington, D.C.: Office of the Chief of Military History, U.S. Army, 1966), p. 24.

27. A. Barbeau and F. Henri, *The Unknown Soldiers,* pp. 6-8; J. L. and

H. Scheiber, "The Wilson Administration and the Wartime Mobilization of Black Americans," *Labor History* 10, 3 (1969), pp. 438, 447.

28. See, for example, L. D. Reddick, "The Negro Policy of the U.S. Army," *Journal of Negro History* 34, 1 (1949), p. 22. See also A. Barbeau and F. Henri, *The Unknown Soldiers.*

29. L. D. Reddick, "The Negro Policy of the U.S. Army"; A. Barbeau and F. Henri, *The Unknown Soldiers*; J. P. Davis, *American Negro Reference Book* (New York: Prentice-Hall, 1966), pp. 619ff.

30. A. Barbeau and F. Henri, *The Unknown Soldiers,* pp. 23-26.

31. Ibid., pp. 26-30.

32. Ibid., chs. 5, 7, 8; L. D. Reddick, "The Negro Policy of the U.S. Army," pp. 23-24.

33. See, for example, R. H. Brisbane, *The Black Vanguard: The Origins of the Negro Social Revolution, 1900-60* (Valley Forge, Pa.: Judson, 1970), for the reactions of the black community to W. E. B. du Bois's editorial "Close Ranks," *Crisis* (July 1918); also see L. H. Fishel and B. Quarles, *The Black American*, pp. 410-12.

34. On these points, see, for example, U. Lee, *The Employment of Negro Troops in World War II,* pp. 15-20; J. P. Davis, *American Negro Reference Book*, pp. 625-26.

35. L. D. Reddick, "The Negro Policy of the U.S. Army," p. 24; U. Lee, *The Employment of Negro Troops in World War II*, pp. 16, 44-45.

36. U. Lee, *The Employment of Negro Troops in World War II*, pp. 25, 28; J. P. Davis, *American Negro Reference Book,* p. 626; R. Stillman, *The Integration of the Negro in the Armed Forces* (New York: Praeger, 1968), p. 10.

37. U. Lee, *The Employment of Negro Troops in World War II*, pp. 44, 49.

38. Ibid., pp. 42-48; R. Dalfiume, *Desegregation of the U.S. Armed Forces: Fighting on Two Fronts, 1939-53* (Kansas City: University of Missouri Press, 1969), pp. 42, 57; J. P. Davis, *American Negro Reference Book,* p. 638.

39. R. Dalfiume, *Desegregation of the U.S. Armed Forces,* pp. 59-60.

40. E. Ginzberg and D. W. Bray, *The Uneducated* (New York: Columbia University Press, 1953), pp. 48-55; R. Dalfiume, *Desegregation of the U.S. Armed Forces,* pp. 56-57, 62, 97; U. Lee, *The Employment of Negro Troops in World War II*, pp. 127-28.

41. *Harpers,* April 1946, p. 334; R. Dalfiume, *Desegregation of the U.S. Armed Forces*, pp. 98, 204-5; D. Mandelbaum, *Soldier Groups and Negro Soldiers* (Berkeley: University of California Press, 1952), pp. 96-97; R. Merton, *Social Theory and Social Structure* (Glencoe, Ill.: Free Press,

1949), discussed the self-fulfilling hypothesis. On the situation in the civilian sector and the military in 1943, see H. Sitkoff, "Racial Militancy and Interracial Violence in the Second World War," *Journal of American History* 58, 3 (1971), pp. 61-81; L. Finkle, "The Conservative Aims of Militant Rhetoric: Black Protest during World War II," *Journal of American History* 60, 3 (1973), pp. 692-713; R. H. Brisbane, *The Black Vanguard,* p. 165; R. Stillman, *The Integration of the Negro,* p. 27; U. Lee, *The Employment of Negro Troops in World War II,* pp. 397-99.

42. R. Dalfiume, *Desegregation of the U.S. Armed Forces,* pp. 93, 95; J. P. Davis, *American Negro Reference Book,* p. 646; R. Stillman, *The Integration of the Negro,* p. 29; U. Lee, *The Employment of Negro Troops in World War II,* pp. 689-95.

43. R. Dalfiume, *Desegregation of the U.S. Armed Forces,* p. 96.

44. Ibid., p. 104; U. Lee, *The Employment of Negro Troops in World War II,* pp. 575-79; R. Stillman, *The Integration of the Negro,* p. 29.

45. Malcolm X, *Malcolm X Speaks* (New York: Grove, 1965), pp. 140-41.

46. *The Journal of Social Issues* 3, 4 (1947), pp. 26-27, 32-39; A. Rose, *The Negro's Morale* (Minneapolis: University of Minnesota Press, 1949); Gunnar Myrdal, *An American Dilemma* (New York: Harper and Row, 1962).

47. S. Stouffer et al., *The American Soldier* (Princeton: Princeton University Press, 1949), p. 542. This trend was strengthened by the removal of the Negro quota in 1950. See R. Dalfiume, *Desegregation of the U.S. Armed Forces*, pp. 202-3, 207, 215.

48. U. Lee, *The Employment of Negro Troops in World War II,* pp. 397-99; R. Stillman, *The Integration of the Negro,* p. 27.

49. R. Dalfiume, *Desegregation of the U.S. Armed Forces,* pp. 202-3.

50. R. Stillman, *The Integration of the Negro,* pp. 44-45, 48-9. See also the *New York Times*, 21 April 1949, 23 May 1950.

51. R. Stillman, *The Integration of the Negro,* p. 62.

52. R. Dalfiume, *Desegregation of the U.S. Armed Forces,* pp. 207, 215. On Project CLEAR, see also L. Bogart, *Social Research and the Desegregation of the U.S. Army* (Chicago: Markham, 1969).

53. R. Dalfiume, *Desegregation of the U.S. Armed Forces,* p. 187.

54. R. Stillman, *The Integration of the Negro,* p. 56.

55. Although an increase in median income occurred, the Negro, in relative terms, only held his own due to the increase in income levels of those that migrated from the South to other regions. On these points, see, for example, E. J. Hughes, "The Negro's New Economic Life," *Fortune* 54, 3 (Sept. 1956); A. Batchelder, "Decline in the Relative

Income of Negro Men," *Quarterly Journal of Economics* 78, 4 (1964); R. Raymond, "Changes in the Relative Economic Status of Non-Whites," *Western Economic Journal* 7, 1 (1969). Denial of equal employment opportunity is dealt with in G. Becker, *The Economics of Discrimination* (Chicago: University of Chicago Press, 1957).

On the Gesell report, see R. Stillman, *The Integration of the Negro,* pp. 108-9. See also *U.S. News and World Report,* 19 Aug. 1963, p. 49.

56. Cited in R. Stillman, *The Integration of the Negro,* pp. 109, 121.

57. J. P. Davis, *American Negro Reference Book,* p. 658.

58. Ibid., p. 659; R. Stillman, *The Integration of the Negro,* p. 111.

59. R. Stillman, *The Integration of the Negro,* p. 117. See also *U.S. News and World Report,* 19 Aug. 1963.

60. J. P. Davis, *American Negro Reference Book,* pp. 659-60; P. T. Murray, "Blacks and the Draft," *Journal of Black Studies* 1 (1971), pp. 57-76; S. H. Hays, "Military Training in the U.S. Today," *Current History* 55, 323 (1968); Marshall Commission Report, in *Current History* 55, 323 (1968); *New York Times,* 17 Feb. 1969. On Project 100,000, see C. R. Coble, "Social Action Programs in the Department of Defense" (Ph.D. diss., University of North Carolina at Chapel Hill, 1969).

61. C. C. Moskos, "Racial Integration in the Armed Forces," *American Journal of Sociology* 72, 2 (1966), p. 138. See also L. Broom and N. Glenn, *Transformation of the Negro American* (New York: Norton, 1967), pp. 181-82; *Civil Rights 1963,* Report of the U.S. Commission on Civil Rights (Washington, D.C., 1964), p. 179; *Manpower Report of the President* (Washington, D.C., 1965), p. 204. Although during the years 1948-1952 (Truman administration), the ratio of Negro to white unemployment was 1.7 to 1.0, during the period 1953-1960 inclusive (Eisenhower administration), the ratio averaged 2.1 to 1.0. In 1958, for example, a structural change in unemployment hit the Negro community very hard, with the rate going over 10 percent overall (male and female); the level wasn't to return to less than 10 percent until 1964.

62. *Manpower Research Notes,* 71-3, 71-4, April 1971: "Advancement Rates of Career Enlisted Personnel by Race and Years of Service"; "Promotion Opportunities of 1st Term Enlisted Personnel by Race, Aptitude, Educational Level, and Military Occupation," Directorate for Manpower Research, Office of the Assistant Secretary of Defense for Manpower and Reserve Affairs (Washington D.C., 1971). The survey cited was of Negro and white air force NCOs, conducted by Alice Yohalem, principal investigator, under the aegis of Conservation of Human Resources Group, Columbia University, New York, Eli Ginzberg, director.

63. See, for example, W. Mason, "The Effect of Military Achievement on the Subsequent Civilian Attainment of Veterans" (Ph.D. diss., University of Chicago, 1970); J. S. Coleman et al., "Occupational Status Changes of Blacks and Non-Blacks during the First 10 Years of Occupational Experience," Reports No. 76 (Aug. 1970), 122 (Dec. 1971), and 123 (Jan. 1972), compiled by the Center for the Social Organization of Schools (Baltimore: Johns Hopkins University); J. Ladinsky, "A Survey of Socially and Economically Disadvantaged Vietnam Era Veterans" (Washington, D.C.: U.S. Bureau of the Budget, 1969).

The "transferability" of technical training to civilian occupations by draftees or enlistees may be limited due to the short period of service (especially in the former case). If the draftee or enlistee *doesn't* continue his technical training in the military, the training he did receive during his period of service is not helpful at all, since it is on the level of a high school vocational course, in most instances, rather than on a technical school level in terms of civilian equivalency. The only way he could continue his training, however, is by reenlisting after his first tour of duty. On these points, see, for example, H. Wool, "The Armed Services as a Training Institution," in E. Ginzberg, ed., *The Nation's Children* (New York: Columbia University Press, 1960), pp. 175-80.

As A. Etzioni noted, "The amount of socialization required by an organization depends, of course, on the degree to which organizational behavior differs from behavior the participants have learned elsewhere," in *A Comparative Analysis of Complex Organizations* (Glencoe, Ill.: Free Press, 1961), p. 146.

64. On the general problem of "transferability" and "convertability," see, for example, H. Wool, *The Military Specialist* (Baltimore: Johns Hopkins University Press, 1968).

65. A. Guttman, "Politics and the Military Ethic," *American Scholar* 34, 2 (1965); K. M. Weigert, "Stratification, Ideology, and Opportunity Beliefs among Black Soldiers," *Public Opinion Quarterly* 28, 1 (1974), pp. 57ff.; J. Howard and I. Couchman, "The American Blacks and Military Service," *Forensic Quarterly* 42 (1968), pp. 458-59.

66. C. C. Moskos, "Racial Integration"; K. Lang, "Technology and Career Management in the Armed Forces," in M. Janowitz, ed., *The New Military* (New York: Sage, 1964), pp. 61-68. On the difficulties of Negro career NCO veterans, see P. Jacobs, "Bringing Up the Rear," in A. Ross and H. Hill, eds., *Employment, Race, and Poverty* (New York: Harcourt, Brace, 1967), pp. 109-14. In this context, "channeling" due to AFQT-AGCT (aptitude-intelligence) test results during the 1960s is discussed in C. C. Moskos, "The Negro and the Draft," in R. W. Little,

ed., *Selective Service and American Society* (New York: Sage, 1969), pp. 150-151. On the problem of Negro officers, see R. Stillman, *The Integration of the Negro*, pp. 86ff.

67. See, for example, H. A. Marmion, *The Case Against an All-Volunteer Army* (Chicago: University of Chicago Press, 1971); J. Miller, *Why the Draft? The Case for a Volunteer Army* (New York: Penguin, 1968); T. E. Borcherding, "Neglected Social Costs of a Volunteer Military," *American Economic Review* 61 (1971); M. Janowitz, "American Democracy and Military Service," *Transaction* 4 (1967); idem, "Volunteer Armed Forces and Military Purpose," *Foreign Affairs* (1972); idem, "Toward an All Voluntary Military," *The Public Interest* 27 (1972); *The Gates Commission* (VOLAR) *Report* and *Studies* prepared for it (Washington, D.C., 1970-1971); W. F. Ford and R. Tollinson, "Notes on the Color of the Volunteer Army," *Social Science Quarterly* 50, 3 (1969); K. H. Kim et al., *The All Volunteer Army* (New York: Praeger, 1971), besides earlier arguments in S. Tax, ed., *The Draft* (Chicago: University of Chicago Press, 1967).

This is the argument of S. Canby in *Military Manpower Procurement* (New York: D. C. Heath, Lexington Books, 1972), pp. 67-72. On this proposal, see the *Times* (London) report of 14 March 1973 made by Henry Stanhope, its defense correspondant.

My concept of the "Sepoy" model is that an overwhelming majority of the officers in the Volunteer Army will be white, whereas the majority of NCOs will be black (see S. Cohen, *The Indian Army* [Berkeley: University of California Press, 1971] for a description of how the Sepoy system functioned in the British Indian Army). There is a growing retention problem among Negro junior officers, as noted in 1971 by the then chief of staff, Gen. William Westmoreland, who attributed it to the growing competitiveness of the civilian sector for educated and trained blacks. The attractiveness of a military career in the "new" all-volunteer army may yet reverse this trend. If it does not, however, the Sepoy model may emerge in even a stronger form than proposed here. For Westmoreland's comments, see H. Johnson and G. C. Wilson, *Army in Anguish* (New York: Washington Post Report, 1972), p. 105. The source for data up to 1972 is *The Negro in the Armed Forces,* a statistical fact book (Washington, D.C.: Office of the Assistant Secretary of Defense for Manpower and Reserve Affairs—Equal Opportunity, 15 Sept. 1971 and 31 Dec. 1972 [Supplement]). The data for 1949-1954 were obtained from *Civil Rights 1963* (Washington, D.C.: U.S. Commission on Civil Rights, 1964), p. 221. Data for 1976-1980 were obtained from Reports *3035* and *3694* for

1976 and 1980 (Washington, D.C.: Office of the Assistant Secretary of Defense for Manpower and Reserve Affairs—Equal Opportunity, 1980).

68. On these points, see J. S. Butler, "Assessing Black Enlisted Participation in the Army," *Social Problems* 23 (1976), pp. 558-66; idem, "Inequality in the Military," *American Sociological Review* 41 (1976), pp. 807-18; idem, "Unsanctioned Institutional Racism in the U.S. Army" (Ph.D. diss., Northwestern University, 1974). See also P. Nordlie et al., *Measuring Changes in Institutional Racial Discrimination in the Army*, Technical Paper 270 (Washington, D.C.: Army Research Institute for the Behavioral Sciences, 1975); K. Weigert, "Stratification, Ideology, and Opportunity Beliefs among Black Soldiers"; J. S. White, "Race Relations in the Army," *Military Review* 50 (1970); J. F. Borus et al., "Racial Perceptions in the Army," *American Journal of Psychiatry* 128, 11 (1972). For an account of racial disturbances in the U.S. Navy during the late 1960s and early 1970s, see J. D. Foner, *Blacks and the Military in American History* (New York: Praeger, 1974), pp. 271ff.

69. M. Janowitz and C. Moskos, "Five Years of the All Volunteer Force: 1973-1978," *Armed Forces and Society* 5, 2 (1979), pp. 215-16, n. 23.

70. Cf. A. Barbeau and F. Henri, *The Unknown Soldiers,* p. xii.

6

OVERVIEW: CROSS-NATIONAL GENERALIZATIONS AND WORLD PERSPECTIVE

INTRODUCTION

A number of general characteristics regarding the military participation of minority groups emerge from the case studies presented in the preceding chapters. In addition, there are specific variations between the cases that must be noted and accounted for so that generalizations across cases can be acceptable and valid. Furthermore, the correspondence of these cross-national generalizations to the military-minority relationship in other countries has to be considered and their implications gauged accordingly.

The first part of this chapter, therefore, describes and analyzes the nature and characteristics of minority-military service emerging from the case studies by dealing with them in terms of (a) *patterns*, (b) *parameters*, and (c) *politicization* of minority-military participation. With regard to (a), the starting point for describing and analyzing patterns of participation is the continuity or discontinuity of minority-military participation with societal patterns of organization, cohesion, or cleavage. Alternatively, a third situation can emerge within which there is a combination of continuities and discontinuities; this case is also discussed. As for (b), parameters of participation are dealt with in terms of variant forms of unit organization, on the one hand, and phenomena such as quota systems and minority-manpower channeling, on the other hand. Regarding (c), the situations within which politicization can take place are described, and this process is illustrated accordingly. Also stressed is the importance of the politicization process, which both determines the situation of the minority in military service overall and reflects underlying minority-societal relations. In addition, a number of "acceleration effects" that emerge are described and illustrated by reference to the cases considered.

The second part of this chapter describes and attempts to account for intercase variations between the United States and the United Kingdom, on the one hand, and between Belgium and Canada, on the other hand. This is done by reference to factors affecting the military-minority-societal interaction such as residence and the demographic situation in the respective case, the nature of the intergroup relationship and the self-perception of the groups involved, and the existence of formal and informal political and socioeconomic structures dividing groups. Finally, the third part of this chapter places the cross-national generalizations made in world perspective by reference to similar situations in other national contexts.

THE NATURE AND CHARACTERISTICS OF MINORITY-MILITARY SERVICE

PATTERNS OF MILITARY PARTICIPATION

In a recent paper, Charles Moskos outlined a developmental approach to the problem of analyzing emergent trends on the level of the general military-societal interaction. Moskos outlined three developmental "models" in this regard: (1) the convergent or civilianized military, (2) the divergent or traditional military, and (3) the segmented or pluralistic military.[1]

With regard to the first model, Moskos attributed "the growing convergence between military and civilian forms of social organization" to the influence of sophisticated weapons and forms of military technology, with the result that the trend toward more complex technology and larger scales of organization induced both rationalization and bureaucratization in the military's organizational system. This engendered a need not only for technical but managerial competence. Notwithstanding the professionalization of the officer corps, the military in this case exhibits a trend "away from authority based on domination towards a managerial philosophy placing greater stress on performance and individual initiative."

In his model of a divergent, or traditional, military, Moskos proposed a "developmental construct which emphasizes the increasing differentiation between military and civilian social organization." This situation, in his view, results from societal trends and "indigenous efforts" within the military "toward institutional autonomy." According to Moskos, some indicators of divergence include the narrowing of the social base of recruitment to the officer corps; a trend toward the monopolization of the officer corps by members of military "families" or graduates of military academies; an increasing gap in the level of education of officers vis-à-vis other ranks; and the peaking of the obvious trend of increasing military technological specialization and the resultant lessening of skills transferability between the military and civilian sectors. Moskos claimed that in this case, although a significant shift from combat and labor occupations occurred in the military of most developed countries in the decade following World War II, after that period, there was relative stability in military skills structure and requirements, since the more technical jobs were likely to become automated, with a resultant increase in the relative number of combat-related occupations. In addition, in this case, the increased use of civilians in support services would also increase the relative number of "traditional military occupations."

Other indicators include the use of the military for social-welfare or occupational-training schemes, that, in Moskos's view, "can only lead to a greater social distance between officers and the ranks." Furthermore, abandoning the citizen-soldier approach is also an indicator of divergence, and using foreign troops in mercenary capabilities would be another sign of a military that is diverging from the civilian society. But, Moskos claimed, the most crucial indication of divergence can be seen in ideological terms. For example, perceived attacks on its honor and the fostering of dissent among its ranks from the outside may result in a defensive reaction on the part of the military, directed against their sources, and induce "a fundamental turning inward in its relations to the civilian structures and values . . . of society." The result of this would be that while civilian institutions could be "heading toward more participative definition and control," the military, at the same time, would be following "a more conventional and authoritarian social organization."

The third model Moskos proposed is that of "the segmented or pluralistic military." In this case, "the military establishment accommodates and orders the otherwise opposing set of empirical indicators associated with the civilianized or traditional models," or "simply put, the pluralistic military will be both convergent and divergent with civilian society; it will simultaneously display organizational trends which are civilianized and traditional." Moskos stressed, however, that in such a case, the military would "not be an alloy of opposing trends, but a compartmentalization of these trends." In his view, this model does not involve "a homogeneous military somewhere between the civilianized and traditional poles. Rather, the emergent military will be internally segmented into areas which will be either more convergent or more divergent," with such developments characterizing both intramilitary and intermilitary organizational patterns. Thus in this case, the branches of the military that would exhibit the most divergent or traditional characteristics would be combat and labor-support units and maybe elements at senior command level that would "continue to cultivate the ideas of soldierly honor and the mystique of the armed forces." In addition, the tendency toward adopting noncivilian values would be the outcome of patterns of self-recruitment among junior officers, with this trend being "reinforced by the dominant conservatism of career officers and noncoms."

Branches where technical occupations predominate, on the other hand, would, according to Moskos, exhibit "civilianized or convergent features" in this case, so "those with specialized education or training will be attracted to the service in a civilian rather than a military capacity and will gauge military employment in terms of marketplace standards." As a result, the social composition of the compartmentalized segments of the pluralistic military that are "civilianized" would, in his view, "resemble that of those performing equivalent roles in the larger economy." The outcome of this, Moskos claimed, would probably be internal bifurcation "along civilianized and traditional lines," with the "traditional or divergent sector" stressing "customary modes of military organization," while the "convergent sector" would operate "on principles common to civil administration and corporate structures."

In dealing with the implications of his three proposed models, Moskos noted that a convergent military could not only "easily lose that elan so necessary for the functioning of a military organization," but in such a case, movement "toward more recognition of individual rights and less rigidity in social control would, in all likelihood, seriously disaffect career personnel while making military service only marginally more palatable to its resistant members." On the other hand, a divergent military "would most likely be incapable of either maintaining the organization at its required complexity, or attracting the kind of membership necessary for effective performance." More importantly, in his view, "a traditional military in a rapidly changing society could develop anti-civilian values tearing the basic fabric of democratic ideology." In conclusion, therefore, Moskos contended that it is the segmented or pluralistic model of the military, with its characteristic of "compartmentalization," that presents the most appealing format for an armed forces structure since it would "maintain organizational effectiveness along with being consonant in the main with civilian values." Finally, Moskos claimed, "the model of an emergent military with intra-institutional pluralism may have broader applicability to the framework of the larger societal system."

An approach similar to that of Moskos could also be formulated with regard to patterns of minority-military participation. Developmental patterns in this case can be described as (a) continuous, (b) discontinuous, or (c) parallel to the prevailing minority-societal relationship. The *continuous pattern* is that in which the nature and characteristics of minority-military participation not only correspond to the societal situation of the minority but result from the deliberate projection of the minority-societal relationship onto the military organization. This can occur with or without reference to the interests of the minority group itself, that is, either by choice or fiat depending on the underlying structure of minority-societal relations. The former situation, that is, continuity by choice, can be seen in the present-day pattern of separate units and *dual* military structures in the Belgian and Canadian cases. The latter situation, that is, continuity by fiat, can be illustrated by reference to the pattern of exclusion and segregation in the United States armed forces before 1948, which was maintained despite the objection of both Negroes and whites. Separate regiments also existed in the British colonial army, for example, the West India and West Indies regiments, the Gold Coast Regiment, and the Kenya African Rifles, and although new commonwealth immigrants in H. M. Forces do not serve in separate regiments today, they *are* to be found concentrated in specific regiments as noted above. The separate unit tradition is still carried on, however, as seen in the continued existence of the Gurkha Regiment.

The *discontinuous pattern* is that where minority-military participation diverges from the prevailing societal-minority relationship as a result of factors either external to the military organization or emanating from its own needs and interests. The discontinuity, however, may have positive or negative aspects with regard to what the minority group sees as its own interests. The former situation, that is, positive discontinuity, can be seen in the process of integration of the United States armed forces that resulted from external pressures and only to a very limited extent from military initiative, with the military even claiming that it was justified in maintaining segregation since this merely reflected the prevalent practice in the civilian sector. Once the United States armed forces saw the value of integration in terms of military effectiveness, however, it led civilian society in terms of the extent of integration implemented. The situation of negative discontinuity can be seen in the status of English in the Canadian forces and that of French in the Belgian armed forces before the establishment of a dual military structure in both cases. In these cases, not only were the languages of the dominant groups—that is, English in Canada, Walloons in Belgium—the sole operational and command languages, but most if not all training was conducted in them, despite the existence of two distinct linguistic communities in both cases, recognition of French in Canada and Flemish (Dutch) in Belgium as "official" languages, and even the existence of separate units in the military composed of men from the various language groups.

The *parallel pattern* of minority-military participation is that where the minority's situation in the military, although reflecting the societal situation for the most part, may contain elements of discontinuity. The distinction between the continuous pattern and the parallel pattern is that in the former case, societal cleavages and institutions are fully projected onto the military organizations, so no discontinuities can emerge. As noted, however, external factors may bring about discontinuity between the minority's situation outside and within the military. When subsequent developments bring the situations into line, there may still exist specific discontinuities that are maintained, so the parallel pattern emerges. Alternatively, the parallel pattern can emerge directly from the continuous pattern of minority-military participation. In this case, there are no discontinuities between the minority situation within and outside the military, that is, here the existence of parallel cleavages and structures reflecting those in society does not result from the ipso facto projection of the societal cleavage structure upon the military. Rather, it emanates from both military considerations and from the minority's own interests vis-à-vis military service, that is, the desired extent and form of participation as perceived by the minority group itself and its members. The parallel pattern can be seen in both the present-day situation of the Negro in the United States armed forces and the colored immigrant in H. M. Forces, where, in the former case, the civilian sector has "caught up" with the military as regards integration and mobility prospects for Negroes, and in the latter case, the situation of the colored immigrant serving in H. M. Forces is neither better nor worse than his situation outside. In the

United States case, then, the developmental process went from continuity through discontinuity to the parallel pattern, and in the British case, it went directly from the continuous to parallel situation.

In the cases of Canada and Belgium, on the other hand, the developmental process proceeded from discontinuous to continuous. In the future, however, both of these cases may tend toward the parallel pattern as their dual military structures rely less for justification on considerations of political expedience and more on those of military effectiveness. It may be, then, that the developmental pattern toward which minority-military participation in our case studies tends is the parallel one, and, as such, it can be considered as the "equilibrium" pattern of participation. This does not mean, however, that the parallel pattern is the optimal one as regards either the military's or minority's interests. Rather, if the parallel pattern is the "equilibrium" pattern in the developmental process toward which our cases have tended, then a "projective fallacy" occurs if these cases are approached on the basis of the formal organizational, systemically based model proposed by Edward Shils, Lucien Pye, and even Morris Janowitz, among others, insofar as this model predicts that the military-minority equilibrium pattern would be discontinuous, and not parallel, as we have suggested.

PARAMETERS OF MINORITY-MILITARY PARTICIPATION

Unit Organization and Participation Situations

The variant forms of unit organization as they relate to minority-military participation emanate, in our view, from a continuum of group boundary maintenance, which ranges from a situation of singular focus, on the one extreme, to multiple enclosure on the other.[2] Following from this, we can specify a continuum of participation situations or forms of unit organization reflecting the group boundary continuum. The situation corresponding to the extreme of singular focus, then, would be that of total *exclusion*, and multiple enclosure would be reflected in the situation of a *dual* or *plural* military structure. Between these situations are ranged those of *segregated*, *integrated*, and *separate* units, the first reflecting, to a certain extent, singular focus and the last reflecting, again, to a certain extent, multiple enclosure.

Now, as a number of observers have noted, minority-military participation in either segregated or separate units does not necessarily lead to ineffective combat performance. However, this seems to depend on (a) the minority group's orientation toward its military role, (b) its identification with the goals of the polity and the military organization in the armed conflict, and (c) its attitude toward the nature of unit organization and participation. In the United States case, for example, although both Nisei Japanese-Americans and Negro airmen served in segregated combat units during World War II, these units proved to be successful. The reason for this, according to Moskos, was twofold. First, the men selected for these units were of much higher quality, as measured by aptitude test scores, than those who served in the average white unit. The second, and perhaps even more important, factor, "was that for the men in these units segregation was perceived as a challenge which they could and did meet." However, segregation affected the morale and performance of most black troops during both world wars and the initial stage of the Korean conflict, since it was seen by them "not as an opportunity for achievement but as an assurance of personal defeat."[3]

In contrast, the success of separate units such as the Gurkha in the British army has been noted by many observers. The case of the Maori in New Zealand can also be cited as one in which a separate unit proved to be effective in combat situations and where the group involved actually requested to serve in its own distinct unit, rather than participate on an integrated basis. The prolonged efforts by both French-Canadians and Flemish-Belgians to serve in separate units has been explained by the desire of these groups to be commanded in their own language. Thus in both Canada and Belgium, dual military structures have been formed accordingly. In the case of Switzerland, a multiple military structure has been set up to enable German-, French-, and Italian-Swiss to be commanded in their respective languages.

It seems, therefore, that for minorities serving in either separate or segregated units, the key elements in successful performance are those listed above (a-c). On the other hand, as Moskos noted, in cases such as that of the Gurkhas, for example, that is, where units are based on "particular ethnic groups where fighting prowess appears to be a strongly valued cultural feature . . . occupational commitment to a military career qua career rather than ideological considerations seems to account for high performance standards."[4]

Quotas and Channeling

Additional characteristics regarding the military service of minority groups can be delineated within the framework of policy and indicative parameters of participation. With regard to *policy parameters*, these include both explicit and implicit elements. The most widespread explicit policy elements are (a) *quotas* specifying desired levels of minority participation overall or in certain occupations, branches, arms, corps, or ranks, and (b) *proscription* of minority-group members from these military categories or, alternatively, exclusion from military service overall.

The most common implicit policy parameter element is the *channeling* of minority group members into or away from various military occupations, service branches or corps, and so on. Channeling away from certain military occupations can result, for example, from entry requirements that minority-group members are unable to fulfill, for example, educational or technical background. Alternatively, they can be channeled into other occupations, for example, combat or service support, by lower entry requirements or specific incentives, such as financial benefits.

In a recent paper, Joseph Blake discussed the channeling process in terms of selective recruitment into a specific military occupation, in this case, combat service. In dealing with "the organization as an instrument of violence: the military case," Blake noted that,

Any organization which serves as an instrument of violence maintains as part of its structure a role or roles designed specifically to be the "carrier of the deed," the deed being the actual commission of the act of violence. A problem then faced by the organization is the need to fill these roles with individuals capable of committing violence and continuing action afterward. This problem may be solved in one of two ways. The organization may initiate a program of selective recruitment designed to draw individuals already having the capacity to commit violence (i.e. already socialized into violence) . . . (or) draw individuals who have not been socialized into violence, then to subject these individuals to process that will so socialize them. . . .[5]

The nature and extent of *indicative* parameters can be seen, for example, in the interservice differentials that exist with regard to minority-military participation, notwithstanding the underlying transformation of the military organization and the effect that functional orientation has had upon this development. Thus when we look at specific service branches, we see significant differences in the structure of rank distribution, something that will affect the rank distribution of those minority-group members in the service itself. For example, in the United States case, the overall rank structure of the marine corps is different from that of the navy and air force, and concomitantly, so is the rank distribution of Negroes in that service branch. In the British case, on the other hand, the rank structure of the army still follows the "traditional pattern," in contrast to the U.S. Army, which had developed the rank structure of a "bureaucratic organization." Thus, as we saw above, the rank distribution pattern of minority-group members in the two armies was different. However, as noted, factors such as differential promotion policies and institutional "standards," or differential career patterns for, say, "tradesman" in the United Kingdom case, as against "specialist" in the United States case, or both of them against "combat-occupation" career patterns can also affect both the rank and occupational distribution patterns of minority-group members.

POLITICIZATION OF MINORITY-MILITARY PARTICIPATION

The introduction of issues arising from minority-military service into the sphere of political debate and decision making can be considered as the crucial factor affecting minority-military participation. The process of politicization may come about during periods of sustained conflict such as wars, rebellions, or revolutions.

Alternatively, it can also result from problems of minority-military participation becoming issues in electoral campaigns or the focus of promises made by politicians in return for the political support of the minority group's leaders and the votes of its members.

In the case of war, for example, the politicization process with regard to minority-military service can take the theme of "quid pro quo," that is, full support of the war effort on the part of the minority and its leadership in return for full citizenship rights or other benefits for minority-group members. Alternatively, it can take the theme of "fighting on two fronts," that is, fighting for freedom and justice abroad or in defense of the country and, at the same time, fighting for the attainment of full citizenship rights perceived by that group being denied the minority at home.

Now, although being a resident or citizen in a country does not necessarily confer full citizenship or civil rights, it may, in some cases, place the obligation of military service upon the resident or group in residence. Individual or group perception of what *should* take place as a result of loyal military service, that is, acceptance as "first-class" citizens and all that such a process entails, that is, attaining full civil rights, however, is not necessarily perceived by those who decide whether or not the group or its members should participate in military service. Other considerations take precedence over this aspect of participation, considerations such as manpower needs, the "suitability" of minority-group members for service in general or in certain occupations, the effect of the minority group's participation on morale in general and on morale in the armed forces itself, and so on. In some cases, the relationship between loyal miliary service and conferral of full citizenship rights perceived by that group being denied them may also be perceived by those who make the decision about the nature and extent of minority-group participation, and thus the decision to exclude the group may be made. This decision, however, may be, in turn, affected by "fears" about the effects of training or arming minority-group members on "public safety" or "public morale" or, again, the effect that inclusion of the minority group may have on the morale of the armed forces in general or the performance of the service branch or branches involved. When manpower pressures deemed so, however, in most cases, minority manpower was used, and specific objections were either "rationalized" or disregarded entirely.[6]

Thus at the point at which "defense of freedom" and "freedom from colonial rule" coincided at the close of World War II, the British were faced with both claims from overseas colonies and resident minority-group members for change in return for loyal military service—in the former case, independence; in the latter case, the conferral of full citizenship rights and benefits. The struggle of Negro Americans for the right to fight, in return for which they expected to become first-class citizens, developed as early as the Civil War, and "fighting on two fronts," for freedom and democracy abroad and civil rights at home, became the dominant theme in the Negro community during the two world wars. In the Belgian case, the slogan "a Free Flanders in a Free Belgium" emerged during World War I when the situation on the home front so affected the Flemish soldiers in the trenches that they formed a separatist movement and political party (VNV) to continue the struggle for language equality after the war. In Canada the theme of fighting on two fronts also strongly emerged, as we have seen, when linguistic and educational rights were demanded by French-Canadians in return for their military participation, both voluntary and compulsory.

Recently, Cynthia Enloe dealt with the process in a different light, claiming in effect that the politicization of minority-military participation may, in fact, enable potential intergroup conflict regarding it to be resolved before the task becomes too difficult to cope with:

Changing the ethnic composition of the military may be least resisted if it is tackled at a time when inter-ethnic hostilities have not yet reached the point of open conflict. That is, it is most politically feasible at a time when the military does not seem crucial for central regime survival. Thus, in both Belgium and Canada over the last several years, there have been official programs to increase the numbers and officer proportions of previously underrepresented groups, Flemings in Belgium and Francophones in Canada. Both efforts are the result of recent politicized mobilization by the underrepresented groups, not of the independent foresight of the central regimes. . . .[7]

ACCELERATION EFFECTS AND MINORITY-MILITARY PARTICIPATION

A final point relates to a phenomenon emanating from m military participation regarding processes affecting minority within the operational framework of the relationship bet "military participation ratio" and changes in the social of the country involved. Briefly, this entails the propos as the intensity of sustained conflict generates manpower the extent of both overall military participation an participation in military service increases. As a result of common experience forged in the temporarily "militarized" society—experience shared both in military service and civilian settings, that common purpose and objectives, the development of a "comm denominator" pervading wartime society—the social struc tends to be less rigid upon the cessation of hostilities, resulting in a higher degree of upward social mobility than had previously occurred, a "social levelling" process in effect having taken place, resulting in an increasing "blurring" of "class lines" and, to a certain extent, a "flattening" of the "social pyramid." The degree of upward mobility for the minority group and its members, therefore, is "accelerated" in the process, the group and its members attaining a greater degree of upward mobility than had existed before the conflict, due to the general "social leveling" process that had occurred as a result of it.

The original "military participation ratio" theory was first proposed by Stanislaw Andreski. Since then, various studies have, in turn, either called it into question or given it tenuous support, such as the work of Philip Abrams, on the one hand, who, in the British case, at least, showed that the effect of World War I on British society as a whole did not correspond to that predicted by the theory; and that of Neil Wynn, on the other hand, who claimed that the effect of World War II on the Negro in the United States case is a good example of Andreski's theory at work, although in qualified form. Here, we can introduce an "accelerator" to account for certain changes brought about in minority-group status that *may* result from sustained conflict and their participation in it. The "social-accelerator" principle has appeared in various guises; however, the one most suitable here is, in fact, the formulation of Chalmers Johnson in his book *Revolution and the Social System* and expanded in his work on *Revolutionary Change.*[8]

An alternative view to that provided by adopting the "social-accelerator" principle is that the very "intensity of conflict" may delay consideration of pressing social issues until after a complete cessation of hostilities. Thus in the case of the French-Canadians, for example, World War II "delayed for a while the great debate about the economic and social reforms needed to improve the lot of the French-Canadians in Quebec." Even in the United States case, only very limited action in the area of social reform vis-à-vis the Negro took place in the *civilian* sector until a complete return to "normalcy" after World War II. This effect, however, is to be expected as a corollary to the military participation ratio theory in that the more intense the conflict, the less social reform that will take place while it is going on. In this context, the conflict can be either external or internal; what matters is the intensity of the conflict itself. The burden of national defense, then, for example, is cited in the case of Israel to explain the inability of the country to deal effectively with its pressing social problems and the deprivation faced by a significant number of Oriental Jews. In Northern Ireland, on the other hand, social reform and provision of de facto equal opportunity for all citizens has been delayed by the growing intensity of the intercommunal strife of the last two decades. The outcome of World War I in political terms in Belgium was to institutionalize the class and religious divisions in that country, thus opening the way for the language problem to establish itself as the cardinal issue dividing it, but extensive socioeconomic reforms only occurred after World War II. In Yugoslavia, on the other hand, the severity of interethnic conflict reached its peak during World War II, when irregular forces of the various nationalities committed acts of violence against each other, going to the extreme of massacre and atrocities against civilians, so "when national strife was . . . curbed at the end of the war it was not as the result of a reconciliation of national differences but because the Communists . . . drastically limited the scope given the expressions of national discontent" and the extent of social reforms vis-à-vis the national minorities.[9]

In any event, what of the structural and organizational changes in the military itself and the effect of *these* changes on the nature and extent of minority-group participation, and to what degree has the "accelerator" principle, proposed by Johnson among others, affected the nature and characteristics of minority-military participation? Regarding the first point, the interrelationship between changes in military technology and changes in the system and structure of military organization has been noted in a number of cases. Weapons, communications, and logistic systems that demand advanced technological skills developed and inexorably changed the "traditional" pattern of military organization, or rather, the system and structure of military organization has changed along with and become complementary to the new military technology.

With the changes in rank and career patterns and occupational structure came changes in the nature and extent of minority-group participation in military service. Essentially, a situation analogous to and working within the framework of the military-participation-ratio process of social change mentioned above was taking place. As each conflict brought about new military technology and further changes in the system and structure of military organization, so opportunities for minority-group participation changed, with more and more *potential* opportunities for upward mobility resulting from changes in the rank and occupational structure, accelerated by the developments in military technology during and as a result of the conflict itself. In effect, then, as each conflict brought about a new technology changing military structure and systems of organization, so each conflict brought about changes in the system of social organization in the society as a whole, resulting in changes in minority-military participation and changes in the position, potential, and acceptance of position by the minority group and its members. An illustration of this process may be seen in the expansion of "middle-level management," that is, NCO positions at the enlisted level, in the United States case, for example, opening up opportunities for Negroes to rise in the ranks and fill them to a greater extent.

As for the second point, however, notwithstanding the new opportunities that may open up to minority-group soldiers as a result of the process outlined above, another phenomenon may intervene, that is, occupational channeling resulting in minority-group members being concentrated in specific military occupations as a result of, for example, low or inadequate educational attainment or background that, in turn, results from societal deprivation or traditional cultural patterns.

Thus although the changing rank structure—that resulted from changes in military technology and organization—may have opened up opportunities for minority-group members, at the same time, these same changes in technology and skills structure also may have brought about the concentration of minority-group members in specific military occupations. In the United States case, for example, elements of this "*dual accelerator*" were noticed in the 1960s by Charles Moskos, who observed that "whereas in World War II, low educational attainments kept most Negroes in support rather than combat units," other reasons for which have been mentioned above, "these same educational handicaps operate in the middle 1960's to overconcentrate Negro soldiers in combat duty." The same can be said of the British case, where the West Indian, who comprises most of colored servicemen in the army, was limited to serving in labor-support units in both World Wars I and II, for the most part, and they are now overconcentrated in combat-related occupations, being "job channeled," as noted above. Barring the situation of exclusion, the "dual accelerator," however, cannot operate within the context of a dual military structure as extant, for example, in present-day Belgium and Canada, although in the latter case, as noted, French-Candians found themselves channeled into combat and service-support occupations and away from technical occupations before the establishment of the dual military structure in that country.[10]

INTERCASE VARIATIONS AND
CROSS-NATIONAL ANALYSIS

BRITAIN AND THE UNITED STATES

Acknowledging the caveats of prominent observers of both British and American race and ethnic relations as regards comparing the two cases, we must first stress fundamental differences that affected the development of "colored" participation in the British armed forces and "nonwhite" participation in the American military. A major difference lies in the historico-demographic background of the respective case, which affected both the nature and significance of minority-military participation or nonparticipation accordingly.

Although there has been a "black presence" in both England and America since the seventeenth century, the "colored" population of Britain has always been (and probably always will be) considerably smaller, both in absolute and relative terms, than the "nonwhite" population in the United States. Both "colored" and Negro soldiers have served in the military forces of the respective countries over the past three centuries, be it from colonial militia in Massachusetts or Jamaica to Vietnam or Ulster. But at times they were excluded from service completely or from certain occupations; segregated into separate units; discriminated against in wages, promotion opportunities, and use of amenities; or channeled deliberately into certain occupations that were deemed "suitable" for men of their "calibre." However, those "new commonwealth" soldiers who served in H. M. Forces were, until the post-World War II era, almost always nonresident in Great Britain and were thus recruited, for the most part, in their areas of origin. Furthermore, there were no significant communities of new commonwealth peoples in the United Kingdom until after World War II and the advent of large-scale immigration of these groups. In the United States case, on the other hand, most of the "nonwhite" communities whose members did participate in military service were resident in the United States itself.[11]

In the case of residence, therefore, the element of individual and group "acceptance" as first-class citizens assumes importance, especially when the group involved has not been generally accepted as "part" of the "nation." The question of national integration has a dual meaning in the case of minorities in the situations considered above. Although "some groups are allowed and encouraged to merge their group distinctiveness and identity" into the populace as a whole, "certain other groups . . . are not." In striving for "national integration" under the "principle of amalgamation," then, certain groups are not included in the process, although this, again, is usually due in some part to the demographic characteristics of the case under consideration. Thus although in the United Kingdom, the relatively small Negro population was "virtually assimilated" by 1850, no such process took place in the United States.[12]

However, although no racial "caste lines" can be said to exist in either the United States or United Kingdom at this point, one would not expect such a phenomenon to repeat itself with respect to the "colored" immigrant communities in the multiracial Britain of today. Although Negroes, Asians, and other groups in the United States were never included in the desire to "promote the amalgamation of ethnic groups," in the British case, it probably would not be far from the truth to say that although the West Indian, for example, believes he is just as much a Briton as any white in the indigenous population, this feeling probably would not be shared by his white British counterpart, who would be of the opinion that West Indians, along with Asians and others, are neither "kith" nor "kin."[13]

Another difference emerges, then, between the two cases, again, resulting from the factor of residence. In the United States case, the relatively longer period of minority-group residence places an emphasis upon *inclusion*, a point not yet reached (but rapidly being approached) in the British case, where the focus is still upon *acceptance*. However, the connotation of these terms is somewhat more complex than both what the "dictionary meanings" and the "Parsonian sense" imply. The existence of a Negro community was "accepted" in the United States as a "fact of life." The problem was that if it were truly "accepted" as part of the nation rather than as a "fact" to be "tolerated" at best (no "final solution" being thought of, as in other cases), the necessity for emphasis on "inclusion," in the Parsonian sense, need never have taken place. The interrelationship between "acceptance," military participation, and the perceived significance of military service in the British case is best reflected in the words of a disillusioned and bitter Jamaican veteran living in Nottingham in 1968:

In 1944 I was a serviceman in the British air force fighting for freedom and democracy. In 1947, I became a settler in Nottingham. In the 1958 race riots I became a coloured man. In the 1962 Commonwealth Immigrant's Act I became a coloured immigrant. And in 1968, I am an unwanted coloured immigrant.[14]

In the United States case, a brief historical digression should be enough to illustrate this point. The American military itself, in pressing its "campaign" for universal military training (UMT) during the 1920s advocated the use of military service for "nation-building, national-integration programs," arguments that have been repeated in the debates over UMT at the end of World War II and again and again since then. As Samuel Huntington noted:

The most extreme instances of the military denying themselves and advocating a military program for non-military reasons, were in their post-World War I campaign for UMT. As the prospects for congressional approval for such a plan rapidly receded after 1920, the arguments advanced in its favor became more and more removed from military requirements. In the end the officers were advancing UMT as more or less the universal panacea for all the social ills which beset America. It would strengthen national unity, *promote the amalgamation of ethnic groups*, and encourage democracy and tolerance. It would be physically beneficial and would virtually eliminate illiteracy in the United States. Far from injuring industry or retarding the development of occupational skills, it would have just the reverse effects. The Army would discharge its recruits with a basic training in law, commerce, transport, engineering, or any one of a number of other technical fields. Most important were the moral benefits to be derived from UMT. . . . Loyalty, patriotism, honor, discipline, fairness, a respect for law, could be inculcated in the youth of the nation through UMT. In short, the officers proved conclusively the need for UMT for every reason except military ones.[15]

Thus although the desire to "promote the amalgamation of ethnic groups" could be stressed in the *Infantry Journal* (a professional journal that not only reflected the norms at the U.S. Army School of Infantry but also helped to shape the opinion "of most of the officer corps" at the time), the Negro, not being an "American" as such, was neither to be included in the "principle of amalgamation" nor to be on the receiving end of "tolerance" (except to be "tolerated" at best). The consequences of "omission" (or exclusion) at this point, and the cumulative effect of "forgetting" the Negro from the end of Reconstruction onwards, were only to be felt four decades later, when "inclusion" and the attainment of full civil rights were demanded by disillusioned Negro Americans. They realized, after service in two world wars and in all wars America had fought until then (and since), that although citizenship implies an obligation to military service, military service does not necessarily bring the rewards of citizenship, that is, civil rights and equality of opportunity.[16]

Another result of the residence factor in the cases we are considering appears in the ability of a resident group to put pressure, in electoral terms and disruptive capabilities, on both the political and military establishments to bring about changes in institutional policies and practices, that is, to politicize minority-military participation (the degree to which they are successful, however, depends very much upon the specific characteristics of the situation at the time the pressure is brought to bear). Thus although some protest about the system of military organization regarding "colored" servicemen and the military tasks they were allowed or not allowed to perform did appear in the British case, the West Indies Regiment, for example, notwithstanding the fine combat record of its predecessor, was turned into a labor battalion during World War I. That there was no concentrated effort made to change the situation was due to the fact that there was no significant West Indian community resident in England to put pressure on the War Office and government to make a change.[17]

In the United States case, on the other hand, the situation was different. Concentrated pressure from Negro organizations; threats of refusal to register for the draft or be inducted; and electoral pressure from the Negro community on politicians, both Negro and white, from the local congressman up to and including the president himself, whether Wilson, Roosevelt, or Truman, brought the problems into public focus. The result was that after "close scrutiny" of the situation in each specific case, whether occupational exclusion or quota, exclusion from the officer corps or officer training, or segregation in the United States armed forces itself, the military authorities did finally change their policies and practices.[18]

Now, although it should be noted that the American military actually believed in the value of segregation and occupational exclusion until "proven" wrong by studies such as "Project CLEAR" (conducted at the time of the Korean War), what had occurred was that a fundamental belief in Negro inability to perform any military function except those involving "labor" tasks resulted in a series of self-fulfilling prophecies regarding the combat experience of separate Negro units in World Wars I and II. Another factor was the fear that integration would harm the morale of white soldiers, who would tend to resent having to serve alongside Negroes. The reason most often given for segregation in the United States military, however, was that the policy and practice reflected only what was perceived as public opinion by the decision makers in the military establishment. The institutional policies and practices that followed as a result are seen in the fact that,

Leading circles in the armed services had long answered demands for an end to segregation of Negroes on the part of the military by pointing to examples of discrimination against them in civilian life in parts of the United States, and by asserting that it was not in the high interest of national defense for the armed forces to engage in "sociological experiments." . . . By this reasoning they justified on-base segregation of Negro servicemen themselves, and obviously they could find no warrant whatsoever for meeting the demands of some civil rights groups that the Negro serviceman and his family be guaranteed full citizenship rights on and off base by affirmative action of their military commanders.

Thus although segregation *in* the United States armed forces was ended in "de jure" terms in 1948 and in "de facto" terms by 1954, the "attack" on *off-base* discrimination against Negro servicemen was not begun by the Pentagon until 1963.[19]

In terms of the reaction of the communities themselves to "rejection," denial of participation, or exclusion from the military, what has happened in the United States case is a good example of what can result, that is, militant activism as regards the attainment of civil rights in the civilian sector and politicization of minority-military participation. In the British case, although the degree of "fragmentation" among colored immigrant communities is similar to that in the case of minority groups in the United States, a continued "rejection" of these communities could lead to a process in which, as noted, "the immigrant sees himself less a West Indian or Sikh in English Society, and more as a black man in white society." The consequences of this are only too predictable.[20]

Now, competent observers of the military in both the United States and United Kingdom have noted the potential function of the military in terms of "basic education and youth socialization," making parallels between programs such as "Project 100,000" in the United States case and the "nation-building, national-integration" and basic education and socialization programs undertaken in other national contexts. One observer recently even advocated something similar to Project 100,000 for the British case, although not consciously including the immigrant community as a potential participant (similar to the "forgetting" of the Negro in the UMT case cited above). In the United States case, however, it must be recognized that Project 100,000 was first a way of increasing the supply of military manpower and only second a "social-engineering" project. The effect of the Project 100,000 experiment and its end-of-service counterpart—Project TRANSITION (conversion-transfer of military acquired-skills project)—are currently being assessed in the United States; however, preliminary results indicate that those Negroes who participated in the Project 100,000 experiment maintain the benefits derived *only* when they remain in military service, since even the benefits of TRANSITION seem to dissipate over time for those Negroes who decide to "have a go" in the civilian sector.[21]

As for the comparative prospects upon return to civilian life of Negro soldiers as against "colored" servicemen in Britain, first, Negroes separating from the military in the United States, despite all of the factors that inhibit their upward mobility, still seem to be in a somewhat better position for converting or transferring their military-acquired skills into civilian job opportunities than "colored" servicemen in the United Kingdom. Second, although a good proportion of "trades" acquired in the British army are recognized by the British trade unions, and employers, as being comparable to trade training in the civilian sector, "colored" personnel may find, as do Negroes in the United States case, upon separating from military service that labor-market discrimination outweighs the level of the skills acquired, resulting in unemployment or underemployment. Thus without proper guidance upon transition to civilian life in the United Kingdom, it is to be expected that problems of "colored" veterans, similar to those of Negro veterans in the United States case, will arise.[22]

To sum up, in late December 1972, it was reported that the then Conservative government was considering a proposal to ensure the unrestricted right of entry for Australians, Canadians, New Zealanders, and others (of "old" commonwealth origin) who fought in the 1939-1945 war. The home secretary, however, pointed out to those senior Conservative MPs who proposed the measure "that such a concession could not be restricted to one or two countries (and that) Indians, Pakistanis, and West Indians with similar service would also have to be granted the same rights," and thus was reported "to be pessimistic about the prospects for devising an acceptable formula on this basis." With regard to Britain's multiethnic society itself, Cynthia Enloe, in a recent paper on the role of the British military, noted that with respect to the Scots and Irish at least, the military had served to a certain extent as an "integrator." As regards the "colored" serviceman, however, we only have to cite Pvt. Errol Geohagen, a West Indian serving in Ulster in 1971. Geohagen, who was born in Barbados and lived in Wanstead, London, "joined the Army because he was excited by the adverts showing British troops in exotic far-away countries." He joined the Queen's Regiment, whose large proportion of West Indians was noted above, and was posted along with his regiment to Belfast. According to Geohagen, although life for a black British soldier in Ulster was indeed difficult, there was at least some consolation, for in his words, "the girls here are friendlier than in England. There is less color prejudice."[23]

In the United States case, in contrast to the "benign neglect" of the racial problem in the United Kingdom military, according to Charles Moskos, at least, "that black soldiers may find they owe higher fealty to the black community than to the U.S. military is a possibility that haunts commanders." But Moskos continued:

The likelihood of such an eventuality . . . will be serious only if the Army is regularly summoned into action in black ghettos. Sensitive to the civil rights issue and the spectre of black power in the military, the armed forces have been surprisingly mild in their handling of black servicemen involved in racial incidents. Most likely there will not be a widespread organized black resistance within the armed forces—barring repeated ghetto interventions—as long as the military follows its present course of internal racially egalitarian policies and allowing moderate leeway for manifestation of black solidarity among troops.[24]

Whether or not United States military policies and practices are "racially egalitarian" is, however, a moot point, since, as John Butler noted, based on his study of rank and occupational distribution patterns of black enlisted men, "the unequal distribution of blacks across ranks decreases over time but remains noticeable into the present. Blacks are underrepresented in technical occupations even when mental group level is controlled." Butler continued, "it can be said that the differential treatment of the black enlisted man has made some positive change over the years." However, he concluded, "Although the Army has made great strides towards racial equality, and has a package of programs which no other institution can match, its black personnel have yet to achieve full participation."[25]

If this is the case, over three decades after the desegregation of the U.S. Army, what does the future hold? In an article dealing with the "racial composition in the all-volunteer force" in the United States, Janowitz and Moskos approached the problem. In effect, they anticipated that if present trends continue, the military, at the enlisted ranks, will become suitable only for minority group and/or poorly educated white youth. However, in making specific proposals to remedy the situation—such as reducing the size of the armed forces and raising educational standards, viewing the military as an educational institution for minorities, linking service in combat units with educational opportunities to attract white youth and reduce the proportion of blacks—even Janowitz and Moskos overlooked the question of labor-market discrimination working against Negro veterans in the United States in terms of racist hiring, and labor union practices, and so on. Thus, as Butler contended, until such issues can be dealt with, "growing black participation in the American military should be viewed as a social problem by sociologists of the military."[26]

BELGIUM AND CANADA

Max Weber's corporate-group concept could be applied here, since as Walter Zenner noted, the minority group resembles a corporate group in that an individual is simply a member or is not. According to Weber.

A social relationship which is either closed or limits the admission of outsiders by rules will be called a corporate group (verband) so far as its order is enforced by the action of specific individuals whose regular function this is . . . more precisely, it exists so far as there is a possibility that certain persons will act in such a way as to tend to carry out the order governing the group; that is, that persons are present who can be counted on to act in this way whenever the occasion arises.

Thus three structural aspects of corporateness can be distinguished: (1) group spokesmen and leadership; (2) self-imposed segregation, to varying extents, in residential, educational, and social terms; and (3) cultural exclusiveness.[27] Walter Zenner noted that the corporate group has the general objective of maintaining a boundary in order to defend a "patrimony" and thereby "continuity of possession to an estate which consists of things, people or both."

In a paper entitled "Pluralism and the Polity: A Theoretical Explanation," Pierre Van den Berghe, in concise and lucid terms, offered an inclusive concept of pluralism that is most suitable here. He maintained that "societies are pluralistic insofar as they exhibit, to a greater or lesser degree, two basic features: (1) segmentation into corporate groups that frequently, thought not necessarily, have different cultures or subcultures; and (2) a social structure compartmentalized into analogous, parallel, non-complementary but distinguishable sets of institutions." He continued:

Additional characteristics frequently associated with pluralism are the following: (1) relative absence of value consensus; (2) relative presence of cultural heterogeneity; (3) relative presence of conflict between the significant corporate groups; (4) relative autonomy between parts of the social system; (5) relative importance of coercion and economic interdependence as basis of social integration; (6) political domination by one of the corporate groups over the others; and (7) primacy of segmental, utilitarian non-affective, and functionally specific relationships between corporate groups and of total, non-utilitarian, affective, diffuse ties within such groups.

He then suggested that a distinction be made between "cultural" and "social" pluralism, but said that "while the two forms of pluralism tend to go together, groups may remain structurally pluralistic even though contact has greatly reduced cultural pluralism," considering social and structural pluralism to be the same form.

With regard to cultural pluralism, Van den Berghe made the cogent observation that it varies from maximally pluralistic societal systems, that is, where the groups "belong to unrelated cultural traditions," to minimally pluralistic systems, that is, societies where group differences are "subculturally" based, in his view, corresponding to "differences based on age, sex, class, race, or caste." He also proposed an intermediate form that can be called "segmented pluralism." Finally, he claimed that "within a given society, all of these three main levels of cultural pluralism can co-exist," citing the South African case, where "for example . . . the distinction between an Afrikaner and a Zulu is one of maximal pluralism, between an Afrikaner and an English-speaking white an intermediate one (i.e. segmented pluralism), and between an Afrikaans-speaking white and an Africaans-speaking Coloured a minimal one." Thus rather than proposing the variants of pluralism as diametrically opposite in type, he asserted that of "crucial importance . . . (is) whether the lines of cleavage between groups are parallel or orthogonal to each other."[28]

In both the Belgian and Canadian cases, we can see the existence of corporate groups; in the former situation the Flemings and Walloons, in the latter the French-Canadians and their English-Canadian counterparts. In both cases, the patrimony involved is language, and efforts made by the respective groups to defend their patrimony have been described in the case studies themselves. As for the "plural" nature of both Belgian and Canadian societies, we have already noted that the former case has been cited as one of "segmented pluralism." In the latter case, one competent observer termed the Canadian situation as one of "double pluralism" accordingly.[29]

Now, over three decades ago, Pierre Bie dealt with French-Canadian and Flemish nationalism in a seminal study conducted at the Institute for Economic and Social Research at the University of Louvain, Belgium. Bie found that although comparisons could be made between the two cases, the latter situation was complicated by the development of a parallel Walloon nationalism, so, in effect, in the Belgian case, one is dealing with two "minority groups"—one "psychological," the Flemish; and one demographic, the Walloons. In contrast, in the Canadian case, the French-Canadians were the minority and the English-Canadians were the dominant group. In historico-demographic perspective, however, this was not always the case in Canada, and one can cite English-Canadian fears of domination by the more numerous French-Canadians until the mid-nineteenth century, when large-scale migration significantly altered the demographic structure in that country. In the Belgian case, the Flemish always composed the numerical majority, but the Flemish elite was Francophone. Thus notwithstanding the demographic majority of Flemish speakers, French was the predominant language in Belgium until the success of the Flemish movement and the creation of a dual linguistic structure in Belgium.

French-Canadians have always put forward Flemish nationalism as an example to follow, from Bourassa, as we have seen above, to Jean Marc Leger, the editor of the French-Canadian nationalist newspaper *Le Devoir*. Leger, in the words of one observer, was "fascinated" by the Flemish "lesson of admirable intransigence," citing "the division of the Belgian Army into two sections with a common bilingual general staff," and praising "the Flemish for persevering until integral bilingualism had been achieved in everything relating to the central government," or, in his words, "fanaticism is indispensable for minorities who mean to survive." Indeed, a significant historical difference between the Belgian and Canadian cases can be seen in the fact that a dual military structure was instituted in Belgium almost three decades before the establishment of a similar structure in Canada.[30]

In retrospect, more differentiates the Belgian and Canadian cases than links them. First, as noted, as a result of industrialization and accelerated economic development in Flanders after World War II, the Flemish are now finally coming to terms with their psychological "minority complex." The situation of the Walloons, who dominated the overall Belgian economic structure, has more or less reversed itself, but they still tend to dominate the key region of economic activity, that is, Brussels. Thus the movement toward Flemish separatism per se has lost momentum, and the focus of Flemish nationalist activity has switched to the Brussels conurbation as noted. In the Canadian case, on the other hand, the process of industrialization and accelerated economic development following World War II in Quebec has actually increased momentum toward French-Canadian separatism, and the nationalist movement in French Canada now focuses its energies in this direction.

Second, although in the Belgian case we are dealing with a dual national linguistic structure overall, that is, in education, military organization, economic development, and so on, and the existence of separate formal structures, such as ministries and governmental bureaucracies, they still operate within a national framework, that is, they are responsible to the Belgian government and parliament. In the Canadian case, on the other hand, Quebec has been linked to other provinces by confederative ties alone, having its own provincial representative assembly, government and ministries, and prime minister. Thus, for example, although defense matters have been concentrated in the hands of the federal government and parliament in Ottawa, Quebec is, in fact, much more independent, and has always been, in running its own affairs, both domestic and "foreign," than either Flanders or Wallonia. Thus the separatist tendency is much stronger in the Canadian case than in the Belgian one. Finally, in Belgium we are dealing with two regionally based linguistic groups who are aware of the fact that neither of their regions could probably survive, either politically or economically, as independent entities. In Canada, on the other hand, French-Canadian nationalists have always been, and are still, convinced that, given proper conditions, Quebec could survive and even prosper on its own. As noted above, however, whether or not this is true remains to be seen.

WORLD PERSPECTIVE: ARMED FORCES IN SEGMENTED AND POLYETHNIC SOCIETIES

SEGMENTED SOCIETIES

The existence of segmented societies is a worldwide phenomenon, and in many of them, there is a pattern of continuity or parallelism between the societal system of organization and that in the military, so articulated military structures exist in these cases accordingly.

Switzerland

Switzerland is a case whose linguistic situation is often held in comparison to the Belgian and Canadian cases. In Switzerland the military is organized along cantonal lines, so units are ipso facto unilingual, due to the demographic structure of the cantons themselves, and thus three languages are, in fact, used in the military: German, French, and Italian.

Now, the Swiss army is, for the most part, an army of militiamen and not a professional army. All of its members—that is, all Swiss male citizens aged twenty to fifty except for those who are either exempted or pay a compensation tax if unable to serve due to physical inability and so on—are called for reserve duty after their basic compulsory military service and training every year for specified periods according to rank, occupation, and service branch. The Swiss constitution prohibits the maintenance of a standing army, except for the existence of permanent cadre such as instructors, officers and NCOs, and corps and divisional commanders. In addition, an allowance is made in the case of the air defense command, which has one permanent reconnaissance-interceptor squadron always on stand-by alert and one army brigade that guards the Alpine fortifications and passes.

The linguistic breakdown of the Swiss armed forces reflects the relative proportions of the three linguistic groups in the country, that is, some 75 percent German, 20 percent French, 4 percent Italian, and 1 percent Romanish speakers (the latter from the Jura region of Bern canton). Out of the twelve divisions in the Swiss army, three are Francophone, and the rest German speaking. An Italian-speaking infantry regiment, artillery battlion, engineering and medical companies, and a frontier-force battalion are attached to German-speaking divisions. Both Italian- and Francophone-Swiss are, however, limited in respect to where they can actually serve. For example, there are no Italian units in the air force nor Francophone communications equipment repair units. Some specialist companies are bilingual, and the servicemen are also required to be bilingual, but Francophone- and Italian-Swiss who also speak German are actively sought to balance these units, which are predominantly staffed by soldiers from German-speaking cantons. As regards the infantry and artillery corps, recruits are trained near home. In the specialist corps, recruits are trained in regional schools according to their language.

In NCO and officer-training schools, courses are held in German and to a limited extent in French, and each cadet is examined in his own language. Officers are recruited on a cantonal-regional basis, and thus the officer corps reflects the population proportions of the respective linguistic groups. There are no language examinations in the army, and line officers up to the level of divisional commander are chosen on a linguistic basis corresponding to the language of the respective division. Staff officers in the operations and training branches are also chosen on a linguistic basis, except for the chiefs of operations and training, who are always from different language groups (there is no chief of staff or commanding general in the Swiss Army or Air Force, except in wartime or time of national mobilization, and this position is, in fact, an elective one, that is, the chief of staff is elected by the federal parliament).

However, although all military directives, regulations, and so on are published in both German and French, and most translated into Italian also, there is usually some delay between publication in German and translation into French and Italian. A special problem presents itself in the case of the Romanish-speaking group that lives in the Jura region northwest of the federal capital Bern. Although this is not the place to go into details regarding relations between the Jurassiens and the German-speaking Bernois in Bern canton, or the Jura problem and separatist movement, a not insignificant number of Jurassiens refuse to serve in the Swiss military, and those who do serve are attached to a French-speaking regiment and Francophone Alpine frontier-force brigade.

To sum up, the Swiss military can be considered to parallel the situation in the civilian sector, where there is a "consociational" form of segmented pluralism according to most observers. However, although the articulated military in the Swiss case reflects the system of societal organization, there still exist problems regarding Francophone-, Italian-Swiss, and Jurassien servicemen as noted.[31]

South Africa

Of the white population in South Africa, the Afrikaners comprise about 60 percent and the white English-speaking group some 40 percent. The South African military is recruited almost entirely from the white group and largely from among the Afrikaners. Afrikaner nationalists are in almost all key positions of authority in the miltary, and as the South African military spokesman noted in 1974, 85 percent of the army's permanent force staff were Afrikaans speaking, 75 percent of the air force permanent staff were Afrikaners, and, interestingly, 50 percent of the South African navy's permanent staff were Afrikaans speaking. In the same year, the *active* strength of the armed forces was some 48,000, of which one-third were permanent personnel. The strength of the standing army (*not* including reserves) in that year was about 35,000, of which only 20 percent were permanent personnel; and in the air force, with a strength of 8,500, 65 percent were regular personnel; and in the navy, with an active strength of 4,500 over 70 percent were regular personnel.

There is universal white conscription in South Africa, and thus both Afrikaners and English speakers in the ranks are proportional to their percentages in the white population. The ethos of the South African army, however, is far from universalistic, having an anti-British tradition and strong attachments to the Afrikaner nationalist cause. However, recently this ethnic-military relationship has been questioned by the Afrikaner elite and political leadership, who have attempted to shift the official ideology from Afrikaner to white nationalism. Thus the regime in South Africa became uneasy with the narrow identification of most of the armed forces with the predominant white group and attempted to expand English-speaking participation beyond short-term conscription and national service. Special recruiting drives aimed at the English-speaking group have been undertaken accordingly to overcome this group's feeling of detachment from the South African military, except for the navy, and also to overcome the English-speaking group's feeling that they "are not wanted" and have little opportunity for advancement and promotion.

As Cynthia Enloe noted, however, "it may prove difficult to transform Afrikaner nationalism into a wider white nationalism. This could weaken the military by depriving it of skilled manpower it needs as it expands and by depriving it of the broader civilian support it will need if it becomes the decisive instrument for sustaining the current system of (white) minority rule."[32]

With regard to the military service of "nonwhites" in South Africa, they are neither considered by the military there to constitute a single group, nor are they treated as such. South Africans of Indian origin and coloreds served during both world wars, albeit in noncombat capacities, as part of the South African forces. Indeed, their military service has provided them with a major point in their argument with the white establishment for granting them full citizenship rights. In 1963 a Colored Corps was set up to provide extra manpower needed by the growing South African army and navy. By 1972 its status as a separate unit was changed, and it was amalgamated into the permanent force. In fact, although a noncombat unit, its members were given weapons training. Three years later, the Cape Corps Service Battalion, a reserve force, was established, and after a year's training in the Cape Corps, the colored soldier was eligible to serve in the permanent force. Thus by 1975, when the first colored soldiers were commissioned as lieutenants in the South African Defense Force, the first "nonwhite" officers in its history, colored recruits were already serving in both the regular army and navy, although they were still barred from service in the air force.

As mentioned above, South Africans of Indian origin also provided military manpower. In mid-1974 the South African military formed an Indian Corps, ostensibly at the request of Indian leaders and ex-servicemen's organizations for the establishment of an Indian unit along the lines of the Colored Corps. Similar to the case of the Colored Corps, the Indian Corps personnel were to be used in noncombatant auxiliary capacities, although they were to be given weapons training.

The increasing use of black Africans in the South African military not only contradicts the historical objection of the Boers to their recruitment, but their assignment to combat-related occupations and deployment along the borders actually highlights a paradox regarding their military participation. This paradox emanates from the fact that the blacks were actually being assigned to fulfill occupations such as armed guard duty at military installations and take part in antiguerrilla operations along the border, while their ostensibly more "reliable" and "less threatening" colored and Indian counterparts were performing only auxiliary noncombat functions. According to Cynthia Enloe, this paradoxical situation only "underscores the contradiction running throughout the Nationalist Party ruling formula; the expansion of capacity—whether industrial or military—drives the white leadership to depend more and more on the largest mobilizable sector of the population, the Africans, for the sake of preventing the deterioration of white dominance."[33]

Malaysia

In Malaysia there are two main ethnic groups: the Malays, who comprise 50 percent of the population; and the Chinese, who constitute some 37 percent. There are also Indians, Pakistanis, Eurasians, and Europeans, who make up the remaining 13 percent of the population.

The segmented character of the country and the historic domination of the Malays is reflected in the armed forces structure and organization. Recruitment into the armed forces was initially restricted to Malays, and, notwithstanding the government's efforts to bring about a sense of common purpose and the formation of some multiracial units, Malays continued to dominate the armed forces through the 1960s. This was particularly evident in the army, where recruitment into the Royal Malay Regiment, which comprised most of the ground forces, was restricted to Malays. All other army units and the air force and navy were multiracial but conformed to the specified racial proportions of 40 percent Malay, 40 percent Chinese, and 20 percent Indian and others. In the Royal Malay Air Force, there was a significant departure from these percentages in the officer corps, where 50 percent were Chinese as against 33 percent Malay, although the overall ratios were maintained, and in the enlisted ranks the percentages were reversed. Thus with regard to senior armed forces officers, it is not surprising that some 65 percent are Malay, and only 35 percent non-Malay.

Although the air force and navy, as well as technical units in the army, have been the main channels for Chinese and Indian participation and promotion (the navy even having an Indian commander), the predominant role of the Malaysian army and the Malay Regiment, comprising 80 percent of total army strength, greatly affects the potential for non-Malay officers advancement.

This, in addition to the trend for non-Malay officers to be found in staff, rather than line positions, clearly limits their policymaking role and influence.

Thus as Cynthia Enloe noted, "Malaysia is certainly not extraordinary as a case in which ethnicity has shaped the composition and role of the national military . . . yet as the military has become a more critical factor in the country's political calculus, the ethnic composition of the military's personnel has been diversified." This basic ambivalence, she noted, may actually be of deliberate nature since, according to her, "at the same time that (the Malay civilian leadership) desires a military force capable of maintaining civic order, it wants a military command it deems reliable and compliant—i.e. a military led by Malays."[34]

Czechoslovakia and Yugoslavia

In the case of Czechoslovakia, the Czechs form some 68 percent of the population and the Slovaks some 26 percent, with other nationalities comprising the remaining 6 percent. In the military, the Czechs are overrepresented in the officer corps, where they form some 80 percent, as against 20 percent Slovaks, a ratio that did not change over the 1950s and 1960s. However, according to one observer of the Czechoslovak military, "the difference between the overall nationality ratio and the composition of officers according to nationality is not great . . . (and) the nationality differences in the composition of the officer corps are gradually disappearing" as Slovak officers advance in rank.[35]

The situation in Yugoslavia, on the other hand, is somewhat more problematic. Here, the Serbs form about 42 percent of the population and the Croats some 23 percent, with the remaining 35 percent being made up of a dozen or so smaller ethnic groups, the most significant being the Slovenes, Macedonians, and Montenegrins, who are ethnically related to the Serbs. Despite the Serbs comprising only a bit more than 40 percent of the population, however, between 70 and 80 percent of the officer corps in the Yugoslav military are Serbian in origin. In addition, although the Montenegrins form only 3 percent of the population, they comprise 15 percent of the senior government employees, with the Serbs themselves making up over 65 percent of federal officials.

During World War II, Serbs, Croats, and Slovenes fought in their own units using their own language and having their own commanders. In the late 1940s, after the Communist takeover, it was decided to integrate these units and centralize the army with Serbo-Croat as its official language. Despite this and other measures to integrate Yugoslavia's ethnic groups undertaken by Tito, Croatian nationalism and separatism is still rife, both within Yugoslavia and among Croats living outside the country.[36]

POLYETHNIC SOCIETIES

In a number of polyethnic societies, the nature and characteristics of the minority situation is similar to that observed in the United States and United Kingdom cases above, and they follow the parallel pattern of minority-military participation. Such cases include that of the Negro and mulatto in Brazil; the Indian and mestizo in Peru, Mexico, and Bolivia; and Indians and mestizos in other countries of Latin America.

In both civilian society and in the military in Latin America, more opportunities have been open to those of European origin than to "people of color" in every national army in Latin America (except for Haiti, which is almost exclusively populated by Negroes and mulattos), and the percentage of officers of European ethnic origin is much higher than the percentage of this group in the population. The predominance of this group in the officer corps is, however, gradually decreasing. In Peru, for example, mestizos form most of the officers corps, as in Mexico, El Salvador, and Paraguay. In Venezuela a growing number of senior officers are of Negro origin. Except for Colombia, where the officer corps still originates from the upper middle class, "there is evidence that the white predominance is breaking down"; however, "whiteness will continue, short of revolution, to be a factor for many years." The main reason for this process is the tendency toward the expansion of the officer corps recruiting base to include the lower social strata, where the mestizos, Indians, Negros, and mulattos are to be found. In Ecuador, for example, officers of lower class origin form the same percentage as those of upper class origin.[37]

In Peru, Indians form some 45 percent of the population;

mestizos, 50 percent, and whites, the rest. While the majority of officers are mestizos, there is interservice differentiation regarding the ethnic composition of the officer corps, since although army officers are largely mestizo in origin, naval and air force officers originate mainly from the white upper class.[38]

In Mexico, Indians comprise some 30 percent of the population; mestizos, 60 percent, and whites of European origin, 10 percent. With regard to the officer corps, most are of mestizo origin, since admissions procedures and requirements at the National Military Academy tend to screen out Indians, but since some officers enter from the ranks, they may be presumed to be of lower class, that is, Indian origin. Although there is deep opposition to compulsory military service among the Indians, due to the historic method of dragooning them into service, there is no problem with Indian recruitment in the Mexican army, since there are many benefits involved in such service for both the Indian and his family, ranging from financial incentives to literacy training and education.[39]

Indians in Bolivia form some 65 percent of the population, with mestizos comprising some 30 percent, and whites of European origin, 5 percent. Class and race distinctions were quite evident in the pre-1952 (revolution) army. The officer corps originated from both mestizos and whites of European origin, and the ranks were composed of Indian conscripts. The Chaco border conflict (1932-1936) between Bolivia and Paraguay, which Bolivia eventually lost, did, however, change the attitudes of the white and mestizo officers toward the Indian soldiers, since they found themselves dependent on the same Indians whom they had, until then, "despised." The Indians, for their part, learned of the ideas of equality during their war service, and didn't forget the lesson, and as one observer put it, "it was Indian participation in the Chaco War which made possible the rapid growth of an autonomous Indian organization . . . if they were equal in their obligation to the nation, how could their privileges be less?" After the 1960 revolution and the reinstitution of compulsory military service, the Bolivian military took on the function of providing literacy and basic educational training for the Indian conscripts, becoming, in the words of one observer, "the most national institution in the country." The officer corps, however, still remains, for the most part, mestizo in origin, despite the military's "role expansion."[40]

In Brazil, which has often been compared to the United States, whites form 54 percent of the population; mulattos, 38 percent; Negroes, 7 percent; and other groups (Indians, Asians), 1 percent. The military, however, is composed mostly of whites in the officer corps and mulattos at the NCO level. Interservice differentials in racial participation are also evident. The Brazilian navy traditionally "considered itself aristocratic and ethnically pure," that is, no Negroes or mulattos, and the army was republican and democratically oriented, so its "officers were of more moderate social origin, some of them having Negro or Indian blood in their veins." As John Johnson noted, "Naval officers freely acknowledge that their service has been racially discriminatory" against both Negroes and mulattos. Although many observers claim that Brazil is "free from racial discrimination," the Brazilian armed forces, at least, still do not have Negroes in their hierarchy.[41]

In both segmented and polyethnic societies, the military can often exacerbate, rather than resolve, conflict. This may occur if regimes deliberately regulate the ethnic composition so that the weaker groups become alienated from both the military and polity. Concomitantly, differential recruitment and promotion often bring the dominant group to view the military as "its own," and it therefore opposes the minority group's demands for greater participation. As Enloe wrote,

The resolution of inter-ethnic conflict demands that armies . . . be examined not as neutral instruments that cope with problems, but as potential causes of problems as well. Not all the ethnic imbalances in state security forces are the result of deliberate policy design—but more than a few are. Any lasting resolution of ethnic conflict may require that the distribution of political authority and influence in society be basically reordered and that, as part of that reordering, the . . . military be ethnically reconstituted at the top and the bottom. Resolution of inter-ethnic conflict and state-ethnic conflict will be tenuous if the security that is achieved is merely state security and not security for each of the state's resident communities.[42]

In summary, then, we can make the following points. First, it would seem that the military in countries characterized by segmented pluralism and polyethnicity has not fulfilled, for the most part, the "national-integration" role attributed to the military in general by many observers. Second, although a number of observers have stressed the discontinuity of the military and civilian society, for example, the "universalistic" nature of the military as against the "particularistic" nature of civilian society and so on, it seems that in the case of minority-military participation, the more prevalent pattern is one of continuity or parallelism. In addition, the parallel pattern may, in fact, be the equilibrium pattern of minority-military service. However, this hypothesis would have to be operationalized and empirically tested, if possible, to be confirmed. But if this hypothesis is indeed correct, a "projective fallacy" regarding use of the formal organizational model proposed by Shils, Pye, and even Janowitz, among others, can be said to exist, insofar as it predicts that the equilibrium pattern of minority-military participation is discontinuity, rather than parallelism, as I have suggested.

Finally, in the cases of armed forces in segmented societies dealt with above, there exists dual or multiple military structures along linguistic or ethnoracial lines, and separate units have also been maintained in some cases of polyethnicity. Now, as has been noted by many observers, sociological theory does not maintain that separate units necessarily weaken the effectiveness of the military organization. Rather, what may be important is the goals of the group or groups involved. Thus separate units have succeeded in many cases, and in other cases, they have failed and prevented socially cohesive groups from developing. An analysis of the factors affecting the success or failure of separate units and dual or multiple military structures as against integrated units and unitary military structures is beyond the scope of this work. However, systematic comparative research along such lines could reveal new information and processes that could, in turn, be of great interest to sociologists of the military.[43]

NOTES

1. C. C. Moskos, "The Emergent Military: Civil, Traditional or Plural?" *Pacific Sociological Review* 16, 2 (1973), pp. 255-80. Moskos also dealt

with the United States case specifically in "Armed Forces and American Society: Convergence or Divergence," in C. Moskos, ed. *Public Opinion and the Military Establishment* (Beverly Hills: Sage, 1971), pp. 273ff.

2. On this, see W. Young, "Multidimensionality and Minoriticity: Towards a Taxonomy of Minority-Societal Relations," *Rivista di Sociologia* (Rome) 28 (1974), pp. 6-9.

3. C. C. Moskos, "Minority Groups in Military Organization," in R. W. Little, ed., *Handbook of Military Institutions* (Beverly Hills: Sage, 1971), p. 280.

4. Ibid. On the Swiss case, see note 31.

5. J. Blake, "The Organization as an Instrument of Violence: The Military Case," *Sociological Quarterly* 11, 3 (1970), p. 337.

6. Morris Janowitz discussed the general problem of the relationship between military service and citizenship in "Military Institutions and Citizenship in Western Societies" (Paper presented at the British Inter-University Seminar on Armed Forces and Society Meeting, 1973).

7. C. Enloe, "Police and Military in the Resolution of Ethnic Conflict," *Annals of the American Academy of Political and Social Science* 433 (1977), p. 144.

8. S. Andreski, *Military Organization and Society* (London: Routledge and Kegan Paul, 1954). See also A. Marwick, *Britain in the Century of Total War* (London: Bodley Head, 1968); idem, *War and Social Change in the 20th Century* (London: Macmillan, 1974). P. Abrams, "The Failure of Social Reform," *Past and Present* 26 (1963), restated Andreski's theory as follows: "there is some kind of meaningful correlation between the social 'size' of a war and the process of social reform and levelling," but "in its crude form, the military participation ratio theory of social reform will not do. If it is to have any value, it must allow for the fact that different groups in society participate in a war effort to different degrees, with widely varying power to influence consequential political decisions and with a very different sense of what participation means to them," pp. 45, 62. For some illustrations of this, see N. Wynn, "The Impact of the Second World War on the American Negro," *Journal of Contemporary History* 6, 2 (1971), pp. 42-53. On the "accelerator," see C. Johnson, *Revolution and the Social System* (Stanford: Stanford University Press, 1964), p. 12; and idem, *Revolutionary Change* (London: University of London Press, 1968).

9. M. Brunet, "The French-Canadians Search for a Fatherland," in P. Russell, ed., *Nationalism in Canada* (Toronto: McGraw-Hill, 1966), p. 56. R. Rothman, "Education and Participation in the Israeli Defence

Forces," *Jewish Social Studies* 34, 2 (1972), described the role of the Israeli Army in alleviating the situation of the Oriental Jew in Israel via compensatory education programs. Cynthia Enloe dealt with the extent of the conflict in Northern Ireland and the role of the security forces there in "Police and Military in Ulster: Peace-keeping or Peace-subverting Forces?" *Journal of Peace Research* 15, 3, (1978). On the Belgian case, see D. W. Urwin, "Societal Cleavages and Political Parties in Belgium," *Political Studies* 18, 3 (1970), p. 329. The situation in Yugoslavia is described by P. Shoup in *Communism and the Yugoslav National Question* (New York: Columbia University Press, 1968), quote from p. 10.

10. C. C. Moskos, "The Negro and the Draft," p. 151.

11. The exception being Puerto Ricans, Filipinos, and indigenous forces serving with United States troops in Viet Nam such as Koreans and Vietnamese-Thai-Lao tribes, to cite some recent examples. On the Puerto Rican case, see, for example, E. King, *The Death of the Army* (New York: Saturday Review Press, 1972), pp. 83-94. On the Filipino case, see, for example, D. Duff and R. Arthur, "Between Two Worlds: Filipinos in the U.S. Navy," *American Journal of Psychiatry* 123, 7 (1967). Although no detailed material is available in the United Kingdom case regarding the record of military service of resident Negroes, some impressionistic material is presented in J. Walvin, *Black and White: The Negro and English Society* (London: Allen Lane, 1973).

12. A. Rose, "Race and Ethnic Relations," in R. Merton and R. Nisbet, eds., *Contemporary Social Problems*, 2nd ed. (New York: Harcourt, Brace and World, 1966), p. 411. This term is used by Samuel Huntington in describing the "role-expansion" functions advocated by the United States military in the post-World War I era. See S. Huntington, *The Soldier and the State* (Cambridge: Harvard, Belknap, 1957), pp. 285-86. See also J. Walvin, *Black and White,* p. 197.

13. On these points, see, for example, E. J. B. Rose et al., *Colour and Citizenship* (Oxford: Oxford University Press, 1969); W. Daniel, *Racial Discrimination in Britain* (London: Penguin, 1968); S. Abbott, *The Prevention of Racial Dicrimination in Britain* (Oxford: Oxford University Press, 1971), all of which discuss the problem. A more recent work is that of a second-generation West Indian, C. Mullard, *Black Britain* (London: Allen and Unwin, 1973). Good reportage is contained in D. Humphry and G. John, *Because They're Black* (London: Penguin, 1972), and a comparative analysis of the United States and British cases is given in I. Katznelson, *Black Men, White Cities: Race, Politics, and Migration in the U.S. 1900-30 and Britain 1948-68* (Oxford: Oxford University Press, 1973). See

also J. Rex and R. Moore, *Race, Community, and Conflict* (Oxford: Oxford University Press, 1967), pp. 100, 156, who noted that in the West Indian case, at least, "West Indians come to England as to their mother country." On the identity problem of second-generation West Indians, see Rose et al., *Colour and Citizenship*, ch. 24, pp. 476-91.

14. T. Parsons defined *inclusion* in his article "Full Citizenship for the Negro American?" *Daedalus* 94 (1965), pp. 1009-54, starting from the premise that the Negro American does not have "full citizenship," by which he meant "full citizenship in the societal community." He defined *societal community* as a "society which is at the same time a community," going on to point out that "the Negro, although a member of American society, is not 'included' in the American community." What would such "inclusion" involve? Parsons listed three basic requirements: (1) equal civil rights; (2) a full sharing in the pursuit of the collective goals of the society, in the process of government and the exercise of power; and (3) equality of the resources and capacities necessary to make "equal rights" into fully equal opportunities. "Inclusion," in Parson's sense, however, does not imply assimilation. He acknowledged that religious and ethnic groups will continue to have their own attitudes and organizations and that this "pluralism" or cultural diversity is a necessary part of American life. However, under conditions of "inclusion," allegiance to one's ethnic or religious group will be one involvement that cuts across many other involvements of the same people. But Parsons was concerned above all with the exclusion of the Negro from "full citizenship" and with the process of inclusion that he believed to be necessary. The Negro's chief ambition, he argued, is to be included instead of rejected or forgotten.

Quote cited in J. Heilpern and D. Hiro, "The Town We Were Told Was Tolerant," *Observer* (London), 1 Dec. 1968, p. 11. In this context, it is interesting that although West Indians, as mentioned above, have the highest degree of identification with the "British way of life," they have suffered the most from racial discrimination in Britain. As "the most comprehensive survey of racial discrimination in Britain" concluded: "Of the three coloured groups (West Indians, Indians, and Pakistanis), the experience of the West Indians has been the worst. To a considerable extent, this is due to their higher expectations on arrival and their greater desire to participate in a British pattern of life. This has caused them greater exposure to rejection and rebuff, and therefore to have a greater feeling that discrimination occurs." See *Racial Discrimination* (London: Political and Economic Planning, 1967), pp. 8ff.

15. See, for example, J. Swomley, *The Military Establishment* (Boston:

Beacon, 1964); C. Ackley, *The Modern Military in American Society* (New York: Westminster, 1972); W. R. Kintner *Forging a New Sword* (New York: Harper, 1958); A. Ekirch, *The Civilian and the Military* (Oxford: Oxford University Press, 1956); L. Smith, *Democracy and Military Power* (Chicago: University of Chicago Press, 1951); S. Huntington, *The Soldier and the State*, pp. 285-86.

16. S. Huntington, *The Soldier and the State,* pp. 204, 255, 286; R. Weighley, *History of the United States Army* (New York: Macmillan, 1967). See also R. Logan, *The Betrayal of the Negro* (New York: Macmillan, 1969). Negro organizations actively opposed UMT after World War II. See J. Swomley, *The Military Establishment,* pp. 71-75.

17. For a description of what occurred in the United Kingdom case, see C. L. Joseph, "The British West Indies Regiment: 1914-18," *Journal of Caribbean History* 2 (1971); J. Walvin, *Black and White,* p. 212; and R. J. MacDonald, "Dr. H. A. Moody and the League of Coloured Peoples," *Race* 14, 3 (1973), pp. 300-301.

18. For an account of the United States case during the Wilson administration, see J. L. Scheiber and H. Scheiber, "The Wilson Administration and the Wartime Mobilization of Black Americans," *Labor History* 10, 3 (1969). For the Roosevelt and Truman administrations, see R. Dalfiume, *Desegregation of the U.S. Armed Forces: Fighting on Two Fronts, 1939-53* (Kansas City: University of Missouri Press, 1969), pp. 32-43, 139-48, 174. The developing political power of the Negro community is also discussed by B. Quarles in *The Negro in the Making of America* (New York: Macmillan, 1964), who noted that to FDR, "the winning of the colored vote was important, since the Negro by 1940 had come to hold the balance of power in some ten states outside the South" (p. 213). Dalfiume showed that although Roosevelt was confident of victory in 1940, he still wanted the Negro in his camp and thus "wooed" Negro votes by promises and concessions of fuller participation in military service. The Negro vote was, however, crucial to Truman in 1948, and both he and his advisers realized this early on, as Dalfiume pointed out. Other studies analyzing the growing political strength of the Negro *as a result* of his northward migration (and migration to the Midwest and Far West) and concomitant urban concentration include: O. Glantz, "The Negro Voter in Northern Industrial Cities," *Western Political Quarterly* 12 (1960); and M. Kilson, "Political Change in the Negro Ghetto 1900-1940's," in M. Kilson, *Key Issues in the Afro-American Experience* (New York: Harcourt, Brace, 1971), pp. 167-92.

19. On Project "CLEAR," see L. Bogart, *Social Research and the Desegregation of the U.S. Army* (Chicago: Markham, 1969); L. D. Reddick,

"The Negro Policy of the U.S. Army," *Journal of Negro History* 34, 1 (1949), p. 23; R. Logan, *The Negro in the United States* (New York: Peter Smith, 1970), pp. 75-78; D. Mandelbaum, *Soldier Groups and Negro Soldiers* (Berkeley: University of Calif. Press, 1952), pp. 96-97; B. Quarles, *The Negro in the Making of America,* pp. 183-85; E. Kenworthy, "The Case against Army Segregation," *Annals of the American Academy of Political and Social Science* 275 (1951), p. 27. See also the text of a speech given by Gen. Omar Bradley as reported by Hanson Baldwin in the *New York Times,* 8 Aug. 1948. For a general discussion of "self-fulfilling prophecies" in relation to manpower utilization, see R. Merton, *Social Theory and Social Structure* (Glencoe Ill.: Free Press, 1949).

See also J. P. Davis, ed., *American Negro Reference Book* (New York: Prentice-Hall, 1966), pp. 656-57, on the problem of on- and off-base discrimination. D. Sutton also dealt with this problem in "The Military Mission against Off-Base Segregation," in C. Moskos, ed., *Public Opinion and the Military Establishment* (Beverly Hills: Sage, 1971).

20. N. Glazer, "Race Relations in Britain—An American Perspective," *Sociology* 6, 1 (1972), p. 98; D. Kramer, "White versus Coloured in Britain," *Social Research* 36, 4 (1969), pp. 589-90. It is important to recall and stress the difference between West Indian Negroes and the resident Negro community in Britain, since although a high proportion of the "resident Negro community" is of West Indian origin, it has basically "acculturated itself" to the status of less than first-class citizens in the Parsonian sense. The new West Indian immigrant community, with its higher expectations of opportunity upon arrival in Britain, has become bitterly disillusioned with the "whole scene," which may account for the recent increasing trend in those returning to the Caribbean. On these points, see J. Walvin, *Black and White*; I. Katznelson, *Black Men, White Cities*. See also, for example, the feeling expressed by J. A. Brathwaite, *A Black British Soldier* (Toronto: World, 1969).

21. See, for example, M. Janowitz, "Basic Education and Youth Socialization," in R. W. Little, ed., *Handbook of Military Institutions*; J. C. M. Baynes, *The Soldier in Modern Society* (London: Eyre Methuen, 1972), pp. 168-73. See also the *Economist* (London), 10 March 1973; C. R. Coble, "Social Action Programs in the Department of Defense" (Ph.D. diss., University of North Carolina, 1969). J. Ladinsky, *A Survey of Economically Disadvantaged Vietnam Era Veterans* (Washington, D.C.: U.S. Bureau of the Budget, 1969), noted the *low* proportion of Negroes who have participated in Project "TRANSITION."

22. J. C. M. Baynes, *The Soldier in Modern Society*, pp. 83-84. United Kingdom censuses 1961, 1966, 1971 show a high West Indian

concentration in lower income status and blue-collar and service occupations. The discharge procedure in the United Kingdom has only recently been reformed. See the *Times* (London), 29 March 1973.

23. *Sunday Telegraph* (London), 24 Dec. 1972; Cynthia Enloe, "The Military—A Sleeper in British Politics" (Paper presented at Northeastern Political Science Association Meeting, Rutgers University, Nov. 1975), pp. 5-6; Ian Mather, "What It's Like to Be British and Black . . . in Ulster," *Daily Mail* (London), 3 Dec. 1971.

24. C. Moskos, "Armed Forces and American Society: Convergence or Divergence," in C. Moskos, ed., *Public Opinion and the Military Establishment* (Beverly Hills: Sage, 1971), pp. 280-281.

25. J. Butler, "Assessing Black Enlisted Participation in the Army," *Social Problems* 23 (1976), pp. 558, 565.

26. M. Janowitz and C. Moskos, "Racial Composition in the All-Volunteer Forces," *Armed Forces and Society* 1 (1974), pp. 109-23; J. Butler, "Assessing Black Enlisted Participation in the Army," p. 560.

27. W. Zenner, "Ethnic Assimilation and the Corporate Group," in M. Kurokawa, ed., *Minority Responses* (New York: Random House, 1970), p. 111; M. Weber, *The Theory of Social and Economic Organization* (Oxford: Oxford University Press, 1947), pp. 145-46.

28. P. Van den Berghe, "Pluralism and the Polity: A Theoretical Explanation," in L. Kuper and M. Smith, eds., *Pluralism in Africa* (Berkeley: University of Calif. Press, 1969), pp. 67-81, especially p. 69.

29. R. Ossenberg, "Social Pluralism in Quebec: Continuity, Change, and Conflict," in R. Ossenberg, ed., *Canadian Society: Pluralism, Change and Conflict* (Ontario: Prentice-Hall, 1971), p. 103-7.

30. E. Corbett, *Quebec Confronts Canada* (Baltimore: Johns Hopkins University Press, 1968), p. 105; *Le Devoir* (Montreal), 22 June 1963.

31. H. Kurz, "Die sprachenfrage in unserer armee," *Der Fourier* (Switz: Gersau, Nov. 1961), pp. 405-9; "Essai sur les questions linguistiques en Suisse," *Revue Militaire Suisse* 118, 1 (1973), pp. 6-7, 10; G. Rapp, "L'attitude actuelle de le jeunesse a l'egard de la defense nationale," *Revue Militaire Suisse* 118, 7 (July 1973), pp. 289-303; H. Kurz, "Analysis of the Swiss Military Establishment" (Berne: Department Militaire Federal, 1973); G. Soloveychik, *Switzerland in Perspective* (Oxford: Oxford University Press, 1954),p. 66; "The Jura Separatists," *Race Today*, Dec. 1972, p. 397. In 1974 the Jurassiens voted for a separate canton, the first since 1830 in Switzerland, thus ending the struggle that had started after the region was absorbed into Berne canton in 1815 by the Treaty of Vienna. See the *Times* (London), 24 June 1974. Note that Romanish is a local dialect of French. For a survey of the Jura problem, see

Kenneth McRae, *Switzerland: Example of Cultural Coexistence* (Toronto: Canadian Institute of International Affairs, 1964).

For a description of the "consociational" form of segmented pluralism in the Swiss case, see H. Daalder, "On Building Consociational Nations: The Cases of the Netherlands and Switzerland," *International Social Science Journal* 23, 3 (1971).

32. C. Enloe, "Ethnic Factors in the Evolution of the South African Military" (Paper presented at the annual meeting of the African Studies Association, San Francisco, Oct. 1975), pp. 6-8; J. Butler, "Social Status, Ethnic Division, and Political Conflict in New Nations: Afrikaners and Englishmen in South Africa," in W. Bell and W. E. Freeman, eds., *Ethnicity and Nation Building* (Beverly Hills: Sage, 1971), pp. 147-69; S. Katzenellenbogen, "South Africa and the War of 1914-18," in M. R. D. Foot, ed., *War and Society* (London: Elek, 1973), pp. 107-21; D. Denoon, "Participation in the Boer War," in B. A. Ogot, ed., *War and Society in Africa* (London: Cass, 1972), pp. 109-21; P. Van den Berghe, *South Africa: A Study in Conflict* (Chicago: Wesleyan University Press, 1965), pp. 98ff.

33. C. Enloe, "Ethnic Factors in the Evolution of the South African Military," pp. 9-12.

34. C. Enloe, "Civilian Control of the Military: Implications in the Plural Societies of Guyana and Malaysia" (Paper presented at the Inter-University Seminar on Armed Forces and Society Meeting, SUNY-Buffalo, Oct. 1974), pp. 15, 42-43; idem, "Malaysia's Military in the Interplay of Economic and Ethnic Change" (Paper presented at Association for Asian Studies Meeting, Hartford, Conn., Nov. 1975), pp. 18-19; J. Henderson, *Area Handbook for Malaysia* (Washington, D.C.: American University Foreign Area Studies, 1970), p. 558; Government of Malaysia, *Official Yearbook* (Kuala Lumpur, 1972), pp. 25ff.

35. J. Cvriek, "Social Change in the Officer Corps of the Czechoslovak Peoples Army," in J. van Doorn, ed., *Military Professions and Military Regimes* (The Hague: Mouton, 1969), pp. 103ff.; Miloslav Rechciql, ed. *Czechoslovakia—Past and Present*, vol. 1, *Political, Social, and Economic Aspects* (The Hague: Mouton, 1968), especially Joseph Hajda, "Czech Federalist Heritage: A Historical Perspective," pp. 736-43.

36. P. Shoup, *Communism and the Yugoslav National Question* (New York: Columbia University Press, 1968); J. Fisher, *Yugoslavia—A Multinational State* (San Francisco: Chandler, 1966); A. Rubenstein, "Yugoslavia's Pluralism at the Crossroads," *Plural Societies* 4, 1 (1973), pp. 31-42; P. Lendvai, "Yugoslavia in Crisis," *Encounter* 39, 2 (1972), pp. 71-75; N. Pasic, "Factors in the Formation of Nations in the Balkans and among the South Slavs"; R. Remington, "Armed Forces and Society in

Yugoslavia," in C. Kelleher, ed., *Political-Military Systems: Comparative Perspectives* (Beverly Hills: Sage, 1974), pp. 163-90.

37. J. Johnson, *The Military and Society in Latin America* (Stanford: Stanford University Press, 1964), ch. 4, pp. 105-6, 237-38; J. Pitt-Rivers, "Race in Latin America," *Archives Européanées de Sociologie* 14 (1973).

38. D. Chaplin, "Peruvian Social Mobility: Revolutionary and Developmental Potential," *Journal of Inter-American Studies* 10, 4 (1966), pp. 567-68; L. North, *Civil-Military Relations in Argentina, Chile, and Peru* (Berkeley: University of California Press, 1966), pp. 54-63; P. Mason, "Gradualism in Peru," *Race* 8, 1 (1966), pp. 43-61; S. Clissold, "The Indian Problem in Latin America: Changing Attitudes in the Andean Republics," *Race* 7, 1 (1965), pp. 47-57.

39. D. Borbolla, "The Mexican Indian Today," in A. Williams, ed., *Mexico Today* (Tampa: University of Florida Press, 1964), p. 123-25; and in the same volume, K. Schmitt, "The Role of the Military in Contemporary Mexico," pp. 54-55; W. Borah, "Race and Class in Mexico," *Pacific Historical Review* 23, 4 (1954), pp. 331-43; B. Kaplan, "Ethnic Identification in an Indian Mestizo Community," *Phylon* 14, 2 (1953), pp. 179-86; E. Wolf, "Aspects of Group Relations in a Complex Society: Mexico," *American Anthropologist* 58 (1956).

40. R. Patch, "Peasantry and National Revolution: Bolivia," in K. Silvert, ed., *Expectant Peoples* (New York: Random House, 1963), pp. 106, 110-11, 117-18, 120; R. Alexander, *The Bolivian National Revolution* (New Brunswick, N.J.: Rutgers University Press, 1958), pp. 145ff.; J. Malloy, *Bolivia: The Uncompleted Revolution* (Pittsburgh: University of Pittsburgh Press, 1970), pp. 296-303.

41. J. Johnson, *The Military and Society in Latin America*, p. 193; J. Zamor, "Social Mobility of Negroes in Brazil," *Journal of Inter-American Studies* 12, 2 (1970), pp. 242-54; R. Poppino, *Brazil* (Oxford: Oxford University Press, 1968), pp. 306-7; G. Freyre, *Mansions and Shanties: The Making of Modern Brazil* (New York: Knopf, 1963), pp. 368-71; O. Ianni, *Crisis in Brazil* (Cambridge: Cambridge University Press, 1970); F. Fernandes, *The Negro in Brazilian Society* (Cambridge: Cambridge University Press, 1969); R. Bastide, "Race Relations in Brazil," *International Social Science Bulletin* 9 (1957), pp. 495-512; M. Harris, "The Structural Significance of Brazilian Racial Categories," *Sociologia* 25 (1963), pp. 203-9.

42. C. Enloe, "Police and Military in the Resolution of Ethnic Conflict," pp. 148-49.

43. M. Janowitz, "The Military Establishment: Organization and Disorganization," in R. K. Merton and R. A. Nisbet, eds, *Contemporary Social Problems*, 1st ed. (New York: Harcourt, Brace and World, 1961), pp. 542-43.

APPENDIX:
MINORITIES: A BIBLIOGRAPHIC
ESSAY AND REVIEW

I.

What constitutes a "minority" has been the focus of social scientists for some time. Besides case studies of specific group-contact situations, theoretical and operational distinctions have been made between "national minorities" and "minority groups" and numerous definitions proposed as to what a *minority* really is. Even in distinguishing between these two "fundamental types," certain anomalies arise, as a result of which we can consider the former "type" as a "special case" of a generalized "minority type," which encompasses both. However, the first point that is usually made in the literature on minorities is that no statistical connotation need be attached to the term *minority*, since due to certain factors arising out of the specific case under consideration, a group that is a demographic "majority" in a certain geographical area may be, in fact, "subordinate" or, in other words, have "minority status." Alternatively, if no group forms the demographic "majority," but there is one group that is "subordinate," this group would be the "minority" (if more than one group in this category, they would be the minorities).

Secondly, when there exists a real or perceived inequality in access to political and economic prerogatives, that group which *both* recognizes its "subordinate" position and is "engaged in a struggle for upward mobility" may be termed a *minority group*. Third, in some cases, there exists an association between membership in a "minority group" and socioeconomic status, an "intersection" between certain socioeconomic status levels (as defined and measured by income and occupation) and the group as a segment of the labor force and total population. In other words, group differentiation perpetuates itself in the social structure and these groups are found stratified, to some degree, in some hierarchical ordering or along "class lines." The degree to which the group and its members find themselves "strongly clustered" around a certain income level or the degree to which its occupational distribution is "skewed" in the direction of lower income and lower status occupations is, however, a function of several complex and interactive variables.

Now, the groups that have been dealt with in previous chapters exhibit "minority characteristics" in that they are differentiable; they have been and in some cases still are the subjects of discrimination and prejudice, both institutional and interpersonal, directed at both the individual and group levels, and the specific characteristics of the cases conform to the points made above regarding stratification, status recognition, and upward mobility.

II.

Arnold Rose noted that "according to the best information," the term *minority group* as distinguished from *national minority* was introduced into sociology by Donald Young in his book *American Minority Peoples* (see A. Rose, "Race and Ethnic Relations," in R. K. Merton and R. A. Nisbet, eds., *Contemporary Social Problems,* 2nd ed. ([New York: Harcourt, Brace and World, 1966], p. 410, n. 3). Rose, in the *International Encyclopedia of the Social Sciences*, vol. 10 (New York: Collier-Macmillan, 1968), defined *minorities* as "a group of people—differentiated from others in the same society by race, nationality, religion, or language—who both think of themselves as a differentiated group and are thought of by others as a differentiated group with negative connotations. Further, they are relatively lacking in power and hence are subjected to certain exclusions, discriminations, and other differential treatment."

Rose contended that although the term *national minority* can be used to describe a number of group cases in Europe and elsewhere, it is inapplicable to the case of the various racial and ethnic groups that comprise, for example, the population of the United States. This limit in usage follows, he asserted, from the nature of the relationship between national minorities and the developing nation-states of Europe:

as modern political boundaries replaced historical ones, the territories covered by political nations soon ceased to be exactly the territories inhabited by the historical nationality groups. . . . Since the modern conception of political nation included the belief that it was to serve the interests of a particular nationality, the smaller groups within the physical boundaries of a nation became known as minorities. . . . Each person was a member of a nationality group determined by his ancestry, not by the country within whose borders he happened to dwell. If his nationality group was dominant in the political control of a nation, he was a member of a majority group. If his nationality group was not dominant, he was a member of a minority group and he had a different status determined both by law and by custom.

In the United States, on the other hand, Rose asserted, "the interests of a particular nationality" are not held uppermost as against those of any other group, nor does any "particular nationality" have overall political control, thus the necessity for the use of a separate term—*minority groups*—to describe certain racial or ethnic elements in the population (pp. 409-10).

As he said in the *International Encyclopedia of the Social Sciences* (hereafter cited as *IESS*), what is vital is a "set of attitudes—those of group identification from within the group and those of prejudice from without—and a set of behaviours, those of self-segregation from within the group and those of discrimination and exclusion from without." However, even at this stage, he advocated disuse of the term *minorities* in favor of *subordinate groups*, since "Many nations have no single 'majority group' in terms of numbers, thus it is necessary either to counterpose a 'minority' to a 'dominant' group in terms of power, or to abandon the term 'minority' altogether and call it a subordinate group" (p. 365).

On the other hand, John Rex noted that,

Charles Wagley and Marvin Harris come nearest to a precise definition of minorities which is nonetheless wide enough to cover the necessary ground when they say that (i) minorities are subordinate elements of complex state societies, (ii) minorities have special physical or cultural traits which are held in low esteem by dominant segments of the society, (iii) minorities are self-conscious units bound together by the special traits which their members share and by the special disabilties which these bring, (iv) membership in a minority is transmitted by a rule of descent which is capable of affiliating succeeding generations even in the absence of readily apparent special cultural or physical traits, (v) minority peoples, by choice or necessity, tend to marry within the group [J. Rex, *Race Relations in Sociological Theory* (London: Weidenfeld and Nicholson, 1970), pp. 25-26, citing Charles Wagley and Marvin Harris, *Minorities in the New World* (New York: Columbia University Press, 1964), p. 32].

Operational definitions of *minorities* range from those proposed in a report submitted by the United Nations secretary general in 1950, entitled "The Definition and Classification of Minorities" (extracts from which are given in Julius Lewin, *The Struggle for Racial Equality* [London: Longmans, 1967], pp. 163-65), to the Soviet concept of *national minorities* or *nationalities* as "administratively recognized ethnic groups" (see P. G. Rubel, "Ethnic Identity among the Soviet Nationalities," in E. Allworth, ed., *Soviet Nationality Problems* [New York: Columbia University Press, 1971], p. 224). Both Rubel and Vaclav Lamser ("A Sociological Approach to Soviet Nationality Problems," in E. Allworth, ed., *Soviet Nationality Problems*) stressed the difference between the analytical and operational when dealing with the conceptualization of what constitutes "minorities," with Rubel stressing the point made originally by Wagley and Harris: even when regarding Soviet "nationalities," that is, when economic and political considerations are introduced by means of a positional and power definition, one can, as did Wagley and Harris, see most (or all) ethnic groups as minorities.

Following from the distinction made by Rose between the two "types" noted above, one can only distinguish a single factor as being the "differentiating" factor, that is, the additional factor of interaction—identification and a reaction of self-identification inherent in the situation of the "minority group." This distinction, however, is not sufficient for our purposes, since many groups that would be considered "national minorities" exhibit the characteristics of "minority groups" as such, but their continued existence, life-style, and political aspirations tend to run counter to the traditional pattern of "majority-minority" relations.

It seems, therefore, that one must look in another direction for the distinction sought. It is here that Weber's conceptions of "corporate group" and, concomitantly, "monopolization" come to mind and, in modified form, seem to provide the ordinal framework for analytical distinctions between the two "minority types" that Rose proposed exist. Walter Zenner cited Morton Fried's use of "corporate group" in that it is a group that "maintains continuity of possession to an estate which consists of things, people, or both" (that is, "monopolization" in Weberian terms). See Max Weber's *Wirtschaft und Gesellschaft* (Tubingen: J. C. B. Mohr, 1922), pt. 3, pp. 183ff.; and E. M. Manasse, "Max Weber on Race," *Social Research*, June 1947, p. 216. Zenner also showed how Eric Wolf used Fried's view of corporate groups in terms of "continuity of possession to an estate" in the existence of a "patrimony to defend" (W. P. Zenner, "Ethnic Assimilation and the Corporate Group," in M. Kurokawa, ed., *Minority Responses* [New York: Random House, 1970], pp. 107, 110).

If we include "cultural heritage" in this "patrimony," this usage fits well as regards "national minorities," where the groups concerned exhibit a high degree of willingness to "defend" their "patrimony." A "national minority," then, would be a group that exhibits *formal* "corporateness," in both structural and functional terms, to a higher degree than a "minority group," within the broader framework of a corporate political system, be it nation-state or empire. The degree of formal corporateness exhibited, combined with the interpretation of its object, would determine, then, the minority "type" being studied (for a description of the formal structural aspects of corporateness, see W. P. Zenner, "Ethnic Assimilation," pp. 106-8, 111-12). This ordinal differentiation holds, furthermore, even when the minority group resembles a corporate group in that an individual is simply a member or is not (p. 111) as "one development in the modern world . . . has been the constitution of the dominant ethnic group in a state as a corporate ethnicity. The nation state, after all, fits Weber's definition of the corporate group. Each state defines its rules of membership. In many cases, this is defined to favor the dominant ethnic group in the state" (see Rose *IESS*). In terms of empires, however, "decentralized-group corporateness" among "nationalities" may be tolerated, or even advocated, by the central governing group. The classic example of this is the Ottoman millet system. In specific case studies, however, one must differentiate carefully between factors perpetuating "defense of patrimony" among various groups.

Although the view taken above is supported by a critical analysis of the definitions provided by both Louis Wirth in his seminal article, "The Problem of Minority Groups" (reprinted in M. Kurokawa, ed., *Minority Responses*), and Arnold Rose, there still remains an inherent vagueness in the use of the term *minority group* due to the widespread acceptance of the definitions offered by these two observers. As Oliver Cox noted, "Wirth even speaks of 'where the minority occupies the position of a caste.' " echoed by Rose, who in his *IESS* article calls a group such as the *Eta* ("outcaste Japanese") a "caste minority" (p. 367). Again, power and positional arguments are the most cogent when considering factors "in minority group formation and perpetuation" (on this point, see, for example, P. G. Rubel, "Ethnic Identity among the Soviet Nationalities," p. 224. See also O. C. Cox, *Caste, Class, and Race* [New York: Monthly Review Press, 1959]), factors that both Wirth and Rose tended to relegate to secondary positions, although Rose eventually recognized its importance. For example, although Wirth defined a *minority* as a "group of people who, because of their physical or cultural characteristics, are singled out from others in the society in which they live for differential and unequal treatment, and who therefore regard themselves as objects of collective discrimination," Cox noted that "this definition, which probably had to be as inclusive as it is because of the tremendous scope of the non-significantly modified concept 'group' promises and accomplishes a confusing discussion" (O. C. Cox, *Caste, Class, and Race*, p. 402, n. 24). Wirth continued, "The existence of a minority in a society implies the existence of a corresponding dominant group with higher social status and greater privileges. Minority status carries with it the exclusion from full participation in the life of the society" (L. Wirth, in M. Kurokawa, ed., *Minority Responses*, p. 34).

Now, although both Wirth and Rose recognized a "subordinate-superordinate (dominant)" element in their definitional considerations, with Rose himself opting for the abandonment of the term *minority* itself, nowhere does either one mention the element of struggle for upward mobility within the context of the power and positional relationships in the society at large, that is, in terms of access to economic and political prerogatives. To take a case in point, women as a group can be considered a "minority" in power terms, but what of "minority-group" women such as Negro women in the United States? Should one consider them a "dual minority," that is, a group having a *status position* reinforced by the fact that they are both black and women at the same time? Looking at the occupational distribution of Negro women tends to confirm this "dual minority" status. An overwhelming number of Negro women in the United States civilian labor force are still engaged mostly in service and laborer jobs while their white counterparts are engaged in clerical and other white-collar occupations.

The problem of the interrelationship between minority-group "formation," on the one hand, and "minority-group characteristics," on the other hand, then, is further complicated by the problem of "minority status" and the basis upon which it is ascribed. Again, it is Donald Young who noted, in reference to American "minority groups" at least, that "the group membership visibility necessary if ascription of minority status is to be effective in establishing and maintaining a hierarchical social system in intergroup relations may be a consequence of either cultural or genetic variance" or both (see his "The Socialization of American Minority Peoples," in D. Goslin, ed., *Handbook of Socialization Theory and Research* [Chicago: Rand-McNally, 1969], pp. 1104-5). Here, however, we see a justification of Cox's criticism that "very much of the responsiblility for the medley of incongruous ideas about race relations and nationality groups frequently encountered in Donald Young's *American Minority Peoples* is no doubt due to the false lead of the ill-defined concept 'minority peoples' itself." For as Pierre Van den Berghe, among others, has noted, the categories dichotomized by Young often overlap (on this point, see P. Van den Berghe, *Race and Racism* [New York: Wiley, 1967], pp. 9-11. See also O. C. Cox, *Caste, Class and Race*, p. 402).

The volume of literature dealing with these problems is, however, far too large to enable full citation here. A developmentally oriented review of the literature contains, in fact, enough material for a thesis in itself. One point must be stressed, however, regarding definitional considerations: the role that power, in political and economic terms, plays in minority-group formation, perpetuation, *and* mobility. As S. M. Lipset and H. L. Zetterberg noted in 1966, "political power as a vehicle for other kinds of social mobility," for example, minority-group mobility, "has so far been a neglected area of research" (S. M. Lipset and H. L. Zetterberg, "A Theory of Social Mobility," in L. Coser and B. Rosenberg, eds., *Sociological Theory* [New York: Macmillan, 1966], p. 442). Important studies on the overall problem of the interrelationship between stratification, differentiation, ethnicity, status, hierarchy, race, caste, class, and so on can be found in the works of Max Weber, W. G. Runciman, W. L. Warner, Leonard Plotnicov and Arthur Tuden, M. G. Smith and Leo Kuper, Louis Dumond, Donald Horowitz, E. K. Francis, O. D. Duncan, Philip Mason, Michael Banton, Pierre Van den Berghe, Melvin Tumin, John Rex, Richard Schermerhorn, Ernest Barth and Donald Noel, Donald Rothschild, G. E. Simpson and J. M. Yinger (although they accept Wirth's minority definition outright; see J. Rex, *Race Relations in Sociological Theory,* p. 25), and in a collection entitled *Caste and Race: Comparative Approaches,* edited by Anthony de Reuck and Julie Knight (London: Ciba, 1966), which includes work by George De Vos, Gerald Berreman, and others. General works include those of Everett Hughes, Raymond Mack, and Milton Gordon.

Another question is raised if, however, the group in question is a "subordinate nation" within a larger administrative unit and if it is administratively recognized as such. In this case, it seems to constitute a "national minority" in definitional terms, but this is further complicated by the question, "what constitutes a nation?" It seems, at the most general level of analysis, that ibn Khaldun was, in fact, on the right track when he proposed that it was *asabiyah* ("fundamental group loyalty and group consciousness") that was at the basis of nationhood. (On these points, see W. L. Young, "Ibn Khaldun et l'etat Islamique," *Cahiers Internationaux de Sociologie* 55 [June-Dec. 1973], pp. 315-20).

Power-positional and stratification relationships resulting in minority-group formation are dealt with in M. Harris, "Caste, Class, and Minority," *Social Forces* 37, 3 (1959), especially p. 253; M. S. Das and F. G. Acuff, "The Caste Controversy in Comparative Perspective: India and the U.S.," *International Journal of Comparative Sociology* 11, 1 (1970); V. S. D. Souza, "Caste and Class: A Reinterpretation," *Journal of Asian and African*

Studies 2, 3-4 (1967); A. Beteille, "Race, Caste, and Ethnic Identity," *International Social Science Journal* 23, 4 (1971); W. G. Runciman, *Relative Deprivation and Social Justice* (London: Routledge and Kegan Paul, 1966).

Milton Gordon used the term *ethclass* to denote the intersection of ethnic group membership and socioeconomic status in *Assimilation in American Life* (Oxford: Oxford University Press, 1964). The existence of "plural societies" complicates universal generalization along this line; however, the general problem of stratification and differentiation in such cases is dealt with in D. L. Horowitz, "Three Dimensions"; L. Plotnicov and A. Tuden, eds., *Essays in Comparative Social Stratification* (Pittsburgh: University of Pittsburgh Press, 1970); L. Kuper and M. G. Smith, *Pluralism in Africa* (Berkeley: University of California Press, 1969); and earlier works by M. G. Smith, Burton Benedict, Harry Hoetink, Leo Despres, and J. S. Furnivall on plural societies in the Caribbean and Asia.

D. L. Horowitz, A. B. Hollingshead, and J. W. van der Zanden proposed similar models, with van der Zanden complementing the proposal that "a social structure may be differentiated (vertically, i.e., compartmentalized) along racial, ethnic, and religious lines and each of these (vertical) cleavages in turn is differentiated (horizontally) by a series of strata or classes that are encompassed within it' (see A. B. Hollingshead, "Trends in Social Stratification," *American Sociological Review* 18 [1952]). "Thus, religious, ethnic, and racial groups are not arranged in a simple higher and lower ranking with respect of the class stratification system. Each of the religious, ethnic, and racial groups tends to span a range of higher and lower positions within the class structure, sometimes from top to bottom, sometimes within a narrower range" (p. 244; J. W. van der Zanden, *American Minority Relations* [New York: Ronald Press, 1966]). On these points, also see T. Shibutani and K. M. Kwan, *Ethnic Stratification* (New York: Macmillan, 1965); H. M. Blalock, *Towards a Theory of Minority-Group Relations* (New York: Wiley, 1967); O. D. Duncan, "Minorities and the Process of Stratification," *American Sociological Review* 33 (1968); G. E. Simpson and J. M. Yinger, *Racial and Cultural Minorities* (New York: Harper and Row, 1965). A very good treatment of the United States case and general issues can be found in James Colemans's *Resources for Social Change* (New York: Wiley, 1971), which deals with the problem of the acquisition of "power" in economic and political terms, indicating the problem involved and proposing equitable and acceptable solutions in terms of redistribution of resources.

As for the issue of race and ethnic relations in general perspective, that is, the intergroup relations aspect of the problem again, the volume of material is too large to cite in full here. Good early works on these points, however, are E. C. and H. M. Hughes's *Where Peoples Meet: Racial and Ethnic Frontiers* (Glencoe, Ill.: Free Pess, 1952); G. W. Allport, *The Nature of Prejudice* (Cambridge: Harvard University Press, 1954); E. K. Francis, "Variables in the Formation of So-Called Minority Groups," *American Journal of Sociolgy* 60 (1954-1955). Recent work along these lines may be found in the writings of Philip Mason, Michael Banton, H. M. Blalock, Minako Kurokawa, Celia Heller, and Pierre Van den Berghe. An interesting approach is also taken by Irwin Rinder in his paper "Minority Orientations: An Approach to Intergroup Relations Theory Through Social Psychology," in M. Kurokawa, *Minority Responses*; and by E. Barth and D. Noel, "Conceptual Frameworks for the Analysis of Race Relations: An Evaluation," *Social Forces* 50 (1972).

The important point in our case studies is the focus upon *differentiable* groups. A number of observers have made the important point that when dealing with such groups, unless their differentiating characteristics are given "ascriptive social meaning," these features are not the concern of social science. The result of this is, in some cases, hierarchical ordering along occupational lines. In terms of other groups, when such features as physical charactersistics or language divide men hierarchically, it can be said that they acquire social meaning.

In these terms, differentiable groups can be called "collectivities," being based upon members who share positions and consciousness, have similar "vantage points," and therefore "objective interests," and are "meaningful stratification units." This has been stressed by Amitai Etzioni, who defines a *collectivity* as

a macroscopic unit that has the potential capacity to act by drawing on a set of macroscopic normative bonds which tie the members of a stratification category . . . the cohesion of a collectivity is not based on face to face contact. Unlike class position in the stratification structure, the position of a collectivity is not necessarily horizontal nor is its prime base necessarily economic.

On these points, see A. Etzioni, *The Active Society* (New York: Free Press, 1968), pp. 98, 439. See also P. Van den Berghe, *Race and Racism*, and L. Kuper, "Political Changes in Plural Societies."

To sum up, the amount of work attempting to deal with what constitutes a minority group and the implications of the alternate approaches is indeed massive. As such, in this appendix, I have attempted to deal with some cardinal elements regarding the problem of what constitutes such a group, and I hope that this has shed at least some additional light on a question that is still relevant for investigation and analysis by social scientists.

BIBLIOGRAPHY

BOOKS

Abbott, S. *The Prevention of Racial Discrimination in Britain.* Oxford: Oxford University Press, 1971.

Ackley, C. *The Modern Military in American Society.* New York: Westminster, 1972.

Alexander, R. *The Bolivian National Revolution.* New Brunswick, N.J.: Rutgers University Press, 1958.

Andreski, S. *Military Organization and Society.* London: Routledge and Kegan Paul, 1954.

Barbeau, A., and Henri, F. *The Unknown Soldiers.* Philadelphia: Temple University Press, 1974.

Barber, B. *Social Stratification* (New York: Harcourt, Brace, 1957).

Barber, D. H. *Africans in Khaki* (London: Edinburgh House Press, 1948).

Baynes, J. C. M. *The Soldier in Modern Society*, London: Methuen, 1972).

Beck, J. M. *Contemporary Canada.* Durham, N.C.: Duke University Press, 1968.

Becker, G. *The Economics of Discrimination.* Chicago: University of Chicago Press, 1957.

Be'eri, E. *Army Officers in Arab Politics and Society.* London: Praeger, 1970.

Bennigsen, A., and Lemercier-Quelquejay, C. *Islam in the Soviet Union.* London: Pall Mall, 1967.

Berger, C., ed. *Conscription 1917.* Toronto: University of Toronto Press, 1969.

Bidwell, R. *Morocco under Colonial Rule.* London: Cass, 1973.

Bie, P. *Le Fait Canadian Français: Etude Comparative des Nationalismes Flamand et Canadien Français.* Louvain: University of Louvain Press, 1948.

Bloom, L. *The Social Psychology of Race Relations.* London: Allen and Unwin, 1971.

Boak, A. E. R. *Manpower Shortage and the Fall of the Roman Empire in the West.* Ann Arbor: University of Michigan Press, 1955.

Bogart, L. *Social Research and the Desegregation of the U.S. Army.* Chicago: Markham, 1969.

Brathwaite, J. *A Black British Soldier.* Toronto: World, 1969.

Brisbane, R. H. *The Black Vanguard: The Origins of the Negro Social Revolution, 1900-60.* Valley Forge, Pa.: Judson, 1970.

Broom, L., and Glenn, N. *Transformation of the Negro American.* New York: Norton, 1967.

Brunet, M. *Canadians et Canadiens.* Montreal: Fides, 1954.

Brunt, P. A. *Italian Manpower: 225 B.C.-14 A.D.* Oxford: Clarendon Press, 1971.

Canby, S. *Military Manpower Procurement.* New York: D. C. Heath, Lexington Books, 1972.

Careless, J., and Brown, R., eds. *The Canadians 1867-1967.* Toronto: Macmillan, 1967.

Caulfield, J. E. *One Hundred Years History of the Second Battallion of the West India Regiment.* London: Forster Groom and Co., 1899.

Challener, R. *The French Theory of the Nation in Arms.* New York: Columbia University Press, 1955.

Chamberlain, M. E. *Britain and India: The Interaction of Two Peoples.* London: David and Charles, 1974.

Chaput, M. *J'ai choisi de me battre.* Montreal: Club du Livre du Quebec, 1965.

Chirol, V. *India.* London: Ernest Benn, 1926.

Clemner, D. *The Prison Community.* New York: Rhinehart, 1958.

Clough, S. B. *A History of the Flemish Movement in Belgium.* New York: Smith, 1930.

Cody, J. F. *Official History of the Twenty-Eighth (Maori) Battallion.* Wellington, N.Z.: War History Branch, Dept. of Internal Affairs, 1956.

Cohen, S. *The Indian Army.* Berkeley: University of California Press, 1971.

Collins, S. *Coloured Minorities.* London: Butterworth, 1957.

Corbett, E. *Quebec Confronts Canada.* Baltimore: Johns Hopkins University Press, 1968.

Coulon, M. *L'Autonomie Culturelle en Belgique.* Paris: Plisner, 1961.

Cowan, J. *The Maoris in the Great War.* Wellington, N.Z.: Whitcombe and Tombs, 1926.

Craddock, R. *The Dilemma in India.* London: Constable, 1929.

Creagh, O'Moore. *Indian Studies.* London: Hutchinson, 1919.

Daalder, H. *The Role of the Military in the Emerging Countries.* The Hague: Mouton, 1963.

Dalfiume, R. *Desegregation of the U.S. Armed Forces: Fighting on Two Fronts, 1939-53.* Kansas City: University of Missouri Press, 1969.

Daniel, W. *Racial Discrimination in Britain.* London: Penguin, 1968.

Davidson, B. *Black British.* Oxford: Oxford University Press, 1966.

Davis, J. P. *American Negro Reference Book.* New York: Prentice-Hall, 1966.

Davis, S. C. *The French War Machine.* London: Allen and Unwin, 1937.

_____. *Reservoirs of Men: A History of the Black Troops of French West Africa.* Geneva: Kundig, 1934.

Deakin, N. *Colour, Citizenship, and British Society.* London: Panther, 1970.

De Meuss, A. *History of the Belgians.* Translated by G. Gordon. London: Thames and Hudson, 1962.

De Vos, G., and Wagatsuma, H. *Japan's Invisible Race.* Berkeley: University of California Press, 1966.

Dore, R. P., ed. *Aspects of Social Change in Modern Japan.* Princeton: Princeton University Press, 1967.

Douglass, F. *Two Speeches by Frederick Douglass.* New York: Rochester, 1857.

Eayrs, J. *The Art of the Possible.* Toronto: University of Toronto Press, 1961.

_____. *In Defense of Canada.* Toronto: University of Toronto Press, 1972.

Eisenstadt, S. N. *The Political Systems of Empires.* Glencoe, Ill.: Free Press, 1963.

Ekirch, A. *The Civilian and the Military.* Oxford: Oxford University Press, 1956.

Ellis, A. B. *History of the First West India Regiment.* London: Chapman and Hall, 1885.

Etzioni, A. *A Comparative Analysis of Complex Organizations.* Glencoe, Ill.: Free Press, 1961.

Fernandes, F. *The Negro in Brazilian Society.* Cambridge: Cambridge University Press, 1969.

Finer, S. *The Man on Horseback.* London: Pall Mall, 1967.

Fishel, L. H., and Quarles, B. *The Black American: A Documentary History.* New York: Morrow, 1970.

Fisher, J. *Yugoslavia—A Multinational State.* San Francisco: Chandler, 1966.

Fitzherbert, K. *West Indian Children in London.* London: Bell, 1967.

Foner, J. D. *Blacks and the Military in American History.* New York: Praeger, 1974.

Fortescu, J. *History of the British Army.* London: Macmillan, 1899-1927.

_____. *Military History.* Cambridge: Cambridge University Press, 1914.

Freyre, G. *Mansions and Shanties: The Making of Modern Brazil.* New York: Knopf, 1963.

Gann, L. H., and Duignan, P. *Burden of Empire.* London: Pall Mall, 1968.

Garder, M. *A History of the Soviet Army.* London: Pall Mall, 1966.

Ghosh, K. K. *The Indian National Army.* Meerut: Asia Pub., 1969.

Gilloin, R. *De l'Alsace à la Flandre.* Paris: Prométhée, 1930.

Ginzberg, E., and Bray, D. W. *The Uneducated.* New York: Columbia University Press, 1953.

Glaser, B., and Strauss, A. *The Discovery of Grounded Theory: Strategies for Qualitative Research.* Chicago: Aldine, 1967.

Glass, D. *London's Newcomers: The West Indian Migrants.* Cambridge: Harvard University Press, 1961.

Goffman, E. *Asylums.* New York: Anchor, 1961.

Golant, W. *The Long Afternoon: British India 1601-1947.* London: Hamish Hamilton, 1975.

Goris, J. A. *Belgium.* Berkeley: University of California Press, 1945.

Granatstein, J. *Conscription.* Toronto: Ryerson Press, 1969.

Greene, L. *The Negro in Colonial New England.* New York: Columbia University Press, 1942.

Gregory, R. G. *India and East Africa: A History of Race Relations within the British Empire, 1890-1939.* Oxford: Oxford University Press, 1971.

Gutteridge, W. *Military Institutions and Power in the New States.* London: Pall Mall, 1964.

Hamilton, W., ed. *The Transfer of Institutions.* Durham, N.C.: Duke University Press, 1964.

Hamshere, C. *The British in the Caribbean.* London: Wiedenfeld and Nicholson, 1972.

Haywood, A., and Clarke, F. A. S. *History of the West African Frontier Force.* London: Gale and Polden, 1964.

Henderson, J. *Area Handbook for Malaysia.* Washington, D.C.: American University Foreign Area Studies, 1970.

Hepple, B. *Race, Jobs, and the Law.* London: Penguin, 1968.

Higginson, T. W. *Army Life in a Black Regiment.* East Lansing: Michigan State University Press, 1960.

Hiro, D. *The Indian Family in Britain.* London: Community Relations Commission, 1967.

Horowitz, I. L. *Three Worlds of Development.* Oxford: Oxford University Press, 1966.

Humphry, D., and John, G. *Because They're Black.* London: Penguin, 1972.

Huntington, S. *The Soldier and the State.* Cambridge: Harvard, Belknap, 1957.

Ianni, O. *Crisis in Brazil.* Cambridge: Cambridge University Press, 1970.

James, A. G. *Sikh Children in Britain.* Oxford: Oxford University Press, 1974.

Janowitz, M. *The Military in the Political Development of New Nations.* Chicago: University of Chicago Press, 1964.

_____. *The Professional Soldier.* New York: Free Press, 1964.

Johnson, C. *Revolution and the Social System.* Stanford: Stanford University Press, 1964.

_____. *Revolutionary Change.* London: University of London Press, 1968.

Johnson, H., and Wilson, G. C. *Army in Anguish.* New York: Washington Post Report, 1972.

Johnson, J. *The Military and Society in Latin America.* Stanford: Stanford University Press, 1964.

Katznelson, I. *Black Men, White Cities: Race, Politics, and Migration in the U.S. 1900-30 and Britain 1948-68.* Oxford: Oxford University Press, 1973.

Kilson, M., ed., *Key Issues in the Afro-American Experience.* New York: Harcourt, Brace, 1971.

Kim, K. H. et al. *The Volunteer Army.* New York: Praeger, 1971.

King, E. *The Death of the Army.* New York: Saturday Review Press, 1972.

Kintner, W. *Forging a New Sword.* New York: Harper, 1958.

Lee, U. *The Employment of Negro Troops in World War II.* Washington, D.C.: Office of the Chief of Military History, U.S. Army, 1966.

Lester, A., and Bindman, G. *Race and Law.* London: Longmans, 1972.

Levy, M. *Modernization and the Structure of Societies.* Vol. 2. Princeton: Princeton University Press, 1966.

Little, K. L. *Negroes in Britain.* London: Routledge and Kegan Paul, 1947.

Little, R. W., ed. *Handbook of Military Institutions.* Beverly Hills: Sage, 1972.

Litwack, L. *The Negro in the Free States.* Chicago: University of Chicago Press, 1961.

Lloyd, C. *The British Seaman: 1200-1860.* London: Collins, 1968.

Logan, R. *The Betrayal of the Negro.* New York: Macmillan, 1969.

_____. *The Negro in the United States.* New York: Peter Smith, 1970.

Malcolm X. *Malcolm X Speaks.* New York: Grove, 1965.

Mallinson, V. *Belgium.* London: Benn, 1969.

_____. *Power and Politics in Belgian Education.* London: Heinemann, 1963.

Mallory, J. *The Structure of Canadian Government.* Toronto: Macmillan, 1971.

Malloy, J. *Bolivia: The Uncompleted Revolution.* Pittsburgh: University of Pittsburgh Press, 1970.

Mandelbaum, D. *Soldier Groups and Negro Soldiers.* Berkeley: University of California Press, 1952.

March, J. G., ed. *Handbook of Social Organizations.* Chicago: Rand-McNally, 1964.

Marmion, H. *The Case Against an All-Volunteer Army.* Chicago: University of Chicago Press, 1971.

Marwick, A. *Britain in the Century of Total War.* London: Bodley Head, 1968.

_____. *War and Social Change in the 20th Century.* London: Macmillan, 1974.

Mason, P. *A Matter of Honour.* London: Cape, 1974.

Massey, H. *The Canadian Military: A Profile.* Montreal: Copp-Clark, 1972.

McMullen, R. *Soldier and Civilian in the Later Roman Empire.* Cambridge: Harvard University Press, 1963.

McPherson, J. *The Negro's Civil War.* New York: Random House, 1965.

McWilliams, W., ed. *Garrisons and Government.* San Francisco: Chandler, 1967.

Merton, R. *Social Theory and Social Structure.* Glencoe, Ill.: Free Press, 1949.

Miller, J. *Why the Draft? The Case for a Volunteer Army.* New York: Penguin, 1968.

Mitchell, R. H. *The Korean Minority in Japan.* Berkeley: University of California Press, 1967.

Mockler, A. *Mercenaries.* London: MacDonald, 1970.

Morton, D. *French Canada and the War.* Toronto: Erindale, 1970.

Morton, M. *The Canadian Identity.* Toronto: University of Toronto Press, 1961.

Mosca, G. *The Ruling Class.* New York: McGraw-Hill, 1939.

Moskos, C. *Public Opinion and the Military Establishment.* Beverly Hills: Sage, 1971.

Mullard, C. *Black Britain.* London: Allen and Unwin, 1973.

North, L. *Civil-Military Relations in Argentina, Chile, and Peru.* Berkeley: University of California, 1966.

Ossenberg, R., ed., *Canadian Society: Pluralism, Change, and Conflict.* Ontario: Prentice-Hall, 1971.

Parker, H. M. D. *The Roman Legions.* Oxford: Oxford University Press, 1928.

Patterson, S. *Dark Strangers.* London: Penguin, 1965.

_____. *Immigration and Race Relations.* Oxford: Oxford University Press, 1969.

Peach, C. *West Indian Migration to Britain: A Social Geography.* Oxford: Oxford University Press, 1968.

Penlington, N., ed. *On Canada.* Toronto: University of Toronto Press, 1971.

Plonski, H. A., and Kaiser, E., eds. *The Negro Almanac.* New York: Bellwether, 1971.

Plotnicov, L., and Tuden, A., eds. *Essays in Comparative Social Stratification.* Pittsburgh: University of Pittsburgh Press, 1970.

Political and Economic Planning. *Racial Discrimination.* London, 1967.

Poppino, R. *Brazil.* Oxford: Oxford University Press, 1968.

Porter, J. *The Vertical Mosaic.* Toronto: University of Toronto Press, 1965.

Quarles, B. *The Negro in the Making of America.* New York: Macmillan, 1964.

Quinn, H. *The Union Nationale.* Toronto: University of Toronto Press, 1963.

Rabushka, A., and Shepsle, K. A. *Politics in Plural Societies.* Columbus, Ohio: Merrill, 1972.

Rechciql, M. *Czechoslovakia—Past and Present.* The Hague: Mouton, 1968.

Rex, J., and Moore, R. *Race, Community and Conflict.* Oxford: Oxford University Press, 1967.

Richmond, A. H. *Colour Prejudice in Britain.* London: Routledge and Kegan Paul, 1954.

Rose, A. *The Negro's Morale.* Minneapolis: University of Minnesota Press, 1949.

Rose, E. J. B. et al. *Colour and Citizenship.* Oxford: Oxford University Press, 1969.

Russell, A. G. *Colour, Race, and Empire.* London: Kennikat Press, 1944-1973.

Russell, P., ed. *Nationalism in Canada.* Toronto: McGraw Hill, 1966.

Sanger, R. *The Arabian Peninsula.* Ithaca: Cornell University Press, 1956.

Saywell, J., ed. *Canadian Annual Review.* Toronto: University of Toronto Press, 1969.

Schermerhorn, R. A. *Comparative Ethnic Relations.* New York: Random House, 1970.

Selvin, H. *The Effects of Leadership.* New York: Free Press, 1960.

Shoup, P. *Communism and the Yugoslav National Question.* New York: Columbia University Press, 1968.

Simpson, S. *Belgium in Transition.* Collection published in hardback volume of *Annals of the American Academy of Political and Social Science* 247 (Sept. 1946).

Smith, L. *Democracy and Miltary Power.* Chicago: University of Chicago Press, 1951.

Smith, M. G. *Government in Zazzau.* Oxford: Oxford University Press, 1960.

Smith, T. L., and Fuji, Y. *The Acculturation of Japanese Immigrants in Brazil.* Tampa: University of Florida Press, 1959.

Snowden, F. A. *Blacks in Antiquity.* Cambridge: Harvard University Press, 1971.

Soloveytchik, G. *Switzerland in Perspective.* Oxford: Oxford University Press, 1954.

Sorrenson, M. *Maori and European Since 1870.* Auckland, N.Z.: Heinemann, 1967.

Stillman, R. *The Integration of the Negro in the Armed Forces.* New York: Praeger, 1968.

Stouffer, S. et al. *The American Soldier.* Princeton: Princeton University Press, 1949.

Swomley, J. *The Military Establishment.* Boston: Beacon, 1964.

Tax, S., ed. *The Draft.* Chicago: University of Chicago Press, 1967.

Thomson, D. *Europe Since Napoleon.* London: Penguin, 1972.

Tinker, H. *A New System of Slavery: The Export of Indian Labor Overseas.* Oxford: Oxford University Press, 1974.

Tobias, H., and Woodhouse, C., eds. *Minorities and Politics.* Santa Fe: University of New Mexico Press, 1969.

Tsurumi, K. *Social Change and the Individual: Japan Before and After Defeat in World War II.* Princeton: Princeton University Press, 1970.

Vagts, A. *A History of Militarism.* London: Hollis and Carter, 1959.

Van den Berghe, P. *South Africa: A Study in Conflict.* Chicago: Wesleyan University Press, 1965.

Verrier, A. *An Army for the 1960's: A Study in National Policy.* London: Secker and Warburg, 1966.

Wade, M. *The French Canadians 1760-1967.* Rev. ed. Toronto: Macmillan, 1968.

Walvin, J. *Black and White: The Negro and English Society.* London: Allen Lane, 1973.

Watson, G. R. *The Roman Soldier.* London: Thames and Hudson, 1969.

Weber, M. *The Theory of Social and Economic Organization.* Oxford: Oxford University Press, 1947.

Webster, G. *The Roman Imperial Army.* London: Black, 1969.

Weighley, R. *History of the United States Army.* New York: Macmillan, 1967.

Wheeler, G. *Racial Problems in Soviet Muslim Asia.* Oxford: Oxford University Press, 1962.

White, D. *The Growth of the Red Army.* Princeton: Princeton University Press, 1944.

Willame, J. C. *Patrimonialism and Political Change in the Congo.* Stanford: Stanford University Press, 1972.

Williams, G. *A History of Negro Troops in the War of Rebellion.* New York: Krauss Reprint, 1888.

Wilson, J. *The Black Phalanx.* Hartford, Conn: Connecticut Historical Society, 1890.

Wool, H. *The Military Specialist.* Baltimore: Johns Hopkins University Press, 1968.

ARTICLES

Abrams, P. "The Failure of Social Reform." *Past and Present* 26 (1963).

_____. "The Late Profession of Arms." *European Journal of Sociology* 6 (1965).

Allen, J. F. W. "An African Army: Some Possibilities." *Journal of the Royal United Service Institution* 58 (1918).

Allen, S., and Smith, C. "Race and Ethnicity in Class Formation: A Comparison of West Indian and Asian Workers." In F. Parkin, ed. *The Social Analysis of Class Structure.* London: Tavistock, 1974.

Amelunxen, C. "The History of the German Speaking Minority Group in Belgium." *Plural Societies* (The Hague) 2, 4 (1971).

Angell, N. "France and the Black Power." *Contemporary Review* 121 (1922).

Banton, M. "The Changing Position of the Negro in Britain." *Phylon* 14, 1 (1953).

Bastide, R. "Race Relations in Brazil." *International Social Science Bulletin* 9 (1957).

Batchelder, A. "Decline in the Relative Income of Negro Men." *Quarterly Journal of Economics* 78, 4 (1964).

Blake, J. "The Organization as an Instrument of Violence: The Military Case." *Sociological Quarterly* 11, 3 (1970).

Blassingame, J. "Recruitment of Negro Troops in Missouri during the Civil War." *Missouri Historical Review* 57 (1964).

Borah, W. "Race and Class in Mexico." *Pacific Historical Review* 23, 4 (1954).

Borbolla, D. "The Mexican Indian Today." In *Mexico Today,* ed. A. Williams. Tampa: University of Florida Press, 1964.

Borcherding, T. E. "Neglected Social Costs of a Volunteer Military." *American Economic Review* 61 (1971).

Borus, J. F. et al. "Racial Perceptions in the Army." *American Journal of Psychiatry* 128, 11 (1972).

Brown, J. M. "War and the Colonial Relationship: Britain, India, and the War of 1914-1918." In *War and Society,* ed. M. R. D. Foot. London: Paul Elek, 1973.

Brunet, M. "The French-Canadian Search for a Fatherland." In *Nationalism in Canada,* ed. P. Russell. Toronto: McGraw-Hill, 1966.

Butler, J. "Afrikaners and Englishmen in South Africa." In *Ethnicity and Nation Building,* ed. W. Bell and W. Freeman. Beverly Hills: Sage, 1971.

Butler, J. S. "Assessing Black Enlisted Participation in the Army." *Social Problems* 23 (1976).

———. "Inequality in the Military." *American Sociological Review* 41 (1976).

Cardoso, J. "The Black Man as a Soldier." In *The Negro Impact on Western Civilization,* ed. J. Roucek and T. Kiernan. New York: Philosophical Library, 1970.

Chaplin, D. "Peruvian Social Mobility: Revolutionary and Developmental Potential." *Journal of Inter-American Studies* 10, 4 (1966).

Cheesman, G. L. "The Auxilia of the Roman Imperial Army." *Studia Historica* 59 (1968).

Clarke, F. A. S. "The West African Frontier Force." *Army Quarterly,* 55, 1 (1947).

Clissold, S. "The Indian Problem in Latin America: Changing Attitudes in the Andean Republics." *Race* 7, 1 (1965).

Clough, S. B. "The Flemish Movement." In J. A. Goris, ed. *Belgium.* Berkeley: University of California Press, 1945.

Cohen, A. "The Army in Palestine in the 18th Century." *Bulletin of the School of Oriental and African Studies* 23, 1 (1971).

Cohen, S. "The Untouchable Soldier: Caste, Politics, and the Indian Army." *Journal of Asian Studies* 28, 3 (1969).

Cornell, J. "Caste in Japanese Social Stratification." *Monumenta Nipponica* 25, 1-2 (1970).

Crocker, C. A. "Military Dependence: The Colonial Legacy." *Journal of Modern African Studies* 12, 2 (1974).

Crowder, M. "West Africa and the 1914-18 War." *Bulletin de l'Institute Français Afrique Noir* 30, 1 (1968).

Cvriek, J. "Social Changes in the Officer Corps of the Czechoslovak

Peoples Army." In *Military Professions and Military Regimes*, ed. J. van Doorn. The Hague: Mouton, 1969.

Daalder, H. "On Building Consociational Nations: The Cases of the Netherlands and Switzerland. *International Social Science Journal* 23, 3 (1971).

Dahya, B. "Pakistanis in Britain: Transients or Settlers?" *Race* 14, 3 (1973).

Davenport, R. "The Negro in the Army: A Subject of Research." *Journal of Social Issues* 3, 4 (1947).

Denoon, D. "Participation in the Boer War." In *War and Society in Africa,* ed. B. A. Ogot. London: Cass, 1972.

Destree, J. "Lettre au Roi sur la separation de la Wallonie et de la Flandre." *Revue de Belgique,* Aug. 15-Sept. 1, 1912.

Duff, D., and Arthur, R. "Between Two Worlds: Filipinos in the U.S. Navy." *American Journal of Psychiatry* 123, 7 (1967).

Dunn, J. A. "Consociational Democracy and Language Conflict: A Comparison of the Belgian and Swiss Experiences." *Comparative Political Studies* 5, 1 (1972).

_____. "The Revision of the Constitution in Belgium: A Study in the Institutionalization of Ethnic Conflict." *Western Political Quarterly* 27, 1 (1974).

Dyer, B. "Treatment of Colored Union Troops by the Confederates." *Journal of Negro History* 20 (1935).

Eccles, W. "The Social, Economic, and Political Significance of the Military Establishment in New France." *Canadian Historical Review* 52, 1 (1971).

Elkins, W. F. "A Source of Black Nationalism in the Caribbean: The Revolt of the British West Indies Regiment at Taranto, Italy." *Science and Society* 34, 1 (1970).

Enloe, C. "Civilian Control of the Military: Implications in the Plural Societies of Guyana and Malaysia." Paper presented at Inter-University Seminar on Armed Forces and Society Meeting, SUNY-Buffalo, Oct. 1974.

_____. "Ethnic Factors in the Evolution of the South African Military." Paper presented at African Studies Association Meeting, San Francisco, Oct. 1975.

_____. "Malaysia's Military in the Interplay of Economic and Ethnic Change." Paper presented at Association for Asian Studies Meeting, Hartford, Conn., Nov. 1975.

_____. "The Military—A Sleeper in British Politics." Paper presented at Northeastern Political Science Association Meeting, Rutgers University, Nov. 1975.

_____. "Police and Military in the Resolution of Ethnic Conflicts."

Annals of the American Academy of Political and Social Science 433 (1977).

————. "Police and Military in Ulster: Peace-keeping or Peace-subverting Forces?" *Journal of Peach Research* 15, 3 (1978).

Fane, R. "The Return of the Soldier: East Africa." *Journal of the Royal African Society*, 1944.

Feit, E. "Pen, Sword, and People: Military Regimes in the Formation of Political Institutions." *World Politics* 25, 2 (1973).

Feldberg, R. "Political Systems and the Role of the Military." *Sociological Quarterly* 11, 2 (1970).

Finkle, L. "The Conservative Aims of Militant Rhetoric: Black Protest during World War II." *Journal of American History* 60, 3 (1973).

Ford, W. F., and Tollinson, R. "Notes on the Color of the Volunteer Army." *Social Science Quarterly* 50, 3 (1969).

Forsey, E. "Canada: Two Nations or One?" *Canadian Journal of Economics and Political Science* 28, 4 (1962).

Garthoff, R. "The Military as a Social Force." In *The Transformation of Russian Society,* ed. C. E. Black. Cambridge: Harvard University Press, 1960.

Gatewood, W. B. "Black Americans and the Quest for Empire." *Journal of Southern History* 38, 4 (1972).

Glantz, O. "The Negro Voter in Northern Industrial Cities." *Western Political Quarterly* 12 (1960).

Glazer, N. "Race Relations in Britain—An American Perspective." *Sociology* 6, 1 (1972).

Greene, L. "The Negro in the Armed Forces of the U.S." *Negro History Bulletin* 14, 6 (1951).

Gutteridge, W. "The Indianisation of the Indian Army 1918-1945." *Race* 4, 2 (1963).

Guttman, A. "Politics and the Military Ethic." *American Scholar* 34, 2 (1965).

Hanham, H. J. "Religion and Nationality in the Mid-Victorian Army." In *War and Society,* ed. M. R. D. Foot. London: Paul Elek, 1973.

Harris, M. "The Structural Significance of Brazilian Racial Categories." *Sociologia* 25 (1963).

Hays, S. H. "Military Training in the U.S. Today." *Current History* 55, 323 (1968).

Howard, J., and Couchman, I. "The American Blacks and Military Service." *Forensic Quarterly* 42 (1968).

Hughes, E. J. "The Negro's New Economic Life." *Fortune* 54, 3 (Sept. 1956).

Inglehart, R. F., and Woodward, M. "Language Conflicts and Political

Community." *Comparative Studies in Society and History* 10, 1 (1968).

Jacobs, P. "Bringing Up the Rear." In *Employment, Race, and Poverty*, ed. A. Ross and H. Hill. New York: Harcourt, Brace, 1967.

Janowitz, M. "American Democracy and Military Service." *Transaction* 4 (1967).

_____. "Armed Forces and Society in World Perspective." In *Transactions of the Sixth World Conference on Sociology*. Evian, France: International Sociological Association, 1967.

_____. "Basic Education and Youth Socialization." In *Handbook of Military Institutions*, ed. R. W. Little. Beverly Hills: Sage, 1971.

_____. Military Institutions and Citizenship in Western Societies." Paper presented at the British Inter-University Seminar on Armed Forces and Society Meeting, 1973.

_____. "Military Organization.' In *Handbook of Military Institutions*, ed. R. W. Little. Beverly Hills: Sage, 1971.

_____. "Toward an All Volunteer Military." *Public Interest* 27 (1972).

_____. "Volunteer Armed Forces and Military Purpose." *Foreign Affairs*, 1972.

Janowitz, M., and Moskos, C. "Five Years of the All Volunteer Force: 1973-1978." *Armed Forces and Society* 5, 2 (1979).

_____. "Racial Composition in the All-Volunteer Force." *Armed Forces and Society* 1 (1974).

Joseph, C. L. "The British West Indies Regiment: 1914-18." *Journal of Caribbean History* 2 (1971).

Kaegi, W. "Patterns of Political Activity in the Armies of the Byzantine Empire." In *On Military Intervention*, ed. M. Janowitz and J. van Doorn. Vol. 2 of Contributions to Military Sociology. Rotterdam: Rotterdam University Press, 1971.

Kaplan, B. "Ethnic Identification in an Indian Mestizo Community." *Phylon* 14, 2 (1953).

Katzenellenbogen, S. "South Africa and the War of 1914-18." In *War and Society*, ed. M. R. D. Foot. London: Paul Elek, 1973.

Kelly, G. A. "Belgium: New Nationalism in an Old World." *Comparative Politics* 1, 3 (1969).

_____. "Biculturalism and Party Systems in Belgium and Canada." In *Public Policy*, ed. J. D. Montgomery and A. O. Hirschman. Cambridge: Harvard University Press, 1967.

Kenworthy, E. "The Case against Army Segregation." *Annals of the American Academy of Political and Social Science* 275 (1951).

Kiernan, V. G. "Conscription and Society in Europe Before the War of 1914-18." In *War and Society*, ed. M. R. D. Foot. London: Paul Elek, 1973.

Kilson, M. "Political Change in the Negro Ghetto 1900-1940's." In *Key Issues in the Afro-American Experience*, ed. M. Kilson. New York: Harcourt, 1971.

Kramer, D. "White versus Colored in Britain." *Social Research* 36, 4 (1969).

Kurz, H. "Die sprachenfrage in unserer armee." *Der Fourier*. Switz: Gersau, Nov. 1961.

Lang, K. "Military Organization." In *Handbook of Social Organizations*, ed. J. G. March. Chicago: Rand McNally, 1964.

————. "Technology and Career Management in the Military Establishment." In *The New Military*, ed. M. Janowitz. New York: Sage, 1964.

Lendvai, P. "Yugoslavia in Crisis." *Encounter* 39, 2 (1972).

Lewis, G. K. "A Introductory Note to the Study of Race Relations in Britain." *Caribbean Studies* 11, 1 (1971).

————. "Protest among the Immigrants: The Dilemma of Minority Culture." In *Protest and Discontent*, ed. B. Crick and W. Robson. London: Penguin, 1970.

Lewis, M. D. "One Hundred Million Frenchmen: The 'Assimilation' Theory in French Colonial Policy." *Comparative Studies in Society and History* 4, 2 (1961).

Lijphart, A. "Consociational Democracy." *World Politics* 21 (1969).

Lincoln, C. E. "The British Say They Aren't Prejudiced." *New York Times Magazine*, 14 Nov. 1965.

Lorwin, V. R. "Belgium: Religion, Class, and Language in National Politics." In *Political Oppositions in Western Democracies*, ed. R. A. Dahl. New Haven, Conn: Yale University Press, 1966.

————. "Linguistic Pluralism and Language Tensions in Modern Belgium." *Canadian Journal of History* 5 (1970).

————. "Segmented Pluralism: Ideological Cleavage and Political Cohesion in the Smaller European Democracies." *Comparative Politics* 3 (1971).

Macdonald, R. J. "Dr. H. A. Moody and the League of Coloured Peoples." *Race* 14, 3 (1973).

Mallory, J. "The Canadian Dilemma: French and English." *Political Quarterly* 41, 3 (1970).

Marshall Commission Report. *Current History* 55, 323 (1968).

Mason, P. "Gradualism in Peru." *Race* 8, 1 (1966).

McAlister, L. "The Military." In *Continuity and Change in Latin America*, ed. J. J. Johnson. Stanford: Stanford University Press, 1964.

McRae, K. "Switzerland: Example of Cultural Coexistence." *Canadian Institute International Affairs*. Toronto, 1964.

Moskos, C. "Armed Forces and American Society: Convergence or Divergence." In *Public Opinion and the Military Establishment*, ed. C. Moskos. Beverly Hills: Sage, 1971.

_____. "The Emergent Military: Civil, Traditional or Plural." *Pacific Sociological Review* 16, 2 (1973).

_____. "Minority Groups in Military Organizations." In *Handbook of Military Institutions*, ed. R. W. Little. Beverly Hills: Sage, 1971.

_____. "The Negro and the Draft." In *Selective Service and American Society*, ed. R. W. Little. New York: Sage, 1969.

_____. "Racial Integration in the Armed Forces." *American Journal of Sociology* 72, 2 (1966).

Murray, P. T. "Blacks and the Draft." *Journal of Black Studies* 1 (1971).

Newell, W. "Some Problems of Integrating Minorities into Japanese Society." *Journal of Asian and African Studies* 2, 3-4 (1967).

Norbeck, E. "Continuities in Japanese Social Stratification." In *Essays in Comparative Social Stratification*, ed. L. Plotnicov and A. Tuden. Pittsburgh: University of Pittsburgh Press, 1970.

Nove, A. "History, Hierarchy, and Nationalities: Some Observations on the Soviet Social Structure." *Soviet Studies* 21, 1 (1969).

Ossenberg, R. "Social Pluralism in Quebec: Continuity, Change, and Conflict." In *Canadian Society: Pluralism, Change and Conflict*, ed. R. Ossenberg. Ontario: Prentice-Hall, 1971.

Parsons, T. "Full Citizenship for the Negro American?" *Daedalus* 94 (1965).

Pasic, N. "Factors in the Formation of Nations in the Balkans and among the South Slavs." *International Social Science Journal* 23, 3 (1971).

Patch, R. "Peasantry and National Revolution: Bolivia." In *Expectant Peoples*, ed. K. Silvert. New York: Random House, 1963.

Perlmutter, A. "The Praetorian State and the Praetorian Army." *Comparative Politics* 1 (April 1969).

Philipart, A. "Belgium: Language and Class Oppositions." *Government and Opposition* 1 (1966).

Pitt-Rivers, J. "Race in Latin America." *Archives Européanées de Sociologie* 14 (1963).

Platt, W. "The East African Soldier." *The National Review* 126, 755 (1946).

Price, R. M. "A Theoretical Approach to Military Rule in New States." *World Politics* 23, 3 (1971).

Pye, L. "Armies in the Process of Political Modernization." In *The Role of the Military in Underdeveloped Countries*, ed. J. J. Johnson. Princeton: Princeton University Press, 1962.

Rapp, G. "L'attitude actuelle de la jeunesse a l'egard de l'armee et de la defense nationale." *Revue Militaire Suisse* 118, 7 (July 1973).

Raymond, R. "Changes in the Relative Economic Status of Non-Whites." *Western Economic Journal* 7, 1 (1969).

Reddick, L. D. "The Negro Policy of the U.S. Army." *Journal of Negro History* 34, 1 (1949).

Reid, B. G. "Confederate Opponents of Arming the Slaves." *Journal of Mississippi History* 22 (1960).

Remington, R. "Armed Forces and Society in Yugoslavia." In *Political-Military Systems: Comparative Perspectives*, ed. C. Kelleher. Beverly Hills: Sage, 1974.

Rens, I. "Les garanties parlementaires contre la minorisation et la revision constitutionelle en Belgique." *Res Publica* 7, 3 (1965).

Rose, A. "Army Policies Towards Negro Soldiers: A Report on a Success and a Failure." *Journal of Social Issues* 3, 4 (1947).

Rothman, R. "Education and Participation in the Israeli Defence Forces." *Jewish Social Studies* 34, 2 (1972).

Rousseau, F. "The Walloon Movement." In *Belgium in Transition,* ed. S. Simpson. Collection published in hardback volume of *Annals of the American Academy of Political and Social Science* 247 (Sept. 1946).

Rubenstein, A. "Yugoslavia's Pluralism at the Crossroads." *Plural Societies* 4, 1 (1973).

Rutan, G. "Two Views of the Concept of Sovereignty: Canadian-Canadien." *Western Political Quarterly* 24, 3 (1971).

Sabben-Clare, E. E. "African Troops in Asia." *African Affairs* 44, 177 (1945).

Scheiber, J. L., and Scheiber, H. "The Wilson Administration and the Wartime Mobilization of Black Americans." *Labor History* 10, 3 (1969).

Schmitt, K. "The Role of the Military in Contemporary Mexico." In *Mexico Today,* ed. A. Williams. Tampa: University of Florida Press, 1964.

Schwimmer, E. "Why the Maoris Choose the Army." *Te Ao Hou* (New Zealand), 1961.

Selvin, H. "Adult Socialization." In *International Encyclopedia of the Social Sciences.* New York: Macmillan, 1968.

Sherman, W. T. "On Recruiting Negroes." *Army and Navy Journal* 11, 27 (1864).

Shils, E. "The Military in the Political Development of the New States." In *The Role of the Military in Underdeveloped Countries,* ed. J. J. Johnson. Princeton: Princeton University Press, 1962.

Simon, A. "L'influence de l'Eglise sur la vie politique dans l'entre deux guerres." *Res Publica* 4 (1962).

Sitkoff, H. "Racial Militancy and Interracial Violence in the Second World War." *Journal of American History* 58, 3 (1971).

Smith, T. L. "The Redistribution of the Negro Population of the U.S." *Journal of Negro History* 51, 3 (1966).

Spear, A. "The Origins of the Negro Ghetto." In *Key Issues in the Afro-American Experience*, ed. M. Kilson. New York: Harcourt, Brace, 1971.

Spry, G. "Canada: Notes on Two Ideas of Nation in Confrontation." *Journal of Contemporary History* 6, 1 (1971).

Stephens, D.-S., "Our Million Black Army." *The English Review*, 22 Oct. 1916.

Stephenson, N. W. "The Question of Arming the Slaves." *American Historical Review* 18 (1913).

Sutton, D. "The Military Mission Against Off-Base Segregation." In *Public Opinion and the Military Establishment,* ed. C. Moskos. Beverly Hills: Sage, 1971.

Swynnerton, C. R. A. *Army Quarterly* 55, 1 (1947), commentary.

Urwin, D. W. "Societal Cleavages and Political Parties in Belgium." *Political Studies* 18, 3 (1970).

van Bogaert, E. R. C. "Belgium: Two Clashing Cultures." In *Year Book of World Affairs* 23 (1969).

Van den Berghe, P. "Pluralism and the Polity: A Theoretical Explanation." In *Pluralism in Africa,* ed. L. Kuper and M. Smith. Berkeley: University of California Press, 1969.

van den Brande, A. "Elements for a Sociological Analysis of the Impact of the Main Conflicts in Belgian Political Life." *Res Publica* 9, 3 (1967).

Van Doorn, J. "The Officer Corps: A Fusion of Profession and Organization." *European Journal of Sociology* 6 (1965).

van Geyt, G. "The Flemish Movement." In S. Simpson. *Belgium in Transition.* Collection published in hardback volume of *Annals of the American Academy of Political and Social Science* 247 (Sept. 1946).

Watene, P. T. "Statement." *Parliamentary Debates,* New Zealand 34th Parliament, 1st Sess., 23 June 1964.

Webb, W. V. "A Model of Defence Manpower Availability." In *Manpower Research,* ed. I.M.B. Wilson. London: English Universities Press, 1969.

Weigert, K. M. "Stratification, Ideology, and Opportunity Beliefs among Black Soldiers." *Public Opinion Quarterly* 28, 1 (1974).

Wesley, C. "The Employment of Negroes as Soldiers in the Confederate Army." *Journal of Negro History* 4 (1919).

Wheeler, S. "Socialization in Correctional Institutions." In *The Criminal in Confinement*, ed. L. Radinowicz and M. Wolfgang. New York: Basic Books, 1971.

White, J. S. "Race Relations in the Army." *Military Review* 50 (1970).

Willner, A. R. "The Underdeveloped Study of Pollitical Development." *World Politics* 16, 3 (1964).

―――. "Perspectives on Military Elites as Rulers and Wielders of Power." *Journal of Comparative Administration*, 2, 3 (1970).

Wilson, A. J. "Recruitment and Army Careers in the 1970's." *Brassey's Annual* (Defence Review), 1969, ch. 19.

Wilson, F. "French-Canadian Separatism." *Western Poitical Quarterly* 20 (1967).

Wolfe, E. "Aspects of Group Relations in a Complex Society: Mexico." *American Anthropologist* 58 (1956).

Wolfe, T. "The Military." In *Prospects for Soviet Society,* ed. A. Kassof. London: Pall Mall, 1968.

Wool, H. "The Armed Services as a Training Institution." In *The Nation's Children,* ed. E. Ginzberg. New York: Columbia University Press, 1960.

Wynn, N. "The Impact of the Second World War on the American Negro." *Journal of Contemporary History* 6, 2 (1971).

Young, W. "Multidimensionality and Minoriticity: Towards a Taxonomy of Minority-Societal Relations." *Rivista di Sociologia* (Rome) 28 (1974).

Zamor, J. "Social Mobility of Negroes in Brazil." *Journal of Inter-American Studies* 12, 2 (1970).

Zenner, W. "Ethnic Assimilation and the Corporate Group." In *Minority Responses,* ed. M. Kurokawa. New York: Random House, 1970.

Zolberg, A., "The Making of Flemings and Walloons: Belgium—1830-1914." *Journal of Interdisciplinary History* 22 (1974).

DOCUMENTS AND REPORTS

AFHRL Reports TR-72-16; TR-72-19. Alexandria, Va.: U.S. Air Force.

Annual Reports of the Ministry of National Defense, Bruxelles; ACJE/ 2118/71;ACJE/2118/73;ACJE/2118/63.

Canadian Armed Forces: Effective Strength Personnel Report (PPFAGA)— 1972. Ottawa: Dept. of National Defense, Jan. 1973.

Census, 1951, 1961, 1966, 1971. London: Her Majesty's Stationary Office.

Civil Rights 1963. Washington, D.C.: U.S. Commission on Civil Rights, 1964.

Coleman, J. S., et al. "Occupational Status Changes for Blacks and Non-Blacks during the First 10 Years of Occupational Experience," Reports No. 76 (Aug. 1970), 122 (Dec. 1971), and 123 (Jan. 1972). Compiled by the Center for the Social Organization of Schools. Baltimore: Johns Hopkins University.

Forbell, H. *Armed Forces Histories,* Parts 1-3. In *Studies Prepared for the Royal Commission on Bilingualism and Biculturalism.* Division 4, Report No. 20. Ottawa: National Library, 1969.

The Gates Commission Report. Washington, D.C., 1970.

Harding, F. D., and Richards, J. A. "A Descriptive Analysis of the Classification, Assignment, and Separation Systems of the Armed Services." *HumRRO Technical Report 71-8.* Alexandria, Va.

House of Commons, Canada, *Debates.* Vol. 9. 1st Sess., 20 Oct. 1966; *Debates.* Vol. 14. 1st Sess., 4 April 1967; *Debates.* Vol. 30. 1st Sess., 4 Feb. 1971.

Kurz, H. "Analysis of the Swiss Military Establishment." Berne: Department Militaire Federal, 1973.

Ladinsky, J. *A Survey of Socially and Economically Disadvantaged Vietnam Era Veterans.* Washington, D.C.: U.S. Bureau of the Budget, 1969.

Les Motivations des Miliciens à l'Egard de l'Armée et du Service Militaire. Bruxelles: Forces Armées Belges; Centre de Recherches des Facteurs Humains, 1972.

Malaysia—Official Yearbook. Kuala Lumpur, 1972.

Manpower Report of the President. Washington, D.C., 1965.

Manpower Research Notes, 71-3, 71-4. Washington, D.C.: Directorate for Manpower Research, Office of the Assistant Secretary of Defense for Manpower and Reserve Affairs, 1971.

The Negro in the Armed Forces. A Statistical Fact Book. Washington, D.C.: Office of the Assistant Secretary of Defense for Manpower and Reserve Affairs—Equal Opportunity, 1971-1973.

Nordlie, P. et al. *Measuring Changes in Institutional Racial Discrimination in the Army.* Technical Paper 270. Washington, D.C.: Army Research Institute for the Behavioral Sciences, 1975.

Opinions de Miliciens seur leur Passage au Centre de Recrutement et de Selection. Bruxelles: Forces Armées Belges; Centre d'Etudes Sociales, Avril 1963.

Rapport Linguistique (1979) *Chambres des representants* 634, 1 (1 Sept. 1980).

Rapport par la Commission Mixte du Probleme Linguistique au Sein des Forces Armees. Bruxelles: Ministere de la Defense Nationale, 1953.

Recherche sur les Besoins des Officiers Subalternes. Bruxelles: Forces Armées Belges; Centre de Recherches des Facteurs Humains, 1971.

Report of the Royal Commission on Bilingualism and Biculturalism. Final Report—documents. Book 3A, Part 2, "The Work World." Chapter 11, Canadian Forces. Ottawa, Sept. 1969.

Reports "3035" and "3694," 1976 and 1980. Washington, D.C.: Office of Assistant Secretary of Defense for Manpower and Reserve Affairs—Equal Opportunity, 1980.

Stacey, C. P. *Arms, Men and Governments: The War Policies of Canada 1939-45.* Ottawa: Dept. of National Defense, Queens Printer, 1970.

Tucker, G. N. *The Naval Service of Canada: Its Official History.* Ottawa: Dept. of National Defense, Queens Printer, 1952.

NEWSPAPERS AND PERIODICALS

Annales Parliamentaires (Bruxelles, 17 May 1919)
Daily Express (London)
Daily Mail (London)
Daily Telegraph (London)
Economist (London, 7 May 1977)
Economist Survey (Canada, 12 Feb. 1977)
Guardian (London)
International Herald Tribune (Paris)
La Belgique Militaire (Bruxelles, 19 Oct. 1924)
Le Devoir (Quebec)
Le Soir (Bruxelles)
New York Times
Newsweek
Nottingham Evening Post (England)
Observer (London)
Race Relations (London)
Race Today (London)
Revue Militaire Suisse (Geneva)
Sunday Telegraph (London)
Sunday Times (London)
Times (London)
Times History of World War I (London)

Time Magazine
UPI Press Release (Ottawa, 1 March 1971)
U.S. News and World Report
Yorkshire Evening News (England)

UNPUBLISHED MATERIAL

DISSERTATIONS

Berry, M. F. "The Negro Soldier Movement and the Adoption of National Conscription: 1652-1865." Ann Arbor: University of Michigan, 1966.

Butler, J. S. "Unsanctioned Institutional Racism in the U.S. Army." Evanston, Ill: Northwestern University, 1974.

Coble, C. R. "Social Action Programs in the Department of Defense." Chapel Hill, N.C.: University of North Carolina, 1969.

Lord, F. A. "The Federal Volunteer Soldier in the American Civil War." Ann Arbor: University of Michigan, 1949.

Mason, W. "The Effect of Military Achievement on the Subsequent Civilian Attainment of Veterans." Chicago: University of Chicago, 1970.

Philips, T. D. "Black Regulars—Negro Soldiers in the U.S. Army, 1866-91." Madison: University of Wisconsin, 1966.

CORRESPONDENCE:

Balniel to Lane, 31 Oct. 1972 (D/MIN/RB/1742)
Bennison to Young, 18 Dec. 1972 (D/DS14/122/12)
Childs to Young, 13 Oct. 1972 (50/8/8DPRPS)
Pitt-Brooke to Young, 3 Sept. 1980 (D/DS14/102/2/VI)
Wilson to Young, 11 Dec. 1972 (19/1/239)

INDEX

independence (1830) period in, 38-39; process of linguistic "radicalization" in, 61; projection of societal cleavage structure onto military in, 66; prosecution of collaborators after World Wars I and II in, 46, 51; provisions of linguistic laws of 1932 in, 46-47, 58-59; "querelle linguistique" in, 49, 53, 58; Rassemblement Wallon (nationalist) party in, 57, 60, 62-63; reasons for Catholic party's assumption of power (1884-1919) in, 42; regional cultural autonomy in, 60, 62-63; regional cultural councils in, 62-64; regional unilingualism established (1932) in, 47; relationship between Church and Flemish movement in, 42, 48; relationship of Force Publique (Congo) to, 73-75; religion of Flemish (Catholicism) in, 39; religious cleavage in, 42; revival of Flemish cultural activities prior to 1830 in, 39-40; revival of Walloon activism in, 52; revolution of 1830 in, 39; Rexist (facist) movement in, 48-49, 51; "Royal Question" in, 52; school laws in, 41; "School Pact" and "deconfessionalization" of politics in, 53, 63; "School Question" in, 52-53; "segmented pluralism" approach to, 64; severity of language conflict in, 64; Social Christian (Catholic) party (PSC) in, 42-46, 52, 58, 59-63; Socialist party (PSB) in, 43, 45, 52, 58-59, 61-63; student deferments and induction problems, 71-72; "Swiss Cantonal model" and linguistic problems in, 41, 48; "triumph of linguistic extremism" (1968), 61; "unifying power of military" in, 66; universal male suffrage in, 41, 47; Walloon "congress" and "assembly" in, 44;

Walloon demand for constitutional protection from Flemish domination in, 60; Walloon "language" as dialect of French in, 40; "Walloon movement" in pre-World War I period, 40; Walloon nationalist parties in, 60, 61-63; Walloon self-perception in, 51; Walloons as "minority" in, 64-66; workers protest movements in, 42

Black military participation in United States. *See* U.S. Armed Forces. *See also* United States; U.S. Air Force; U.S. Army; U.S. Marine Corps; U.S. Navy

Blake, Joseph: characteristics of "channeling" into combat service according to, 253-54

Bolivia: basic education and "role-expansion" in military of, 281-82; Chaco War (1932-36) between Paraguay and, 281; ethnoracial composition of population in, 281; Indian participation in Chaco War in, 281; Indian participation in military of, 281; origin of officer corps and ranks in pre-1952 army in, 281; revolution (1960) and reinstitution of compulsory military service in, 281

Brazil, 10; ethnoracial composition of military in, 282; ethnoracial composition of population in, 282; interservice differentials in ethnoracial military participation in, 282; Japanese immigrants in, 10; Negroes in, 10, 280, 282; racial discrimination in, 282; racial discrimination in Navy in, 282

Britain: ability of Anglo-Saxon to live with diversity in, 183-84; absence of broad-based organization defending rights of colored community in, 169; acceptance of colored immigrant children into

place of British Indian Army in, 172; empirical data regarding colored personnel in late 1960s in, 177-82; expected versus actual rank distribution of colored soldiers (1968) in, 179, 189 n.72; *Guardian* disclosure of memorandum excluding colored personnel from elite regiments and select units (1964) of, 174; *Guardian* report on order nullifying obstacles to recruitment of colored soldiers (Oct. 1966) in, 174; length of service of colored soldiers and possible increase in popularity among immigrants of, 177; loyalty of Irish troops and Fenian infiltration of, 144-45; manpower shortage after 1870 in Scottish regiments of, 145; manpower shortfalls and suggestions of expanding Gurkha participation in, 172-73; *Nottingham Evening Post* report on continued exclusion of colored personnel from elite regiments (Dec. 1966) of, 174; occupational distribution of colored personnel by MOS (1968) in, 179-80, 189 n.72, n.74; official justification for channeling West Indies regiment into labor duties during World War I in, 148, 264; official justification for discontinuing collection of statistics on colored personnel in, 177, 189 n.70; official justification for quota on colored personnel in, 174-75; participation of Irish and Scots during middle and late colonial periods in, 144-46; possible quota on colored soldiers in event of personnel imbalance in, 175-76; "proper soldiering" and stylized colonial operations of, 172; proportion of Irish and Scottish soldiers (1830-70) in, 144-45; Race Relations Act (1968) and racial

balance in, 175-76; racial tension and disturbances in, 182-83; reanalysis of statistics on colored participation (1968) in, 178-81; reasons for noncombat role of black troops in Europe during World War I in, 149; regimental structure and separate West Indies regiments in, 148; role of African forces in, 172; role in 1960s of, 172; segregation of medical and recreational facilities by color during World War I in, 148; service and size of contingents in India of regular, 143, 160; service in Ulster of colored soldiers in, 183; Stephens proposal (1916) for African combat force to be used on Western front by, 149; *Times* inquiry (1967) finds 4 percent quota and occupational exclusion of colored personnel in, 174, 188 n.66; *Times* report on official 2 percent policy of colored recruitment (1961), 174; *Times* report on parliamentary reply to *Express* disclosure of quota on colored recruits (Dec. 1968) in, 174-75, 188 n.67; treatment of West Indian soldiers during World War I in, 147-48, 264-65; typical career pattern versus colored attainment of expected rank (1968) in, 179, 189 n.72; utilization and combat roles of West African Frontier Force in World Wars I and II in, 147, 149, 161-62; utilization of East African soldiers during World War II by, 161-62; wage discrimination during World War I in West Indian and African regiments of, 157; West Indian regiments as representatives of West Indies in, 148; West Indian troops not integrated into existing regiments during World War I in, 148. *See also* Britain; British Armed Forces; British Indian Army; Canada

French-Canadians during World
War II in, 110-11; Confederation of
all provinces (1867) in, 96;
conservative reaction against Lesage
reforms in Quebec (1966) and Parti
Quebeçois in, 125; cooperation
between English reformers and
French-Canadians in, 93-94; decline
of relative proportion of French-
Canadian population in, 108-9;
development of Canadianism in, 91;
development of minority group
attitudes and behavior among
French-Canadians after
Confederation in, 96; development
of new French-Canadian elite in, 91;
dispatch of French-Canadian
volunteers to Sudan (1884) from, 98;
dual loyalty of English-Canadians
in, 98; Durham proposes
"assimilation" of French-Canadians
in, 92-93; Durham proposes "Union"
of, 93; Durham on Quebec Act and
guarantees to French-Canadians in,
92; Durham Report on, 83, 92-93;
economic characteristics of Quebec
during period 1839-1939 in, 124;
economic transformation and
advancement in Quebec during
period 1939-50 in, 124; effect of
American revolution on Quebec and
English-French Canadian relations
in, 89-90; effect of fall of France
(1940) on French-Canadians in, 111;
effect of French revolution and
Napoleonic wars on, 90; effect of
Militia Act (1777) and imposition of
compulsory service on French-
Canadians, 89; effect of Militia Act
(1812) and War of 1812 on, 90-91;
effect of pro-British American
refugee influx into, 89-90; effect of
Transvaal crisis and Boer War on,
98-99; effects of immediate post-
World War I and Great Depression

on, 109; effects of large scale Irish
and British immigration on, 94-95;
electoral sweep of Liberal party in
Quebec in federal election of 1939
in, 110; English-Canadian and
American control of Quebec's
economy in, 96, 109; English-
Canadian domination of active
militia in, 97; English-Canadian
excesses in Northwest territories in,
97; English-Canadian perception of
inequality of casualties during
World War II in, 116; English-
Canadian politico-military
leadership advocate French-
Canadian brigade but mixed
divisions during World War I in,
107; English-Canadian reaction to
results in Quebec of 1939 provincial
and federal elections in, 110;
establishment of Quebec legislature
in, 96; exemption claims and
noncompliance of French-Canadian
conscripts (1917-18) in, 105-6; extent
of French-Canadian participation in
militia during period 1862-71 in, 97;
failure of reform leads to agrarian
uprising among French-Canadians
and Rebellion of 1837 in, 91-92; first
regular French-Canadian regiment
raised and sees action during 1812
war in, 90-91; FLQ organized and
initiates terrorism (1963) in, 125;
FLQ political activities push Parti
Quebeçois into more radical
positions in, 125; FLQ terrorism
reaches climax (1970) in, 125; FLQ
terrorism results in use of army to
restore order in Quebec during 1970
emergency in, 125-26; French-
Canadian nationalists predict need
for conscription (1914) in, 101;
French-Canadian politicians oppose
increased defense expenditure during
interwar period in, 109; French

French-Canadian recruits in pre-World War II period in, 113; limited advancement of French-Canadian officers during immediate post-World War II period in, 121; link with British RAF of, 108, 112; minor improvements during 1950s resulting from intervention of defense ministry in linguistic policy of, 121; national unity and post-World War II policy of unilingualism in, 121; no official figures on French-Canadian participation during World War II kept by, 113; no provision for training French-Canadians in pre-World War II period in, 113; problem of training Francophone personnel during post-World War II period in, 121; RAF influence increasingly replaced by USAF during post-World War II period in, 121; recruiting facilities in Quebec expanded during World War II by, 113; separate course for Francophone mechanics set up (1941) in, 113; step-up of recruiting program in Quebec after 1940 by, 113; unilingual French-Canadian recruits given intensive English courses prior to technical training during World War II in, 113; use of French in post-World War II period by, 121

Canadian Armed Forces: Anglophone and Francophone participation overall and by service branch in, 129; army as first service established in, 97; Cadieux plan (1968) advocates bilingual structure and quasi-bifurcation of, 123-24; Cadieux plan proposes French as language of work and special provisions for basic training of Francophones in, 123; Central Language school set up (1967) in, 122; conspiracy of silence regarding

role of French-Canadians in development of, 97; Defense White Paper on Unification (1964) of, 122; differential effects regarding Francophone participation in, 128-31; effect of autonomous Quebec on manpower in, 132; effort to overcome low retention rates brings improvement in French-Canadian service conditions (1968) in, 123; English as only official language in 1960s in, 122; English sole operational language in service branches other than army during World War II in, 112; enlistments from Quebec proportional to population during 1950s and 1960s in, 122; extent of French-Canadian enlistment by 1941 in, 112; extent of French-Canadian service during World War I in, 107-8; French-Canadian appointed as chief of staff (1966) of, 121-22; gross rank distribution of active service officers by service branch, linguistic group and type of rank in, 130; gross rank distribution of NCOs and other ranks by service branch, linguistic group and type of rank in, 130; implications of autonomous Quebec for, 132; interwar period most British-oriented in history of, 109; lack and nonrelease of official figures on recruitment and participation by linguistic group during World War I in, 104, 108; limited steps initiated to improve French-Canadian situation (1967) in, 122; low reenlistment rate overall during 1960s in, 123; low reenlistment and retention of French-Canadians during 1950s and 1960s in, 122-23; opposition and controversy over appointment of French-Canadian as chief of staff (1966) of, 122; outcome of effective

Military College set up (1952) by, 119; French-Canadian disincentive to join during formative period of, 97; French-Canadians in Royal Military College of, 97, 102; French language programs for Anglophones initiated (1946) by, 118; French usage during World War II in French-Canadian units of, 117; government applies War Measures Act to combat FLQ terrorism (1970) and restores order in Quebec by using, 126; government policy of maintaining fixed percentage of French-Canadians overseas during World War II and fixed proportion of Francophone personnel and units in immediate post-war period in, 117-18; growth in size prior to 1914 of, 99; heavy casualty rate during World War I and drop in enlistment in, 104; high command recognizes problem of French-Canadian participation during World War II in, 112; high French-Canadian enlistment rate (1939) in reserve units of, 110; interwar status of Twenty-second French-Canadian regiment and situation of Francophone soldiers in, 109; lack of French-Canadian technical background and education cited (1941) as reason for limited service in technical units of, 112; manpower pressures during World War I and formation of French-Canadian battalions in, 103; nature and extent of French-Canadian participation during World War II in, 117; opposition to conscription among French-Canadian officers and men during World War I in, 104; outcome of shortage of Francophone officers in French-Canadian units of UN contingent in Korea of, 119;

participation in Boer War of volunteer and militia contingents of, 99; percentage of Francophones by rank in officer corps (1958) of, 119; plans to organize French-Canadian brigade during both World Wars in, 107, 117; postwar study cites reasons for low French-Canadian enlistment rate during World War II in, 118; problem of French-Canadian advancement in immediate post-World War II period in, 118-19; problem of French-Canadian participation in unilingual Anglophone technical branches (1941) of, 112; promotion problems of unilingual French-Canadian officers during World War II in, 117; purpose and function during initial period after formation of, 97; quota on percentage of Francophone personnel in infantry and other branches set in post-World War II period by, 118; rate of desertion among French-Canadian troops during World War I in, 104; reason for formation of Twenty-second French-Canadian regiment of, 102-3; reasons for small number of French-Canadian officers and NCOs prior to 1914 in, 102; regionally based French-Canadian units formed (1939) by, 112; reorganization after Boer War of, 99; role and combat performance of Twenty-second French-Canadian regiment during World War I as part of Expeditionary Force of, 107; shortage of French-Canadian officers during World War II extends to late 1950s in, 117, 119; transfer of personnel from French- to English-Canadian units in World War I demoralizes French-Canadian recruits in, 104

and Project CLEAR experience on integration in, 215, 218-19, 239 n.52, 265; effect of regimental structure prior to Civil War on Negro participation in, 195; Eisenhower memo on Negro troop use and channeling during World War II by, 210; exclusion of Negroes at outset of World War II from Signal and Air Corps of, 209; Executive Order 9981 (Truman Desegregation Order, 1948) and, 216-19; extent of segregation after Executive Order 9981 in, 219; factors changing "Negro policy" (1948-54) of, 215-16; Fahy Committee (1948-49) recommends desegregation and abolition of racial quota in, 212, 215-17, 219; federal agents recruit Negro brigades (1863) for service in, 196; gap between policy and practice regarding "all-Negro" divisions in, 212; general order (1820) proscribes Negro recruitment in, 194; General Sherman on use of Negro manpower during Civil War in, 197; implications of Conscription Act (1863) for use of Negro troops in, 196; influence of Stimson on Negro manpower policy during World War II of, 209-10; initial lack of officer training program and restrictions on Negro officers during World War I in, 203; job exclusion of Negroes prior to World War II in, 209; job exclusion of Negroes subsequent to Truman Desegregation Order in, 219; Lee proposal for using Negro volunteers in white combat units (1944) in, 213-14; "liberal" manpower approach of civilian analysts and Negro policy (1947) of, 215; limited desegregation and on-base facilities due to racial tension

(1943) in, 212; long-term upper "limit" equilibrium view of VOLAR effect on Negro participation in, 228, 242 n.67; McCloy Committee recommendations on racial tension (1943) in, 213; McCloy views Negro as manpower asset (1944) to, 213-14; manpower needs and policy changes regarding use of Negro troops (1944) in, 213-14; "mercenary" force view of VOLAR effect on Negro participation in, 227, 242 n.67; "Mexican bandit" and "Brownsville" incidents and collective view of Negro soldiers of, 201-2; Militia Act (1792) effectively bars significant Negro participation until 1862 in, 194-95; misrepresentation and misinterpretation of Negro AGCT scores during World War II by, 210-11; Negro AGCT scores justify limited induction and job exclusion during World War II in, 210-11; Negro enlistment and retention in immediate post-World War II period in, 216, 239 n.47; Negro enlistment temporarily halted (1946) due to quota in, 216; Negro overrepresentation at junior and senior NCO levels in, 232-33; Negro participation during post-Civil War period (1866-98) in, 199; Negro participation during Spanish-American War and Philippine insurrection campaign in, 199-201; Negro participation during World War I in, 203; Negro participation in interwar period in, 208; Negro reenlistment and retention prior to World War I in, 202; Negro regiments kept at minimal strength (1931-34) in, 208; Negro service after Bastogne (1945) in "integrated" combat units in, 214; Negro service in Continental Army during Revolution, 193; Negroes as a percentage of total enlisted personnel by rank in, 229; occupational distribution and channeling of Negro enlisted men and NCOs (1964-80) in, 231, 234, 268; outcome of low AGCT Negro concentration in segregated units during World War II in, 210-11, 238 n.41; overall and Negro rank distribution in, 230; perceived and actual effect of integration on unit efficiency (1951-54) in, 218-19; perceived and actual role of Negro troops during Civil War in, 197, 199; performance of Negro air combat units during World War II in, 214; policy prior to World War II on mobilization of Negro manpower for, 208; politicization of Negro participation (1940) in, 209, 265, 287 n.18; possible educational requirement limitation on Negro participation in, 229, 242 n.67; possible effects of VOLAR on Negro participation in, 225, 227-29, 242 n.67; possible reason for increased Negro entry into officer corps (1980) of, 233, 242 n.67; post-World War I Negro manpower policy and utilization plans of, 206-8; problem of civilian control over racial policy (1949) in, 217-18; problem of divided loyalty of Negro soldiers in, 268; problems involved in abolition of racial quota (1950) in, 216-17; prohibition on enlistment, reenlistment, and promotion of Negroes (1931) in, 208; provisions of Militia Act (1862), channeling of and unequal pay for Negroes in, 197; quota and fixed segregated units policy of Negro participation (1866-1931) in, 199, 208; race riots at Southern bases (1943) of, 212;

racial equality and differential treatment of black enlisted man in, 268-69; racial mythology affecting Negro manpower policy and utilization (1920-40) in, 207-9; racially egalitarian policies in, 268; racist attitudes of white officers in Negro units during World War II in, 211-12; racist nature of War College study (1925) on use of Negro manpower by, 207-8; reasons for deficient overseas combat performance of "all-Negro" Ninety-second division during World War I in, 205-6; removal of Negro officers from Negro regiments during World War I in, 203; renewal of enlistment and Negro quota (1934) in, 208; Royall blocks Johnson gradualist approach to integration (1949) in, 217; "self-fulfilling hypothesis" aspect of Ballou Report (1920) and Negro manpower policy of, 206, 287 n.19; "Sepoy model" of Negro participation in, 229, 232, 242 n.67; statistical analysis of Negro participation (1949-80) in, 231-34; Stimson belief in Confederate military mystique and value of white illiterates (1941) in, 211; training program for Negro officers during World War I in, 203; unequal pay policy and morale of Negro troops during Civil War in, 197; variant opinions regarding possible use of Negro manpower (1939-40) in, 209; War College study (1925) and Negro manpower policy and utilization plans of, 207-8

U.S. Marine Corps (USMC): rank structure and rank distribution of Negroes in, 254; reasons for increased Negro entry into officer corps of, 232; statistical analysis of

About the Author

WARREN L. YOUNG is Lecturer in the Sociology of Education and Technology at the Center for Technological Education, Holon, Israel, and Lecturer in Sociology, Ethnic, and Race Relations at the University of Maryland, European Division. His publications include three research monographs and many scholarly articles.